THE BAʿTHIFICATION OF IRAQ

THE BAʿTHIFICATION OF IRAQ

Saddam Hussein's Totalitarianism

By Aaron M. Faust

UNIVERSITY OF TEXAS PRESS, AUSTIN

Aaron M. Faust is a Foreign Affairs Officer at the US Department of State. The views in this book do not necessarily reflect the views of the State Department or the US government.

Printed in the United States of America
First edition, 2015
First paperback edition, 2016

Requests for permission to reproduce material from this work should be sent to:
Permissions
University of Texas Press
P.O. Box 7819
Austin, TX 78713-7819
http://utpress.utexas.edu/index.php/rp-form

♾ The paper used in this book meets the minimum requirements of ANSI/NISO Z39.48-1992 (R1997) (Permanence of Paper).

LIBRARY OF CONGRESS CATALOGING-IN-PUBLICATION DATA

Faust, Aaron M., author.
The Baʿthification of Iraq : Saddam Hussein's totalitarianism / by Aaron M. Faust. — First edition.
pages cm
Includes bibliographical references and index.
ISBN 978-1-4773-0557-7 (cloth : alk. paper)
ISBN 978-1-4773-0558-4 (library e-book)
ISBN 978-1-4773-0559-1 (non-library e-book)
1. Hizb al-Baʿth al-ʿArabi al-Ishtiraki (Iraq)—History. 2. Iraq—Politics and government—1979–1991. 3. Iraq—Politics and government—1991–2003. 4. Hussein, Saddam, 1937–2006. 5. Political parties—Iraq. 6. Totalitarianism. I. Title.
JQ1849.A98B37273 2015
956.7044—dc23 2015013804

doi:10.7560/305577
ISBN 978-1-4773-1217-9 (paperback)

To my parents, Ruth Anne and Halley Faust
My brother, Josh
Aunt Ronni
My daughters, Natalie and Maya
My sons, Adam and Evan
And for Rachel,
My love, my partner, and my inspiration

CONTENTS

List of Abbreviations *ix*

Chronology *xi*

Preface *xv*

Acknowledgments *xxiii*

PART I. **Introduction** *1*

CHAPTER 1 The Inculcation of Loyalty *3*

CHAPTER 2 The Origins of Husseini Baʿthist Totalitarianism *18*

PART II. **Ideology** *31*

CHAPTER 3 Husseini Baʿthism *35*

CHAPTER 4 Culturalization *51*

PART III. **Organization** *69*

CHAPTER 5 The Leader and the Party *73*

CHAPTER 6 The Party State *97*

CHAPTER 7 The Baʿthification of Society *117*

PART IV. **Terror and Enticement** *147*

CHAPTER 8 Terror *151*

CHAPTER 9 Enticement *171*

CONCLUSION **A Total Strategy** *183*

POSTSCRIPT **The Legacy of Baʿthification** *188*

APPENDIX 1 A Work Plan for Coordination between the Party and Mass Organizations in the Field of the Baʿthification of Society *193*

APPENDIX 2 Special Regulations for How to Deal with the Relatives of Criminals Convicted for Political Crimes *203*

Notes 207

Glossary of Arabic Terms 259

Bibliography 267

Index 279

ABBREVIATIONS

BRCC	Baʿth Arab Socialist Party Regional Command Collection
CRRC	Conflict Records Research Center
DMI	Directorate of Military Intelligence (mudīriyyat al-ʾistikhbārāt al-ʿaskariyya)
GDI	General Directorate of Intelligence (mudīriyyat al-mukhābarāt al-ʿāma)
GFIW	General Federation of Iraqi Women (al-ʾittiḥād al-ʿām li-l-nisāʾ al-ʿirāq)
GSD	General Security Directorate (mudīriyyat al-ʾamn al-ʿāma)
ICP	Iraqi Communist Party
ID	Iraqi Dinars
IMF	Iraq Memory Foundation
KDP	Kurdistan Democratic Party
MIA	Missing in Action
PMOs	Professional and Mass Organizations (al-munaẓẓamāt al-mihniyya wa-l-jamāhīriyya)
POWs	Prisoners of War
PUK	Patriotic Union of Kurdistan
RC	Regional Command (al-qiyāda al-quṭriyya)
RCC	Revolutionary Command Council (majlis qiyādat al-thawra)
RG	Republican Guard
SSO	Special Security Organization (jihāz al-ʾamn al-khāṣṣ)

CHRONOLOGY

1914	Great Britain occupies Basra
1920	The San Remo Conference assigns the Mandate for Iraq to Great Britain; a revolt against the Mandate breaks out
1921	The British install King Faysal bin Hussein al-Hashemi as king of Iraq
1932	The British Mandate ends; Iraq gains independence
1933	King Faysal dies; his son, King Ghazi, takes the throne
1936	General Bakr Sidqi leads Iraq's first coup d'état
1939	King Ghazi dies in a car accident; his infant son succeeds him. Abd al-Ilah acts as regent
1941	Rashid Ali al-Kailani leads a coup backed by the "Golden Square" of four military officers, forcing Abd al-Ilah and Nuri al-Said, the British-backed prime minister, to flee. Great Britain subsequently overturns al-Kailani; al-Ilah and Nuri return to Baghdad
1948	Al-Wathba: mass protests against the signing of the Portsmouth Treaty between Iraq and Great Britain highlight popular discontent over foreign influence
1958	The monarchy is overthrown; Abd al-Karim Qasim takes power
1963	Abd al-Salam Arif and the Baʿth Party ally in a military coup d'état to overthrow and execute Qasim. Arif subsequently purges the Baʿth
1966	Abd al-Salam Arif dies in a helicopter crash; his brother, Abd al-Rahman Arif, takes over
1968	The Baʿth and their military allies overthrow Abd al-Rahman Arif; the Baʿth purge the military officers who assisted them
1972	Iraq nationalizes its oil industry
1977	Shiʿi protests throughout the 1970s culminate in their most massive demonstration, known as the Safar Intifada. The Baʿth put down the demonstrations with force after briefly losing control

1979 Saddam Hussein takes over as president from Ahmad Hassan al-Bakr

1980 Iraqi forces invade Iran, starting the Iran–Iraq War; the Baʿth execute popular Shiʿi Ayatollah Muhammad Baqir al-Sadr

1988 The Iran–Iraq War ends

1990 Iraq invades Kuwait; the United Nations imposes sanctions and a trade embargo

1991 The Persian Gulf War takes place. Allied forces expel Iraq from Kuwait. The government crushes popular uprisings in the majority Shiʿi south, but Iraqi Kurdistan slips out of its control

1996 Iraq accepts UN Security Council Resolution 986, the "oil-for-food" program

2003 An American-led coalition invades Iraq; Saddam Hussein is captured. The Baʿthist regime in Iraq ends

0.1. ***Map of Iraq with Governorates under the Baʿth.*** © Aaron M. Faust. Prepared by Bill Nelson.

PREFACE

How did Saddam Hussein and the Baʿth Party rule Iraq? What was life like for their ordinary citizens? This book analyzes these questions based upon the Baʿth Party's internal records—records the Baʿthist regime never intended to reveal to the Iraqi public, let alone the world at large. Specifically, this study looks at a set of documents from the party's central archive, formerly housed at its Regional Command (RC, *al-qiyāda al-quṭriyya*) headquarters in Baghdad. Known as the "Baʿth Arab Socialist Party Regional Command Collection" (BRCC), the Iraq Memory Foundation's (IMF) Kanan Makiya, an Iraqi dissident and exile, discovered the archive in 2003. For four years, IMF employees explored and scanned the BRCC's pages at their offices in Baghdad with the intention of one day including the records in a documentation center in Iraq. Wartime conditions, however, made IMF officials fear for the safety of the BRCC and other documents they had collected. In 2006–2007, the organization arranged for the United States government to transport the IMF's holdings to the United States for scanning and safekeeping. In 2009, the IMF negotiated an agreement with the Hoover Institution Archives on the campus of Stanford University in Palo Alto, California, to receive its collections in order to preserve and make them accessible to scholars until conditions in Iraq allow for their return. The Iraqi government and Hoover subsequently signed a memorandum of understanding to this effect.[1]

All told, the entire "Hizb al-Baʿth al-ʿArabi al-ʾIshtiraki in Iraq [Baʿth Party] records, 1968–2003" collection at Hoover consists of approximately eleven million pages in a series of datasets grouped together by document type and year collected. The particular segment of the BRCC that this study looks at—officially the "Boxfiles dataset" but referred to generically as the "BRCC" throughout—consists of 2,764,631 digitized pages found in 6,420 boxfiles from the years 1979 to 2003. Those years, which correspond to Saddam Hussein's presidency, constitute the time period of this study.[2]

This study focuses on the BRCC files because the Regional Command was the Baʿth Party's highest authoritative body in a one-party totalitarian dictatorship under Saddam Hussein. Hussein kept a close eye on everything that happened in Iraq down to the minutest details. The Baʿth Party served as an extension of his authority, using its web-like cell structure to fan out into every corner of the country and the farthest reaches of state and society. In a regime in which everything was political and no boundaries existed between the governmental and civil, or public and private, spheres, the Baʿth Party became Hussein's chief political instrument—his organ of meta-control.[3] As such, it was not as feared as the security services, as powerful as the army, or as big as the ministerial bureaucracy, but the party monitored and regulated all of these and other government institutions, occasionally duplicated their functions, and maintained a monopoly over civil life and association. Accordingly, the BRCC contains documents about virtually every aspect of life in Hussein's Iraq, providing a panoramic view of his regime.

A large portion of the BRCC archive relates directly to party affairs. Its documents include policy directives and regulations sent from the Party Secretariat down the chain of command as well as replies, reports, and memoranda filed up through the organizational hierarchy. The BRCC contains files related to party branches and committees within other state organs and social groups; correspondence about personnel and administrative matters both within the party and government bureaucracy; communications by the Party Secretariat with the Office of the President (*dīwān al-riʾāsa and riʾāsat al-jumhūriyya*), the Revolutionary Command Council (RCC, *majlis qiyādat al-thawra*), the various security services, the Professional and Mass Organizations (PMOs, *al-munaẓẓamāt al-mihniyya wa-l-jamāhīriyya*), government ministries, and other state appendages; internal organizational and bureaucratic matters, including the creation, dissolution, and amalgamation of party units; statistics of various kinds; files on special programs and initiatives; ideological materials; membership files and investigations into incidents relating to particular individuals; and materials from the party's National Command (*al-qiyāda al-qawmiyya*).[4]

A substantial number of boxfiles also relate to state bodies. These include documents detailing matters presented directly to Hussein and his immediate deputies for their decisions; ministerial files, especially those from the ministries of defense, interior, and culture and media; records of state honors and awards meted out and taken away; accountings of expenditures, procurement, and other financial matters; correspondence related to students accepted into and rejected from the teachers colleges, military academies, and state-run religious schools; reports about prisoners of war (POWs), opposition groups, and criminal matters; programs and official slogans for national ceremonies; files about the activities of the PMOs; petitions from citizens to Hussein, party officials, and ministers; and boxfiles without titles or simply labeled "miscellaneous." Also included within the BRCC, but not under consideration for this study, are the equivalent of middle and high school registers for the entire country, collected by the security services. The registers record basic personal and political information about each student.[5] Additionally, the BRCC includes almost four million pages of membership files. These are the main—although not the only—types of documents included in the BRCC. The boxfiles cover literally thousands of political, economic, social, legal, historical, personal, and other subjects; an exhaustive list cannot be presented here.[6] That the BRCC includes information about so many aspects of life proves that the party constituted the unifying thread within the totalitarian system that Hussein used to control Iraq.

In addition to the IMF collections at the Hoover Institution, the Conflict Records Research Center (CRRC) at the National Defense University in Washington, DC, also opened in 2010. It has tens of thousands of documents and thousands of hours of audio tapes of Hussein discussing affairs of state with his subordinates.[7]

Until these archives opened, scholars of Baʿthist Iraq, usually without access to the country, let alone Baʿthist officials or internal files, used newspaper accounts, broadcast material, Western archives, interviews with exiles, and official Iraqi and international statistics to paint as accurate a picture of the Baʿthist State as possible given the resources at their disposal. Nevertheless, because of the distance between themselves, their sources, and their subjects, their conclusions could not delve beyond a certain depth with a reasonable degree of certainty.[8] That is why until Joseph Sassoon's recent *Saddam Hussein's Baʿth Party* and Dina Rizk Khoury's *Iraq in Wartime*, both of which draw on the IMF collections and, in Sassoon's case, the CRRC material, most in-depth academic works about modern Iraq based on primary sources end in 1958—the year the "Free Officers" overthrew the Hashemite Monarchy.[9] As Makiya wrote in the 1998 edition of his *Republic of Fear*, the first book to analyze the character of Baʿthist Iraq, "Every writer on post-1968 Iraq has to work with severely inadequate information originating in an obsessive official attitude toward 'national security.'"[10] As a result, it was, as Marion Farouk-Sluglett and Peter Sluglett lamented, "extremely hard to discover how Iraq is actually run on a day-to-day basis, how the bureaucracy functions, how essential services are maintained, and so forth."[11]

Fortunately, with the opening of the Hoover records and the CRRC, these statements are no longer true. Today's scholars of Baʿthist Iraq are no longer limited by the nature of their sources, and these sources provide a breathtaking and unprecedented amount of detail in comparison to the information available about other Arab states and, indeed, most autocratic regimes. The BRCC documents permit their readers to see *exactly* how Iraq was run on a day-to-day basis, how the bureaucracy functioned, how essential services were maintained, and how the Baʿthist State and its citizens interacted. What is more, in addition to relying on speeches, official publications, and media accounts, scholars can now see on Baʿth Party or presidential stationary—sometimes in Saddam Hussein's own handwriting—the plans for the regime's policies stated explicitly on the page.

This study builds on the work of scholars such as Amatzia Baram, Ofra Bengio, Charles Tripp, Kanan Makiya, Marion Farouk-Sluglett, Peter Sluglett, Isam al-Khafaji, Faleh A. Jabar, and others. Part of its purpose is to assess the findings of these authors based on the new information that the BRCC archive contains. In many cases, the BRCC confirms their conclusions but adds a rich layer of detail and anecdote that enhances our understanding. In others, the historical record requires modification. In either case, I rely on these scholars for their excellent analyses of the Iraqi press and the interviews they conducted with Iraqis who lived under and worked in the regime. The circumstances under which I wrote this book did not permit interviews or exhaustive media analysis. This study's original contribution is its deep and extensive look at the BRCC conducted over six months of full-time research in the archive, and its analysis of the documents based on the benefit of reading previous scholarship about Baʿthist Iraq and other, similar regimes. Along with its virtues, I am aware of the limitations of this approach. The reader should keep these in mind, in addition to a series of methodological issues the BRCC documents present.

METHODOLOGY

Despite the BRCC's great value, its sheer size, scope, and complexity produce a number of methodological challenges that require scholars of the BRCC—myself included—to attach a degree of provisionality to their findings. First, as Merle Fainsod found in his landmark study of the Smolensk Archive, a Soviet documentary collection one-tenth the size of the BRCC's boxfiles dataset, "The array of documents in the Archive ramifies over so many diverse fields as inevitably to pose a serious problem of organization, selection, and emphasis."[12] The BRCC is so large that even scholars with defined topics cannot know for sure that they did not miss a critical document, or that the information they discovered is representative of the rest of the archive. The Baʿthist records are the product of imperfect humans, and the documents describe their fallible and sometimes mercurial actions. The records contain errors and display lapses in protocol, illustrate erratic application of directives and procedures, and suggest an array of motivations, abilities, and intentions. To quote Fainsod again, "Like a slow-motion camera, the documents in the Archive reveal a tale of infinite complexity."[13] The amount of detail in the BRCC is so rich that there are invariably exceptions to every rule. Without reproducing the BRCC word-for-word, it is impossible to include every exception with each statement of fact or analysis. It will take many years, book-length monographs, and journal articles on narrower subjects than the larger issues that this study addresses before anybody will be able to do a true meta-analysis of Husseini Baʿthist historiography.

How is it possible to tell a coherent story about Baʿthist Iraq based upon such a large and diverse body of information? Scholars will approach this question differently. In my experience, it is impossible to read every page and file absent virtually unlimited time in the Hoover archives. Over six months, I therefore decided to read at least one of every *type* of file in the BRCC to gain a breadth of understanding. I then read *all* of certain kinds of records over varying time periods depending on how deeply I wanted to focus on particular subjects. I looked, for example, through all of the box-files with titles related to the President's Office, Baʿth Party statistics, and religion, and I examined a file from each year, from 1980 to 2003, for all of the party's regional bureaus. In contrast, I read a smaller number of files emanating from party branches, sections, divisions, and cells, and from the government ministries. Since stray sets of documents about particular topics can be found in random places, this does not eliminate the size and complexity problem, but hopefully by reading selective samples and using those to focus my research, I reduced it.

Second, the BRCC is not a complete documentary record of Hussein's Iraq. The BRCC does not contain files about every subject in every year, leaving time gaps in its information. It also has more data about some topics than others. This arises partly from the fact that the BRCC is the Baʿth Party's central archive. Although it contains correspondence with, and carbon copies from, government ministries, the security services, the President's Office, the PMOs, lower level Baʿthist organizations, and many other departments, bureaus, and bodies—and thus provides a good overview of the Baʿthist State as a whole—the bulk of BRCC documents either derive from, or were sent to, the Office of the Party Secretariat (*maktab ʾimānat sirr al-quṭr*). The archive thus provides a centralized, top-down view from the party's perspective. The vantage point from one of the security services, the Education Ministry, or a local party organization would not necessarily change the conclusions presented in this study, but their records would undoubtedly provide alternative angles from which to view Hussein's Iraq.

Third, in addition to being immense, the BRCC is poorly organized and only partially annotated. Whether through filing errors or for other reasons, it is not uncommon to find a document in a boxfile that is entirely unrelated to the boxfile's title. Furthermore, because Hussein micromanaged the country to a great degree, and because the Baʿth Party oversaw all affairs of state and society, documents on subjects large and small, from opposition groups to agriculture, appear in boxfiles for the President's Office, the Party Secretariat, and the Baʿth Party's bureaus, branches, sections, divisions, and cells. For this reason, and due to the BRCC's size, it is impossible for a researcher to declare with a reasonable degree of certainty that he or she has read *all* of the documents about a particular subject.

Fourth, the BRCC documents are replete with inaccurate information and propaganda. Baʿthists wrote their internal documents in the party's idiom, parroting ideological propaganda and praise for Hussein as part of bureaucratic practice and everyday ritual. Baʿthist ideology posited that Hussein and the party's policies were always correct and only failed due to a lack of ideological fervor, poor discipline or organization, or enemy sabotage. Bad news could only occur if an inferior did not execute the leadership's commands properly or allowed the Baʿth's enemies to get the better of them. Unlike in a democratic government where a president or prime minister must answer for the actions of lowly officials, in Baʿthist Iraq inferiors bore the responsibility for their superiors' decisions. The consequences for reporting bad news could be severe and the rewards for good news, great. As a result, lower level officials often lied to their superiors and exaggerated statistics. Citizen petitions sometimes offer different accounts of events than the regime's investigations into them. The documents do not present an objective mirror of reality but a magnification of Hussein and the party's power.

That does not mean, however, as one scholar has argued, that the documents present only "a picture of a state and a party awesome in their ability to monitor and control dissent and skillful in manipulating their resources to reward loyal citizens with a largesse that belied the country's poverty." While the documents contain much propaganda, and certainly exaggerate at times, they do not "represent the party's creation of its own world."[14] In addition to lies and exaggerations, the records contain many honest assessments of the conditions in Baʿthist Iraq and the regime's less than "awesome" authority. In particular, chapters 5, 7, and 8 highlight the deficiencies in Baʿthist control in specific times and places, and with regard to different elements of Iraqi society such as soldiers, women, the tribes, and religion.

Internal party reports almost always contain lists of "positives" (*ʾījābiyyāt*) *and* "negatives" (*salbiyyāt*) about a particular phenomenon in addition to sections extolling the leader, the party, and the nation. Reading the documents, I did not get a sense that Hussein's regime was an all-powerful, perfect totalitarian state, as Hussein would have liked. Rather, the documents lay bare his regime's imperfections, explaining why ideological predictions did not come to pass and offering recommendations for improvement. The archive's heavy use of propaganda can cloud and sometimes mask the reality of events, but propaganda was, in part, a reflection of Iraqis' reality and thus also offers a window into how the regime worked. When analyzing the BRCC, I never took the documents at face value. Instead, by reading widely, deeply, and skeptically; by learning the intricacies, vocabulary, and, most importantly, the logic, of the archive; by studying the tendencies of the regime and the behavior of its officials and citizens; and by triangulating information between documents and with other sources, I try in this study to explain the regime's strategy for ruling the country and the extent to which it did—and did not—succeed.

Finally, other than that of Saddam Hussein and his top deputies, this study does not use the names of the Iraqis mentioned in the BRCC. The recent demise of Hussein's regime and the chaos that followed made the BRCC available to scholars, but that also means that many of those named in the archive are still alive. The political situation in post-Baʿthist Iraq remains fluid, and there is no reason to endanger anybody for reasons that might be within or beyond my imagination. Extreme caution in this regard is therefore warranted.

A NOTE ON TRANSLITERATION

In transliterating from the Arabic of the documents, I have tried to stay faithful to the guidelines set forth by the *International Journal of Middle East Studies*. For names and places, however, I do not use diacritics, and if an Arabic word, place, or name has a common English spelling, I use that instead of the transliterated version.

ACKNOWLEDGMENTS

Writing this book has been a solitary endeavor, but I would never have finished it without the support of family, friends, mentors, and colleagues. First and foremost, my wife, Rachel Alpert, provided unwavering love, support, patience, and encouragement. My parents, Ruth Anne and Halley Faust, uprooted their lives for long periods on multiple occasions to help us take care of our daughters. My brother, Josh Faust, let me invade his apartment for weeks on end while I conducted research at the Hoover Institution Archives. The best reward for finishing this book is the extra time that I will get to spend with my family.

This book grew out of my dissertation at Boston University (BU). I would especially like to thank Betty Anderson, who spent many hours reading drafts, offering advice and constructive criticism, and coaching me through the dissertation, dissertation-to-book, and book proposal processes. My advisor at BU, Herbert Mason, never failed to listen, respond, and advocate for me within the University Professors Program and on applications to support my studies and research. Igor Lukes, who sat on my dissertation committee, directed me toward sources about European history, politics, and totalitarianism, which contributed to the comparative aspects of this book. I would also like to thank Houchang Chehabi for his friendship, mentorship, and tutelage on all things Iranian; Sunil Sharma; Merlin Swartz; and Erik Goldstein. Last but not least, Edna Newmark, Susan Tomassetti, and Martha Wellman Khan made sure that I dotted my "i"s and crossed my "t"s on the way toward graduation.

At the Iraq Memory Foundation (IMF), IMF founder and Brandeis University professor Kanan Makiya warmly supported my interest in the Baʿthist documents from allowing me to first view them at his home in 2007 to assisting my research at Hoover to serving on my dissertation committee. IMF research director Hassan Mneimneh also deserves thanks.

At the Hoover Institution, the companionship and expertise of my friends Ahmed Dhia and Haidar Hadi kept me going through long days in the reading room; their dedication to the IMF documents is inspirational. Former director of the library and archives Richard Sousa facilitated my access to the IMF documents. Current director Eric Wakin has proved equally supportive. Carol Leadenham and her staff in the Hoover reading room fielded my many questions and requests with patience and professionalism. Deborah Ventura and Celeste Szeto provided critical logistical support during my trips to Stanford University. Stephanie Stewart and Vishnu Jani helped me obtain the copies of documents that appear in this book.

Jim Burr and his colleagues at the University of Texas Press have proved a pleasure to work with. I am grateful to the two reviewers of my initial manuscript who submitted helpful comments, which greatly improved the quality of this text.

Financial assistance from the Smith Richardson Foundation's World Politics and Statecraft Fellowship and BU's University Professors Program aided my ability to live in California while I conducted my research. A Fulbright scholarship and National Security Education Program (NSEP) Boren fellowship allowed me to study Arabic full-time in Damascus, Syria, from September 2008 to August 2009, where I gained the language skills to explore the Baʿthist archives. Hopefully the blood being shed by one Baʿthist regime in Syria and in the wake of another in Iraq will soon leave both countries at peace.

PART I. INTRODUCTION

1. THE INCULCATION OF LOYALTY

I hope that his party loyalty is stronger than his familial allegiance.

SADDAM HUSSEIN, ON A BAʿTHIST WHOSE NEPHEWS JOINED AN OPPOSITION PARTY

INTRODUCTION

On March 4, 1984, the secretary of the Arab Baʿth Socialist Party's (*ḥizb al-baʿth al-ʿarabī al-ʾishtirākī*) Wasit branch wrote to the head of Iraq's High Committee for Deserters and Draft Dodgers praising a citizen's act of allegiance to "the land, the nation, and the victorious leader, Saddam Hussein (God keep him) . . . which is without precedent in history, even in the first *Qādisiyya*."[1] A Partisan from the Wasit branch's Saad section, the secretary wrote, tried to convince his son to turn himself in to his army unit after deserting. The son refused, so the Partisan, a sixty-two-year-old bicycle repairman from Suwayra, shot and killed his son while his son slept before turning himself in. "Please be apprised, and present this unrivaled, awesome example of the fidelity of Iraqis to the president (God keep him) so that the president may consider stopping the legal investigations against [the father]," the secretary concluded. Saddam Hussein reviewed the secretary's letter and agreed with the recommendation. Writing his instructions in green ink in the letter's right-hand margin, Hussein pardoned the man, granted him a medal, and had the event included in official documents and films about the Iran–Iraq War.[2]

Contrary to the Wasit branch secretary's assertion, the Baʿth Regional Command Collection (BRCC) documents show that the phenomenon of family members killing or turning each other in to be executed for capital crimes was not uncommon in Hussein's Iraq. A 1985 report to the Baʿth Party's highest administrative unit, the Office of the Party Secretariat, describes thirty-seven "exemplary and honorable cases" where citizens informed on their family members for desertion. A number of these citizens accompanied the detachments sent to apprehend their brethren. One man refused to accept his nephew's body; another killed his brother because the brother would not turn himself in.[3] These incidents continued even after the Iran–Iraq and Gulf wars. In 1993, the father of a Special Republican Guard member threw his son out of the house because he repeatedly ran away from his unit. When the son hit him and attacked his mother in retaliation, the father killed him.[4] In an almost identical incident, in 1995, a man from al-Kut tried to apprehend his son in order to turn him in but could not physically arrest him. He presented himself to the police after shooting his son dead. He too received a pardon for his "act of courage."[5]

In addition to these examples of extreme loyalty, the BRCC tells stories of tribal sheikhs who executed their tribesmen for criminal activity, of Baʿthists who turned in their nephews for joining opposition movements, and of friends who reported their fellows for comments made in confidence.[6] The BRCC contains tens, if not hundreds, of reports about Iraqis who composed oaths of allegiance to Hussein signed in their own blood. Poets wrote odes to his leadership.[7] Hussein's institutions of tyranny—the security services, police, Baʿth Party, and military—required hundreds of thousands (and during the Iran–Iraq and Gulf wars, millions) of officers, volunteers, and conscripts to carry out his wars and domestic operations. Each year, thousands of young people from all regions, sects, and ethnicities applied for admission into the Baʿth's security, police, and military academies. These applicants knew the secret police's penchant for unwarranted arrests, frequent use of torture, and murder, often after "disappearing" their victims. But they still applied. State institutions and their vast bureaucracies needed qualified officials and technocrats. Schools required teachers. The streets had to be swept, and the Baʿth found an ample supply of willing *mukhtārīn*, or local watchmen, to keep an eye on their neighbors. Finally, the Baʿth Party needed members. In the 1970s, the Baʿth counted its membership in the hundreds of thousands.[8] By 1986, BRCC statistics show that the party's roles had grown to over 1.6 million people at all levels of party membership; by 2002, they contained four million, or almost 16 percent of the population.[9] Even if most of the people mentioned above never killed or carried out oppression themselves, they worked for the system that did, thereby either explicitly or tacitly affirming it. Saddam Hussein ruled Iraq as a dictator, often micromanaging mundane affairs in far-flung provinces, but the BRCC documents demonstrate that he could not have survived as president from 1979 to 2003 without creating a wide base of support at all levels of government and throughout society.

Why did millions of Iraqis participate in Hussein's government, go along with his social policies, and regularly demonstrate their fealty to him and the Baʿth Party, especially when doing so required turning against their religious and ethnic groups, families, and tribes? How did Hussein and the

Baʿth inculcate this kind of loyalty in their citizens? Why did the system of control they constructed prove so durable through uprisings, two wars, and UN sanctions?

Why, moreover, did the same system that elicited so much loyalty also spark resistance, insubordination, and criminal behavior? If, overall, the Baʿthist system worked—it kept the Baʿth in power for thirty-five years, twenty-three of those with Hussein as president—the extent of Hussein and the party's authority varied over time and place. It was never absolute, often inefficient, and despotic enough that many Iraqis fled, defected, and deserted even though they knew the potential consequences for themselves and their families. While in the most extreme cases Iraqis proved willing to kill family members for the regime, BRCC statistics show that the vast majority did not. The Baʿth neutralized their existential opposition, but the party's files contain hundreds—if not thousands—of reports of Baʿthists, policemen, security service personnel, and soldiers killed or injured while investigating crimes, chasing down deserters or opposition party members, and guarding party offices.[10] These offenses occurred so often that the regime promulgated eight amnesties from 1980 to 1999.[11]

If Iraqis generally showed their loyalty, they often did so grudgingly. While many Baʿthists attended meetings, the BRCC reports that significant numbers skipped them and otherwise "shirked" their party duties (*al-tasarrub*). Lower level party organizations did not respond to requests for information in the stipulated time and handled secret party correspondence carelessly. Accounting irregularities occurred because Baʿthists stole from party coffers. The Baʿth frequently had trouble recruiting new members and had to plead with their existing cadre not to take part in "mistaken" or "un-natural" religious practices.[12] After the Iran–Iraq War, soldiers left the party in the hundreds of thousands.[13] When the 1991 uprisings broke out, few party members reported to their posts to defend Baʿthist and government installations.[14] In 1995, the regime had to pay its top officials to attend public ceremonies.[15]

How should we understand the stories of extraordinary allegiance, middling support, and resistance that the BRCC documents tell? How and why did Hussein and the Baʿth achieve such power and influence over Iraqi state, society, and their citizens' individual lives, despite the inefficiencies, corruption, and both tacit and overt opposition that their rule produced?

BAʿTHIFICATION: SADDAM HUSSEIN'S IRAQI TOTALITARIANISM

In analyzing Baʿthist Iraq, much of the prevailing literature has focused on what Marion Farouk-Sluglett and Peter Sluglett call the "highly personalized politics" of Saddam Hussein's emergence as Iraq's strongman following the Baʿth's successful 1968 coup and his takeover of the presidency in 1979.[16] As Amatzia Baram and Ofra Bengio have detailed, Hussein cultivated a loyal inner circle and political and economic elite, based upon longtime party association and the traditional loyalties of family, clan, tribe, sect, and region.[17] The ties inherent in these "primordial" allegiances, combined with Hussein's tendency to shuffle top officials in and out of positions of power, enabled him to consolidate control over the major pillars of his regime: the security services, the Baʿth Party, the military, and the oil industry. Charles Tripp's work has shown how these elites also served as conduits for patronage, creating clientelist networks that fanned out into a "shadow state" representing "the real nexus of power" behind the government.[18] In his analysis of the BRCC documents, Joseph Sassoon shows that kin and clan connections were critical to Hussein's grip on authority. In one of its own documents, an official in Hussein's most powerful security service, the Special Security Organization (SSO, *jihāz al-ʾamn al-khāṣṣ*), attributed the SSO's efficiency to "total loyalty based on kinship and the substantial rewards enjoyed by employees."[19]

The research for this study confirms the work of these scholars about how Hussein held the Baʿthist elite together through kin and clan connections, clientelism and patronage, and a policy of "carrot and stick." Nevertheless, the tactics that Hussein used to manipulate his inner circle do not explain how he cultivated such a large support base within all segments of society, a base that the documents reveal stretched beyond the personal and patronage networks of the "shadow state." Why would a lowly bicycle repairman from Suwayra, who did not occupy a top party position, and who had no personal connection to Hussein, shoot his son out of loyalty to the regime? Why would thousands of Kurds join the National Defense Regiments (*ʾafwāj al-difāʿ al-waṭanī*), a Kurdish militia created by the Baʿth to help suppress the Kurdish population? Why would Shiʿi taxi drivers and hoteliers living in the holy shrine cities of Najaf and Karbala collaborate with the Baʿth Party and security services to root out their co-religionists in opposition parties, and to suppress popular Shiʿi rites during the holy month of Muharram?[20]

For Kanan Makiya, the answers to these questions lie in the totalitarian "Republic of Fear" that Hussein and the Baʿth created through their extensive use of violence. As Makiya wrote, "Violence generates the fear that creates the complicity that constitutes the power, which first passed to the party and then to Saddam Husain in the form of his authority."[21] The Baʿth, Makiya argued, employed violence as a direct application of the ideology of party founder, Michel Aflaq, who justified harsh tactics against the Baʿth's enemies in the name of pan-Arabism.[22] Since violence both perpetuated and legitimized Baʿthist rule, the party had to use violence even after Makiya believes it eliminated all opposition and established its "absolutist leadership." The Baʿth consequently continued to assert their enemies' existence in order to rationalize their brutality. As Makiya explained:

> Tyrannies and dictatorships resort to violence when their authority is placed in jeopardy. But for the Baʿth, violence is no longer merely the ultimate sanction used periodically against a genuine opposition. The Baʿth invent their enemies; violence—not the threat of it—is institutionalized, forever reproducing and intensifying that all-pervasive climate of suspicion, fear, and complicity so characteristic of their polity.[23]

As a result, Makiya wrote in the 1998 introduction to his book, "Expansion of the means of violence . . . had undergone the classic inversion: from being a means to an end, the elimination of opponents and the exercise of raw power, they became horrific ends in themselves." This produced "a polity made up of citizens who positively expected to be tortured under certain circumstances."[24] To paraphrase the totalitarian theorist Hannah Arendt, violence was the essence of the Baʿth's form of government.[25]

Information gleaned from the BRCC documents supports much of the Republic of Fear thesis but also contradicts it in many ways. As this study shows, fear played a large part in Baʿthist Iraq and violence played a role in creating it. Violence was not the only factor that produced fear, however, and the production of fear was not the primary purpose behind the Baʿth's violence. As discussed throughout this book, Iraqis complied with the regime—but also resisted it—in response to a wider array of stimuli than Hussein's organs of terror produced.

This study supports the claim that Baʿthist Iraq was "totalitarian" but follows a definition of the term that recognizes that no regime can wield unlimited authority, elicit unremitting allegiance, and eliminate *all* opposition. As Richard Overy has noted, "the paradigm of completely unrestricted power, exercised in a coherent, centralized polity by men of exceptional ruthlessness who brooked no limitations or dissent was, and remains, a political-science fantasy."[26] Instead of as a regime type that actually *achieves* total power, historians today define "totalitarianism" as the *aspiration* to apply an exclusivist, utopian, populist ideology. No totalitarian dictator—not even Adolf Hitler or Joseph Stalin—has ever fully realized this aspiration.[27] The ideology that inspires it nonetheless lends itself to *a strategy of rule* that leads totalitarian leaders to seek a monopoly over political power and thought based in the popular legitimacy they claim comes from their unique ability to advance the collective welfare of their nations. Unlike authoritarian leaders who govern by the logic of "might makes right," or "*Oderint Dum Metuant*" ("Let them hate as long as they fear"), totalitarian rulers want their citizens to love big brother.[28] They want to have their cake and eat it too: to retain autocratic power in the name—and at the behest—of "the people" or "the masses."[29] Yet because the necessities of retaining autocratic power invariably require the oppression of at least some of a ruler's citizens, because no ruler can obtain all of his citizens' approval, and because a ruler cannot abolish *all* opponents and alternative political ideas, a wide gap inevitably emerges between a totalitarian ruler's utopian promises and claims of mass support and the illiberal, imperfect reality his citizens experience. Acknowledging this gap would debunk the ideological claims at the core of a totalitarian regime's legitimacy. The strategy that totalitarian rulers apply therefore consists of coercing and eliciting support from their citizens and eliminating institutional and human elements in society that refuse to be co-opted. This allows them to simultaneously work toward their conception of an ideal society, consolidate and perpetuate their political power, and prove the popular legitimacy they assert. When a ruler pursues these goals with *sufficient resources* and the *willingness to employ any and all means necessary* to achieve them—violent, peaceful, bureaucratic, ideological, organizational, cultural, religious, and more—a totalitarian strategy is born. In theory, this strategy enjoys the active support of the masses, mobilized by the party, and led by the leader for the glory of their unified nation. In practice, it becomes the forced simulation of mass popular consent.

When defined in this way, "totalitarianism" is a useful tool for historical analysis because it explains why Hussein and the Baʿth operated as they did instead of just describing the extent of their authority in a given time and place.[30] From a comparative perspective, it identifies the common modus operandi of Hussein's Iraq, Stalin's Russia, Hitler's Germany, Mao's China, North Korea, and most of Eastern Europe from 1945 to 1953. Simultaneously, it recognizes that these regimes emerged out of distinct historical and cultural contexts; they were not identical.

Calling these regimes "totalitarian" nonetheless differentiates them from their authoritarian cousins. Totalitarianism and authoritarianism share autocratic traits, but their strategies of rule differ. Totalitarian regimes rule by politicizing and mobilizing their citizens, by attempting to turn everyone into active supporters: "A totalitarian regime not only rules 'from the outside' through violence, it also seeks the full and unconditional loyalty of the individual citizen."[31] Authoritarian regimes, on the other hand, demobilize large segments of their populations to keep them out of politics, permitting a "limited political pluralism" so long as nothing threatens their authority.[32]

The term "totalitarian" can also mark different periods or geographies in the same regime's time in government. As Arendt argued, after Stalin died the Soviet Union went through a period of "detotalitarization" when the arts returned and dissidents could plead "not guilty" in court.[33] While maintaining many of the same methods of rule, the Soviet regime began to moderate its aspirations—that is, it no longer pursued *total* control—a trend that advanced in fits and starts, eventually culminating in perestroika. For its part, Hussein's regime never pursued the same comprehensive strategy in the Kurdish and marsh regions as it did in the rest of Iraq.

The totalitarian strategy that Hussein and the Baʿth used to rule Iraq was called "Baʿthification" (*tabʿīth*). The main purpose behind Baʿthification was to inculcate loyalty in the Iraqi populace by making the brand of Baʿthist ideology employed by the regime during Hussein's presidency—Husseini Baʿthism—the primary basis for political and social order and the supreme source for individual and collective identity. Husseini Baʿthism consisted of a mixture of ideological and personal motives deriving from the utopian, totalitarian aspirations of traditional Baʿthist thought and the selfish and pragmatic necessities required for Hussein and the Baʿthist elite to retain power within the context of modern Iraqi history and culture. Baʿthification was a particularly Iraqi phenomenon in which Hussein manipulated Iraqis' tribal and familial conceptions of honor, and religious and ethnic sensibilities, interweaving them with classic totalitarian methods to solidify his control.[34]

As with other totalitarian regimes in history, the Iraqi Baʿth aimed to create a "new man" (*al-ʾinsān al-jadīd*) in a "new society" (*al-mujtamaʿ al-jadīd*), to transform the nature of human beings in order to advance the fortunes of Saddam Hussein's person; the values of the Baʿth's July 17–30, 1968, revolution; and the collective welfare of the Iraqi and Arab nations.[35] During Hussein's presidency, the Baʿthist propaganda machine fused these three elements—the leader, the party, and the nation—into one myth-symbol complex representative of Iraqi patriotism and national identity. Throughout this study I refer to this myth-symbol complex as the "Baʿthist Trinity." It formed the real content of the ideology behind Hussein's regime from 1979 to 2003, as opposed to the purely idealistic principles of the Baʿth's traditional slogan: "Unity, Freedom, and Socialism." Each symbol within the Baʿthist Trinity equated to the other so that pledging allegiance to one demonstrated an Iraqi's loyalty to all. Conversely, the Baʿth considered an attack on Hussein or the party to be "national treason."[36]

Baʿthification was thus a fusion of an idealistic aspiration to mold Iraq's heterogeneous population into one nation united behind Husseini Baʿthist principles and a strategy for Saddam Hussein to establish and perpetuate his dictatorship. Ideally, if Hussein could transform Iraqi society into a Husseini Baʿthist society—if he could "Husseini Baʿthize" it, or "Baʿthize" it for short—he would not need to use force to control the population.

The Iraqi Baʿth considered itself a "vanguard" (*ṭalīʿa*) and "leading party" (*al-ḥizb al-qāʾid*), which derived its legitimacy from popular support and the ability to advance the welfare of "the people" (*al-shaʿb*) or "the masses" (*al-jamāhīr*).[37] As Hussein put it, "The relationship between the party and the masses is a living dialectical relationship, for the party without the masses remains merely an elite, and the masses without the party remain merely raw material and a broken capacity (*ṭāqa muʿaṭṭala*) led astray amid the turmoil of the daily progress of events."[38] Like the Baʿth's relationship with the Iraqi state, Baʿthist ideology held that the masses needed the party to give them direction. In turn, the party needed the masses to supply it with members, fight in its wars, partake in its rituals, and otherwise support its initiatives. Whether sincere, coerced, or elicited, mass support justified the Baʿth's totalitarian strategy because the party's rationale for using such strict control was to advance the people's welfare. The Baʿth thus had to demonstrate that the people felt their welfare was in fact being improved. This is why the Baʿth did not content themselves with authoritarian means—with simply suppressing their citizens—and why they did not tolerate neutrality.[39] Instead, the Baʿth spent considerable effort mobilizing their citizenry to participate in the party's rituals, wars, and initiatives, and they expected Iraqis to exhibit active support in these venues to prove their loyalty.

Despite Hussein and the Baʿth's efforts, the oppressive realities of life under their rule belied their progressive narrative. Perhaps because of this obvious gap between rhetoric and reality, the secondary literature has largely denied both classical and Husseini Baʿthist ideology a significant role in the history of Hussein's presidency. Hanna Batatu, for example, argues that the theories of the most influential Baʿthist philosopher in Iraq, Michel Aflaq, "do not add up to an entirely consistent point of view."[40] Similarly, Marion Farouk-Sluglett and Peter Sluglett criticize Majid Khadduri for discussing the post-1968 Iraqi Baʿth in ideological terms, "as if the Baʿth had a coherent set of ideological principles."[41] Only Makiya finds fault with this "reluctance to come to terms with the coherence of the Baʿth," arguing that "ʿAflaq's early ideas had to have been followed through by later Baʿthi leaders."[42] What do the documents suggest?

The attack against Baʿthist ideology as a cover for self-serving action is true if Hussein's policies from 1979 to 2003 are judged against the purely theoretical principles preached by Aflaq and his cofounders in the 1940s and if Hussein never really meant anything he said about his ideological desire to pursue Iraq's greatness or Arab unity. But Hussein did not try to apply traditional Baʿthist ideology during his presidency. Instead, he pursued a Husseini Baʿthist version. Recordings of Hussein's private conversations, moreover, show that he tended to say the same things in public as he did behind closed doors.[43] He consistently expressed his belief in the Baʿth Party's message in addition to asserting that only under his leadership could the party steer Iraq toward a better future. In his rhetoric, Hussein consequently kept the ideological elements of classical Aflaqian Baʿthism that legitimized the party's attempt to seek total power while transferring that power to himself in the form of a leadership cult. The production of this cult rationalized the move from "collective leadership" (*al-qiyāda al-jamāʿiyya*) under his predecessor, Ahmad Hassan al-Bakr, to making Hussein "*the* leader" (*al-qāʾid*) of the country.[44] Hussein could therefore justify the use of any means necessary to retain power because according to the logic of Husseini Baʿthism, anything that he did was good for Iraq by virtue of the fact that he did it. Just as the Italian Fascist philosopher Giovanni Gentile defined the "real 'views' of [Benito Mussolini]" as "those which he formulates and executes at one and the same time," Hussein's words and deeds became Husseini Baʿthist doctrine.[45] It is too simple, therefore, to say that Hussein was motivated purely by either personal or ideological reasons because in Baʿthist Iraq those reasons were the selfsame thing. Anything that Hussein said immediately became the official philosophy of all facets of Baʿthist society.

Understanding the principles of Husseini Baʿthism, regardless of their objective truth or the extent to which the population believed them, is critical to comprehend the logic behind the regime's Baʿthification policies and how the Baʿthist State functioned. Husseini Baʿthism provided a logical and moral consistency to what, on its face, was an incoherent and immoral state of affairs. It provided the message behind the Baʿthist liturgy, into which the party indoctrinated its members and citizens. It directed and ordered the Baʿth Party apparatus and, in turn, the party's organization of society. Husseini Baʿthism identified the Baʿth's enemies, countenanced the violence used against them, and validated the preferential treatment given to Baʿth Party members and independent loyalists. In a regime where political considerations were paramount, Husseini Baʿthism stood in for the traditional roles of law, religion, and culture as the sources of legal, ethical, and normative rules in society. As such, ideology was central to the maintenance of Hussein and the party's power even if, as Eric Davis suggests, Baʿthist philosophy "was not taken particularly seriously by the political elite under Saddam."[46] In an intellectual sense, few Iraqis, it seems, truly believed in Baʿthist principles. Those principles nevertheless ordered the environment around them, so they were well served to study them in order to survive in the system. As the Polish dissident Leszek Kolakowski said about ideology behind the Iron Curtain, "It is a paradox that this ideology, in which practically everybody has ceased to believe—those who propagate it, those who profit from it, and those who must listen to it—is still a matter of the most vital importance for the continuing existence of this political system."[47] When the United States and its allies removed Iraq's Baʿthist exoskeleton in 2003, Iraq disintegrated. The reasons for this go beyond a "de-Baʿthification" policy that removed the army, a cadre of technocrats, and high-level officials critical to maintaining the Iraqi state. The BRCC documents show that by 2003, Baʿthification had destroyed or emasculated most of Iraq's pre–1968 governmental, civil, social, and familial institutions and value systems, and had transformed or replaced them with Husseini Baʿthist versions. In addition to stripping the state of expertise and manpower, de-Baʿthification removed the underpinnings of a society conditioned for thirty-five years to operate according to Baʿthist—and for twenty-three years, Husseini Baʿthist—dictates.

MEASURES AND METHODS

Practically, Baʿthification manifested itself in a set of policies and tactics designed to coerce and elicit support for Hussein's regime, and to eliminate alternatives to it. Employing the Baʿth Party as his chief political instrument, Hussein attempted to transform every state and social institution, civil society organization, private family, and individual person in Iraq into a Baʿthist entity or a Baʿth Party member—or to otherwise solicit the institution or individual's loyalty. Baʿthification also required ridding Iraq entirely of alternative political organizations and ideas, and forcing Iraqis to, at least outwardly, subordinate their social, economic, religious, cultural, familial, and individual bonds to Hussein and the Baʿth Party—in addition to their personal inclinations, beliefs, and creativities. As a piece of literature put out by the party's Euphrates bureau in 1985, entitled "A Plan for the Baʿthification of Society" (*khiṭat tabʿīth al-mujtamaʿ*), stated, Baʿthist organizations were "to put in place new measures and methods of mobilization that would lead the masses of the people in their entirety to rally around the revolution and to create absolute loyalty (*al-wilāʾ al-muṭlaq*) to the party and the leader."[48] During Hussein's presidency, the BRCC records show that loyalty—or, more accurately, Hussein and the Baʿth's *perception*

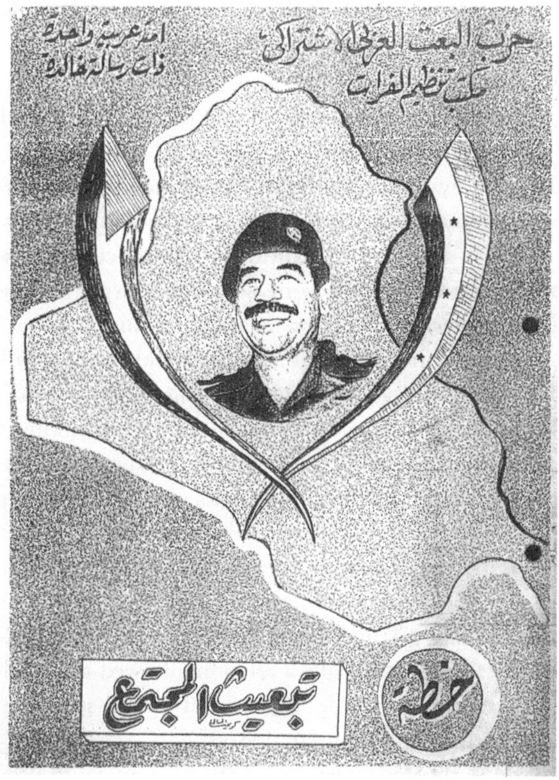

FIGURE I.1. ***The Cover Page to a 1985 Euphrates Bureau Study Entitled, "A Plan for the Baʿthification of Society."*** Source: BRCC, 111-3-2: 5. Courtesy of Hoover Institution Library & Archives, Stanford University.

of a person's loyalty—dictated his or her fate more than any other factor, including his or her familial, tribal, ethnic, sectarian, or local background.

The "measures and methods" that Hussein employed to Baʿthize the country fell under four general rubrics: ideology, organization, terror, and enticement. These four categories of controls are analyzed briefly below and in-depth throughout this book. Although each chapter scrutinizes aspects of these controls so as to better flesh out their characteristics, in reality, the controls overlapped and reinforced one another. Combined, the BRCC documents show that the boundaries these controls placed on permissible action and thought trapped many Iraqis in an environment that channeled their behavior into avenues supportive of the regime. At the same time, the severe consequences that accrued to Hussein's opponents meant that once his regime identified a person as an enemy, the person had little choice but to turn to a life of crime, resistance, or exile.

The language employed by the BRCC's authors demonstrates that Hussein and the Baʿth viewed themselves in quasi-religious terms, as nationalist missionaries sent to save the Arab and Iraqi nations by preaching their Husseini Baʿthist faith to the masses. Since the Baʿth believed they held a monopoly over historical truth, anybody who held an alternative view was not necessarily evil but unenlightened, somebody who did not possess "sufficient awareness that the way of the Baʿth is the right way to serve the people and the nation."[49] Accordingly, the documents' authors explain the core of the Baʿth Party's mission as to "explain" (*tawḍīḥ*) Husseini Baʿthist principles to the masses in order to "indoctrinate" (*tawʿīyya*), "culturalize" (*tathqīf*), and "frame" (*taʾṭīr*), or mold, them into Baʿthist believers who would "mobilize" (*taʿbiʾa*) behind the regime's policies. As a result, the Baʿth leaned heavily on ideological propaganda, cultural production, and a plethora of rituals in all areas of life. The Baʿth designed their indoctrination and culturalization campaigns to imbue an emotional, spiritual, and intellectual faith in Husseini Baʿthism. In an ideal world, this faith would take the place of Iraqis' traditional allegiances and manifest itself in their active and unprompted political support. The particular character of Baʿthist ideology, which Aflaq claimed was "a general philosophy in life" (*falsafa ʿāma fī-l-ḥayāt*), like a religion, allowed the Baʿth to stake a claim to control anything they desired, and Hussein's success amassing so much power allowed him to aspire to do so.[50]

Hand in hand with indoctrination, Baʿthification sought to "organize" Iraqi state and society in their totality so that both the forms and content of all governmental, civil, social, and private institutions and relationships supported the claims of Husseini Baʿthist ideology. Hussein used the Baʿth Party to take over the Iraqi state—to make it into the Party State—and then to use the resources at the Party State's disposal to incorporate social institutions and individuals into the party, state, and the Baʿth's ersatz civil society associations, the "Professional and Mass Organizations" (PMOs). Hussein did this by co-opting or replacing top state officials and social leaders with Baʿthists; recruiting; instituting bureaucratic, administrative, and regulatory controls over Iraq's previously independent social institutions such as the country's tribes and religious establishments; and implementing laws and regulations that controlled normally private matters such as marriage. As with the Nazi policy of *Gleichschaltung*, or the integration and synchronization of German society, organization affected Iraqis' tangible, day-to-day interactions by influencing them to act obediently through the countless, repetitive, institutionalized practices of the "infrastructural power" of the state.[51]

Terror and enticement facilitated indoctrination and organization by, in the former case, clearing Iraq's public and private spaces of organized opposition and alternative worldviews, and, in the latter, by providing positive incentives to support the process of Baʿthification. As with Baʿthification's other means, Hussein used violence primarily for instrumental purposes: as a tool to eliminate people and groups in society that he perceived as a threat to his authority, and as a deterrent to crime and attacks against his regime, which he considered tantamount to political opposition. The fact that Hussein held arbitrary (albeit not absolute) power with few legal or other checks on his authority meant that, like Stalin, he frequently employed violence to eliminate anybody that he merely suspected of disloyalty.[52] No consequences accrued from his use of violence, so it was better to be safe than sorry. As a result, Hussein or another Baʿthist official's irritation or paranoia could lead to the killing, torture, or incarceration of innocent citizens and longtime regime supporters alike. That does not mean, however, that violence became the raison d'être of the Husseini Baʿthist system of governance. Violence was, rather, a byproduct of the arbitrary nature of the system, which included a broad definition of Hussein and the Baʿth Party's enemies.

Equally as important to the Baʿth's use of terror was an established regime of awards, medals, honors, and statuses that brought their winners financial, professional, academic, health, social, and other benefits. Hussein and the Baʿth employed these in tandem with violence and surveillance as incentives for Iraqis to pledge their fealty. Iraqis called this phenomenon "*tarhīb wa-l-targhīb*," or "terror and enticement."[53] The combination of these two elements cemented many Iraqis' loyalties. Terror and enticement offered a stark choice: oppose the regime and face the consequences or support it and live what passed for a normal life in Baʿthist Iraq. As with people everywhere, the BRCC shows that Iraqis wanted to provide for their families, put a roof over their heads, ensure themselves and their children good educational and professional opportunities, move up the social ladder, and live with dignity. Terror and enticement made it so that everybody had something to lose *and* something to gain if they played by the regime's rules. Baʿthist Iraq *was* a "Republic of Fear," but it was not only fear of violence. It was also fear of hunger, homelessness, poverty, and the loss of respect, honor, and opportunity.[54]

Terror and enticement worked particularly well because a person's actions affected the fate of his extended family, and vice-versa. As a result, if for no other reason, an individual who cared about his kin submitted to the Baʿth's rules. Conversely, families had an incentive to preserve their collective welfare by policing their members. When a relative crossed the regime, the BRCC shows that families severed ties with him quickly and decisively in prominent displays of loyalty meant to reassert their allegiance—like the family members who killed their relatives. Especially in a society that greatly valued individual and communal honor—be it familial, tribal, national, or religious—forcing Iraqis to downgrade these normally robust allegiances in favor of Hussein and the Baʿth pressured them to commit otherwise unthinkable acts against their brethren on the regime's behalf. As the process of Baʿthification persisted, these acts happened so frequently that over time they became common. Terror and enticement thus contributed to a normative environment produced by the incentives inherent in its rewards and punishments whereby many Iraqis felt compelled to act for the benefit of the Baʿthist Trinity.

STRATEGY AND TACTICS

The BRCC documents show that Hussein never abandoned Baʿthification as his ruling strategy throughout his tenure as president. This conclusion contradicts the conventional narrative. The narrative holds that in the early 1990s Hussein downgraded the Baʿth Party and began to accommodate and curry favor with tribal and religious elements in society as a way to hold onto power and reassert his legitimacy. Proponents of this view assert that these actions transgressed traditional Baʿthist values, which were antitribal and secular. The regime, they argue, consequently gave up on Baʿthification and totalitarianism.[55] As Makiya wrote in the 1998 introduction to his book, "*Republic of Fear* . . . describes a state system that no longer exists in post–Gulf War Iraq. The war, the uprising that followed on its heels, and seven terrible years of sanctions and economic privation have seen to that. Nothing in Iraq is as it was in the heyday of the regime's absolutism."[56] Instead, the Baʿth regime maintained its power by encouraging Iraqis "to fear one another" and by "inculcating sectarianism, confessionalism, and tribalism as its new instruments of rule."[57]

While Hussein might have added these instruments to his repertoire, the BRCC documents do not support the view that they constituted a shift away from Baʿthification. Instead, they reflect a regime on its heels, knocked off-balance by the size of its defeat in the Gulf War, the popular uprisings that followed, and UN sanctions. In dire financial straits and without the manpower necessary to fully implement Baʿthification, Hussein played to tribal values and religious trends in order to usurp the authority and legitimacy that came with projecting an image of a strong tribal and religious leader. Thus, Hussein and the Baʿth's organs of propaganda emphasized tribal and religious rhetoric, and the regime embraced overt policies to back up its words. Among other measures, Hussein invited tribal sheikhs to the Republican Palace for the first time in March 1991 and embarked on a "Faith Campaign" in 1993. As part of the latter, even Baʿth Party members had to take religious exams.[58] In some ways, therefore, Hussein did "tribalize" and "Islamize" his regime.[59] Yet, evidence from the BRCC shows that simultaneous to Hussein's adoption of tribal and religious characteristics, he intensified the Baʿthist regime's longstanding efforts to co-opt tribal and religious leaders and remove sheikhs and imams unwilling to submit to the regime's dictates. Hussein also worked to instill Husseini Baʿthist ideological and organizing principles in tribal and religious worldviews and institutions, and to assume the mantle of tribal and religious legitimacies in order to bring both elements more firmly under his regime's direct control. In other words, instead of supplanting Husseini Baʿthism for tribalism and Islamism, Hussein subsumed them inside Husseini Baʿthist ideology and the Baʿthist State.[60] This does not mean that Hussein succeeded at Baʿthizing every tribe and religious entity, or that the Baʿthification of tribes and religious establishments proceeded perfectly according to a secret master plan; far from it. Improvisation and failure marked all of the regime's Baʿthification policies at times, particularly in the early to mid-1990s.[61] But the BRCC records show that the way in which Hussein approached and employed tribal and religious elements during this period conformed to his general Baʿthification strategy. Juan Linz has called political parties or movements that aspire to total control but do not achieve it "defective or arrested totalitarian systems."[62] Baʿthist Iraq as a whole can be characterized as such in the early to mid-1990s, and in the Kurdish areas, marshlands, and much of rural Iraq throughout the Baʿth's tenure.

As the early 1990s era illustrates, it is important to understand both the successes and failures of Baʿthification to gain an accurate picture of life under Husseini Baʿthist rule. Even if Baʿthification did not always succeed, the regime's attempt to apply it with fluctuating capabilities to Iraqi culture, individuals, families, state and social institutions, and demographic groups, all of which wavered between acceptance and resistance in different times and places, largely dictated the many realities that Iraqis lived from 1979 to 2003.[63] Baʿthification is therefore a useful conceptual framework with which to analyze, explain, and describe Hussein's Iraq.

Baʿthification did not result from a vacuum. It emerged as a set of policy choices that the Baʿth Party's leaders made after they took power in 1968—choices that Hussein took to extremes during his presidency and which must be set against the backdrop of the specific historical and social contexts out of which the Baʿth Party emerged, Hussein's personal proclivities, and the Baʿth's ideological and organizational foundations.

2. THE ORIGINS OF HUSSEINI BAʿTHIST TOTALITARIANISM

INTRODUCTION

The Baʿthification of Iraq began shortly after the Baʿth Party assumed power in 1968. Only when Saddam Hussein took over the presidency from Ahmad Hassan al-Bakr in 1979, however, did Iraq change from a Baʿthist oligarchy into a Husseini Baʿthist dictatorship—from a regime focused on the party's power to a strategy designed primarily to promote and safeguard Hussein's personal authority, using the party as his chief political instrument.[1] The BRCC documents reflect these dual currents of continuity and change. On the one hand, the few BRCC records from before Hussein's presidency evince a similar literary style to those that come afterward. All of the documents contain the party's traditional catchphrases and conventions. The party and state bureaucracies functioned according to the same general system in both eras, and the Baʿth's underlying ruling strategy—Baʿthification—did not change.[2] On the other hand, before Hussein's official ascendance, the documents do not contain the same kind of fawning praise for him as those following his assumption of power; they retain the façade of collective leadership that al-Bakr cultivated. Albeit clearly the country's strongman from the mid-1970s onward, Hussein did not feel authoritative enough to remove this façade until he eliminated the last of his party rivals and deposed al-Bakr.

Hussein's totalitarianism resulted from three main factors. First, the Baʿth succeeded in taking and holding power in 1968 because they learned from history that to gain and retain power in Iraq they had to take the violent and conspiratorial means used by their predecessors to new heights in order to stave off countercoups. The Baʿth did not want to succumb to the same types of political intrigue that brought down their forebears and doomed their initial experience in power in 1963. Second, from within the Baʿth Party, Hussein established his power by being more ruthless and paranoid than the rest, and by methodically building up and bringing under his personal control the party apparatus and security services. It is hard to imagine Baʿthification taking on the extreme character that it did during Hussein's presidency without taking into account Hussein's background, personality, and unique ability to wield the instruments of power available to him. Third, both the organizational structure and ideology that the Baʿth brought with them to power lent themselves to an autocratic and controlling fashion of governance. Combined, these three ingredients—fertile historical ground, Hussein's personality, and traditional Baʿthist organization and ideology—mixed in the right proportions to produce Husseini Baʿthist totalitarianism.

STUDENTS OF HISTORY

The historical trends behind Baʿthification reach back to the dissolution of the Ottoman Empire at the end of World War I and the creation of modern Iraq as an emanation of British policy. In Ottoman times, Sunni Islamic religion, culture, and political institutions acted as a unifying social force throughout the empire. Iraq's Shiʿis and Kurds lived as small communities on the Ottoman Empire's fringes. Great Britain took an interest in the three Ottoman provinces of Basra, Baghdad, and Mosul, because they lay on the route to Britain's colonies in India. After the British captured these provinces in World War I, they tried to safeguard this route by retaining the ruling order left by the Ottomans in a new nation-state under British tutelage. Accordingly, the British installed a monarchy led by King Faysal bin Hussein al-Hashemi, the son of the Sharif of Mecca. The Hashemite Monarchy was a Sunni institution supported by an urban coalition of former Ottoman notables, officials, landowners, and tribal sheikhs.[3] In the age of nation-states, Wilsonian self-determination, and Marxist-Leninist populism, however, a Sunni minority government installed and aided by an imperial power in an ostensibly democratic country proved to be an anachronism. The monarchy largely excluded the majority Shiʿi community from politics, and its pan-Arab ideology denied the Kurds—who had a distinct culture, language, and identity—a place in the national narrative.[4]

Within the monarchy's ruling Sunni elite, Iraq's political, economic, and cultural institutions did not peacefully mediate between factions. As a result, political struggles took place outside of Iraq's institutions through pure power plays, for which the support of Great Britain or the Iraqi army proved decisive.[5] Throughout the monarchy (1921 to 1958) and the republican period of Iraqi leaders Abd al-Karim Qasim (1958 to 1963) and the Arif brothers (1963 to 1968), no political faction could summon enough support from its own political or social base to rule alone. Attaining power required alliances.[6] Once an alliance served its purpose, however, allies inevitably turned on each other.[7] In the process, the faction that emerged triumphant winnowed its support base and angered the other faction that it squeezed out. This made it necessary to take preemptive action against countercoup attempts and to ensure that a ruler's inner circle remained loyal. The latter was done by parceling out jobs, state contracts, and other forms of patronage. These incentives filtered down through clientelist networks, which usually corresponded to the "primordial" loyalties of kin, clan, tribe, ethnicity, and sect, even if they outwardly revolved around political principles or social interest groups.[8]

The consolidation of a ruler's inner circle and patronage networks cemented his authority, but it delegitimized him in the long run because the autocratic means required to gain power within Iraq's political system made it difficult to keep. A pattern therefore developed whereby each ruler had to enforce his political dominance through authoritarian means and exclusive systems of patronage while, at the same time, attempting to forge a unified nation out of a heterogeneous population that felt dispossessed, and, in the Kurds' case, had national, separatist aspirations of their own.[9] This proved a recipe for political dysfunction, violence, corruption, paranoia, and duplicity.

This historical backdrop, and the political culture it produced, partially accounts for the Baʿth Party's totalitarian tendencies. The Baʿth proved to be excellent students of Iraqi history. They learned the autocratic steps necessary to execute their 1968 coup d'état and how to consolidate power afterward. They also studied the mistakes of their predecessors and their failed experience in 1963. In that year, the Baʿth succeeded in staging a coup, but their military co-conspirators, led by Abd al-Salam ʿArif, later purged them, an event aided by the Baʿth's internal squabbling. This taught the Baʿth the necessity of attaining a loyal foothold in the military, the need to maintain internal party discipline, and the value of setting up parallel paramilitary and security organizations to balance and maintain surveillance over the Iraqi army.[10]

As a result, after being purged in 1963, the Baʿth built up a military network, taking advantage of a small group of mainly Sunni, Tikriti Baʿthist officers, including Saddam Hussein's relative, Ahmad Hassan al-Bakr. Al-Bakr used the Tikriti military network after 1963 to edge out Salah al-Saʿdi's civilian faction within the Baʿth's intraparty struggles in the mid-1960s. He then exploited his position to make non-Baʿthist allies in the army, who conspired with the Baʿth to depose Abd al-Salam's brother, Abd al-Rahman ʿArif, on July 17, 1968. (Abd al-Salam died in a helicopter crash in 1966).[11]

After the 1968 coup's success, the Baʿthist leadership acted quickly against their officer allies. Within two weeks, the Baʿth Party's leaders had exiled the most senior military commanders that assisted them.[12] The Baʿth refer to this period in which they pulled off two successive coups to take sole possession of power as the "July 17–30 revolution" (*thawrat 17–30 tamūz*). Over the course of the next year, the party replaced the military's senior leadership and some 2,000 other officers with Baʿthists and other loyalists via a series of purges, retirements, rotations, and murders.[13]

With top military positions in Baʿthist hands, the party consolidated its control over the entire organization through ideological indoctrination and surveillance by the party and security services. As the Baʿth's Eighth Regional Congress report from 1974 claimed, the party aimed to ensure "that [the military] would always be completely identified with the popular movement under the leadership of the Party." This made the military into the party's appendage, guaranteeing the Baʿth's supremacy. As such, the Baʿth transformed the military into an "ideological army" (*jaysh ʿaqāʾidī*) under the instruction of the party's Directorate of Political Guidance (*mudīriyyat al-tawjih al-siyāsī*), set up in 1973.[14] In addition, the Baʿth placed party cells inside each army unit, as did the security and intelligence services. Applying the carrot as well as the stick, the Baʿth used oil revenues throughout the 1970s to vastly expand and modernize the military.[15]

The steps that the Baʿth took toward the military at the beginning of their rule revealed the basic elements of Baʿthification. When party leaders wanted to exert control over a state or social institution, they co-opted or replaced its leadership with Baʿthists and placed the organization under Baʿthist surveillance and administration. At the same time, they indoctrinated the people within the institution into Baʿthist ideology and supplied material incentives to secure their loyalty.

Additionally, the Baʿth worked to silence all opposing voices within the political arena, turning Iraq into a one-party state. The Iraqi Communist Party (ICP) was the Baʿth's great nemesis in the 1950s and 1960s. It came in for particularly harsh treatment. From 1968 until 1974, the Baʿth toyed with the ICP, variously permitting it to organize and then cracking down as a way to leverage the ICP for the Baʿth to improve relations with the Soviet Union. Once the Baʿth Party's leaders felt strong enough, they tried to eradicate the ICP in a campaign of arrests, torture, and murder, including the execution of twenty-one communists in 1978.[16] The communists retained a minor underground presence in Iraq throughout the party's tenure, but they never came close to threatening the Baʿth's grip on power. Neither did any other opposition party.

The intelligence and security services were the chief instruments of terror in Iraq. Saddam Hussein unofficially led these organizations, which grew both in numbers and size in the 1970s. Before 1968, two state security services existed: the General Security Directorate (GSD, *mudīriyyat al-ʾamn al-ʿāma*) and the Directorate of Military Intelligence (DMI, *mudīriyyat al-ʾistikhbārāt al-ʿaskariyya*). Once the party came to power, Hussein opened the Office of Public Relations (*maktab al-ʿalāqāt al-ʿāma*), a small and secret service. In 1972, when Hussein felt threatened by the rise of his protégé, Nazim Kazzar, as the head of the GSD, he turned the Office of Public Relations into a parallel force called the General Directorate of Intelligence (GDI, *mudīriyyat al-mukhābarāt al-ʿāma*). Hussein installed his friend, Saadun Shakir al-Azzawi, a member of the Baʿth Party Regional Command (RC, *al-qiyāda al-quṭriyya*), as GDI director, and placed his half-brothers, Barzan and Sabʿawi al-Tikriti, as apprentices in high positions.[17]

In addition to these three organizations, in 1984 Hussein added what became the most powerful security service in Iraq: the Special Security Organization (SSO, *jihāz al-ʾamn al-khāṣṣ*). The SSO reported directly to Hussein, guarded and spied on top regime officials, and gradually took over many of the most sensitive intelligence operations once carried out by the GSD.[18] Other specialized services existed too such as the Special Protection Apparatus (*jihāz al-himāya al-khāṣa*), which guarded the president. It consisted of fifteen- and sixteen-year-old boys from poor Tikriti backgrounds who received special training for three years before they entered the service. Even though the *himāya* protected al-Bakr, its young men owed their jobs, arranged marriages, possessions, social status, and salaries to Hussein. In turn, they remained intensely loyal to him and kept al-Bakr contained. This allowed Hussein to gather power for himself.[19]

Hussein used his position atop the security and intelligence services to win power struggles within the party and to consolidate his personal power over the Iraqi state. In 1969, Hussein became deputy chairman of the Revolutionary Command Council (RCC, *majlis qiyādat al-thawra*), the state's top political body, to which he added Deputy Secretary-General of the party's highest authority, the RC. At this time, Hussein also erected parallel "advisory offices" (*al-makātib al-ʾistishāriyya*), which usurped the policymaking roles of regular state institutions and ministries. These advisory offices were linked to the RCC, had their own budgets, and were staffed by high-ranking Baʿth Party members or technocrats who were friends of Hussein.[20] In 1976, al-Bakr named Hussein a general in the army despite having no military experience.[21] In 1977, the RC voted to appoint him head of the party committee in charge of Iraq's oil policy and revenues.[22] In the same year, Hussein expanded the RCC to include all members of the Baʿth's Regional Command, fusing the state's top political body with that of the party. Hussein thus gained complete control over, or major footholds in, all of Iraq's most important political and economic institutions. According to former Planning Minister Jawad Hashim, few important areas of the state reported to al-Bakr by the late 1970s.[23]

As occurred with his predecessors, the more power that Hussein gathered for himself, the more his kin and clan support base narrowed. By the end of the 1970s, almost all of the top officials in his government came from tribes whose home territories lay in the "Sunni triangle," which emanated from Baghdad out in a northwesterly direction through Salah al-Din and Anbar provinces between the Tigris and Euphrates rivers up to Mosul.[24] Yet, the clan and regional ties that persuaded Hussein to install members of these tribes also made them dangerous to him since they occupied positions of power within his regime. No large-scale popular uprising has ever overthrown an Iraqi leader. Only internal intrigue and foreign powers—the British in 1941 and Americans in 2003—have caused their downfall. Hussein never dispensed with these tribes, but each time he retired, shamed, or killed one of their members, he triggered vendettas against himself, winnowing his base further.[25] Relying on an ever-thinning inner circle insulated Hussein from plots, but the number of his loyal backers decreased over time.

The nationalization of Iraq's oil industry in 1972 provided a medium-term fix for this problem. Combined with a worldwide oil price rise in the same year, the increased revenue gave al-Bakr and Hussein the means to flood the tribal networks that they relied on the most with patronage.[26] By the end of 1975, Iraq's oil revenue reached eight billion dollars, allowing them to hand out state contracts, business licenses, and other benefits that, by-and-large, kept their supporters happy and created a group of nouveau-riche Baʿthist elite.[27]

To diversify and deepen their bases of support, al-Bakr and Hussein used these oil revenues to expand their webs of patronage and allegiance to the entire population. The 1970s saw the Baʿth construct a massive social welfare system. Incomes rose sharply, access to education and literacy improved, and medical services and consumer goods became more widely available. The size of the middle and working classes increased, and the Baʿth should be credited with modernizing the state.[28] As a result, few ordinary Iraqis, by now used to the game of musical chairs that characterized Iraq's political leadership, noticed the noose tightening around their necks. As one Iraqi explained, "During the early and mid 1970s the majority of the population in Iraq was content and enjoying some economic benefits from the Baʿath government. If they knew of atrocities, they chose to look the other way, as did many Western and regional governments."[29] The stability and relative prosperity that Baʿthist rule brought in its first decade led many Iraqis to overlook the freedoms that the party curtailed and the Baʿth's increasingly violent suppression of dissent.

With the onset of the Iran–Iraq War, however, Iraqis had little reason to continue to ignore the strict controls placed on their lives. The war placed unprecedented demands on Iraqis to maintain the war effort and started the country on an economic downslide. This was especially true as the group of Baʿthist elites and their patronage networks did not share the same wartime burdens as the rest of the population but continued to enrich themselves at the country's expense. Hussein always claimed to rule on behalf of all Iraqis, but even some diehard Baʿthists began to doubt that claim.[30] A wide gap emerged between Baʿthist rhetoric and reality at the beginning of the 1980s. The need to square this circle—to preserve the minority ruling order and simultaneously justify it on the basis of popular consent—provided another impetus for Baʿthification. All of Iraq's rulers have faced this dilemma to varying degrees. What made Hussein's government totalitarian was the strategy he used to overcome this predicament, in contrast to his predecessors. Whereas during the monarchical and republican periods, the ruling elites suppressed society in order to maintain their political authority, Hussein attempted to transform society so that Iraqis would naturally support his ruling order. This alternative response to a common historical predicament resulted from two factors: Hussein's personality and the organizational structure and ideology of the Baʿth Party.

SADDAM HUSSEIN

It is impossible to know how, or if, Iraq's political history would have turned out differently if somebody besides Hussein had taken over from al-Bakr, just as Soviet history might have differed if Stalin had not succeeded Lenin. But even al-Bakr recognized that Hussein's younger generation of Baʿthists leaned more on torture, arrests, and murder than his own.[31] Hussein emerged from within this younger generation by being more paranoid and ruthless than the rest.[32] As Isaiah Berlin pointed out, many socialist and nationalist leaders have advocated similar visions for their societies. They have not all pursued their goals, however, with the same kind of extreme tactics that leaders such as Stalin, Hitler, and Hussein did.[33] Like his predecessors, the inherent pressures of governing Iraq pushed Hussein to employ an autocratic form of governance. Unlike them, however, Hussein opted for a totalitarian strategy because it suited his personality, background, and connection to the Baʿth Party.

Psychological profiles of Hussein point to the early loss of his father, his abuse at the hands of his stepfather as a young child, and his poor, rural origins from a small town near Tikrit, al-ʿUja, where tribal honor codes predominated, as early determinants of his egotistic and coldblooded character.[34] Drawing on these facts and his behavior as president, one such profile diagnosed Hussein as a "malignant narcissist" because of a lack of conscience, "unconstrained aggression," paranoia, and delusions of grandeur.[35] Hussein evinced his willingness to kill and go to extremes that Iraq's other rulers would not in order to achieve his objectives.

Hussein first made a name for himself within the Baʿth Party for his part in the party's 1959 assassination attempt on former Iraqi president Abd al-Karim Qasim, in which Hussein supposedly extracted a stray bullet from his leg while escaping from the scene. In exile afterward in Syria and Egypt, Hussein returned to Iraq in 1963 during the first Baʿthist government. In 1964, he defended party founder Michel Aflaq against another party faction at the Baʿth's acrimonious Sixth National Congress in Damascus, Syria, after which Aflaq recommended him for promotion to a top position in the Iraqi Baʿth.[36] Around this time, Hussein developed an internal security organization used to protect the party from enemies and "for assassinations of members of other political groups as well as fellow *Ba'ath* Party members."[37] Hussein's character and experience with clandestine organization and operations complemented al-Bakr's position in the military and respected leader-mediator role within the party, which Hussein needed as a gateway to establish his reputation within both institutions.[38]

Hussein's background and emergence via the security services made his connection to the Baʿth Party critical to establish his leadership, because neither his humble origins nor his brutal methods of conspiracy contained inherently legitimizing elements or large social bases of support. In a society that valued noble lineage, Hussein's was unremarkable and even derided by some Iraqis.[39] The security services proved useful for power plays within the Baʿth Party, to target opposition groups, and to police the populace, but a regime that rested on such a thin social and geographic base could not survive on fear and repression alone. The political scientist Juan Linz has found that authoritarian leaders tend to come from an established ruling order. They are counterrevolutionaries whose institutional positions, prestige among their elite peers, and social connections prove sufficient to consolidate power. Totalitarian leaders, by contrast, have generally been younger, antibourgeoisie, civilian revolutionaries who did not have connections to the establishment. As such, they "could only gain power and consolidate it by creating a mass movement, a party, its militias and ancillary organizations."[40] Totalitarian leaders had to manufacture their social bases by organizing and mobilizing the population and by leaning heavily on ideological rhetoric to replace the prevailing weltanschuung with their own. They did not want to merely overthrow a political leadership but to overturn the entire political and social order that excluded them from positions of privilege. For the Baʿth, and especially for Hussein's generation within the party, this required not just replacing one establishment ruler for another, as during the revolving chair cabinets of the monarchy, or one military officer for another, as during the Qasim and Arif periods. Instead, it meant reconstructing Iraqi state, society, and culture in a way that would establish Hussein and his cohort as the new Iraqi elite, capable of enforcing their hegemony through coercion and patronage but also via the soft power of cultural and institutional practices.

THE BAʿTH PARTY

The Baʿth Party's organizational structure and ideology complemented the historical and personal factors described above. Its organizational apparatus mirrored the Soviet Communist Party's pyramid structure. At the lowest level, the Baʿth Party consisted of small cells of members overseen by higher divisions, sections, branches, and bureaus, the latter of which reported directly to the Office of the Party Secretariat. The Party Secretariat was the central executive and administrative arm of the Baʿthist leadership, composed of a General Secretary and Regional Command. Growing the party's organizational apparatus allowed the Baʿth's leaders to create a nationwide loyal network of supporters larger than the limited number of people within al-Bakr and Hussein's tribal and regional alliances. Although Sunni Arabs from the Tikrit area dominated the Baʿth's highest leadership positions, and the party kept track of the nationality and tribal, regional, and religious affiliations of its members, the BRCC documents show that the Baʿth recruited throughout the country from each ethnic and sectarian group. The party's cell-like hierarchy proved ideal for creating webs of surveillance and mobilization within neighborhoods, businesses, schools, the army, state ministries, and unions, and among social groups and demographics. By extending their apparatus over the entire country and including Iraqis of all stripes in the party and Professional and Mass Organizations, the Baʿth's leaders attempted to make up for their outsider social status and to unify Iraq's heterogeneous population behind their ideas for a broader national identity. They also hoped to add an extra layer of political and social control that did not exist in the monarchical or republican periods in order to safeguard their regime.

Baʿthist ideology provided patriotic and moral justifications for growing the party apparatus, reasons that went beyond the sustenance of a one-man dictatorship. Until the end of their reign in Iraq, two slogans adorned

Baʿth Party letterhead: "unity, freedom, and socialism" (*waḥda, ḥurriyya, wa-l-ʾishtirākiyya*), and "one Arab nation with an eternal message" (*ʾumma ʿarabiyya wāḥida dhāt risāla khālida*). "Unity," as the second slogan indicated, referred to Arab unity. The original Baʿth Party constitution from 1947 claimed the Arabs to be both a political and cultural nation that would naturally choose to live in one unified state if not for imperialist interference: "Any differences existing among [the Arab nation's] sons are accidental and unimportant. They will all disappear with the awakening of the Arab consciousness." Loyalty to the Arab nation was the only larger identity permitted under the constitution; "religious, communal, tribal, racial, or regional factions" were prohibited.[41] Accordingly, when the Baʿth came to power they officially banned references to tribal affiliation within the party and made it illegal for public figures to use their tribal, regional, or clan names.[42] Saddam Hussein al-Tikriti, for instance, became simply Saddam Hussein. The Baʿth implemented this policy in order to abolish divisive political and social markers attached to Iraqis' names. In reality, however, the gesture was symbolic. The many government and party forms that Iraqis had to fill out asked for personal details that included the supposedly taboo information. The forms often requested details about a person's spouse and relatives as well. The Baʿth kept this intelligence in their citizens' files and used it to conduct background checks.[43]

The Baʿth Party's definition of "freedom" differed from the democratic concept of the protection of individual liberties as the basis for a free society. The first clause of the second "principle" of the constitution claimed that "Freedom of speech, freedom of assembly, freedom of belief, as well as artistic freedom, are sacred. No authority can diminish them." The second clause, however, attached a caveat to these rights: "The value of the citizen is measured—once all opportunities have been given them—by the action they take to further the progress and prosperity of the Arab nation, *without regard to any other criterion*."[44] Put differently, a citizen of the Arab nation derived his or her personal value from actions intended to advance the welfare of the collective. As the Nazis used to say: "*Gemeinnutz geht vor Eigennutz* (The welfare of the community precedes the welfare of the individual)."[45] A pamphlet put out by a branch of the Baʿth party in 1995 showed that this was still the case:

> Party relationships are principle relationships on all levels of the party. It is revealed through them that the party takes the individual's place, the welfare of the party takes the place of the individual's welfare, and the party's decision takes the place of personal opinion. The connection between speech and action, between methods and the goal, between

thought and practice, and between the mean and the end are the most distinctive characteristics of the Baʿth.[46]

Accordingly, Baʿthist ideologues believed that individual liberties could be sacrificed in the national interest. Conveniently, the national interest corresponded to "those individuals and associations that are in agreement with the aims of the Arab nation, i.e., the party."[47] The party could thus regulate individual freedoms and define the country's course of development. In a one-party state, this justified the Baʿth's aspiration to exercise unbridled authority over every aspect of Iraqi state and society.

Baʿthist ideology posited that the bond between the individual and the Arab nation was *sacred*; nothing could abrogate it. If the welfare of the Arab nation—and, hence, the party—took priority over its citizens' individual lives, it followed that individuals should sacrifice themselves for the sake of the nation and the party. "Sacrifice for the sake of nationalism leads to heroism," Aflaq wrote, "for he who sacrifices everything for his people, in defense of its past glory and future welfare, is more elevated in spirit and richer in his life than he who makes a sacrifice for the sake of one person."[48] Conversely, when an individual's interests opposed the nation's, the Baʿth had the moral authority to kill them. This authority extended not just to action but thought. A successful national action leads, Aflaq believed, "to a powerful hate, a hate unto death of those persons who embody an idea contrary to the idea of [the nationalist]. . . . An inimical theory is not found on its own; it is embodied in individuals who must be annihilated so that it too may be annihilated."[49]

Expunging alternative ideas in addition to behavior led to policies designed to create a national consciousness favorable to the Baʿth's preferred political and social order, and to prevent ideas antithetical to that order from seeping into Iraqis' minds. This effort went so far as to include the regulation of private morality and family matters previously left out of the state's control. The Baʿth believed that the state, ruled by the party, ought to extend beyond the public into the private sphere—or, rather, to abolish the private sphere and make everything public. As a result, normally personal decisions became state interests. The Baʿth defined marriage, for example, as a "national duty." As a result, "the state must encourage it, facilitate it, and control it."[50] "Freedom," in the Baʿth's mind, meant the subordination of all individual rights—even private rights—to the will of the collective.

As the Baʿth's constitution stated, the party considered itself a "popular party. It believes that the value of the state is the outcome of the will of the masses from which it issues and that this value is sacred only to the extent that the masses have exercised their choice freely."[51] For the masses to choose freely, however, they needed to be both physically and mentally uninhibited. In the former case, that required emancipation from imperialism. In the latter, it referred to the reawakening of Arab minds, the resurrection (the meaning of *baʿth*) of their consciousness as a people able to determine their own destiny. Since Baʿth Party members had already undergone this awakening, it was up to them to show unenlightened Arabs what their true interests were—"to force them to be free."[52] This definition of freedom, of course, was in actuality its antithesis. In the historical context of Baʿthist Iraq, it contributed to totalitarianism.

"Socialism" for the Baʿth corresponded more to other third-world "isms" than to a traditional Marxist program. In the 1970s, the Baʿth instituted land reforms, erected a social services system, nationalized Iraq's oil industry, and created a state-run economy.[53] They never attempted to dispense with capitalism or abolish private property, however.[54] On the contrary, as Farouk-Sluglett and Sluglett have shown, the Baʿth remained committed to "maintaining and sustaining the existing capitalist economic order."[55] In practice, the focus of Baʿthist socialism lay primarily in the desire for political, economic, and social justice and an end to imperialist domination over the Arab nation instead of transforming the relationship between workers and the means of production. As the party's constitution stated: "Socialism constitutes, in fact, the ideal social order which will allow the Arab people to realize its possibilities and to enable its genius to flourish, and which will ensure for the nation constant progress in its material and moral output."[56] Since the Baʿth regarded its policies as inherently good for the country, "socialism" could be whatever group of socioeconomic policies they desired. As the Baʿth's Ninth Regional Congress report made clear in 1982, socialism could even encompass the privatization of state assets so long as the results furthered the regime's political objectives.[57]

Typified by its position on socialism, the vagueness of classical Baʿthist ideology proved both a help and a hindrance to the Baʿth in establishing their regime. On the one hand, Baʿthism's lack of concrete prescriptions left the party rudderless after its initial takeover. As the 1974 congress report said, in 1968 "The Party in fact had no ready example to follow, linking practical application with detailed programs. All the Party had was faith and a wealth of experience full of lessons and, at times, bitterness."[58] On the other hand, Baʿthist ideology's lack of specificity made it malleable and open to reinterpretation based on contemporary needs. Hussein claimed in the late 1970s that "the Ba'th Party has since its assumption of power in Iraq in the July 17–30, 1968, Revolution, embarked on enriching its own theory. This was quite necessary to meet the new circumstances and needs posed by a new phase of its long course of struggle."[59] As the two chapters in part II detail, the BRCC documents show that after Hussein assumed the presidency he took advantage of Baʿthist ideology's malleability, its assertions of legitimacy, and the moral authority it posited to create a "new theory" that combined Aflaq's "total philosophy" and Hussein's personality cult. This "Husseini Baʿthism" allowed Hussein to continue to profess the party's traditional slogans, but it also buttressed his personal power through a campaign of propaganda and indoctrination—or culturalization—designed to make his ideology stick.

PART II. IDEOLOGY

When a reader opens a BRCC file, she steps into a self-contained universe where "normal" common sense does not apply; an environment governed by its own language, rituals, logic, and ethics; a place where each word and action buttresses Saddam Hussein and the Baʿth Party's authority and asserts their legitimacy. Accordingly, the BRCC employs a vocabulary that is at once bureaucratic and ideological. Party slogans and pithy quotes from Hussein adorn the tops of all party and ministry letterhead, even in drafts and handwritten notes. They find their ways into party reports, administrative memoranda, and citizen petitions. Certain adjectives always pare with specific nouns, indicating the regime's official line. Hyperbolic superlatives attach to particular Baʿthist enterprises so that they become part of the term that symbolizes it, leaving no doubt as to their "greatness," regardless of their efficacy or outcome. Every piece of party correspondence begins with "Comradely greetings" (*taḥiyya rifāqiyya*) and reminds its recipient to "keep struggling" (*dumtum li-l-niḍāl*) at the end, framing the body of the text and creating a physical, standardized space that orients both the writer and reader within the Baʿthist idiom. Within this highly stylized setting, freedom of expression consists of clever turns of phrase and creative praise for the party, leader, and nation: the Husseini Baʿthist Trinity. Loyalty to the Trinity is cast as the overriding goal of existence, even to the point of self-sacrifice. Indeed, its exaltation often consumes more ink than the substance of the message itself. In the face of the Trinity's glorification, opposition seems absurd.

The same circumscribed worldview that underlies the BRCC's literary styles and conventions mirrors itself in the individual and collective rituals of fealty that the archive describes Iraqi citizens took part in on a daily basis. These rituals were many and varied. Children and Baʿth Party members took tests on Husseini Baʿthism in order to receive good marks in school or a party promotion.[1] Iraqis discussed Hussein's most recent speeches at party meetings, in union gatherings, and in public lectures and seminars.[2]

People who left the country wrote intelligence reports upon their return detailing their activities and explaining the superiority of the Baʿthist system compared to the country they visited.[3] Petitioners to Hussein, the party, and the government inevitably began and ended their requests with excessive fawning.[4] The number of recorded oaths of loyalty that Iraqis sent to Hussein written in blood runs into the hundreds. On Baʿthist anniversaries and national holidays Iraqis participated en masse in carefully orchestrated ceremonies where they chanted slogans written for the occasion by the Baʿth Party and the Ministry of Culture and Media (*wizārat al-thaqāfa wa-l-ʾiʿlām*). Those who did not take part read about the event in newspapers, magazines, and journals, watched it on television, walked by banners adorned with official mottos while going about their daily activities, and discussed the event in designated times set aside before the workday began. Like the ubiquitous posters of Hussein's pictures plastered throughout the country in public spaces and on the walls of businesses and private residences, the regime sought to infuse every aspect of life with a Husseini Baʿthist ethos. The BRCC's authors placed every activity and thought into context. They constantly affirmed and reaffirmed that state and society existed to venerate and advance the interests of the Baʿthist Trinity.

Why do the BRCC records evince such an ideological character? What purposes lay behind the constant and concerted use of ideological language, symbolism, rituals, and ceremonies? Why did Saddam Hussein surround himself with such an outsized cult of personality? What effects, if any, did living in a carefully controlled environment constructed out of Baʿthist propaganda have on the Iraqi population?

Part II of this study argues that the nature of the BRCC's literary styles, conventions, and rituals demonstrate two general phenomena. First, during Hussein's presidency, the ideology professed by the Baʿthist regime evolved from a party-focused general philosophy into a personality cult and prescription for political action and control. Chapter 3 therefore examines how Hussein refashioned Baʿthist ideology by retaining the legitimizing elements of Baʿth Party founder Michel Aflaq's theories while transferring those properties to himself and using them to justify his regime's policies. Husseini Baʿthist ideology was the keystone that provided political, intellectual, moral, and emotional coherence to the four categories of controls that made up the more tangible aspects of Baʿthification.

Second, as chapter 4 explains, the BRCC's contents showcase an extensive ideological indoctrination and propaganda—or "culturalization"—campaign designed to transform Iraqis into Baʿthists by imbuing the population with a genuine faith in Husseini Baʿthist principles. This required reorienting Iraqis' conceptions of what constituted a just and "natural" society to conform to both the utopian aspirations of Husseini Baʿthism and the reality of everyday life under Hussein. The cultural inputs and commonly accepted myths that informed Iraqis' worldviews—their religious beliefs and dogmas, tribal honor codes, local customs, and historical heritage—therefore had to be changed or subordinated to the Baʿthist Trinity. As a result, Hussein tried to make Husseini Baʿthism the sole source of Iraqi culture—to, in effect, transform it into Husseini Baʿthist culture. By controlling culture he could manipulate the psychological framework that helped Iraqis make sense of the Baʿthist environment that enveloped them. He could thus control individuals' behavior. If he controlled behavior he could control society, and if he controlled society he could have his cake and eat it too: his regime would retain its authority and elicit the consent required from the populace to legitimize the maintenance of his rule.

3. HUSSEINI BAʿTHISM

Our creed is thought, belief, and practice.

SADDAM HUSSEIN

INTRODUCTION

Ronald Grigor Suny has explained how Joseph Stalin consolidated his personal control over the Soviet Union after Lenin died, outmaneuvering his rivals through "the naked exercise of unrestrained power." Simultaneously, Stalin also

> worked to create authority and acceptance, borrowing from and supplementing the repertoire of justifications from Lenin's day. While appropriating the mantle of Lenin and much of the rhetoric of Bolshevism, however, Stalin revised, suppressed, and even reversed much of the legacy of Lenin. Internationalism turned into nationalism; the *smychka* between the workers and the peasants was buried in the ferocity of collectivization; radical transformation of the family and the place of women ended with reassertion of the most conservative "family values." And in the process almost all of Lenin's closest associates fell victim to the self-proclaimed keeper of the Leninist flame.[1]

A remarkably similar process to the one that Suny describes in Stalinist Russia occurred in Baʿthist Iraq. Saddam Hussein consolidated his power through his relationship to Iraqi president Ahmad Hassan al-Bakr, his grip over the security and intelligence services, and his willingness to take ruthless measures against his political and ideological rivals within the Baʿth Party. All the while, he maintained that his actions corresponded to the wishes of al-Bakr, the principle of "collective leadership," and the philosophies of Baʿthist founder Michel Aflaq.[2] While Hussein always asserted his commitment to pan-Arabism during his presidency, in reality he adopted an Iraq-centric focus.[3] Women saw a relative emancipation under the Baʿth in the 1970s. Under Hussein, however, the more conservative tribal and Islamic conceptions of gender roles held sway. If, therefore, "there was a fundamental discontinuity between Bolshevism and Stalinism," there was also a discontinuity between the Baʿthisms of al-Bakr and Aflaq and the Baʿthism of Saddam Hussein.[4] Since Hussein's Baʿthism did not derive purely from original Baʿthist thought, because it differed in certain respects from the Baʿthism practiced in Syria at the same time, and because Hussein's personality cult occupied such a large role within it, I refer to it as "Husseini Baʿthism." Husseini Baʿthism was the actual philosophy applied by Hussein's regime during his presidency. Consequently, the success or authenticity of Hussein's policies should be judged against it as opposed to other forms of Baʿthism.

What did Husseini Baʿthism consist of? The BRCC shows that it was made up of three broad elements. First, Hussein retained the language, catchphrases, and moral imperative of the party's founding theories, as propounded by Aflaq. To make Baʿthist ideology his own, however, Hussein introduced two additional concepts: his cult of personality and the notion of "applying" (*taṭbīq*) Baʿthist ideals, or "putting them into practice" (*mumārasa*) by "constructing" (*bināʾ*) a strong Baʿthist human being, society, and nation in all their facets. These two additions went hand-in-hand because each strengthened Hussein's role within the Baʿthist State. Hussein's personality cult made him into the Baʿth's chief prophet, giving him exclusive insight into the monopoly on historical truth that underlay the party's claims to legitimacy. With this power, Hussein's emphasis on the "application" of Baʿthist ideology allowed him to interpret Aflaq's vague principles as he wished. If ideology was the keystone of the Baʿthist system, by placing himself at the center of party ideology, Hussein sat at the apex of the regime where, to paraphrase Vaclav Havel, the center of power was identical to the center of truth.[5] Husseini Baʿthism not only gave Hussein unquestionable authority, it made the continuance of his authority necessary to maintain the Baʿthist regime and to achieve Baʿthist ideology's utopian goals.

A NEW STAGE

In 1986, the deputy head of the Baʿth Party's Office of Culture and Media (*maktab al-thaqāfa wa-l-ʾiʿlām*) sent Hussein a twenty-seven page syllabus of readings to be used in the "cultural" training of party members. The syllabus contained what the office considered the basic literature of the party in addition to selected articles from *The Arab Revolution*, a party magazine. The "basic literature" came from four sources: the writings and speeches of Aflaq, those of Hussein, party documents issued by national and regional conferences, and historical party declarations, including a group from the 1963 Baʿthist classic, *Nidal al-Baʿth* (The Baʿthist Struggle).[6] Of these, Aflaq and Hussein's contributions made up almost all the passages. Hussein approved the syllabus. It contained what under his leadership was the Baʿth Party's intellectual canon, produced so that its members would "understand fully the different ideological, organizational, and political aspects that are required of a party comrade."[7]

The nature of the syllabus illustrates the progressive yet reverential character of Husseini Baʿthist ideology whereby the Baʿth sought to retain the original concepts and catchphrases of traditional Baʿthism but claimed the right to further Aflaq's theories and interpret them according to the Baʿth's needs when putting them into practice. The founding principles of the party, as laid out by Aflaq, retain a prominent place in the more theoretical sections. His writings are the only ones contained in the parts on "The Character of Baʿthist Thought," "Arab Nationalism and the Nationalist Theory," "The Concept of Revolution" (*al-ʾinqilābiyya*), and "The Relationship between Unity, Freedom, and Socialism." Hussein's speeches and writings, in contrast, almost exclusively make up the more practical sections and articles. Whereas an item by Aflaq is the required reading for "Our Socialism versus Communist Socialism," Hussein's writings fill "Socialism Applied," "Theory, Strategy, and Tactics," and "Issues of the Revolution Applied."[8]

The names given to Aflaq and Hussein in the BRCC reinforce this division between past and present, theory and practice. Until his death in 1989, Aflaq remained the secretary of the Baʿth's symbolic National Command. Hussein was his deputy and secretary of the more powerful but technically inferior Regional Command. Publicly, the regime venerated Aflaq as "the Founding Leader" (*al-qāʾid al-muʾassis*), giving him credit for his *previous* role as the driving force behind the party. The BRCC documents, on the other hand, call Hussein "the leader" (*al-qāʾid*), often with one of his titles or a common Baʿthist moniker attached, such as *al-munāḍil*, "The Struggler." Hussein, in other words, was the *current* political leader. Introducing these types of distinctions allowed Hussein to keep parts of Baʿthist heritage that served his purposes but to claim the right to alter others in what his regime called a "new stage" (*marḥala jadīda*) of the nation's development. It too gave Aflaq esteem but eliminated the possibility that he or any other respected former party leader could challenge Hussein based on their Baʿthist credentials. Hussein retained parts of Aflaq's theories for other reasons too. To totally dismiss the party's original concepts would have left no justification to maintain the Baʿth Party's structural apparatus, which Hussein needed to organize state and society. It would also have deprived him of rhetorical weapons in the fight against his internal and external enemies.

More importantly, however, the principles of Aflaqian Baʿthism contained legitimizing instruments that Hussein could not find elsewhere. Hussein's legitimacy was inextricably tied to the Baʿth Party's. He did not have natural legitimacy with which to rule based upon his own background or the autocratic means that he used to gain and hold onto power. He emerged from within the party and thus could not dispense with the party slogans that he had promoted vigorously in the past. Otherwise, he opened himself up to charges of hypocrisy akin to those that contributed to the downfall of his predecessors. He thus needed to preserve the appearance that the Husseini version of the Baʿth had not eschewed the principles of the party's founders.

Those principles contained a theoretical appeal to many, as explained by former Baʿthist Diya al-Din al-Majmai:

> The leaders of the Baʿth and its ideologues promised big goals that represented the dreams of every upstanding (*sharīf*) Arab. At the forefront of these were "unity" (and who doesn't love the unity of the Arabs, which would lead to their strength in the face of their enemies); "freedom," emancipation from imperialism and the release of intellectual, cultural, and religious freedoms, and the freedom of each man in all of his choices; then "socialism" and the achievement of social justice, providing opportunity to all citizens equally.[9]

Nevertheless, after over a decade in power, the Baʿth Party's many broken promises left Iraqis like al-Majmai disillusioned:

> In truth, I was one of those men who was destined to be a Baʿthist. . . . However, after a number of years, I balked (*waqaftu*) at the many crimes the Baʿth committed against the goals it professed (*ḍid al-ʾahdāf allatī yarfaʿuhu*). It conspired against any true Arab solidarity or approximation of unity. [Baʿthist leaders] claimed to work to free Palestine or the eastern front, but they increased discord (*al-fitan*) and problems with their Arab brothers. . . . They announced the existence of freedom in the media by television and radio and newspapers, but in reality they suppressed all freedom to the point where a man could not reveal his true opinions and thoughts even in his house within earshot of his wife and children. . . . As for socialism (which became private under the Baʿth), suffice it to say that the Baʿth's practices made each Iraqi at the mercy of private property (*al-milkiyya*) and capitalism, because the regime's cronies (*zabāniyat al-niẓām*) and the relatives of the tyrant and

> especially his family took over everything and gave the people a taste of ignominy. . . .
>
> Beginning in the 1970s, many Baʿthist comrades began to ask themselves and each other: what has become of the principles, slogans, and goals of the Baʿth?[10]

The ideological legitimacy of classical Baʿthism remained important to Hussein because the logic inherent in Aflaq's original theories helped to bridge the gap al-Majmai describes between Hussein's professed beliefs and his obviously self-serving policies. As the leader of a movement that sought to awaken Iraqis to the historical truth of Arab nationalism for Iraqis' own benefit, the Baʿth Party's monopoly over the right to interpret historical truth gave its actions legitimacy, ipso facto. Instead of conforming to its principles, therefore, this put the Baʿth Party, for all intents and purposes, above its theory, making its actions its principles. As the Baʿth's leaders learned when Abd al-Salam Arif purged them in 1963, their first priority had to be the "preservation of the revolution."[11] From the start of their rule in 1968, they saw no contradiction in pursuing pragmatic ends over purely ideological goals because the maintenance of their rule was a prerequisite to one day achieving their utopian aims. When Hussein took over the party he retained this logic, using the Baʿth's ideological language to justify his actions, even if those actions were on their face antithetical to the Baʿth's stated ideals. Likewise, Aflaqian Baʿthism provided moral legitimacy for Hussein's rule. Aflaq based his theories in what he claimed to be the laws of history. Hussein consequently argued that his right to rule derived from historical necessity, an assertion that he used to cover up the self-serving and hypocritical aspects of his regime.

The moral legitimacy that Hussein posited provided Iraqis an excuse to support him. People will only carry out acts they would otherwise consider reprehensible on somebody else's behalf—or debase themselves by supporting a system that does—if they feel that they are acting within established norms, that their behavior falls within a reasonable ethical framework. Ideologies, the Italian political theorist Gaetano Mosca observed, "answer a real need in man's social nature; and this need, so universally felt, of governing and knowing that one is governed not on the basis of mere material or intellectual force, but on the basis of a moral principle, has beyond any doubt a practical and a real importance."[12] As a result, "In each dictatorship," Richard Overy has written about Stalin and Hitler's regimes, "a unique moral universe was constructed in order to justify and explain what appear otherwise to be the most sordid and arbitrary of acts."[13] Husseini Baʿthism provided this same kind of "moral universe" to explain away Hussein's seemingly severe and hypocritical policies, a universe in which Iraqis who supported him could find refuge in order to avoid the shame and guilt that would have normally accompanied the betrayal of old loyalties. Instead, Husseini Baʿthism characterized their support as patriotism. To the extent that many Iraqis at least outwardly accepted the regime's ideological rationalizations, the moral legitimacy inherent in Aflaq's theories permitted Iraqis to take the actions necessary to survive in the Baʿthist system—actions that meant taking part, or becoming complicit in, the very policies that denied their collective liberty and facilitated the maintenance of Hussein's rule.

SADDAM HUSSEIN'S CULT OF PERSONALITY

As far back as 1980, Amatzia Baram identified Hussein's effort to supplant the Baʿthism of Aflaq and al-Bakr with his own.[14] From at least the mid-1970s, it became known both domestically and internationally "that [Hussein], rather than Hasan al-Bakr, was the dominant figure in the regime."[15] It was thus not surprising when Hussein officially took over from al-Bakr in July 1979. The way in which he did so set the tone for the remainder of his presidency. A closed meeting of the Baʿth Party leadership followed al-Bakr's resignation. At the meeting, the leadership was shown a videotape of one RCC member, Muhyi Abd al-Husain Rashid, confessing to participation in a Syrian plot to overthrow Hussein. He fingered a number of other Baʿth Party members who were sitting in the audience. Upon calling their names, guards came and took them out of the auditorium, often while screaming Hussein's praises. Hussein then took the podium and, while smoking a cigar and wiping tears from his eyes, implicated others. When he finished, Hussein required the remaining Baʿth Party members to shoot their comrades, choosing relatives to kill each other and neighbors to kill neighbors. All in all, twenty-two people were shot, thirty-three were sentenced to prison, and thirteen were let go. The Baʿth distributed copies of the film to other party members. Choking back tears, Hussein warned the crowd, and, in effect, the country: "He who betrays his nation (*qawm*), we have nothing for him except the sword."[16] The nature of the purge, however, indicated that it was not just the Baʿth Party or the nation that required Iraqis' allegiance—it was Hussein's person.[17] And, indeed, the BRCC boxfiles show that Hussein's cult of personality, or leadership complex, was already well established in 1979; by the end of the party's Ninth Regional Conference in 1982, it existed in full force.[18]

The main purpose behind Hussein's leadership cult was to affirm and cement his untouchable, absolute authority as the sole legitimate leader of the country. Hussein derived this power as the head of the Baʿth Party, which claimed to lead the Arab and Iraqi nations. Hussein's person consequently became a symbol associated with Iraqi patriotism, Arab nationalism, and the personal and collective honor attached to these values under which all of Iraq's sects and ethnicities could theoretically unite. As a 1989 party report, entitled "A plan in order to confirm the execution of the values and principles that were included in the speech of the Struggler Leader Saddam Hussein (God save him)," put it:

> [Baʿthist principles and values] build the party into an edifice of struggle to be able . . . to tackle all of the important struggling tasks because of the party's great historical role in the life of the nation (*ʾumma*). These principles and values build the new society to be cohesive, homogeneous (*mutajānisan*), productive, and civilized. They govern its movement and the development of its values and traditions, which the Comrade Leader Symbol Saddam Hussein heads with the revolutionary party that leads the march toward the best possible outcome for eternity.[19]

Like the Baʿth Party did with its authority, Hussein posited his greatness and then rewrote history to support this claim. Already at the 1974 party conference, the Baʿth began to provide rationalizations for moving beyond the unspecific nature of an idealist ideology to one that justified their pragmatic actions. The conference report mentioned the need "to avoid generalities . . . to exert the greatest possible effort to formulate a realistic and clear revolutionary programme which would unify the will of the Party and the masses, leaving no room for possibly conflicting interpretations."[20] The move to distinguish their theory from those developed before 1968 required a new story to support the Baʿth's changes. This meant not only justifying those changes based on practical considerations but also reinterpreting history to bring its laws in line with the Baʿth's fresh narrative. "The many schools and interpretations and great events of history," Hussein said in a 1977 speech, "enable every one to pick out what he likes from history to support his own approach. Arab history is no exception."[21] History, like everything else, was a tool in the Baʿth's service; its facts were subjective and could be engineered according to necessity.

The emergence of Hussein's personality cult went hand-in-hand with giving him a central role in party history. The 1974 conference report does not mention Hussein once other than giving his name under his picture at the beginning of the publication.[22] By contrast, the Ninth Congress Report from 1982 mentions Hussein's name, his nicknames, and his titles over a thousand times.[23] The report puts him at the center of every event and development in party history. Contrary to all objective evidence, it claims that Hussein was the "ringleader" (*al-mudabbir*) and "mind" behind the Baʿth's revolutionary plan (*al-ʿaql al-mukhaṭṭiṭ*). Hussein led the first tank that stormed the Republican Palace. On July 30, 1968, he was "the true leader of the revolution" (*huwa qāʾid al-thawra ḥaqqan*) who purged the Baʿth's nonparty co-conspirators. By sniffing out subsequent plots, Hussein solved the historical problem that bedeviled previous Baʿth regimes in Iraq and Syria: how to retain power. Hussein thought up and carried out the plan to nationalize Iraq's oil industry. He solved the Kurdish issue by establishing the "autonomous region" (*mantaqat al-ḥukm al-dhātī*). He gave birth to Iraq's nuclear strategy. He developed the armed forces. He established the office of propaganda and media and turned it into a superior cultural center. He built the internal structure of the party before and after the revolution. He thought up and initiated all of the party's domestic and foreign policies.[24] Whereas in a previous phase general principles sufficed, the report made clear that the Ninth Congress represented the beginning of a new phase in Baʿthism, one that required more specific policies.[25] Hussein issued these policies, which gave the party a clear path forward: "Indeed, we say with objectivity and sincerity that it has become entirely clear, the true face of the party and its revolutionary experience in the country (*quṭr*) . . . has begun to move forward according to the natural path."[26] That natural path always included Hussein taking the official reins of the party eventually. His leadership was a historical necessity, and the report gave him the title of "The Leader—The Necessity" (*al-qāʾid—al-ḍarūra*).[27] The same force of history that the Baʿth Party claimed for its ideology lay at the root of the legitimacy of Hussein's leadership complex.

The BRCC documents showcase the same narrative espoused in the Ninth Congress report, which places Hussein at the center of Baʿth Party and Iraqi history since 1968.[28] The records explain Hussein's exceptional traits. They depict him, at once, to have an uncanny ability to predict future events and thus create current policies to stave off potential problems and thwart enemies. This ability makes him one of the best military leaders of all time. In 2000, for example, a party member sent Hussein a one-sentence appeal for a transfer to the party's Office of Students and Youth. Preceding the sentence, he wrote the following:

> I present my request to you, Sir (*siyādatakum*), asking and soliciting your noble fatherly kindness in order to take some of your dear time, a limited audience so as to present to you, into your noble hands, a modest study entitled, "A Perspective on the Characteristics of the Successful Leadership of the Leading Comrade Saddam Hussein," (*naẓra fī khaṣāʾiṣ al-qiyāda al-nājiḥa li-l-rafīq al-qāʾid ṣaddām ḥusayn*) which won first

> place. It deals with the role of the Comrade Leader Saddam Hussein as one of the most distinguished military and historical leaders, not just on the national (*quṭr*) but also the Arab and world levels. It also highlights the most distinctive personal traits of the Leading Comrade Saddam Hussein as a leader who, by way of his permanent presence and bravery, influences all critical situations (*al-mawāqif al-ḥarija*). He made correct decisions in battles during Saddam's Glorious *Qādisiyya* and The Eternal Mother of All Battles. The Leader Symbol (*al-qāʾid al-ramaz*) is distinguished by rare courage, intelligence, leadership, a unique faculty to predict and account for current and future positions with a high degree of accuracy and renowned discernment, an unusual ability (*qudra khāriqa*) at renewal and creativity in the different aspects of life, in famous military thought and, likewise, in ancient and modern history.[29]

In this passage and others, Hussein is depicted as unusually brave, creative, smart, and thoughtful, a workaholic possessing limitless energy and consumed by the need to advance the nation's progress and his love for the country. He gives superior advice on virtually every subject imaginable, from art to science, politics, economics, personal hygiene and health, women's affairs, and agriculture.[30] No subject, large or small, escapes his knowledge, interest, or opinion. He knows all about everything. He was central to what was, what is, and what will be. As another petitioner wrote,

> If men possessing noble and manly qualities are rare in history, then you, Sir, are one of those few men. But you have something on them (*laku dālu ʿulayhim*). You exhibit these noble qualities with uncommon ease. . . .
>
> Whenever any Iraqi man or woman feels as if injustice has fallen upon them, they turn to you in any place and hope that you will protect them in the name of justice, Arabness, generosity, magnanimity, and nobility. O' Sir, I found within myself a strength that cannot be repelled (*la rāddin laha*) because I compose [my petition] and send it up with confidence, surety, and true knowledge that is the source of my hope, which extends powerfully, purely, without any imperfections. How could it be otherwise? Life has taught me that those naturally disposed to generosity are the first to do famous deeds . . . Saddam Hussein, the leader of the people and the shepherd of their destiny, the first among the generous, and the symbol flag (*al-ʿalam al-ramaz*) in their ships.[31]

Just as traditional Baʿthist ideology claimed for itself an unquestionable interpretation of historical truth, in this petition, the author depicted Hussein as the perfection of humanity in history, possessing just qualities.

Iraqis frequently sent petitions to Hussein when they could not find redress for wrongs committed against them through regular legal, party, or other channels. The phrases "you are our refuge" (*malādhna*) and "we turn to you" (*naljaʾ ʾilayk*) appear repeatedly in citizen petitions. In this way, although he was ultimately responsible for the corrupt bureaucracy that ill served Iraqis without personal connections in government or the party, Hussein stayed above the fray. He could consequently take credit for the state and party's accomplishments but also deny responsibility for their wrongs, chiding them when necessary and offering an outlet for appeal when all other avenues had been blocked. The juxtaposition of Hussein's justice against a corrupt state made his star shine even more.

The titles that the Baʿth Party and Iraqi citizens bestowed on Hussein magnified his status. They mythologized his person and made him, literally, into the "symbol" of the nation, people, and party. Although the passage predates the event, the above petitioner's term for Hussein as the "symbol flag" of Iraqis foretold the inscription of "God is Great" in Hussein's handwriting on the Iraqi flag during the Gulf War.[32] By connecting Hussein to the nation, the party made participation in Hussein's cult akin to performing patriotic acts. Citizens also gave his name to their children in droves. One document from September 1, 2002, reported that there had been 14,148 babies named Saddam born thus far that year.[33]

The language contained in the BRCC documents imbues Hussein with a sacred, prophetic character. Except in the earliest records, each time a BRCC document mentions Hussein's name or one of his titles, the phrase "God save him and keep him" (*ḥafẓuhu allāh wa raʿāhu*) follows.[34] Hussein's name appears so often in the BRCC that the phrase becomes ingrained in a reader's mind. When it does not appear, it raises a red flag, and one instantly wonders if any consequences accrued to the writer. The only other names in the BRCC documents that enjoy similar treatment are those of God, the Prophet Muhammad, and the Shiʿi imams, each of which is traditionally followed by a short blessing. This was not an accident. The Baʿth explicitly compared Hussein to Muslim prophets. In a 1995 report about the events of the Shiʿi holiday of Muharram, for example, which commemorates the martyrdom of Imam Hussein, the Director of the Office of the Party Secretariat suggested "honoring the readers of the *ḥusayniyyāt* (Shiʿi religious centers) who had an exceptional role in making a link between the bravery of Imam Hussein (peace be upon him) and the bravery of his descendant (*ḥafīd*), the leader (God save him), who faced down the aggression of 33 countries and achieved a victory."[35] In this quotation, the director repeated the Baʿthist canard that Saddam Hussein and Imam Hussein were related through a genealogical line going back to Imam Hussein's father,

Imam Ali, the fourth Muslim Caliph.[36] By comparing Hussein to Muslim prophets instead of deifying him, the director imbued Hussein with the quality of prophets who are at once human and fallible but who also channel God's unquestionable word. This fit in with his role as interpreter of Aflaq's traditional message, creator and applier of new party principles, repository of historical truth, and the leader of the Baʿth Party and Iraqi and Arab nations. Like the prophet Muhammad, Hussein combined the leadership of Iraq's spiritual and political community in his person.[37]

Repetition reinforced the narrative of Hussein's personality cult. The BRCC's authors repeat Hussein's titles ad nauseam, mirroring his all-pervasive visual presence in Iraqi society at-large. The BRCC contains an entire file about the "poster committee" (*lajnat al-jadāriyāt*) within the Ministry of Culture and Media, which was responsible for hanging placards of Hussein around the country.[38] In addition to posters, Hussein appeared in murals, paintings, advertisements, movies, television shows, books, and poetry.[39] A considerable amount of cultural output revolved around his person.[40]

Hussein's sayings too appeared everywhere, including on government and party letterhead in the late 1990s. Many of these sayings were banal or in the tradition of folk wisdom. "Don't get close to anybody who thinks that you disdain him," for example, appeared on the Party Secretariat's letterhead. Others gave real insight into Hussein's mindset: "Keep your enemy in front of your eyes and anticipate his actions; don't let him go behind your back." Another saying constituted pure doublespeak given the political character of the Baʿth's justice system. "I have judged, and I will judge, with impartiality (*ʿadl*). Bias does not weigh on my calculations. It does not allow a criminal to escape punishment who does not hope to reform himself," appeared on the Justice Ministry's letterhead.[41]

In addition to lauding Hussein's virtues, the Baʿth furthered his cult by making his person inviolate. The regime considered anybody who did not heed Hussein's words, or attacked him verbally in public, as a traitor who deserved to die. The BRCC records a number of these cases, including an instance from 1983 in which a soldier at the war front repeatedly insulted Hussein in his unit, mocked the awarding of medals of bravery to a number of officers, and claimed that some of the officers took bribes from soldiers so that the officers would place the soldiers in the back lines of battle, giving them a better chance of survival. When he was informed of the case, Hussein ordered military intelligence to execute the soldier by firing squad.[42] In 1986, the regime officially made insulting the President of the Republic (Hussein), his replacement, the Revolutionary Command Council, the Baʿth Party, the National Assembly (*al-majlis al-waṭanī*), or the

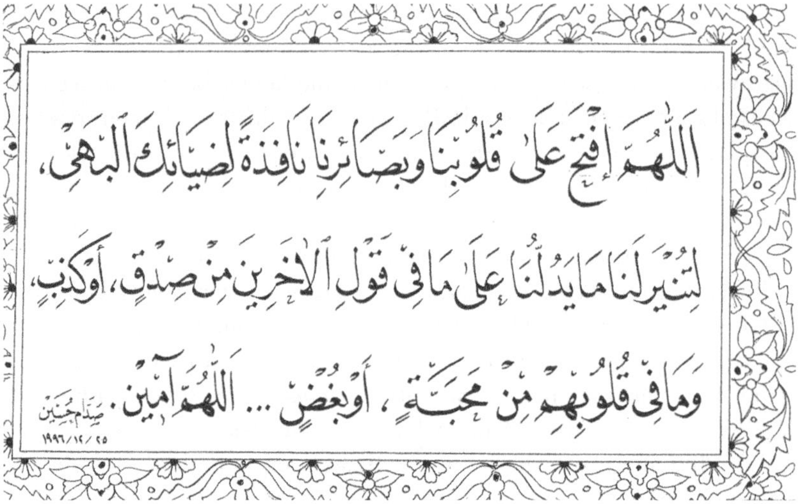

FIGURE 3.1. ***An Invocation by Saddam Hussein, Written in the Style of a Qurʾānic Sura.*** The document appears in a boxfile entitled "Sayings of the Leader Comrade (God save him)." The invocation reads: "O' Lord, open for our hearts and insights a window to your radiant light in order to illuminate what indicates for us in the speech of others what is truth, or falsehood, and what in their hearts is love, or hatred . . . O' Lord, amen. Saddam Hussein, 25/12/1996." Source: BRCC, 025-1-7: 200. Courtesy of Hoover Institution Library & Archives, Stanford University.

Iraqi government punishable by life in prison. The crime became a capital offense "if the insult or the attack is done in an egregious fashion (*bi shakl sāfir*) and with the intent to stir up popular opinion against the regime (*al-sulṭa*)."[43] In 1987, a General Security Directorate (GSD) report told the story of an investigation into the breaking of a picture of Hussein, which hung on a wall in a factory. A factory worker turned in the factory's technical director for supposedly throwing the picture, shattering its protective glass. When the GSD looked into the matter, they found no wrongdoing. They concluded that the picture simply dropped when the director handed it to another worker so that the picture would not be harmed during renovations. The GSD did not recommend punitive action. The fact, however, that merely harming the glass covering Hussein's picture—not even the picture itself—prompted somebody to report the incident, and that the security services then fully investigated, illustrates the sensitivity the regime had to perceived slights to Hussein and the extreme care citizens had to take with regard to the "Leader President."[44]

The seriousness that surrounded symbols or depictions of Hussein extended to his words. Whenever Hussein spoke, whatever he said immediately became required reading or listening. When Hussein gave a speech, the Ministry of Culture and Media subsequently printed tens or hundreds of thousands of copies of the text and distributed it to the party and the Professional and Mass Organizations (PMOs).[45] As the head of the office of the party's Southern Bureau wrote to the branches under his purview in 1985,

> The publications of the comrade leader struggler, Saddam Hussein (God save him), play a large intellectual role in spreading and deepening the thought of the party and its literature. They give reality work to be applied in the political, economic, military, and cultural fields. This thought has become a great teacher and a big intellectual program. Therefore, the following should be done:
>
> 1. Comrades should acquire every piece of literature and publication that the Comrade Leader issues.
> 2. The cultural committees should enrich the party libraries with these publications.
> 3. The cultural committees must prepare a special program of cultural debates (*munāẓarāt*) to discuss the literature of the Comrade Leader. This program should include members of the section and division leaderships and the party organizations descending to the circles of partisans and supporters.
> 4. The section and division leaderships should follow all of the comrades and the party apparatus to ensure their acquisition of these publications, and the branch leaderships should see to it that this occurs.[46]

As directives like this one show, the Baʿth turned Hussein into the party's chief ideologue even before Aflaq died.[47] As one party petitioner to Hussein wrote, "I am one of those who believe before anything that your speech . . . is the principle program for the ideas of our leading party and its aspirations to prove its judiciousness, the depth of its knowledge, and the integrity of its intentions. They are slogans that we all unite under for the sake of the great Iraq, for building it, advancing it, for its victory and its passage."[48]

Statements like these were not just flattering rhetoric. They expressed the reality of daily life whereby Iraqis who wanted to succeed academically, professionally, or in the party hierarchy had to praise Hussein, study his speeches, and repeat his words on exams, petitions, and in official governmental and party correspondence. The Baʿthist from above who requested a transfer to the Office of Students and Youth, for example, participated in an essay competition about Hussein's leadership traits, which required him to brainstorm and describe Hussein's qualities in a persuasive fashion. Similarly, an elementary school exam for sixth-graders in Arabic language from 2002 asked students to write about one of the following two subjects (figure 3.2):

1. "We learn, we fight, we achieve (*nubdiʿ*) for the sake of the country (*al-waṭan*) and our inspiration (*mulhimna*), the leader Saddam Hussein (God save him and keep him). Express yourself about this subject and clarify in your answer the importance of knowledge (*ʿilm*) in our daily lives, and in protecting the country and defending our Arab nation."
2. "Describe your town or village."

In the grammar section of the same test, students had to fill in the word "the leader" voweled correctly in the sentence: "The recommendations of *the leader* are lessons for life."[49] Within the party, a "cultural" test for members of divisional leaderships required participants to answer three of these questions within three hours:

1. "Discuss the role of the comrade Leader Saddam Hussein (God save him) in facing the instance of the thirtieth military aggression (*al-ʿudwān al-ʿaskarī al-thalāthīnī*) in fighting the Eternal Mother of All Battles."
2. "Discuss the goals of the message of the comrade Leader Saddam Hussein (God save him) to the members of the council of ministers on the date (of 2/12/1995), strengthening your answer by mentioning its basic results."
3. "Relate the fundamental aspects for the achievement of Arab solidarity as appeared in the words of the comrade Leader Saddam Hussein (God save him)."
4. "Clarify, in brief, the strategic elements to strengthen the Arab nation (*li-ʾiqtidār al-waṭan al-ʿarabī*)."[50]

Even if the Iraqis who participated in these competitions and took these tests did not believe the words they wrote, the fact that Hussein's regime could make them recite its official slogans and repeat the party's lines proved the regime's power over them, not least because these exercises created a public record of complicity and obedience. Repeatedly singing Hussein's praises became ritual, ingraining the concept of Hussein's "necessity" in normative social practice.

Within this atmosphere of all-pervasive and excessive fawning, it is not surprising that the BRCC records contain many acts of seemingly unsolicited allegiance to Hussein by Iraqi citizens. In this category, perhaps the most common act was the presentation of oaths of loyalty to Hussein written in their authors' blood (*wathīqat ʿahd bi-l-damm*). Hussein received the oaths from every segment of society: students, tribal sheikhs, the women's

بسم الله الرحمن الرحيم

الامتحانات العامة للدراسة الابتدائية — جمهورية العراق / وزارة التربية

الدور الأول ١٤٢٣ هـ / ٢٠٠٢ م — الزمن : ساعتان ونصف

اللغـــة العربيـــة

الإنشـــاء : اكتب في **أحد** الموضوعين الآتيين : (٣٠ درجة)

١-نتعلّم .. نُقاتلُ .. نُبدعُ من أجلِ الوطن ومُلهمنا القائد **صدام حسين** (حفظه الله ورعاه) .

عبّر عن هذا الموضوع وبيّن فيه أهمية العلم في حياتنا اليومية ، وفي حمايةِ الوطن والدفاع عن امتنا العربية .

٢-صف مدينتَكَ أو قريتَكَ .

القواعـد : أجب عن **سؤالين** فقط : (٥٠ درجة)

س١ : أ) أجعل (النكرة) معرفةً و (المعرفةَ) نكرةً فيما يأتي : .(١٠ درجات)

١- رَفعتْ تلميذة العلَمَ . ٢- يزرعُ الفلاّحُ قمحاً . ٣- استيقظَ عامل .

ب) استخرج الاسماء المنصوبة من الجمل الآتية واذكر سببَ نصبها ثم بيّن علامة نصبها . (١٥ درجة)

١- ليتَ المتفوقاتِ كثيرات . ٢- ارتدي الملابسَ الصوفيةَ شتاءً . ٣- أمست الطائرتانِ محلقتينِ .

س٢ : أ) املأ كُلَّ فراغٍ مما يأتي بكلمةٍ مناسبةٍ تختارها من بين الاقواس . (١٥ درجة)

١- وصايا ..... دروس للحياةِ . (القائدُ ، القائدَ ، القائدِ)

٢- علِمتُ ..... أمَّ المعاركِ اختبار للهممِ . (إنَّ ، أنَّ ، لكنَّ)

٣- أتمنى أن ..... فريقُنا . (يفوزُ ، يفوزَ ، يفُزْ)

٤- يحترمُ الطلابُ ..... . (المعلمانِ ، المعلمونَ ، المعلمينَ)

٥- ..... طائراتُنا أهدافَ العدوِّ بدقةٍ . (تضربُ ، يَضربُ ، ضَربَ)

ب) رتب كلمات كُلِّ سطرٍ فيما يأتي بحيث يُصبحُ جملةً فعليةً . (١٠ درجات)

١- التلاميذُ ، العلَمِ ، المدرسةِ ، وقفَ ، ساحةِ ، في ، لتحيةِ .

٢- أعداءَهم ، الأسودِ ، يُقاتلُ ، قتال ، العراقيون .

س٣ : أ) أعرب ما تحته خط مما يأتي : (١٥ درجة)

١- استعرضَ <u>جيشُ</u> القُدسِ <u>أمامَ</u> القائدِ . ٢- أكرمَ <u>المتفوقانِ</u> .

٢-<u>الفلسطينيون</u> <u>عائدونَ</u> إلى وطنهم .

ب) ١- هات الأفعال الخمسة من الفعل (يفرحُ) . (٥ درجات)

٢- أجمع المفردات الآتية : الطيّار ، زينب ، قانون ، الماجدة ، مسجد . (٥ درجات)

المحفوظات والنصوص : أجب عن سؤالٍ **واحدٍ** فقط (٢٠ درجة)

س١ : أكتب **خمسةَ** أبياتٍ من الشعرِ مما حفظتهُ في كتاب القراءة العربية للصف السادس واذكر عنوان القصيدة واسم الشاعِر .

س٢ : أكتب **خمسةَ** أسطرٍ من النثر مما حفظته في كتاب القراءة العربية للصف السادس ، مع ذكر عنوان واسم القائلْ .

FIGURE 3.2. *An Elementary School Exam for Sixth Graders in Arabic Language from 2002.* In addition to the examples above, the test also asks students in the grammar section to vowel the following sentences correctly: "I learned *that* the Mother of All Battles is a test of mettle"; "I hope that our team will *win*"; "The students respect the *teachers*"; "Our planes hit the enemy targets precisely"; "The Jerusalem Army paraded in front of the leader"; "Honor those of outstanding achievement"; and "The Palestinians are returning to their homeland." Source: BRCC, 018-5-2: 32. Courtesy of Hoover Institution Library & Archives, Stanford University.

federation, the artists' union, party branches, and so forth.[51] One, from the "vanguard and youth of Maysan Province," from 1983, reads like this:

> Sir, the Leader President, knight of the Arab nation (*fāris al-ʾumma*), the Honorable Struggler Saddam Hussein,
>
> With our blood, we write an oath of loyalty and great love to our leader and the knight of our nation, the comrade struggler Saddam Hussein, in the name of the vanguard and youth (*ṭalāʾiʿ wa-futuwwa wa shabāb*) of Maysan, confirming our allegiance (*al-bayʿa*) and march (*al-sayr*) behind your leadership for the *Qādisiyya* of honor and dignity until the final victory over the enemies of the impostor Khomeini.
>
> Congratulations to you from the depths of our hearts in the days of victories that your soldiers, the soldiers of the *Qādisiyya*, have achieved in the theater of honor and dignity. May God give you victory and success.[52]

The BRCC documents do not indicate that the regime required or suggested that Iraqis write these oaths. Often the people who sent them seemed to want to ensure the state's good graces. At other times, they appeared unsure if they had crossed one of the regime's blurry red lines and decided to confirm their loyalty. Some of the oaths and other acts of allegiance recorded in the BRCC were undoubtedly heartfelt. In 2002, a woman appeared suddenly at the party's al-Zubayr branch headquarters and asked if she could place henna on Saddam's picture. When asked why, she explained that her son, who had been sick, vowed to place the henna but died before he could do so. After he passed away, she decided to carry out his wish. "Please, O' shield and protector of Iraq!" (*dakhīlak yā bakht al-ʿirāq wa ḥāmīhi*) she reportedly cried while placing the henna on the picture.[53] When denied access to alternative views and subjected to an intense indoctrination and propaganda campaign, some Iraqis developed genuine affection for Hussein. As one young Iraqi woman from a rural village told Fanar Haddad, "I used to love Saddam because I knew nothing else."[54]

4. CULTURALIZATION

Culture regulates our lives at every turn. From the moment we are born until we die there is, whether we are conscious of it or not, constant pressure upon us to follow certain types of behavior that other men have created for us. . . . Mothers of small children know how unnaturally most of this comes to us—how little regard we have, until we are "culturalized"

CLYDE KLUCKHOHN, *MIRROR FOR MAN*

INTRODUCTION

"When one hears of state planning in the Soviet Union one usually thinks of factories, steel plants, large grain farms and cotton plantations, tractors and other accessories of industrialization," wrote the American historian and journalist William Henry Chamberlin in 1932. "What is perhaps not generally realized is that man himself is the first and most important objective of Soviet planning and that the tendency to replace man, the individual, by collective man, the product of social groups and forces, is one of the most important and interesting currents in Soviet life." As a result, Chamberlin said, Soviet leaders had established "a gigantic mechanism of social, economic, educational and propaganda forces which tend to repress many old aspects of human personality and to remold it in the image of Marx and Lenin." Subject to these forces, "even the strongest individuality" could not help but be "modified to a greater or lesser extent by the political, economic, social and intellectual atmosphere surrounding it."[1] In Germany too, Adolf Hitler emphasized the creation of a "new man" by wrapping the German people in the spirit of National Socialism. As Timothy S. Brown explained, "The [National Socialist] revolution was not to be socioeconomic but cultural, biological, and above all racial."[2]

Regardless of the specific content of a totalitarian regime's ideology, all totalitarian rulers have used propaganda and indoctrination to shape their citizens' worldviews. As Chamberlin noted, culture shapes man's environment because it affects how humans see the world and act purposefully within it. Controlling culture thus helps a totalitarian ruler control his citizens' behavior and elicit consent for his rule without the resort to violence. "Cultural uniformity," I. L. Kandel observed in relation to Nazi Germany, "becomes . . . an essential aspect of political uniformity, and the machinery is set up to see that cultural uniformity shall be secured without question."[3] By laying the foundational principles and norms on which society operates, a carefully controlled program of cultural production and engineering prepares the groundwork for the long-term maintenance of totalitarian government.

Other types of governments, of course, also manipulate culture in order to establish their hegemony. What distinguishes totalitarianism is the aspiration to control *all* cultural sources and patterns in a society, be they religious, philosophical, aesthetic, scientific, ideological, historical, tribal, regional, athletic, or otherwise.[4] In all cases, the most important thing is for each cultural element to support the ideological claims and political policies of the totalitarian regime. For this reason, citizens cannot play "chess for the sake of chess" or conduct a science experiment purely to advance human knowledge.[5] At least ostensibly, they must carry out every action in the name of the totalitarian political program, and the results of their actions cannot contradict the regime's ideology.

The rulers of a totalitarian state, in other words, seek to transform society's existing culture into a "political culture." That is, after they establish the culture of their political system, they extend that system into all spheres of society, exploding the boundaries between public and private, imbuing even family and personal matters with a political character. Many scholars call totalitarian ideologies "political religions" because they resemble religious belief systems, contain canonical texts, and produce liturgies.[6] I prefer the term "political culture" because no totalitarian ruler has ever claimed to start a new religion, because totalitarian ideologies derive the sources of their legitimacy from history instead of the divine (indeed, they are usually secular), and because totalitarian propaganda and ritual encompasses more than just religious practices.

Scholarship on totalitarian ideological programs shows that political cultures exhibit traits of the environments from which they emanate. Totalitarian movements emerge from distinct historical and cultural contexts, and totalitarian rulers bring to power the values and customs they grew up with. No matter how vigorously promoted, it is difficult to impose an entirely alien ideology on any society. The degree to which a population will accept a new worldview depends in no small part on the extent to which that worldview looks like, or shares traits with, the old one. This necessitates adopting or repurposing existing social and cultural practices, even if the reason for doing so is to supplant them. As George Mosse illustrated, the Nazis created a "morning festival" on Sundays where propagandists led the audience in patriotic songs designed to keep people away from the Church. The morning festivals also served to appropriate the power of Christian tradition, indoctrinate through public ritual, and draw authority from the common habit within German culture of attending a sacred ceremony on Sundays. Similarly, in China, Jiping Zuo relates that "the fanatical attitude that the masses held toward Mao's 'Little Red Book' resembled people's attitude toward animistic magic in the past. As people in traditional Chinese society believed in the power of magic, the masses in the Cultural Revolution believed that the 'Little Red Book' would save them from all trouble."[7] Political cultures thus draw their power to seduce from the utopian aspiration to a better future *and* from their resemblance to existing cultural systems.

The BRCC documents show that the creation of a Husseini Baʿthist political culture constituted a key element of Baʿthification. In party reports, Baʿthist authors speak explicitly about "a strategic campaign to frame (*taʾṭīr*) society and Baʿthize (*tabʿīth*) it by instilling the values of the party and its principles in the masses of the people."[8] The Baʿth referred to this campaign under the general rubric of "culturalization" (*tathqīf*), a term the BRCC's authors frequently paired and interchanged with "indoctrination" (*tawʿīyya*). Like the Soviets and Nazis, the Baʿth theorized that by subjecting Iraqis to constant propaganda and indoctrination in the media, in popular culture, and in school—and by forcing them to consistently engage in individual and collective rites where they had to express their allegiance to the Baʿthist Trinity—the population would "absorb" (*ʾistīʿāb*) Husseini Baʿthist principles, and the Baʿthist ethos would become an organic part of the Iraqi soul. To aid this process, Hussein and the Baʿth appropriated and manipulated established myths, customs, norms, values, and vocabularies from Iraq's religious, tribal, ethnic, and local cultures. If they could harness the tendencies to think, feel, believe, and act in the particular ways that any cultural environment imparts to the individuals immersed in it, Hussein and the Baʿth hoped that Iraqis would support their regime out of their citizens' own motivations instead of through coercion or oppression.

CULTURE AND CULTURALIZATION

The concept of "culture" (*thaqāfa*) occupies a central place within Baʿth Party documents. Beginning at least in 1982, if not before, each Baʿth Party branch had a "cultural committee" (*lajna thaqāfiyya*) tasked with educating party members about Baʿthist ideology and spreading the party's message to the masses.[9] One such committee from the party's Baghdad branch explained the reasoning behind the Baʿth's emphasis on culture in a 1984 report:

> Culture in our party occupies a place of exceptional importance because it is a basic means to prepare the Baʿthist struggler intellectually for his struggle (*niḍāliyyan*), starting from the unity of the Baʿth's concept of thought and practice. This unity is embodied in knowledge about, and awareness of, the thought of the party in order to arrive at absolute faith in it. Faith is reflected in the living practice of the Baʿthist struggler and in how he embodies these principles in the reality of the nation (*ʾumma*) by way of his change in a revolutionary direction.
>
> The party has expressed this importance in various forms and practices. All of them, however, express the party's special understanding for the culture of the revolution. That is, the party does not look at culture as mere knowledge or an academic acquisition but looks at it as living practice that expresses the embodiment of the principles [of the party] in reality and in what confirms the fact that the Baʿth is a pioneering revolutionary vanguard that leads the masses toward a new tomorrow and resurrects the nation's civilized qualities.[10]

From this and other passages in the BRCC, it is clear that culturalization consisted of a three-step process that the regime believed would lead to a Husseini Baʿthist political culture in Iraqi society.

First, the Baʿth would indoctrinate their members. To do this, the 1984 Baghdad branch report offered ten "means of culturalization" (*wasāʾil al-tathqīf*) as prototypical elements of Baʿthist indoctrination, describing to the Baghdad Bureau Command "the most notable" cultural activities carried out by Baghdad party organizations in recent times. Cultural subjects occupied the first place on party meeting agendas, the report claimed, and every party organization convened a cultural seminar (*nadwa*) on a regular basis.[11] In order to "create a spirit of competition between members" and encourage "their absorption of cultural subjects" the committee put on a series of "cultural competitions" that pitted party organizations against one another. A series of continuing education classes took place so as to strengthen and develop members' cultural knowledge. The party conducted the classes in one of the Baghdad Bureau's newly opened "party preparatory schools" (*madāris al-ʾiʿdād al-ḥizbī*) over two semesters each year and used the grades students received to hand out promotions and demotions. To enable research into Baʿthist culture, and to promote "self-culturalization" (*al-tathqīf al-dhātī*), the Baghdad Cultural Committee claimed to have refreshed the libraries of party organizations with books on Baʿthist thought and national (both Iraqi and Arab) history. This, the committee maintained, was partly in order to satisfy Hussein's directive for cultural committee members to present research papers and to set up teams of researchers who would produce scholarly work on Baʿthist history and ideology. Finally, the report mentioned that the Saddam branch of the Baghdad Bureau ordered all of the party organizations under its command to lecture their partisans and supporters about cultural programs; to take them on field trips to Baʿthist museums, exhibits, panoramas, and the monuments of the martyr and unknown soldier; and to engage them in producing their own posters, festivals, and exhibits. All of these activities, the report argued, reinforced and deepened the cultural knowledge of the Baʿthists who participated in them. Indeed, the creation of a competent "vanguard" (*ṭalīʿa*) or leadership "cadre" (*kādir*), which could spread propaganda and recruit from the population, was a prerequisite for culturalization to succeed.[12]

Second, a Baʿthist had to prove his faith and serve as an example to others by acting on his beliefs and carrying Baʿthist principles into everyday life. As one party slogan went: "The Baʿthist and his family are examples in their behavior and discipline."[13] The party regularly evaluated its members. One of the criteria for assessment was the "cultural level and the extent to which [the member] has absorbed the thought of the party."[14] "Confirmation of the struggling, leading role of a true Baʿthist," an internal party pamphlet explained,

> is evident in his view toward all of life as an arena in which he expresses his belonging and his thought . . . indeed, the expression of the integrity of his Baʿthness (*baʿthiyatihi*) and his commitment to struggle lies in how he carries the party as a distinctive state of being throughout life. The party, for him, should not just be attendance at meetings after which he transforms into another person with no connection to the party whose thoughts and behavior do not give expression to [Baʿthism].[15]

The party saw Baʿthism as a worldview and way of life as opposed to just a political program: something that inspired a Baʿthist's political, economic, and social views, his artistic and cultural output, his beliefs, and the way he acted in public and private.

The third step required transferring (*naql*) Husseini Baʿthist culture from the party to the populace. Hussein emphasized that the principles and directives he voiced should be "applied" (*taṭbīq*), "executed" (*tanfīdh*), and put into practice (*mumārasa*) in daily life. He believed, in line with the title of a speech he gave shortly after becoming president, that "By Thought and Practice and the Living Example, Faith is Achieved."[16] If Iraqis actively and repeatedly parroted the regime's slogans and carried out its rites, their collective behavior would create a set of national myths and symbols, and their individual behavior would shape their personal dispositions and motivations, in ways that led them to have "faith" in Husseini Baʿthism.[17] Ideally, "faith" would constitute genuine belief that would advance the party's aspiration to turn Iraqis into Baʿthists and create a unified nation founded on loyalty to the Baʿthist Trinity. More practically, Hussein hoped to establish his political authority by ingraining cultural patterns and tendencies in Iraqis' minds and bodies.

The Baʿth attempted to transfer their ideology to the population through a dual campaign of propaganda and ritual, each of which reinforced the other. Propaganda contributed to mass mobilization (*taʿbiʾa*) by telling and convincing Iraqis when, how, and why to support the regime's policies. Conversely, mobilizing Iraqis to partake in Baʿthist rites and ceremonies reinforced the myths of Baʿthist propaganda. "A Study about Mass Mobilization," for instance, written by the Baghdad Bureau Command in 1987, advocated

> Taking an interest in implanting national (*qawmiyya*) and socialist concepts for the sake of enriching and developing the [Baʿthist] march (*masīra*), and focusing on the cultural aspect of mass mobilization activities so that the masses will absorb (*ʾistīʿāb*) the Baʿthist creed completely, arriving at a unity of comprehension and opinion (*mawqif*) [about Baʿthist ideology]. As a result, citizens will take positions on a daily basis that are practical expressions of [Baʿthist ideology] when dealing with the details of daily life. This will contribute to raising the spirit of mobilization among the masses.
>
> Many of the initiatives that have been employed by the party and mass organizations have aimed to increase the effectiveness of popular mobilization and to raise it to the level of thwarting the extent of the [Iranian] aggression and its evil ambitions.[18]

As this last sentence indicates, culturalization would not only convince Iraqis of the Baʿth's virtues, it would also shield them from the ideological rhetoric of enemies such as Iran. Citizens who internalized the Baʿth's message, a 1984 party report argued, "assess other intellectual currents and political positions in relation to the principles of the party, its positions, and its decisions."[19] When considered by the un-indoctrinated mind, opposition rhetoric could poke holes in the logic of Husseini Baʿthism. But if Iraqis considered Husseini Baʿthism's tenets to be authoritative moral precepts, they would automatically reject alternative ideas on principle because those ideas would not coincide with the Husseini Baʿthist worldview. As Isaiah Berlin observed, the "training of individuals incapable of being troubled by questions which, when raised and discussed, endanger the stability of the system . . . is the intellectual outlook which attends the rise of totalitarian ideologies."[20] Hussein and the Baʿth sought to produce this same type of outlook in Iraq. The specific policies and tactics that they employed to do so are the topics of the remainder of the chapter.

PROPAGANDA AND INDOCTRINATION

Writers with experience living in totalitarian regimes have remarked on the constancy, repetitiveness, and zealousness with which propagandists deliver their messages and how this affects the people subject to indoctrination. Stephen H. Roberts, an Australian scholar who spent three years living in and studying Nazi Germany before World War II, found that "It is very hard, even for a foreigner, to resist [Nazi propaganda's] messages, so convincingly are they delivered, because fervid partisanship permits an emotional intensity out of the question in a system where objective impartiality is sought."[21] "Not only the members of the party and the more or less indifferent masses," wrote Carl Friedrich and Zbigniew Brzezinski, "but even the more or less determined enemies of the regime, fall prey to [totalitarian propaganda's] insistent clamor, to the endless repetition of the same phrases and the same allegations. A general pattern of thought, almost a style of thinking, proves increasingly irresistible as the regime continues in power."[22]

Husseini Baʿthist propaganda aimed to engender a "style of thinking" commensurate with the regime's worldview, and the BRCC documents show that the party's organs of indoctrination delivered their ideological messages with the same "emotional intensity," "insistent clamor," and "endless repetition" of carefully cultivated phrases and images that the Nazis and Soviets did. By way of example, in 1984 the Euphrates Bureau issued a study entitled, "Ways to Culturalize the Masses (Mass Mobilization)" [*ʾasālīb al-tathqīf al-jamāhīrī (al-taʿbiʾa al-jamāhīriyya)*]. As the title indicates, Hussein believed that by manipulating culture he could elicit popular support, and he tasked the Baʿth Party with overseeing his culturalization effort. In the study, the Euphrates Bureau describes itself as an "educational, cultural, and media organization," which aspired to integrate the party and the masses through "the process of mobilization, indoctrination, and culturalization." As a result, the bureau focused on ways to attract the populace's attention and emphasize the party's basic messages in an attempt to both draw Iraqis into the Baʿthist fold and communicate the regime's desires. The best way to do this, the study argued, was via media and cultural productions aimed especially at youth and carried out in conjunction with the Professional and Mass Organizations.[23] The study characterized media as television, radio, newspapers, and videos of ideologically inspired content, especially programs featuring Hussein. Beyond media, the Euphrates Bureau study defined "mass indoctrination and culturalization" to comprise "pictures, paintings, songs, odes, caricatures, exhibitions, sport competitions, folklore, leaflets, posters, publications, and anything that leads to mass mobilization which can possibly be exploited and benefited from." To furnish the content for these items, the Baʿth patronized journalists, documentary and movie producers, artists, writers, and poets who had to join official unions and comply with the regime's various agencies of "culture and media" in order to practice their craft.[24]

In addition to serving as an agent of indoctrination, the language and images of Husseini Baʿthist propaganda acted as a means of public discourse within the state and society, and between the two. Hussein and the Baʿth communicated with the populace through this Baʿthized vocabulary, and the populace used it to respond. This conversation occurred in both directions. Occasionally, individuals in society pushed back and forced the government to listen, but even in those cases the fact that the conversation took place within the Baʿth's imposed idiom indicated the overwhelming power that Hussein and the party held.

Words act as symbols for ideas or things. In context, they also elicit particular emotions and attitudes, are connected to behavioral tendencies, and carry moral connotations. Words thus contribute to shape culture and individual and collective psychology.[25] In Hussein's Iraq, the Baʿthist idiom worked hand-in-hand with the coercive mechanisms that the regime used to control state and society. If the latter placed physical boundaries around the populace, the former consisted of a series of "code words" that defined appropriate thought and conduct, laid out rewards for obedience, and warned of punishments for defiance.[26] By examining the words the regime used to describe something, Iraqis knew immediately whether it was "good" or "bad." The ideological vocabulary that characterizes the BRCC records told Iraqis the rules the regime expected them to follow.

One of the ways that the Baʿth regime indicated its approval of a subject was by placing a particular superlative or positive adjective after the subject's name. Three of the Baʿth's favorite positive adjectives were "glorious" (*majīd*), "great" (*ʿaẓīm*), and "eternal" (*khālid*). The Baʿth frequently referred to the 1968 revolution as "the glorious revolution." The Iran–Iraq War was "Saddam's Glorious *Qādisiyya*" (*qādisiyyat ṣaddām al-majīda*), and the Baʿth called the Gulf War "The Eternal Mother of All Battles" (*'umm al-maʿārik al-khālida*). Finally, one of the official slogans when Hussein opened the "Saddam River" in 1992 claimed that "With Iraq's creative minds we produced the eternal Saddam River."[27]

The regime repeated these phrases so often that the adjectives became part of the names of the events they described. The adjectives almost always occur attached to their subjects in both internal Baʿth Party correspondence and citizen petitions, proving that Iraqis understood the vocabulary they had to use when interacting with the party and the state. The Baʿthist idiom thus became a form of doublespeak, masking the actual character of a particular subject, person, or event. In the case of the Iran–Iraq War, every Iraqi had a friend or relative at the front and knew at least one of Iraq's approximately 125,000 dead or 255,000 wounded.[28] For eight years, the wounded filled hospitals, and the BRCC records make clear that southern residents lived in a war zone.[29] Millions of people served on the front lines or in support positions. Iraqis knew the true character of the war.[30] Yet, they were constantly told, and had to parrot back, the claim that the war was "glorious." The parameters of permissible discourse, and the tangible consequences that would accrue to themselves and their families if they contradicted the regime's propaganda, made it prudent to accept the government's line.[31]

The regime further signaled its intentions to the populace by imbuing sets of words with contrasting positive and negative connotations. Merely labeling something as an "experience" (*tajriba*) or a "phenomenon" (*ẓāhira*), for example, told the public how they should orient their mindset and actions toward it.[32] In a party report detailing the positive aspects of a plebiscite supporting Hussein in 1995, the Party Secretariat referred to the event as "the experience of the Day of the Big March" (*tajribat yawm al-zaḥf al-kabīr*).[33] The BRCC's authors similarly called the 1968 revolution "the experience of the great July 17–30 revolution" (*tajribat thawrat 17–30 tamūz al-ʿaẓīma*). The Baʿth further claimed legitimacy for themselves in 1984 by highlighting their "living expertise and experience that the leadership of the party and the revolution possesses, and its close interaction with reality."[34] By playing up their "experience," the Baʿth sought to burnish their leadership credentials, not least by asserting that their goals and policies derived from first-hand knowledge about the actual state of the world—knowledge they could use to address the needs and aspirations of Iraqis.[35]

In contrast, the word "phenomenon" connoted something negative or abnormal. The Baʿth frequently referred to the same subjects that they labeled "phenomena" as "unnatural" (*ghayr ṭabīʿī*).[36] The Baʿth used "phenomenon" in relation to desertion from the army (*ẓāhirat al-hurūb*), absence and tardiness at party meetings (*ẓāhirat al-ghiyāb wa-l-takhalluf ʿan ḥuḍūr al-ʾijtimāʿāt al-ḥizbiyya*), and joining the party just to accrue its benefits (*ẓāhirat al-ʾintimāʾ al-maṣlaḥī li-l-ḥizb*). Likewise, the terrible economic conditions that Iraq suffered in the 1990s brought on "the phenomenon of beggary" (*ẓāhirat al-tasawwul*).[37]

In a religious context, the distinction between "experience" and "phenomenon" highlights a further aspect of the Baʿth's culturalization campaign: the appropriation of existing cultural symbols and myths in Iraqi society for the Baʿth's own purposes. Within a list of "general slogans" prepared for the Prophet's 2002 birthday celebration, the Baʿth called Muhammad's revelation "the greatest experience of faith that our glorious nation has lived" (*ʾaʿẓam tajriba ʾīmāniyya ʿāshathā ʾummatnā al-majīda*).[38] Alternatively, the Baʿth referred to popular Shiʿi rituals and Sunni Wahhabi practices as elements of a general "religious phenomenon" (*al-ẓāhira al-dīniyya*), which the Baʿth distinguished from true religious "faith" (*ʾīmān*), or Islam.[39] This distinction went back to Aflaq, who claimed a difference "between the truth of religion and the appearance of religion." Aflaq contended that Islam was "a revolutionary movement." By doing so, he rhetorically removed Islam from a religious context and placed it within the Baʿthist idiom. Baʿthist revolutionaries could thus best understand Islam and carry it forward.[40] In this way, Aflaq covered up the Baʿth's blasphemous subordination of Islam to the higher principle of Arab nationalism while rebutting the charge that the party was secular and consequently illegitimate in a religious society. Instead, by appropriating Islam's moral and historical authority, Aflaq placed a claim on Islam's emotional and cultural power to mobilize the Arab people, neutering religious alternatives to the party's message in the process.

The Baʿth drew on Aflaq's theories about religion and their distinctions between positive and negative religious practices to promote the generic concepts of "faith" and "belief" (*ʾīmān*) in Baʿthist ideals. Words have "multivocalities"; they contain ambiguities and thus can mean different things to different people.[41] To a devout Muslim or Christian, "faith" could mean belief in God. To a party member, it might represent his or her belief in Baʿthist ideology. Without mentioning religion, the Baʿth could reference their general support for "faith" and appeal to a broad constituency while satisfying the primary criterion of any ruler in an Islamic culture: the belief in God and Muhammad's message. Consequently, when the Baʿth introduced Islam into official state sanctioned culture in the early 1990s, they called the initiative "The Faith Campaign" (*al-ḥamla al-ʾīmāniyya*); Islam does not appear in the title. The official slogans for the party's celebration of the Prophet's birthday in 2002 included the assertion that "By choosing the Prophet Muhammad (blessings and peace be upon him), the Arabs were chosen as the possessors of faith and the central means (*mīdān*) for the birth of its message." Playing off the commonly used term for Muslims as "believers," which the party also employed to refer to its members, the same slogan went on to claim that "It is the responsibility of the fighting believers (*al-muʾminīn al-mujāhidīn*) to carry [faith] to all of humanity." Whether "believers" and "faith" refer in this slogan to Muslims and Islam, or Baʿthists and Husseini Baʿthism, is intentionally ambiguous. In another motto, the Baʿth made their nationalist values equivalent to but more progressive than Islam while paying homage to Islam and asserting the party's primacy: "The believing, fighting nationalism (*qawmiyya*) is the *new way of belief* to save the Arab nation."[42] "The new way of belief," of course, referred to Baʿthism. By connecting the generic quality of "faith" to a traditional Islamic concept, the Baʿth made faith a proxy for commitment to their cause and linked the familiar belief in Islam with belief in the party's values. In this way, Iraqis did not have to give up their religions or the emotional and orientational satisfactions of the "experience of faith;" they just had to give them a Baʿthist focus. If the Baʿth could convince enough Iraqis to make this adjustment, to see the world through their eyes by reorienting their belief systems, they could shift Iraqi culture into harmony with their ideals. The use of code words like "experience" and "phenomenon" contributed to this effort.[43]

If the regime used ideological language and code words to communicate with the populace, Iraqis also conversed with the regime. This conversation did not take place on equal terms. The regime held the preponderance of power and considered outright objections to its dictates tantamount to treason. Nonetheless, the regime ultimately needed a certain number of citizens to do its bidding. It thus had to apply its rules with a modicum of consistency when rewarding and punishing its supporters and opponents. Iraqis had a small degree of leverage over the Baʿthist State. By couching their objections in Baʿthist language and employing the regime's code words, Iraqis could clarify their loyalties and, in the process, buy credibility to subtly resist, alter, complain, or offer suggestions about the regime's policies. While Iraqis rarely succeeded in thwarting or significantly changing the regime's programs, their conversations with the Baʿthist State often took the form of a negotiation instead of a dictation.[44]

The case of a tribal sheikh who wrote to Hussein in order to be named the official chief of his clan (*fakhdh*) demonstrates the subtlety and ambiguity with which these negotiations took place. In the introduction to his letter, the sheikh left no doubt about his allegiances. He addressed the letter to "Mr. Leader President, strength of Iraq the great and the leader of the glorious victory, the honorable Saddam Hussein (God keep you)." The sheikh consequently placed the subject matter of his request firmly within the parameters of the Baʿth's official line about the "gloriousness" of their wars and Hussein's exalted status in his personality cult. The sheikh then included an original, laudatory poem about Hussein before getting down to business:

> Despite my knowledge of how consumed you are by affairs of state and party, I apologize for taking a moment of your precious time, which is the property of noble Iraqis, and to engage you with a request from your loyal son who is of a family where the names of the great Baʿth and the great Saddam Hussein bring happiness. My father requests that I be confirmed as the head of the albu-[name withheld] clan within the [name withheld] tribe in the district of Samarra. By God, Sir, I don't want to hide from your honorable self that I am one of your loyal sons, faithful to our party and leader and glorious revolution, and one of the influential men of clan albu-[name withheld]. I would provide good opinions (*ḥusn ẓann*) of our leader, our inspiration, and our refuge, the great Saddam Hussein, keeping in mind, Sir, that the clan of albu-[name withheld] has a large membership, all of whom are loyal to our leading party. They always attend the national occasions (*al-munāsabāt al-waṭaniya wa-l-qawmiya*), and we would be, at the signal of the leader symbol, the great Saddam Hussein, sharp swords in your right hand to drive away the enemy apostates (*al-ʾaʿdāʾ al-māriqīn*). We ask God, the exalted, to save you and give you a long life and to grant you mighty victories.[45]

In this request, the sheikh told Hussein that, if confirmed as the head of his clan, he would work within it on Hussein and the party's behalf. Yet, his appeal was conditional and contained a veiled threat. If Hussein did not choose him, he might work against the regime among his tribesmen, which could constitute a thorn in Hussein's side because of his tribe's numbers and martial prowess. If Hussein directed all the means at his disposal against the clan and its tribe he would undoubtedly have been able to subdue them. But would Hussein want to spend the resources and forgo the clan's automatic support just to choose somebody else? Regardless of the answer, the sheikh asked Hussein to contemplate this equation. This kind of give-and-take whereby Iraqis pledged their loyalty in return for official backing constituted a basic agreement between the ruling clique and the rest of society.

RITUAL AND CEREMONY

In addition to media and language, culturalization consisted of a series of rituals and ceremonies designed to instill Husseini Baʿthism in everyday personal and collective practice. One of the best examples of this lay in the Baʿth's cult of martyrdom. By fostering the cult, the Baʿth politicized the normally private and religious affairs surrounding death and the mourning rituals associated with it, drawing an emotional, spiritual, and sacred affair into their national liturgy. The Arabic word that the regime used for "martyr," *shahīd*, originated in Islamic parlance where it refers to Muslims who die in battles with infidels. Muslim martyrs receive direct passage to heaven.[46] "The martyrs are nobler than us all" (*al-shuhadāʾ ʾakram minna jamīʿan*) is one of Hussein's most oft repeated catchphrases in the BRCC, and the archive's authors use the phrase, "those who are nobler than us all," as a euphemism for martyrs.[47] The expression channeled Aflaq's original sentiment that sacrificing oneself for the nation is the highest possible moral act in Baʿthism. In the BRCC, it conferred an elevated political and social status on martyrs and their families, and Iraqis used the fact that family or tribal members had died in war as proof of their loyalty. Three tribal sheikhs claimed in a petition to Hussein, for example, that their tribes "had the honor of participation in the second *Qādisiyya* (the Iran–Iraq War) with two hundred martyrs, martyrs in the name of your justice."[48] As this quotation indicates, Hussein employed the concept of martyrdom to encourage Iraqis to fight in the Iran–Iraq and Gulf wars and to refrain from desertion and dodging military service. By linking a religious concept to a national obligation, moreover, the Baʿth tried to give the families of martyrs solace that their relatives did not die in vain.

The Baʿth reinforced the cult of martyrdom as a collective national duty in mass ceremonies on "Martyr's Day" (December 1) and in ad hoc events organized for political purposes. In 1984, the President's Office circulated a program in advance of Martyr's Day detailing the activities that would take place. First, at morning prayers in both mosques and churches, the "prayer of absence" (*ṣalāt al-ghāʾib*) was "to be performed over the souls of the martyrs." Next, a group of party elites and representatives from the PMOs would lay wreaths at the tomb of the unknown soldier. Then Iraq's air raid sirens would sound for five minutes of reflective silence. The first hour of the work and school days was to be reserved for speeches and poetry readings "to discuss the exploits of our martyrs and their heroism in Saddam's glorious *Qādisiyya*, their role in protecting the land of Iraq and the honor and dignity of Iraqis, the loyalty to the history of the Arab nation and its civilization, and to act as a reminder of the shameful role of the rulers of Tehran in the execution of [Iraqi] prisoners [of war]." The members of party branches, local organizations, and the PMOs would then visit martyrs' families to repeat this message, relate the regime's condolences, and remind the families of the regime's ongoing emotional and financial support. The Ministry of Culture and Media was instructed to cover the events of

Martyr's Day on television, on the radio, and in newspapers so that Iraqis who did not personally participate in the rituals could still observe, listen to, or read about them. Among these programs, newspapers were specifically told to print articles and investigative pieces (*taḥqīqāt*) celebrating the act of martyrdom (*ʾistishhād*) and the martyrs themselves. Art exhibitions and poetry festivals were also to be organized around "subjects that honored martyrdom and the heroic deeds of our armed forces."[49]

The 1984 Martyr's Day program had clear purposes. Its events acted as mourning ceremonies where Iraqis could grieve as a group, where they could find solace in the fact that their individual losses were part of a larger, necessary sacrifice on behalf of the nation. Their martyrs died fighting for the people of Iraq; they died with honor. By ingraining this official narrative, and supporting the emotional and financial needs of the martyr's families, the Baʿth made the moral framework for the war clear. Men could go to fight—and had no excuse not to—because they knew the regime would take care of their families if they died. The Baʿth sought to legitimize themselves by proving that they cared for their people as any rightful populist and Muslim ruler should.

In the Martyr's Day ceremonies, ritual acted as an instrument of culturalization. The BRCC contains a particularly poignant example of how this worked in two documents about Martyr's Day in 1997. The documents leave no doubt that Hussein's regime organized any gathering of more than a few people in Iraq down to the last detail for maximum effect. In the days leading up to Martyr's Day, the President's Office ordered the Iraqi Red Crescent and Iraq's domestic children's organizations to organize a funeral procession for fifty children in coordination with the Health Minister. The procession, the President's Office stated, was to be devoid "of any official signs or manifestations in order to give the impression that the funeral was not organized by the state, just as it has been decided to call citizens to participate in the funeral in an indirect way."[50] Having noticed these seemingly spontaneous displays (or simply going along with the charade), the head of General Security wrote to the president's Secretary for Party Affairs, informing him that

> In recent days, funeral processions have taken place for Iraqi child martyrs of the evil blockade. We have noticed the positive effect of these processions for increasing hatred among the public toward America and, similarly, its effect outside of the country as a result of the reactions relayed by the Arab and world media.
>
> Perhaps we can expand these practices to become more influential on the public so as to increase hatred against America and widen their effect on the personalities and organizations concerned with children out-

side of the country in order to make them a means of pressure and condemnation against America and its positions.[51]

Accordingly, the GSD Director suggested that the Health Ministry collect the bodies of dead children and hoard them instead of giving them to their families in order to build up a critical mass of corpses for a mass funeral procession. The dead children, he said, should be placed in small coffins instead of regular, adult-size ones because they had more of an emotional effect on the observer. Making the connection between patriotic sacrifice and martyrdom, he advocated wrapping an Iraqi flag around the coffins "in order to clarify that the child is a martyr." On the cart that carried each coffin, the director ordered that a large picture of the child be placed on top with his or her name and age written underneath in both Arabic and English, so that an international audience could read the signs. Each cart would lead a procession to a different mosque or church where a funeral rite would be performed with a state or party representative in attendance in addition to members of Arab and Islamic diplomatic missions. Following the individual ceremonies, the coffins would coalesce in one large march toward the square in Baghdad where the regime carried out its national ceremonies (*sāḥat al-ʾiḥtifālāt*). There, Hussein would preside over a ceremony where members of the Revolutionary Command Council, the party, and the PMOs would lay wreaths and flowers on the coffins. An imam would give a fiery speech, and then the bodies would be given to the families. The crowd during the occasion would hold placards blaming America for the children's deaths, again in Arabic and English. The whole process, the director wrote, should be covered live on television and followed up with coverage in the newspapers and in special publications designed for international consumption.[52]

The rituals associated with the "democratic" façade of the Baʿthist regime constituted another category of national ceremonies designed to propagandize. Like the Nazis and Soviets, the Baʿth consistently claimed that they were democratic. Accordingly, they insisted on carrying out national and party elections, holding plebiscites, erecting a National Assembly (*al-majlis al-waṭanī*) and local "People's Councils" (*majālis al-shaʿb*), and promulgating laws and regulations, including new constitutions in 1968, 1970, and a draft constitution that they never ratified in 1990.[53] Why did the regime bother when, in reality, Baʿthist rule constituted the antithesis of democracy, the elections and assemblies were shams, and the rule of law did not exist? As the Director of the Party Secretariat wrote in 1995 about why the regime held a plebiscite (*ʾistiftāʾ*) on Hussein's presidency: "The plebiscite proved that the Iraqi people remain devoted to the original national values that appear throughout its bright history, that they are a people united during crises, and that they are a large cohesive power in the face of challenges by virtue of the secure care of the party. They do not disagree with, nor will they give up on, their national and moral principles or their loyalty to the leader (God keep him)."[54] The regime carried out the plebiscite shortly after two of Hussein's sons-in-law defected to Jordan and during a time of economic privation brought on by UN sanctions. In the face of these adverse circumstances, the plebiscite "proved" the unwavering support of the masses for Hussein and the Baʿth's leadership. Although the result was incredulous—Hussein received 99.96 percent of the vote—nobody could definitively contradict it given an absence of alternative information.[55] Only Hussein's name appeared on the ballot and voting against him carried repercussions. The result of the polling process could thus have been accurate, even if it did not represent the true sentiment of the Iraqi people. Regardless, forcing Iraqis to vote at the polls demonstrated that the regime still had enough power to organize a nation-wide simulation of mass support. The plebiscite simultaneously confirmed that Hussein retained a great deal of authority, posited his legitimacy, and distracted and deterred opponents who hoped to capitalize on the discord within his inner circle and the country's poor economic conditions. Like other national occasions, the plebiscite acted as a venue for Hussein and the Baʿth to make an incredible claim and substantiate it at the same time.

A number of other "occasions" (*munāsabāt*), as the BRCC's authors refer to them, also served as rituals and propaganda tools. April 5, for example, became a national day of remembrance following an Iranian missile attack that hit the "Palace of Martyrs" school (*madrasat balāṭ al-shuhadāʾ*) in 1988, killing tens of children. It later turned into the more general "Day of the Iraqi Child" (*yawm al-ṭifl al-ʿirāqī*) when the Baʿth wanted to pressure the international community to lift its sanctions in the 1990s.[56] Similarly, the Baʿth converted the American and British bombing campaign in December 1998 into a yearly celebration called "The Day of the Glorious Victory" (*yawm al-fatḥ al-mubīn*), using the same Arabic term that appears in Sura 48 of the *Qurʾān*, which refers to when the early Muslims took Mecca in 630 AD.[57] These two occasions, combined with the anniversaries of the Iran–Iraq and Gulf wars, gave the regime opportunities to repeatedly remind the populace that Iran and America harbored evil intentions from which only the Baʿthist State could protect them. The slogans for the 1999 Day of the Iraqi Child, for example, included, "By the thought and the wisdom of the leader, we guarantee the future of our children," and "the blockade is a witness to the imperialist hatred for the children of Iraq."[58]

These rituals and ceremonies were only some of the recurring holidays, remembrances, anniversaries of historical Baʿthist events, and celebrations of Hussein's leadership that accrued throughout his tenure.[59] Together, they defined Iraqi patriotism as allegiance to the Baʿthist Trinity, shaped the national calendar, and gave public life a sense of consistency and order. The Baʿth made the occasions into tests of loyalty by noting if an Iraqi attended them in his or her file. Although each occasion had its own focus, the programs that the Baʿth Party and Ministry of Culture and Media prepared for the occasions all conformed to the same general pattern of the Martyr's Day rituals described above. Indeed, the purpose of the occasion seemed to matter little. Emphases of particular terms changed. The Baʿth at various times included more pan-Arab, tribal, Mesopotamian, or Islamic language in their slogans, but the ceremonies' basic objectives stayed the same: to use the symbols, myths, and values that the Baʿth propagated to culturalize the populace and propagandize to the outside world.

In one sense, the Baʿth's national occasions resembled every other ritual of loyalty that Iraqis performed in their daily lives. The occasions relied heavily on repetition and a panorama of "code words," images, and catchphrases that defined acceptable conduct and thought, reinforcing the Baʿth's authority. In another sense, however, the collective character of the occasions gave them a more powerful quality. The personal rituals that Iraqis carried out on a daily basis atomized them. But at occasions, Iraqis repeated the same slogans in unison, participated in the same marches, listened to the same speeches, and shared the same experiences and emotions as their fellows. As a result, Iraqis became, at least during a ceremony, part of a unified, exclusive community with a shared ethos, undivided by religion, sect, tribe, ethnicity, or class. The occasions affirmed the Baʿth's assertions before everybody's eyes, in public, by the masses. Rhetoric and reality, ideology and practice, united as Hussein intended. Acting collectively in support of the regime implicated everyone yet diffused responsibility onto the crowd. In this way, the Baʿth hoped that their rituals would make it easier for Iraqis to accept the excuse that Husseini Baʿthism offered for supporting Hussein's regime.[60]

Of course, that Hussein and the Baʿth felt the need to institute so many rituals in daily life, and to hold frequent mass ceremonies, showed how quickly the hegemonic effects of the rituals dissipated, and how thoroughly against the grain of objective reality and history the regime's rites went. To solve this problem, the BRCC suggests that the Baʿth tried to make life into a series of rituals and ceremonies designed to destroy as much as possible the time and space when Iraqis were not, in one way or another, part of a rite or otherwise subject to propaganda. The results of culturalization undoubtedly differed on an individual basis, but the question is nevertheless worth posing: how many times did Iraqis participate in the regime's liturgy before the Husseini Baʿthist universe began to become their own?[61]

PART III. ORGANIZATION

> *Organization* (al-tanẓīm) *is not a formal, technical matter isolated from the nature of [Baʿthist] thought and the struggle for its sake. It is, rather, a living form that enables the party to achieve its ideas and pursue them with greater ability and effectiveness in order to change the reality of the Arab nation from the perspective of a total national revival.*
>
> FADIL ABBAS AZZAWI, *AL-BUNIYYA AL-TANZIMIYYA LI-L-HIZB AL-BAʿTH AL-ʿARABI AL-ʾISHTIRAKI* (*THE ORGANIZATIONAL STRUCTURE OF THE ARAB BAʿTH SOCIALIST PARTY*)

In the first half of 1933, the National Socialists in Germany began a policy of *Gleichschaltung*, or the integration and synchronization of German society.[1] *Gleichschaltung* consisted of a series of laws backed by Nazi Storm Troops designed to guarantee the political reliability of all public officials and institutions, civil society organizations, and private citizens. As part of *Gleichschaltung*, the Nazis sifted through the civil service and forced all of the top public officials in national, state, and local positions in Germany to either enlist in the party or resign. They eliminated Germany's federal separation of powers. They abolished all previously independent state and regional offices and councils. They began to appoint local officials from Berlin. At the same time, Adolf Hitler's regime brought Germany's education and judicial systems, political parties, state institutions, media, cultural organizations, professional and voluntary associations, unions, clubs, and economic pressure groups under the Nazis' direct or indirect political control and bureaucratic administration. Even Germany's churches, Hamilton Fish Armstrong wrote in 1933, had begun to form "a new and unified *Reickskirche* (Church of the Empire) to meet the fear of the Nazis." Many Germans complied with the process of *Gleichschaltung* because they feared the consequences of resistance, or because they hoped to resist or influence Nazi policies from within. Between January 30 and May 1, 1933, 1.6 million people joined the party; many others assimilated into the Nazi system.

"The process of co-ordination (*Gleichschaltung*) was less than perfectly carried out," the historian, Richard Evans, wrote. "Nevertheless, the scale and scope of the co-ordination of German society were breathtaking."[2]

The Nazis pursued *Gleichschaltung* for political reasons: to cement their authority by eliminating space for opposition, and to establish an institutional, bureaucratic, and legal basis for their rule. *Gleichschaltung* also had a higher purpose: to make society amenable to indoctrination—"to remold the German psyche and rebuild the German character."[3] As Hannah Arendt pointed out, in totalitarian regimes "Organization and propaganda (rather than terror and propaganda) are two sides of the same coin."[4] Just as ritual reinforces the messages of propaganda, so too can society's architecture, infrastructure, institutions, legal frameworks, and normative practices give tangible shape to ideological assertions. *Gleichschaltung* was a strategy for political control, but it was also part and parcel of the Nazi culturalization project. For this reason, Timothy Brown argues that *Gleichschaltung* had both a practical and broader meaning. Practically, it consisted of the policies described above that facilitated the Nazi takeover of Germany's state, civil, and social institutions. "More broadly, Gleichschaltung represented the attempted Nazification of all aspects of German culture and society."[5]

By the same token, regime officials employed the term "Baʿthification" with a dual meaning. Baʿthification referred to the regime's general strategy to integrate Iraq's heterogeneous individuals, communities, and institutions into one homogenous Husseini Baʿthist nation, unified politically, emotionally, intellectually, morally, spiritually, and culturally. More narrowly and literally, Baʿthification consisted of the organization of Iraqi state and society.

What did "organization" mean in the Baʿthist context? As with *Gleichschaltung*, the BRCC documents show that organization consisted of installing loyalists in as many positions of governmental, civil, economic, and social influence as possible in addition to taking control of the institutions and networks that these individuals presided over or worked in. Just as the Baʿth used propaganda and ritual to culturalize the populace, so too did they attempt to shape Iraqi behavior and consciousness by manipulating the leaders, structures, rules, and values of the state bodies, civil associations, and social and religious institutions that Iraqis interacted with, belonged to, and considered authoritative in the different spheres of their lives. Hussein and the Baʿth reasoned that if the familial, tribal, civil, social, religious, and ethnic groups that an Iraqi belonged to all professed loyalty to the Baʿthist Trinity, then he would too. If an Iraqi had to join the Baʿth Party or maintain a spotless political record in order to keep her job or attain a place at a university, then she would probably comply with the regime. If to avoid persecution and receive the Baʿthist State's patronage an imam had to mention Hussein's name in his Friday sermon and inform on his fellow religious leaders, then he would do so. The BRCC records show that not all Iraqis bowed to the logic of Baʿthist organization, but on a system-wide level the strictures that Hussein and the Baʿth placed on Iraq's state institutions, citizens, and communities proved powerful impetuses to conform. As the sociologist Anthony Giddens has written, "Power may be at its most alarming, and quite often its most horrifying, when applied as a sanction of force. But it is typically at its most intense and durable when running silently through the repetition of institutionalized practices."[6]

Part III of this book details the many ways in which the Baʿth pursued the organization of Iraq, from top to bottom. Chapter 5 explains how Hussein wielded personal power through the administrative and bureaucratic hierarchy of the "Baʿthist State," which consisted of Iraq's traditional government institutions and agencies in addition to the Baʿth Party and its pseudo-civil society associations, the Professional and Mass Organizations (PMOs).[7] Chapter 6 shows how Hussein used the Baʿth Party to ensure the political loyalty of Iraqi state officials and institutions, or how he Baʿthized the Iraqi state, turning it into the "Party State" (*dawlat al-ḥizb*). Chapter 7 subsequently demonstrates how Hussein utilized the elements of the Baʿthist State to "organize" individuals and Iraq's various social and demographic groups into official and unofficial Baʿthist support networks.

5. THE LEADER AND THE PARTY

The fundamental duty of the party apparatus is to execute the decisions and instructions of the leadership of the party and revolution in order to set state and society in motion.

FROM A 1985 NORTHERN BUREAU STUDY ENTITLED, "PRACTICING RESPONSIBILITY FROM THE LOWEST POSITION"

INTRODUCTION

The organization of the Baʿthist State during Saddam Hussein's presidency mirrored the principles of Husseini Baʿthist ideology. Husseini Baʿthism considered Hussein the wellspring of Baʿthist thought and the indispensable leader of Iraq. Accordingly, Hussein made himself into the keystone of the Baʿthist State. He sat atop the state apparatus where he exercised centralized control by virtue of his legal and extralegal powers and the chains of command and information that he developed. Like a keystone, which holds up an arch from its central, highest point, Hussein designed the Baʿthist State so that if he fell, it would collapse too; he made himself integral to the Baʿthist State's structural coherence.

Of course, a keystone also relies on its side stones to bear its weight. Similarly, Hussein's ability to exercise his power depended on the complicity and execution of others capable of ensuring the political reliability of Iraq's citizens and institutions, especially a tight inner circle of trusted officials and the Baʿth Party apparatus (*al-jihāz al-ḥizbī*), which consisted of the regular party and its Professional and Mass Organizations (PMOs). While during the era of Ahmad Hassan al-Bakr, the party claimed to rule Iraq as an institution, Hussein turned the party into an extension of his personal authority. This authority radiated outward and down through the Baʿthist State hierarchy into the far-flung corners of Iraqi society.

The BRCC documents demonstrate that the same extensive organizational apparatus that allowed Hussein to project power far and wide also developed its own institutional and local interests, leaders, dynamics, and inefficiencies. If the centralized structure of the Baʿthist State magnified Hussein's power, it also constrained that power according to the inherent organizational and bureaucratic limitations of the system.

SADDAM HUSSEIN AND THE BAʿTHIST STATE

Hussein's authority accrued from a number of sources. His personal ruthlessness, charisma, and firm grip over—and willingness to use—the security and intelligence services inspired fear and paranoia amid his subordinates and the populace. Rhetorically and emotionally, his place at the center of the Husseini Baʿthist liturgy made him the "necessary" leader of a political and social movement to advance the Arab and Iraqi nations, protect them from enemies, and achieve social justice. Through his access to the spoils of state, he oversaw not only a series of patronage networks but also the government's welfare system, through which he parceled out jobs, state contracts, benefits, and perks in exchange for support. Finally, by the very fact of coming out on top in Iraq's rough and tumble political game, by seizing power, vanquishing his enemies, and imposing his vision and will on the country, he forced Iraqis and outsiders alike to acknowledge his authority.

Hussein also exercised institutional power, which by virtue of his accumulation of official positions gave him untrammeled legal and political authority over the elements of the Baʿthist State. He retained the titles of President of the Revolutionary Command Council (RCC), President of the Republic, Commander-in-Chief of the Armed Forces, and Secretary-General of the Baʿth Party, among other positions. Within the framework of Iraq's 1970 "temporary" constitution, which remained in effect until 2003, this gave Hussein personal control over the legislative, executive, and judicial branches of government. The only theoretical check on his power derived from the requirement to obtain support from a majority of RCC members to pass laws. The RCC was Iraq's highest authoritative body and its chief legislative instrument. RCC meeting minutes found in the BRCC, and audiotapes of RCC discussions, indicate that real consultation and discussion took place in the RCC, but RCC members only voted to approve laws that Hussein endorsed. For its part, the National Assembly could constitutionally propose laws and review those passed by the RCC, but in reality it was toothless. Hussein was Iraq's de facto lawgiver.

In his role as president, Hussein controlled the executive and judicial roles of state. The constitution mandated that the president issue the regulations necessary to execute the constitution and the RCC's legislation.

Tasked with safeguarding the country from internal and external threats as commander-in-chief, Hussein controlled the police, the security and intelligence services, and the military, giving him a monopoly over the state's means of force. Hussein had the power to appoint and dismiss his deputies, ministers, and all other civilian and military employees. As president and head of the RCC, he oversaw the legislation that regulated the judiciary, and he chose or approved all judges. Informally, Hussein even served as Iraq's highest appellate authority. He often set up ad hoc commissions to investigate matters brought to his attention by petition when the regular judicial system failed. The commissions then presented their findings and recommendations for Hussein to produce a final ruling. When a delegation of human rights activists asked in 1983 why defendants sitting before Iraq's Court of the Revolution (*maḥkamat al-thawra*) could not appeal the decisions against them, the Justice Minister responded: "Every Iraqi citizen has the right to challenge the judgment against him by appealing to the President of the Republic to review the judgment. The President of the Republic is akin to the Supreme Court."[1]

With these powers, Hussein forged the Baʿthist State into a hierarchical organization with himself at the top of the Baʿthist State's institutional chains of command and channels of information. The officials at the top of Iraq's institutions could communicate with one another only through the Office of the President. As a result, only Hussein had a complete picture of the Baʿthist State's activities. A perfect illustration of this came in chapter 4, which related the story of the Director of the General Security Directorate (GSD) who witnessed what he thought was a genuinely spontaneous funeral procession for dead children but was actually organized by another government agency. The director suggested in a letter addressed to one of Hussein's secretaries that the regime ought to take advantage of "popular" sentiment and organize more, similar activities, themselves made to look unprompted. This story illustrates how Hussein's system succeeded in isolating individuals and institutions while giving them incentives to act in support of his interests. The GSD director was kept in the dark about plans to organize funeral processions for propagandistic purposes carried out by other agencies and thus did not have contact with whatever other organizations produced them. Yet the structure and incentives within Hussein's system conditioned the director to see the processions as an opportunity to take initiative that would both further Hussein's own aim (stirring up international sentiment against UN sanctions) and potentially reward the director for "taking responsibility" (*ḥaml al-masʾūliyya*) and "creativity" (*ʿibdāʿ*), two qualities Hussein tried to instill in the Baʿthist State's leaders.[2] In this case, Hussein's interests, those of the director, and the institutional incentives inherent in the ruling structure he set up aligned, and the system worked as planned.

Firewalls put in place between organizations gave Hussein alternative sources of information about the state underneath him and allowed him to monitor the interactions between his most powerful institutions: the security services, military, and Baʿth Party. In 1989, Hussein ordered that information from the Baʿth Party's files should not be shared with anybody except for the Party Secretariat and Hussein's Secretary for Party Affairs in the President's Office. The apparent purpose of this directive was to prevent the intelligence services from asking lower-level party organizations for information directly about people they were investigating. Instead, the branch within the security service that wanted the information had to first ask the directorate of the service to ask the Party Secretariat or Hussein's secretary. The Secretariat or secretary would then send the request down the party's chain of command to the Baʿthist organization that had the information. The party organization would then send the requested intelligence back up through the party hierarchy to the Party Secretariat or Secretary for Party Affairs, who would transmit it back over to the security service directorate. The security directorate, in turn, would dispatch the intelligence down its chain of command to the branch or office that originally requested it. This process kept Hussein apprised of ongoing security investigations and helped to root out opposition.

Such a compartmentalized communications structure, however, caused inefficiencies that could detract from Hussein's personal security. The information-sharing process between agencies could be slow, subject to bottlenecks at the top of the Baʿthist State structure where the security service and Baʿth Party chains of command met. The process also suffered from the general lethargy that characterized the speed at which lower level party organizations responded to the Party Secretariat's requests.[3] After receiving the 1989 order, the Directorate of Military Intelligence (DMI) complained that it hampered the DMI's ability to keep watch over individuals who worked in sensitive positions in the armed forces. Voicing similar reservations, the Special Security Organization (SSO) claimed that the order made Hussein's position less secure. The two services, the SSO argued, should thus be exempt from the regulation.[4] The BRCC documents do not say whether Hussein granted the DMI and SSO exemptions, but at least by the early 1990s, members of the security services and the Baʿth Party sat on local "security committees" together, and the regime encouraged more direct information sharing. This likely happened not because Hussein felt comfortable with giving up his oversight but because the security situation in the country deteriorated so much in the early 1990s that he needed to allow his security apparatus more freedom. Although Hussein retained his regime's basic organizational shape throughout his presidency, he also tinkered with its makeup when necessary. As the above example illustrates, state institutions such as the security services could push back against Hussein's directives if they couched their objections in terms of Hussein's best interests. Hussein always had the last word, but by appealing to his paranoia and instinct for self-preservation, the DMI and SSO tried to block a regulation that would have hampered their activities.

Especially during his first decade as president, Hussein evinced a tendency to micromanage. At times, reading the BRCC files on the President's Office seems like observing a local official or magistrate instead of a head of state. The BRCC contains a number of memoranda that describe the types of mundane affairs that Hussein dealt with on a daily basis. On May 24, 1989, the Director of the Party Secretariat and the Presidential Secretary for Party Affairs handed Hussein a typical memo that detailed matters for his attention with blank space underneath each item for Hussein to write in his instructions. On this day, one issue pertained to a Baʿthist who requested the use of a house in Baghdad while he was in town on party business. Hussein allowed him to use one of the houses left behind by an "Iranian" deported from the country (see chapter 8). Another request came from a woman who asked for permission to travel to France to complete medical treatment at her own expense and then to visit her brother in the United Arab Emirates. Hussein wrote "agreed" in the area designated for his comments. Other people wanted to meet with Hussein in person for one reason or another. Hussein approved some of these meetings while rejecting others without providing explanations.[5] On other days, Hussein got involved in minor law enforcement and corruption cases, economic affairs, administrative matters, and even local neighborly and domestic disputes, usually after hearing about them via petition.[6] He exempted citizens from military service, saw to it that Iraqis received their rightful benefits, and answered pleas when citizens felt themselves wronged by state or party officials. Until 1991, Hussein also personally approved all personnel appointments (*taʿayīn*) and transfers (*naql*) in the Baʿthist State from mid-level positions upward. At that time, he delegated this authority to the Party Secretariat's "Organization Committee" (*al-lajna al-tanẓīmiyya*) and the Baʿth's regional bureaus. The only exception to this rule was in the Baghdad Bureau and its branches, where he continued to directly oversee personnel matters.[7] Hussein always took a special interest in affairs around the capital because that is where he lived.

Hussein's micromanagement both caused and resulted from the extreme centralization of power in the Baʿthist State. On the one hand, like the channels of information he fostered, micromanagement kept Hussein more secure because it gave him personal control over many decisions. On the other, it hampered the productivity of the Baʿthist State's institutions. Baʿthist State officials feared making decisions that Hussein might not like because Hussein scrutinized everything closely. As a consequence, they passed any matter that could conceivably get them into trouble up the chain of command until it reached the President's Office and Hussein himself. This resulted in an increasing number of matters to which the President's Office had to attend. By 1986, the number of memoranda handed to Hussein for his decisions—such as the one from 1989 discussed above—reached forty per day (14,038 for the year), a 14 percent increase over 1985. The President's Office as a whole received 347 pieces of correspondence per day (125,214 for the year) from other governmental bodies and sent out 267 (97,557 for the year), increases of 26 and 15 percent over 1985, respectively. Meanwhile, internal memos within the President's Office reached 26,000 in 1986 compared to 20,000 in 1985. To deal with the increased workload, the office expanded its staff from 173 to 229 employees. No numbers were found for other years, but it is unlikely that the workload of the President's Office decreased.[8]

Whether it was to deal with an increasing workload, because Hussein tired of routine affairs, or because he realized that more urgent matters required his time in the wake of the Gulf War and its subsequent uprisings, the BRCC records show that around 1991 Hussein began to delegate. In that year, the President's Office sent a directive to state ministries and the Baʿth Party, entitled, "The Responsibility of State Departments to Solve the Issues of Citizens." In it, the office complained that

> When [the ministries or departments unconnected to a ministry] want to shirk their responsibility to offer a necessary service to a citizen they find an excuse by informing him that what he wants either "conflicts with the instructions of the presidency" or that the matter requires approval from the Comrade Leader (God save him). This occurs even with incidental and simple matters that are at the heart of these departments' duties.

As a result, the directive said that Hussein had ordered state officials to solve citizens' problems "without informing the President's Office." Otherwise, they would be punished.[9]

The only exception to this rule was for citizen petitions. Hussein seems to have liked the petitions because they were a semi-independent source of information about the state of affairs in different parts of the country. The petitions and Hussein's meetings with citizens allowed him to maintain a link to ordinary people and fed into the notion of him as Iraq's benevolent law giver, chief justice, and leader who responded to Iraqis' needs. Hussein repeatedly expressed his desire in the BRCC documents for the Baʿthist State to serve its citizenry because Baʿthism sought to improve the people's welfare and because ignoring the populace's frustrations could create a "great danger" for the regime.[10]

Even with all of the power he accrued, therefore, Hussein was not an absolute dictator. His words had the effect of law, the breach of which could lead to death, and his ruthlessness bred reverence and fear. But no man can personally oversee all affairs of state and simultaneously focus on the maintenance of his political survival. No ruler has perfect information about what is happening in his country everywhere at all times and the ability to act on it. Hussein had to rely on other people and institutions to help him wield the power he amassed. The massive party and state apparatus that Hussein oversaw magnified his power by giving him access to vast resources and allowing him to extend his rule into the furthest corners of society. The Baʿthist State also posed a danger for him, however, because he depended on the individuals and institutions within it. The force that the security services and army used against opposition groups and "enemies" could also be employed to assassinate him or execute a coup. The government officials that he relied on to carry out his orders and dispense the basic services critical to his legitimacy had the ability to sabotage Iraq's bureaucratic machinery and infrastructure. As the sheikh petition discussed in chapter 4 illustrated, even a totalitarian regime rests on an agreement, or tacit understanding, between ruler and ruled whereby in exchange for the latter's support and obedience, the former offers something in return. If the state stopped supplying benefits to its citizenry and, more importantly, if Hussein stopped taking care of the officials who doled out benefits and protected him, it is an open question how long he would have survived.

To help him maintain control over the upper echelons of government, Hussein cultivated a small coterie of family members, tribal relations, and long-time confidants that he shuffled in and out of top positions. Over the course of his reign, however, the people in the first two categories tended to prove either unreliable or incompetent, became too personally ambitious for Hussein's liking, or provoked intrafamily or tribal disputes to the extent that they embarrassed Hussein or threatened the stability of his inner circle. As a result, he progressively narrowed this circle to the point where only a handful of people remained.[11] This immediate circle consisted of his youngest son, Qusay (his oldest son, Uday, proved too erratic and destructive), his personal secretary, Abd Hammud, and a group of men whom Hussein had known since his youth and who rose to power in his wake through the Baʿth Party: Ali Hassan al-Majid, Tariq Aziz, Izzat Ibrahim al-Duri, and Taha Yasin Ramadan. Like Hussein, these four did not have natural power bases of their own in other institutions or society (although al-Majid was a tribal relation). They also tended to come from humble beginnings. As a result, they owed everything to their connection to Hussein. Their fates were inextricably tied to his, and it appears that Hussein trusted them. They, in turn, remained loyal from the beginning of Hussein's rule until its end, outlasting even Hussein's preference for family members in top positions.[12] Their signatures appear repeatedly in the BRCC under the titles of various top party, state, military, and intelligence posts, which Hussein shuffled them in and out of as necessary. When Hussein had a special initiative to undertake, he usually chose one of them to lead it depending on how the task at hand matched their particular skills.

The men in Hussein's inner circle acted as a buffer between him and the lower levels of government as well as channels for patronage, but in neither quantity nor quality did they suffice to assist him in controlling the Baʿthist State outside of its highest posts. Hussein therefore had to give the employees of the state ministries and agencies below him enough freedom to satisfy the government's basic coercive, administrative, and technocratic roles while ensuring that they could not use their collective power against him.[13] He needed to guarantee that, as an organizational whole, the Iraqi state operated with a common political direction and unity of purpose, but that the individuals who worked within it remained atomized so that a small clique could not imitate what the Free Officers did to the monarchy, Arif did to Qasim and the Baʿth, and the Baʿth Party did to Abd al-Rahman Arif. Hussein required an expansive and disciplined organization with which to oversee Iraqi state and society—one institutionally loyal, ideologically committed, and with a stake in maintaining the system by seeing to it that the government executed his desires. Hussein found this organization in the Baʿth Party apparatus.

THE BAʿTH PARTY APPARATUS

As with "culture," the concept of "organization" played an outsized role in the thought and practice of the Baʿth Party. Regular reports sent by lower level Baʿthist officials to their superiors describing the activities that their organizations participated in, and the subjects they discussed at meetings, often list "the organizational aspect" (*al-jānib al-tanẓīmī*) of these activities and discussions first.[14] Individual Baʿthists, meanwhile, referred to themselves as having been "organized" (*munaẓẓam*) when they joined the party: indoctrinated, placed within the party hierarchy, and subjected to the disciplinary constraints of Baʿthist membership.[15] Conversely, the Baʿth spoke in the active voice about "organizing" nonmembers into the party's ranks.[16] As the epigraph to Part III of this study by the Baʿthist ideologue Fadil Abbas Azzawi indicates, the Baʿth did not consider organization a merely "technical matter" but rather "a living form that enables the party to achieve its ideas."[17] Organization allowed the party to put its principles into practice.

The Baʿth Party Structure

Structurally, the party acted as the Baʿthist State's circulatory system. The Party Secretariat was the Baʿthist State's heart. It pumped the political lifeblood out to state institutions and the Iraqi body politic through its arterial bureaus (*tanẓīm*, pl. *tanẓīmāt*), branches (*farʿ*, pl. *furūʿ*), and sections (*shuʿba*, pl. *shuʿab*), and down to its capillary divisions (*firqa*, pl. *furuq*) and cells (*khaliya*, pl. *khalāyā*). The Baʿth referred generically to each individual party unit at all levels of their structural hierarchy as an "organization" (*munaẓẓama*, pl. *munaẓẓamāt*). Cells, the lowest-level organizations, were made up of not more than twelve people in a small geographic area, oftentimes not larger than a city block or a few apartment buildings. Divisions oversaw between three and eleven cells in an urban neighborhood or rural town or region. Sections included two to nine divisions and supervised a large city area or big suburban or rural town. Branches contained at least two sections. Up until the Gulf War and its subsequent uprisings, branches administered entire governorates except in Baghdad where, by 1988, five branches existed. Five regional bureaus sat over the branches during this time period. The bureaus corresponded to the Baghdad metro area and the "Northern" (*shumāl*), "Central" (*wasaṭ*, northwest of Baghdad), "Euphrates" (*furāt*, southeastern), and "Southern" (*junūb*) parts of the country. A sixth Military Bureau (*al-maktab al-ʿaskarī*) oversaw the organizations found within the armed forces. All of the bureaus reported to the Office of the Party Secretariat. In addition to geographic boundaries, some organizations focused on specific demographics such as students or women.[18]

The Baʿth Party changed the number of its organizations throughout the years. It added branches and bureaus, fused and split lower level organizations, and, in the process, repeatedly redrew administrative boundaries. Due to increased security concerns and population growth after the 1991 uprisings, the party created more branches within governorates and assigned two or three governorates to each bureau, increasing the number of civilian bureaus from five to twelve. By 2002, each governorate had its own bureau with the exceptions of two bureaus for Baghdad Governorate, al-Karkh and al-Rasafa, and one bureau that combined the Najaf and al-Qadisiyya governorates. On a nationwide basis, the party's fifteen total bureaus now had a combined 68 branches, 611 sections, 3,791 divisions, and 28,342 cells for a total of 32,809 party organizations.[19]

Each Baʿth Party organization looked like a smaller version of the entire party structure. With some exceptions, each organization retained its own secretary; command; and organizational, cultural, financial, security, and other committees. These commands and committees sent regular reports up the chain of command, attaching lower-level reports to their memoranda so that the Party Secretariat had a complete, stratified set of data about the party at all levels across the country.[20] The Baʿth's organizational structure allowed the Secretariat to issue centralized directives to the party organizations while giving those organizations flexibility to adapt their approaches and activities to local conditions.

Baʿth Party Membership

The Baʿth Party had a series of membership levels. At each, a person had to spend a specific amount of time and demonstrate a particular skill set before being promoted. When a person first joined he did not immediately become a full member but a "supporter" (*muʾayyid*). Above supporters sat "partisans" (*ʾanṣār*, sing. *naṣīr*), followed by "advanced partisans" (*naṣīr mutaqadam*), "nominees" for membership (*murashshaḥ*), "members in training" (*ʿuḍū mutadarrab*), and, finally, "full" or "active" members (*ʿuḍū ʿāmil*). Once a full member was voted into or appointed part of either a division, section, or branch command (*qiyāda*), the party referred to the member accordingly (e.g., "divisional member," *ʿuḍū firqa*). Unless specified, throughout this text the general terms "party members," "members," or "Baʿthists" refer to anybody in the party regardless of their membership status.

The Baʿth kept internal statistics about its membership at the local and national levels, some of which survive in the BRCC. With regard to the former, there are many statistics on individual party organizations and their corresponding geographic areas within the organizations' regular status reports and in the Party Secretariat's records of fusing and splitting up organizations (*al-shaṭr wa-l-ʾistiḥdāth*). These reports and records provide snapshots of the party's reach in particular areas at specific times, but the information is uneven and provides no context to put the numbers into perspective. Even when multiple years of data exist on a single organization it is difficult to draw conclusions because the party constantly fused and split up its organizations and changed their borders.[21] The most that can be said based upon available statistics is that the percentage of the population in the party within civilian, nonstudent organizations ranged widely from a low of 0.4 percent in two respective divisions within the Ta'mim (Kirkuk) branch in 1991, to 25 percent within a division in the Basra branch in 2001. Within that range, most party organizations reported a percentage between about 2 to 12 percent. The party's personnel strength changed, therefore, from area to area and time to time, but it is impossible based on the BRCC's incomplete information between geographic regions—and even within bureaus, branches, and sections—to draw definitive conclusions about which areas these were in different years.[22]

Nationwide statistics provide more opportunity for comparison because they have a common denominator. Table 5.1 shows the total number of people in the country who were in the Baʿth Party for the four years of statistics found in the BRCC, broken down by membership level. To her credit, the 1986 numbers (1.64 million total members) correspond closely to those reported by Christine Moss Helms in 1984 (1.5 million).[23] Notably, the next available year of party statistics, 1997, shows a *decrease* in membership (1.52 million) from 1986, both absolutely and relative to the population. Party membership went from 10.1 percent of the population in 1986 to 6.8 percent in 1997.

Why? Absent reliable statistics from the early 1990s, it is impossible to know for certain, but evidence found for this study suggests that the Baʿth Party lost many adherents after the Iran–Iraq and Gulf wars and experienced a major blow after the 1991 uprisings. This was because the physical and psychological effects of the wars led to a decrease in the desire, or ability, for many Iraqis to join or continue in the party. In 1989, a man wrote a letter entitled, "A Report about Why I Do Not Want to Receive the Honor of [Full] Membership." Begging off by employing the Baʿthist idiom in order to prevent repercussions, the man claimed that he had not achieved a high enough "cultural" or "organizational" level and thus did not feel worthy of becoming a full member. Perhaps more to the point, he also said that he had just been released from the army after twelve years of continuous service and wanted to start a regular life before re-engaging in party activities.[24] In the same year, the Baʿth suggested that the full membership status of a woman be withdrawn despite her previously strong support for the party. The woman, the report claimed, had not attended party meetings in a year because she had to attend to her wounded husband and her children, and to continue to work as a teacher.[25] In 1990, with the Iran–Iraq War over and Hussein beginning to demobilize his forces, the Director of the Party Secretariat sent the President's Office an internal study detailing the numbers of officers and enlisted men who left the party after finishing their military service. (As chapter 6 explains, military officers had to join the party.) In total, the study claimed that 119,556 soldiers had left the

TABLE 5.1.
Total Party Membership, Available Years

	1986	*1997*	*2001*	*2002*
Full members (ʿ*uḍū* ʿ*āmil*)	40,385 (0.25% of Iraq's pop.)	125,198 (0.6%)	231,396 (0.9%)	558,993 (2.2%)
Members in training (ʿ*uḍū mutadarrab*)	20,347	22,732	172,699	No information given
Nominees (*murashshaḥ*)	No information given	15,752	26,395	24,627
Partisans (*naṣīr*)	589,004	427,374	914,478	1,117,222
Supporters (*muʾayyid*)	987,708	924,510	1,769,862	2,318,229
Total party population	1,637,444 (10.1% of the pop.)	1,515,566 (6.8%)	3,114,833 (12.5%)	4,020,761 (15.7%)
Total Iraqi Population	*16,159,000*	*22,207,000*	*24,938,000*	*25,578,000*

SOURCES: "Statistical Summary for the Organizational Offices in the Entire Country for the Month of April 1986," 164-3-1: 87 (1986 data); 062-4-7: 159 (1997 data); 182-4-2: 66 (2001 data); 108-4-6: 19–24 (2002 data). The 2002 numbers contradict Marr's contention, based upon statistics from Faleh A. Jabar ("Iraq Mutates into a Society of Tribalism," *Gulf News*, Aug. 3, 2000), that "By 2003 [the Baʿth Party] may have lost as much as 70 percent of its membership, weakening its capacity as an instrument of control and social engineering" (293). The population statistics are taken from World Bank numbers via Google's "Public Data Explorer": http://www.google.com/publicdata/explore?ds=d5bncppjof8f9_&met_y=sp_pop_totl&idim=country:IRQ&dl=en&hl=en&q=iraq+population+statistics [accessed Nov. 25, 2011].

party completely and a further 26,251 did not officially leave but had begun to shirk their party obligations (*al-mutasarribīn*).[26] The exodus was so massive that although the Baʿth's Organization Committee discussed the study and recommended that Baʿthists meet with the dropouts to persuade them to remain in the party, there was an air of resignation in its directive for "party organizations to deal with the situations that can possibly be corrected. As for the elements that insist on not continuing in the party apparatus, we see no benefit from requiring them to remain since the [party] apparatus is, fundamentally, voluntary struggling work."[27]

Further evidence of a dip in the party's general effectiveness at this time comes from a 1990 study by the Northern Bureau entitled "How to Deal with the Partisans and Supporters Who Ask to Retire from the Party." The study does not provide statistics, but one of the reasons it claims that supporters and partisans had been asking to leave the party was because of the "weakness of the political and cultural level [of the partisans and supporters] *due to the difficult conditions experienced by the party*."[28] An internal 1992 party report written by the "Central Bureaus" (*tanẓīmāt al-wasaṭ*) for Hussein specifically addressed the need to "reverse the psychological situation of the party apparatus and the citizens following the two phases of the thirty-country aggression (*al-ʿudwān al-thalāthīnī*, the Gulf War) and the page of treason and treachery (*ṣafḥat al-khiyāna wa-l-ghadr*, the Baʿth's euphemism for the 1991 uprisings)."[29]

Another document from 1992 points to lower general participation in Baʿthist institutions during the early 1990s and an overall lack of enthusiasm for the party on behalf of the population. In the document, a study entitled "The Reality of the Unions, Federations, and Mass Organizations during the Most Recent Period," the official in charge of the Middle Euphrates Bureau reported that after "the Command" (it is not clear which "command") issued a decree giving people "the right to choose to join a union," Iraqis within the Middle Euphrates Bureau's geographic purview left the PMOs in droves. In fact, the official claimed that the PMOs in his region had become "skeletons without masses" because now that nobody had to join them to practice their professions, few people wanted to participate in their activities.[30]

Taken together, the documents discussed above suggest that many Iraqis saw little reason to join or remain active in the party after the Iran–Iraq War and into the early 1990s. Deep in debt and subject to UN sanctions, the general lack of zeal for the Baʿth resulted from physical and mental fatigue from wartime conditions and the fact that the regime had fewer resources with which to dole out benefits and patronage—and to enforce compliance.[31] The conclusion that some scholars have drawn that the party's fortunes within society decreased in the early to mid-1990s therefore appears to be correct if measured by the fluctuations in the Baʿth's total membership and anecdotal evidence.[32]

By other measures, however, the party gained strength. As table 5.1 demonstrates, even if the Baʿth's total numbers fell between 1986 and 1997, the number of full members rose by 310 percent and more than doubled as a percentage of the population from 0.25 percent to 0.6 percent. Full members always assumed the vast majority of party responsibilities and carried out most of the Baʿth's activities. Their numbers indicate the most zealous core of Baʿthist support. If the party shed some of its outer layers in the 1990s, its core strengthened.

Taken as a whole, moreover, the BRCC archive offers no proof that the party ever lost its importance as Hussein's instrument of political metacontrol, or that Hussein abandoned Baʿthification as his overarching ruling strategy. Nor is there evidence that the party declined relative to other parts of the Baʿthist State. On the contrary, although Baʿthification suffered a blow in some areas, the Baʿthification of Iraq's tribes and religious establishments continued apace and perhaps even accelerated in the early to mid-1990s.

By the late 1990s, the Baʿth's statistics demonstrate that the party had regained whatever influence in society it lost and was stronger than ever. The explosion in party population between 1997 and 2002 was most likely the result of two factors: one related to full members and the other to supporters, the latter of which accounted for over half the increase in total membership over this period. With regard to full members, beginning in 1997 Hussein began to place emphasis on the need to refresh the party's aging population. Table 5.2 provides a breakdown by age of party members in leadership roles for that year. Its numbers correspond with Amatzia Baram's conclusion that, by this time, many younger, lower-level members, partisans, and supporters had become disgruntled for lack of opportunity to move up in the party. As a result, many younger Baʿthists "won" internal party elections for organizational commands, beating out their older comrades. The Baʿth also started to promote younger members before they would normally have been eligible. This created a leadership cadre of Baʿthists who only knew life under Hussein's rule.[33] For their part, the number of supporters likely increased because joining the party became attractive again after Iraq accepted UN resolution 986 in late 1996, allowing the "oil-for-food" program to replenish Hussein's coffers in subsequent years. Oil-for-food gave Hussein the resources to restore many of the benefits that he cut in the early 1990s. Furthermore, to extrapolate from a general trend explored in chapter 6, the Baʿth may have also made joining the

TABLE 5.2.
Age of Party Members in Leadership Roles, 1997

Age	*Secretaries of Branches*	*Members of Party Offices within the Secretariat and Branch Commands*	*Members of Section Commands*	*Members of Division Commands*	*Full Members (not in leadership roles)*
Under 30			1 (0.05%)	12 (0.08%)	3754 (3.5%)
30–35	1 (3%)	2 (0.5%)	15 (0.2%)	615 (4%)	16,108 (15%)
36–40		3 (0.7%)	61 (3%)	1,757 (11%)	18,651 (17%)
41–45		32 (8%)	385 (18%)	4,688 (30%)	28,433 (27%)
46–50	8 (21%)	109 (26%)	734 (34%)	4,594 (29%)	20,441 (19%)
51–55	24 (62%)	190 (45%)	705 (33%)	3,033 (19%)	13,687 (13%)
56–60	6 (15%)	78 (18%)	200 (9%)	852 (5%)	4,337 (4%)
61–65		9 (2%)	28 (1%)	154 (1%)	1,422 (1%)
Total	*39*	*422*	*2,129*	*15,705*	*106,833*

SOURCE: 062-4-7: 154–157.

Baʿth Party compulsory to enroll in ever more academic degree programs or to hold government posts.

Internal Activities and Responsibilities

The Baʿth Party structured its internal activities to create a loyal, unified, committed core of party members capable of Baʿthizing the country. The most central Baʿthist activity was the party meeting, which a 1990 report from the Baghdad Bureau stated "forms the basic pillar of the organizational process with the aim of employing this activity to elevate and execute the party's missions precisely."[34] The meeting served as the center of party life in every organization, a time when members discussed organizational, financial, cultural, and security-related issues; planned internal and public conferences, symposia, and lecture series; prepared for visits to other party organizations, citizen groups, and families; coordinated their activities with the PMOs; delegated responsibilities to committees and individuals; and issued commendations and punishments. The party required regular attendance and participation at meetings, and too many absences could lead to punishment or expulsion.

The meeting was also a time when the party enforced discipline (*ʾinḍibāṭ*). "Discipline in the organizational sense," according to Hussein, meant "observing the party system and knowing its rights and responsibilities."[35] "Observing the party system" referred to the Baʿth Party's numerous administrative and bureaucratic rules, including about the timeliness in which organizations were to respond to correspondence, how information was to flow through the hierarchy, regulations for maintaining secrecy in party affairs, financial reporting, the qualifications required for certain party offices, and when it was appropriate to reward or penalize members. It also related to the jurisdictions of the Baʿth's many offices, committees, and bureaus.[36]

The Baʿth regulated the "rights and responsibilities" of its members strictly. The party regularly assessed its members' observance of rules, their participation in activities, and their general character. The evaluation form for a section in Baghdad in 1999 asked for the following information, among other things:

- What is the extent to which the member manifests the principles of the party in his daily behavior?
- Does he enjoy the trust and respect of his comrades and within the public circles in which he works?
- What are his leadership and organizational capabilities?
- Does he exhibit bravery in the face of adversity, and what is the extent of his ability to make brave decisions?
- What is his general cultural level and the extent to which he has absorbed the thought of the party?
- What activities did he carry out during the period of assessment?

- How many people did he recruit into the party during the period of assessment?
- What was his role in Saddam's Glorious *Qādisiyya* and the Eternal Mother of All Battles (the Iran–Iraq and Gulf wars)?
- Did he participate in the *yawm al-nakhwa* occasion and the popular drills?[37]
- Did he receive party commendations (*tashakkurāt*) during the year?
- Did he receive party punishments during the year?
- What negatives have been recorded about him?

The form then requested general recommendations from the member's superiors.[38] As the questions from this assessment indicate, being a Baʿthist meant undergoing constant tests of loyalty. Baʿth Party membership had many benefits, but joining the party also meant subjecting oneself to continuous evaluation and the party's often burdensome rules.

The Baʿth Party's marriage regulations illustrate the kinds of strictures placed on Baʿthists in both their professional and personal lives. Since many Baʿthists worked in sensitive government posts, marriage had national security considerations. Before a Baʿthist could marry, he had to submit his fiancée's name, profession, age, and address to his local party headquarters in addition to the name of her father and his profession, the names of her siblings, their spouses and professions, and the name of the shariʿa court that would draw up the marriage contract. He also had to provide a copy of the woman's Iraqi identity card.[39] Army officers, all of whom were Baʿthists, followed a similar procedure. Military intelligence investigated their fiancées and passed on the information to the party if they uncovered something suspicious.[40] The Baʿth required this information because they did not want their members to marry "agents" of foreign powers or opposition groups who could corrupt them and their children and possibly work from within the regime to weaken it. The BRCC includes records of many instances in which the party prohibited Baʿthists or military officers from marrying women who had relatives in the Daʿwa or Communist parties.[41] They too could not marry foreigners but only "real" Arabs or Iraqis.[42]

On the other side of the marriage equation, beginning in 1985 the wives of men who deserted from the army, dodged military service, or defected to Iran could, after six months, request divorces from their husbands, whether they were Baʿthists or not. In this way, a woman would not have to continue waiting for her husband to return. Instead, she could remove the stain from her honor for being married to a deserter, prove her loyalty, and make herself available for remarriage, which was the most socially acceptable position for women past a certain age. If her husband returned within a prescribed period, however, he had the right to reverse the divorce.[43]

As part of the nomination process to become full members, the Baʿth also assessed the wives of nominees. If they failed the Baʿth's loyalty tests, their husbands did too.[44] Marriage thus acted as a proxy for loyalty. A 1983 directive said that when "unencouraging" (*ghayr mushajjaʿa*) information about a proposed wife came to light, the party should ask the Baʿthist to call off the marriage. If he did, it showed that he prioritized his allegiances properly. If he consummated the marriage, however, the party should expel him.[45]

In accord with the party's belief that its members should act as moral examples to the rest of the populace and command respect within society, the party also regulated whom a Baʿthist could marry based on the reputations of his fiancée and her family. The party deemed one woman "unsuitable" (*lā yaṣluḥ*), for example, because "her reputation and the reputation of her family are not good from a moral standpoint," and because the family was "morally discredited within the area" where they lived.[46] In the case of a second woman, "morally discredited" or "morally disreputable" (*sāqiṭa khalqiyan*) meant that the woman was not a virgin. Her mother also did not have a good reputation, and her father was known to gamble and drink. The second woman did not pass the national security test either; her cousin was a prisoner of war (POW) in Iran.[47] (As the next chapter explains, the Baʿth were suspicious of POWs.) The Baʿth sometimes required party members whose wives committed adultery to divorce them. Conversely, if a Baʿthist cheated on his spouse, the party punished him, occasionally with expulsion.

Other examples of party controls on individual behavior included having to wear special uniforms when conducting party activities and the need to submit to regular physical exams to make sure that party members were not overweight. In the latter case, gaining weight could result in a demotion. Beginning around 1987, the Baʿth Party gave all of its members an initial exam and then weighed them every six months. If an overweight member did not reduce his weight to an acceptable amount, the party docked him a membership level. By 1989, however, because of a dearth of full members at the branch level, Hussein ordered that people who failed the weigh-in could parade before him and he would decide if they should be demoted.[48]

The BRCC documents demonstrate that party responsibilities and activities took up a significant amount of time. In the Maysan branch alone, between April and September of 2001, the party organizations claimed to have convened 14,858 meetings, 609 symposia, 1,504 visits (*ziyārāt*) to other organizations, and 683 receptions (*ʾistiḍāfāt*) of other organizations' delegations in the "organizational" category of events. The Maysan branch organizations also supposedly recruited 2,573 people into the party, performed forty-four statistical surveys of the branch apparatus (*faḥaṣ al-tanẓīm*), and put on thirty-nine developmental sessions (*al-dawrāt al-taṭwīriyya*). These numbers do not even include all of the activities listed under the "cultural" (*al-jānib al-thaqāfī*), "security" (*al-jānib al-ʾamanī*), or "mass" (*al-jānib al-jamāhīrī*; that is, public) categories.[49] The Maysan branch officials who wrote the report likely exaggerated these statistics, as did many Baʿthist officials in their reports. Nevertheless, the party clearly carried out a large number of activities on a regular basis, and the BRCC contains many anecdotes that show that Baʿthists often had difficulty balancing their party obligations with other aspects of life. At times, this meant members dropped out of the party. At others, the party showed flexibility by relaxing its rules or mandating that meetings not occur too frequently, last too long, or conflict with Baʿthists' professional responsibilities.[50]

THE BAʿTHIFICATION OF CIVIL SOCIETY: THE PROFESSIONAL AND MASS ORGANIZATIONS

If "civil society" is defined as associations of people inhabiting a sphere distinct from the state and economy, then the BRCC contains no evidence that real civil society existed in Baʿthist Iraq.[51] Rather, after taking power, the Baʿth methodically destroyed what remained of Iraq's independent unions, federations, and associations, and used the Baʿth Party to construct new ones in their places. Thus, in the 1970s, the Baʿth created the "central" offices of workers (*maktab al-ʿumāl al-markazī*), peasants (*al-maktab al-filāḥī al-markazī*), professionals (*al-maktab al-mihnī al-markazī*), and students and youth (*maktab al-ṭalaba wa-l-shabāb al-markazī*). In 1988, all four of these offices coalesced under the Central Office of the Professional and Popular Bureau (*al-maktab al-markazī li-l-tanẓīm al-mihnī wa-l-shaʿbī*), known as the Central Office. The Central Office also oversaw the General Federation of Iraqi Women (GFIW, *al-ʾittiḥād al-ʿām li-l-nisāʾ al-ʿirāq*), the People's Councils (*majālis al-shaʿb*, see chapter 6), and all Iraqi and pan-Arab professional associations located in Baghdad such as those for doctors, economists, lawyers, artists, and the like. All together, the Baʿth referred to these various entities within the Central Office as "Professional and Mass Organizations" (PMOs), or "Mass Organizations" for short. Each domestic PMO had branches throughout the nation and in other countries.[52] If there was any doubt that the PMOs were Baʿthist proxies, the Central Office operated out of the Office of the Party Secretariat.

One of the most important documents found for this study is entitled "A Work Plan for Coordination between the Party and Mass Organizations in the Field of the Baʿthification of Society."[53] (See appendix 1 for a full English translation of this document.) As the title suggests, the Baʿth viewed the PMOs as extensions of their Baʿthification effort: "The Mass Organizations play an important and basic role in attracting the masses, mobilizing them, and investing their energies and capabilities in order to strengthen their progress. [The Mass Organizations] solidify and strengthen the mass base of the party and spread Baʿthist values within the mediums in which they work." The PMOs were particularly well suited to do this, the work plan says, because

> they represent a majority of the sectors of our people. They form, in truth, some of the party's most advanced and effective indirect organizational fronts (*wājihāt*) and are more capable of influence within the mediums that they represent. In light of that, it is necessary to ascribe a special and exceptional importance to the work of the Mass Organizations and to benefit from their direct influence according to the individual abilities of each in the process of recruitment and in executing the work plans of the main [party] organizations in the field of the Baʿthification of society.[54]

The work plan reasoned that because individual PMOs focused on particular segments or professions in society, they could most effectively Baʿthize those groups. The Southern branch of the Office of Students and Youth, for example, described in its program for the 1990–1991 school year how it would visit local student union branches and student families, conduct symposia among students, drill them in military matters and academic skills over the summer, and recruit amid students and teachers. These activities, of course, paralleled exactly those undertaken by regular party organizations except that they also included initiatives specifically geared toward students.[55] The offices of peasants, workers, and professionals similarly took into account the conditions within the unions they oversaw, and the GFIW tailored its activities toward women.

In organizational terms, the PMOs' structures followed that of the regular party apparatus. A GFIW report detailing the federation's activities from 1980 to 1983 said that it had expanded into all eighteen governorates, which corresponded to regular party branches at the time. Within each party branch, the GFIW had a number of "union centers" (*marākiz ʾitiḥādiyya*), or satellite offices, totaling 1,030, with 366,210 members throughout the country, primarily between the ages of eighteen and fifty-nine. The structures of the other PMOs had similar administrative shapes.[56]

Within the administrative and geographic areas connected to each regular party branch, the work plan directed the PMOs to coordinate their activities in a "Baʿthification Committee" (*lajnat tabʿīth*). In Baghdad, the committee was to include the heads of the Baghdad branches of the GFIW, the executive office of the National Union of Students and Youth of Iraq, the Union of Peasants Associations, the Worker's Union, and the Teacher's Union. The Baʿthification Committee in each branch served as a link between the party and the PMOs. The committee was to send regular reports to the Baʿthist leadership about the PMOs' combined accomplishments. In turn, the party provided the committee with lists of independents that the party either failed to recruit or who were not eligible to join the party because of something in their or their relatives' past. The committee then distributed the lists to the PMOs, which were to include the independents in their activities.[57]

Like the Baʿth Party apparatus, the PMOs acted as key organs of communication, mobilization, indoctrination, and surveillance. "What are the mass, unionist, and professional organizations except for arms and bridges that link the revolution with the broad masses of the people and their wide popular base?" the author of a report prepared by the GFIW in 1983 asked rhetorically.[58] Making regular citizens participate in Baʿthist rituals established patterns of behavior and occupied them with pro-Baʿthist activities as opposed to leaving them to their own devices. With active party members about 1 percent of the population for most of Hussein's rule, the regular party needed extra hands to organize and execute its programs. In a semiannual report from 1995, the Central Office of Workers therefore detailed how it mobilized and conducted propaganda toward workers in the unions it oversaw to encourage them to vote in Hussein's plebiscite.[59] Not above buying the public's support, the work plan ordered the PMOs to enter Iraqis' homes to ensure that their material requirements were taken care of, and to dispense sums if necessary. In these ways, the PMOs were to "Create a state of awareness and mutual understanding between the party and the masses, which will lead to the people interacting with the leading party so as to produce accomplishments and a favorable reception to the party's initiatives and its daily activity."[60]

The PMOs thus laid the groundwork for the regular party's success by conducting their own organization and culturalization activities. In relation to the latter, as a GFIW report from 1994 stated, "One of the missions of the GFIW is to prepare and execute cultural programs that aim to raise the cultural level of the honorable Iraqi women and implant pure Arab values, which our struggling party has decided should be disseminated and generalized in order to build Baʿthist society, considering that our union is one of the sources of the struggling party."[61] Similarly, the 1990–1991 school year plan from the Office of Students and Youth placed at the forefront of its goals "the preparation of a revolutionary generation armed intellectually and practically with patriotic and nationalist values and morals." This included "deepening love and loyalty to the builder of the glory of the new Iraq, Mr. President Saddam Hussein," increasing the desires of students and youth "to defend the nation and participate in constructing it," to "firmly establish revolutionary values in the souls of the students," and to "achieve a revolutionary education in harmony with Baʿthist values."[62]

While the PMOs were primarily agents of Baʿthification, the BRCC files show that they also attempted to serve the interests of their memberships. BRCC files about the GFIW in particular show that it tried to advance the plight of women in Iraqi society within the framework of the Baʿthist system.[63] A 1983 report the GFIW presented to an international women's union meeting in Hungary listed its achievements with regard to increasing female participation in the workforce, erasing illiteracy among women, improving their health services, and securing new legislation and regulations that gave Iraqi women rights more equal to men.[64] The GFIW also kept statistics and wrote reports about its attempts to address social and family problems that women faced in Iraqi society. A 1993 report about the "family and legal problems" that the GFIW tackled in the first half of the year claimed that the GFIW had provided financial assistance to women who could not make ends meet. The report stated that the federation intervened in twenty-seven cases of marital discord, helping nineteen of the couples to stay together while eight divorced. The GFIW had also helped women navigate the Baʿthist State bureaucracy to attain the benefits due to them as wives of martyrs, prisoners, or those MIA.[65] More generally, the GFIW tried to address the reasons why relatively few women applied for full membership in the party and remarked frequently in its correspondence about the need to improve women's self-confidence so that they could succeed academically and professionally. Albeit with little success, the federation also tried to liberate women from the paternalistic tribal and religious customs and honor codes that kept women from improving their collective lot in Iraqi society. One GFIW report claimed that to improve Iraqi women's collective self-image, the federation needed to "emphasize that women are independent figures and are not subjects or shadows or second class entities without their own opinions."[66]

Besides acting as extensions of the regular party, the Baʿth created the PMOs with the intent to cloak their regime with a layer of popular legitimacy. The Baʿth exploited the PMOs' supposedly nonpartisan status to prove their mass support and the willing participation of independents in party initiatives. As the Director of the Party Secretariat wrote in a letter to Hussein in 1992:

> The political regime that the Arab Baʿth Socialist Party led after the 17–30 July revolution gave . . . a prominent, active, and leading role to the popular, unionist, associational, and professional organizations in all political, economic, social, and cultural fields, and in legislating laws. This means that hundreds of thousands, if not millions, of citizens associated with these organizations, unions, and associations participated in all of these areas. Each of these organizations, unions, and associations are founded on the basis of elections from the bottom to the top, and on patterns of direct secret elections. Indeed, an important number of the commands of these organizations, unions, and associations are not made up of members of our party.[67]

The official Baʿth Party apparatus infiltrated society to a great extent, but the Baʿth saw themselves as an elite "vanguard" that did not intend to incorporate all Iraqis into the party. The PMOs allowed the Baʿth to retain their elite status while simultaneously bringing the masses under their administrative, institutional, and ideological umbrella.

Along with their internal roles, the PMOs played critical parts in the Baʿth's external propaganda. The primary goal of attending an international conference and presenting a report such as the one made by the GFIW in Hungary was always to burnish the regime's image instead of to share the GFIW's experience and to learn from other women's organizations. A GFIW account of a delegation that visited Cuba in 1988 boasted about how GFIW representatives had "seized the opportunity . . . to explain the factors of the Iranian aggression against Iraq" to their Cuban counterparts who, they said, had never heard Iraq's side of the story about the Iran–Iraq War.[68] In this same vein, the regime's directives for putting on international scientific conferences held in Iraq in the 1990s stated that "the purpose for putting on the conference or specific exhibition must be to bolster political relations or to improve Iraq's economic, health, or scientific condition in light of the unjust embargo."[69] Ulterior political motives always underlay the Baʿth's sponsorship of an organization or event.

For these same reasons, during his presidency Hussein hosted the headquarters of over twenty pan-Arab professional unions and associations in Baghdad, including the Arab Dental Federation, the Union of Arab Historians, and the Union of Arab Physicists and Mathematicians.[70] Hussein supported these organizations in exchange for their political backing. Each time they held a conference or issued a statement (always pro-Iraqi), it carried the weight of having been propagated by a regional, pan-Arab civil group instead of the Iraqi government. This, at least, was the party's intention, stated explicitly by the Central Office in a 1990 letter to the president: "Through the activity and the work of the Arab organizations headquartered in Baghdad in the Arab and international arenas, the command of the Office of Unions has identified the unions listed below as possessing exceptional weight because of their importance and influence on their Arab and international counterparts, in addition to their receptiveness and response to our patriotic and national issues."[71] Just like their domestic counterparts, the pan-Arab organizations that the Baʿth hosted provided a mirage of objective approval and legitimacy for the regime's actions.

6. THE PARTY STATE

The state represents no end, but a means.

ADOLF HITLER, *MEIN KAMPF*

What distinguishes the strong relationship between administration and politics in the applications of socialist regimes is that the matter necessitates that the nature and content of the administration act as a tool or a means to achieve the economic and social goals of the revolution.

HISHAM WANDAWI, *AL-ʾIDARA WA-L-SIYASA* (*ADMINISTRATION AND POLITICS*)

INTRODUCTION

In 1978, the Director of the Party Secretariat sent a letter to the Baʿth Party's top officials telling them that "professional responsibilities (*al-mahma al-waẓīfiyya*) in the state are party obligations before they are traditional state employment (*waẓīfa taqlīdiyya*), because working for the state is the arena in which the party's creed and its theory are translated into a practical, tangible reality."[1] Even before Saddam Hussein's presidency, in other words, Baʿth Party leaders saw the Iraqi state as Adolf Hitler did in the epigraph above: as a means to control the country and realize their ideological goals. As such, the Baʿth attempted to transform the Iraqi state into what they called "the Party State" (*dawlat al-ḥizb*). The "Party State," as a divisional member explained in a 1991 memorandum, meant that "the state is the state of the party; the party is not the party of the state"; "loyalty to enduring Baʿthist principles" (*al-wilāʾ li-l-thawābit al-baʿthiyya*) ought to be the state's primary mission.[2] Accordingly, the Baʿth instituted a series of administrative, legal, and institutional policies designed to monitor state officials and institutions and to turn them into devoted Baʿthist entities. For the same reason, the Baʿth Party duplicated government functions, in some cases producing parallel party organizations in order to provide an extra layer of control. Ideally, as the party's Northern Bureau stated in a 1985 report, "total mutual understanding" would prevail between the party and the Iraqi state, resulting in a unified Baʿthist State apparatus devoted to "protecting the revolution and defending its gains and achievements."[3]

Overall, the BRCC documents show that Hussein and the Baʿth successfully brought the Iraqi state under their political control and turned it into a tool for the Baʿthification of society. A governmental and bureaucratic system that placed political considerations above all else, however, did not operate based upon the rule of law. This allowed officials who otherwise faithfully carried out Hussein and the Baʿth's directives to carve out personal fiefs within the system where bribery, extortion, and nepotism reigned. Hussein often spoke out against corruption in the Baʿthist State, but his lackluster attempts to eliminate it show that he accepted corruption so long as it bought him the loyalty of Baʿthist State officials and did not spark popular reactions against his regime.

THE BAʿTHIFICATION OF STATE PERSONNEL

In a 1984 party report, a Southern Bureau official explained that the purpose behind placing Baʿthists in government jobs was "to build the Party State and to solve the problems of the masses."[4] The BRCC documents show that the Baʿth Party and, in many cases, Saddam Hussein personally, oversaw the hiring and appointment of all national and local government officials. Joining the Baʿth was not a prerequisite to secure a government position, but the party placed Baʿthists in most top jobs, vetted independent candidates stringently, and required nonmembers who worked in the state to maintain records of exceptional loyalty.

The Baʿth's records indicate that all state positions related to national security and education beyond the rank-and-file army went to Baʿthists. The authors of internal Baʿth Party correspondence refer to these positions as "locked for the party" (*mughlaq li-ṣāliḥ al-ḥizb*).[5] After it came to power in 1968, the party first Baʿthized the army, quickly training and promoting party activists as officers to replace non-Baʿthists in order to ensure the party's control over the institution. The party similarly Baʿthized security and intelligence service personnel, weeding out any remaining independents over the first twelve to fifteen years of the regime.[6] As the case of one General Security Directorate (GSD) officer suggests, by at least the early 1980s everybody in Iraq assumed that all security service personnel had joined the party. The GSD officer sent a petition to Hussein asking him to correct the officer's party file. The file stated that the officer joined the party in 1978, but he claimed to have done so ten years earlier. "Nobody who is a member of the General Security Directorate is unorganized into the ranks of our struggling party, the Arab Baʿth Socialist Party," the officer wrote. As a result, since he had been working in the GSD since 1970, he asked, rhetorically, "Would it have been permitted for me to remain in General Security for eight years without being organized?"[7] If non-Baʿthists remained in the security services after the early 1980s, they were rare cases.

The fact that the Baʿth "locked" jobs in the teaching corps (*al-hayʾa al-tadrīsiyya*, or, *silk al-taʿlīm wa-l-tadrīs*) in addition to national security positions illustrates the degree to which Hussein viewed education as an important area for ideological indoctrination and social control. As with the military, the BRCC suggests that the Baʿthification of the teaching corps first began shortly after the party came to power in 1968. Some of the few pre-1979 documents in the BRCC show that the Baʿth tried to replace all university professors with party members, settling for loyal independents in cases where not enough Baʿthists yet existed to fill all of the positions, usually in the Kurdish territories. One letter from 1976, for instance, refers to the replacement of communist professors with Baʿthists at Suleimaniyya University, although the Minister of Higher Education and Scientific Research suggested that keeping one communist would benefit the general good because of his administrative and professional capabilities.[8] Also in Suleimaniyya province, a 1978 report bemoaned the continued existence of "communist or reactionary elements" (*al-ʿanāṣir al-shuyūʿiyya ʾaw al-rajaʿiyya*) working in school administrations. "It is suggested," the report's author wrote, "that a plan be formed by the party command in the region and education directorates to replace these elements with elements supportive of the party and the revolution, or independents, since our information indicates that Baʿthists cannot occupy all administrative positions."[9] In no area of the state did the Baʿth's organization occur all at once or even as quickly as the Nazis' *Gleichschaltung*. The organization of the Iraqi state was, rather, a process that began in 1968 and continued throughout Hussein's presidency, proceeding at various paces in different state institutions.

Other than replacing independent officials with Baʿthists, the Baʿthification of sensitive government positions occurred through the process of admitting applicants to the state-run academies that trained Iraq's national security and education officials. The Baʿth referred to all national-security-related institutes under the general rubric of "military academies" (*al-kulliyāt al-ʿaskariyya*). These included the Baʿth's military and intelligence officer training schools, the police academies, judicial training centers, and the process for appointing stewardesses to serve on Iraqi Airways, the national airline.[10] The curriculum in these academies and the teacher's colleges contained a heavy dose of Husseini Baʿthist propaganda. Just as important, the admissions process allowed the Baʿth to seek out "good elements" (sing. *ʿunṣūr jayyid*) that they believed had proper "intellectual and security-related integrity" (*al-salāma al-fikriyya wa-l-ʾamaniyya*).[11]

Although I did not find an explicit directive limiting entry to the military academies to Baʿthists, BRCC files about the admissions process show that being a party member was usually a prerequisite for acceptance and an applicant's independence an almost certain guarantee of denial. In some cases, the academies explicitly barred independents.[12] Committees made up variously of representatives from the party, the PMOs, and the security services conducted extensive background checks into all of the applicants to the academies. These agencies examined their respective institutional files about each applicant and did field work to collect missing information. They then passed the information to the Party Secretariat and the academies' admissions committees.[13]

Needless to say, what Baʿthist State officials discovered about an applicant affected his or her chance of admission, either positively or negatively. For the 2001 school year, the Party Secretariat sent forms for the GSD to fill out within sixty days about each applicant to "the military faculties and institutes, or to volunteer in the armed forces." The forms asked for an applicant's "political direction and party level," "his general behavior and morals," "the reputation of his family and its political orientation," "his nationality" (usually noted as Kurdish, Arab, or Iranian), the political positions he and his family took during the Gulf War and its subsequent uprisings (did they participate in the Iraqi army or the opposition?), and whether or not the applicant had a relative who "conspired against the party and the revolution." The form also asked if the applicant's father was a "Friend of the Leader President" (an honored status), if his father or brother had been martyred, if he had volunteered in the Saddam's Fedayeen militia, and if he had "participated in drilling the sons of the people on *yawm al-nakhwa*."[14]

The tenor of these questions illustrates the kind of traits that the regime looked for in its officials. First and foremost, the Baʿth wanted to know about the applicant's personal background and behavior, which they considered indications of potential future loyalty. Was he a Baʿthist? If so, did he take party work seriously and seek to advance in the organization? Or did he join just to attain party benefits? The Baʿth valued moral rectitude. Did the applicant behave appropriately in social situations? Would he impress the public around him and draw people into the Baʿth, or would he embarrass the party and stain its honor?

Given the importance of family cohesion in Iraqi society, the regime considered the behavior of an applicant's family members as probable clues to his own opinions. Did the morals and political views of an applicant's family affect him? Did the applicant's family have a record of loyalty or opposition to the regime? A boxfile containing forms of information about applicants to the Police Preparatory School (*ʾiʿdādiyyat al-shurṭa*) in 2002 categorized forty-one rejected students as having "unencouraging information" registered against them. Among them, a few had relatives who participated in the post–Gulf War uprisings. Other relations were members of, or had been executed for, joining opposition parties. One applicant had a family member imprisoned for forging official documents. Another's relative stole a car and killed its driver, a nonpolitical crime that resulted in the relative's execution. A suspicious or incomplete family background proved problematic as well. The Baʿth denied an applicant simply for having uncles who lived in Erbil in the Kurdish territories. The negative noted against another applicant stated that "his reputation and that of his family is not good." The Baʿth rejected somebody else because it did not have enough information to justify his acceptance. The party also looked askance at Baʿthists who did not exhibit sufficient commitment or ardor in carrying out their party activities. The forms describe a few applicants as "uncommitted" (*ghayr multazim*) or not having participated in national events such as the military drills undertaken on *yawm al-nakhwa*.[15]

The regime similarly used an applicant's "nationality" as a proxy for the likely extent of his allegiance. The Baʿth preferred "pure" Arabs and Iraqis to those with "Kurdish" or "of Iranian origin" (*tabaʿiyya ʾīrāniyya*) written on their state-issued identity cards, even though the latter were often ethnically Arab but retained the "Iranian" marker as a vestige of Ottoman times.[16] Although the Baʿth publicly denigrated tribalism until 1991, moreover, in the many forms that Iraqis had to fill out, they usually had to record their full names, which included their tribal affiliation. They also had to include their birthplace, their father's name, his town of origin, and sometimes this same information for their spouses and other relatives.[17] The regime was explicitly nonsectarian in its internal discourse and paid lip service to the Kurds as part of the Arab nation. With all of the intelligence that the Baʿth gathered on their citizens, however, they could have easily profiled based on sect, tribe, and region just as they explicitly did for nationality. According to an interview by Isam al-Khafaji of an Iraqi Army captain in 1991, Shiʿis made up no less than 70 percent of security service personnel in Hilla, a majority Shiʿi town, but they did not hold command positions, suggesting that perhaps a glass ceiling for Shiʿis existed in the security services, if not the Baʿthist State as a whole.[18]

All of this said, the 2001 admission criteria demonstrate that a person's native upbringing did not automatically qualify or disqualify him for the academies. Loyalty constituted the most important attribute to the Baʿth.

If a person from a questionable background joined the party and participated actively in its organizations and activities, the Baʿth looked at him favorably. Conversely, candidates from Baʿthist families with otherwise spotless backgrounds might not be admitted if they evinced lax, indifferent, or antiregime behavior. The BRCC shows that exceptions existed to all of the above rules, as personal and political connections as well as bribery could influence admissions committees.

Similar to the military academies, the Baʿth reserved the majority of spots in Iraq's teacher's colleges for party members. A minority went to carefully vetted independents, the number of which decreased over time. Rules for accepting applicants into the teaching academies for 1980 stipulated that at least 60 percent of incoming students had to be Baʿthists. In 1983, Hussein ordered that Baʿthist applicants should have fifteen to twenty points added to their averages so that they could better contest the remaining 40 percent of slots available to independents.[19] Directives issued in 1986 raised the requirement for Baʿthist acceptees to 80 percent. The remaining 20 percent went to Baʿthists that the academies did not accept in the first round of admission and to independents. For academies to accept independents, the 1986 directives stated that the independents had to come from a "known family" (*ʿāʾila maʿarūfa*), all of whose members supported the party. The candidates had to have at least one family member of the first or second degree (parents, children, grandparents, and siblings) who was a full party member. The parents and relatives of candidates needed to be native Iraqis with either "Iraqi" or "Ottoman" listed on their identity cards; nobody of "Iranian origin" could be accepted. To prove their fealty further, accepted independents had to promise to join the Baʿth Party during their first year of study, and they could not graduate until they did so.[20] From at least 1986 onward, therefore, all new teachers coming out of Iraq's teaching academies were Baʿthists.

Similar criteria served as prerequisites for teachers to continue in their profession after graduation. In 1981, the Revolutionary Command Council (RCC) stipulated that all teachers under forty years of age who did not have a relationship with the party had to be transferred outside the teaching corps. In 1988, the RCC ruled that if teachers in some way "proved the absence of their loyalty to Iraq, the leader, and the principles of the glorious 17–30 July revolution," they could be expelled.[21] The behavior of a teacher's family members could also affect their jobs. The Baʿth almost always transferred teachers with relatives in opposition parties either outside one of the two education ministries or to an administrative job within them.[22]

Besides placing loyalists in politically sensitive jobs or national-security-related positions, the Baʿth also retired or transferred relatives of executed political criminals out of these posts. Relatives of the first degree (parents and children) employed in the upper levels of the state or party, the military, one of the security and intelligence services, the police, the teaching corps, the Atomic Energy Agency, the National Computer Center (*al-markaz al-qawmī li-l-ḥāsibāt al-ʾiliktrūniyya*), or the ministries of defense, interior, or foreign affairs were almost always moved out of those institutions or to less sensitive positions within them. The Baʿth had increasing discretion for relatives of the second (grandparents and siblings), third (uncles, aunts, nephews, and nieces on both sides), and fourth degrees (maternal and paternal cousins), and in cases where the Baʿth did not execute a criminal but handed out a lighter sentence.[23]

The BRCC contains hundreds, if not thousands, of these regulations playing themselves out in practice. One boxfile from the Euphrates Bureau in 1984 contains the stories of a teacher and a police officer that the Baʿth fired because their brothers were executed for being Daʿwa Party members.[24] In the same year, the Baʿth retired a woman because her brother's execution caused her severe emotional anguish.[25] Conversely, even though the assessment of an elementary school teacher from Baghdad in 1985 claimed that her brother's death had not affected her, the author of the assessment recommended transferring her anyway to a post outside of education for "precautionary purposes."[26] As this example demonstrates, the party did not always apply the rules for family members dogmatically. When the Baʿthist State executed the brother of an official in the Directorate of Nationality and Civil Affairs (*mudīriyyat al-jinsiyya wa-l-aḥwāl al-madaniyya*) for his membership in the Daʿwa, the Director of the Party Secretariat wrote to Hussein asking that he be brought back from retirement to resume his post. The man duly returned to work.[27] In an analogous case, the Baʿth allowed a former teacher that they moved into the Baʿquba local administration in 1988 to return to her original job even though her husband remained in jail for being a communist.[28]

In nonnational-security-related posts, not every official had to be a Baʿthist, but the party placed its members strategically throughout each government institution so that all of its offices contained party members who could monitor and influence the political direction of their departments. A set of 1994 regulations required all directors of ministry offices and the ministers' secretaries—the ministers' two top bureaucratic officials—to be at least full members in the party, and the directors and secretaries in deputy ministers' offices had to be at least advanced partisans. This kind of structure mirrored the tactic employed by Hafez al-Assad in the army in Baʿthist Syria whereby whenever al-Assad made a Sunni a commander, he appointed an Alawite (the Shiʿi sect from which al-Assad came) as the commander's deputy.[29] Even when the top officials of state organizations did not have to be Baʿthists, the party surrounded them with members in their administrations.

Additionally, when a hiring ministry or agency wanted to appoint somebody to a post not "locked for the party," the ministry or agency had to check with the Baʿth before appointing its preferred candidate. To do this, the hiring office sent a request to the Party Secretariat, which forwarded the letter to the section or division in which the nominee for office lived. The local party organization then filled out a form with the requested information about the candidate and sent it back up the chain of command with a recommendation to confirm or reject the nomination. The Party Secretariat then consulted the President's Office, or Hussein personally, or ruled on the matter itself before informing the ministry of the party's decision.[30] In 2001, for example, the Minister of Education sent the Party Secretariat a letter asking it "to please supply us with full information about [the names of people on a list of directors and teachers from schools in Baghdad], and the members of their families, from a security and social standpoint . . . in order to select some of them as directors of sections in the ministerial *dīwān* and general directorates of education."[31] The party responded by sending back information about all fourteen names, five of whom they listed as independent.[32]

Two examples of the party's relationship with other state institutions not made up entirely of Baʿthists—local government and the National Assembly—illustrate in more detail how the party's vetting process for "unlocked" state positions worked. The Baʿth oversaw the activities of local administrative officials in a number of ways. Each governorate in Iraq had a governor (*muḥāfiẓ*) that served under the Interior Ministry. Within governorates, counties (*qaḍāʾ*) had their own chief officers (*qāʾimmaqām*). Counties contained a series of municipalities (sing. *nāḥiya*) headed by municipal directors (*mudīr al-nāḥiya*). To fill these three offices, the Minister of Local Government (*wazīr al-ḥukm al-maḥallī*) sent a list of nominees to the President's Office for Hussein's review. To select from among the candidates, Hussein used his personal knowledge of the individuals and information that he received from the party about them.[33]

Baʿthists frequently occupied local government offices, particularly governorships. Local office holders who did not join the party, however, came into contact with Baʿthists in their day-to-day activities, either in their own administrations, in the governorate bureaucracy, or on regional committees that included Baʿthists, security service personnel (who were also Baʿthists), and representatives of ministries or agencies relevant to the area in which they worked. As an RCC member who led the Diyala Branch of the party for a month in 1985 commented in his report: "The current relations between the branch command and the administrative (local governmental) apparatus are positive. Direct cooperation occurs between the branch command and the comrade governor, and this applies on the county and municipal levels as well."[34]

Mukhtārīn (sing. *mukhtār*) occupied the administrative level below municipal directors. The Baʿth assigned *mukhtārīn* to keep watch over local districts or neighborhoods (sing. *maḥalla*).[35] *Mukhtārīn* were not all Baʿthists and fell, like their superiors, under the Interior Ministry's jurisdiction. Nevertheless, Baʿthists received preference in being appointed, and the party worked closely with *mukhtārīn* to monitor the population and to maintain connections with average citizens. One of the recommendations from a 1987 "Study on Popular Mobilization and How to Improve It," written by the Baghdad Bureau, instructed the party to "choose *mukhtārīn* in the neighborhoods that are capable and have social influence in the area in order to increase participation in mobilization activities."[36] Other BRCC files confirm the indication in this quote that local Baʿth Party organizations themselves usually nominated *mukhtārīn*. In a case from Baghdad in 1999, one of the nominees that a branch command passed up to the Party Secretariat to replace a retiring *mukhtār* was a non-Baʿthist. The branch found him suitable regardless, however, because "he is one of the good elements and cooperates completely with the party and the security services."[37]

Comparably, the Baʿth vetted candidates for the National Assembly and proffered their own party lists, which included party members and independents. Analogous to their support for the PMOs and pan-Arab organizations, the Baʿth purposefully nominated independents for propaganda purposes so as to prove their democratic leanings and political inclusiveness. Any independent on or off the party's slate that the Baʿth allowed to run had to meet a list of conditions. A BRCC boxfile containing documents about the 1996 National Assembly elections includes assessments of all the people that the Baʿth nominated and who submitted their own names to stand for office. The party bureaus did not use entirely uniform criteria to assess the nominees. Some bureaus rejected partisans because they were not full party members while others nominated them, for example, but overall the criteria were consistent, particularly with regard to independents. Examples of the notations in two independents' assessments—one nominated and one denied—provides a sense for why the party approved or rejected a candidate for the National Assembly and why the Baʿth might approve or disapprove of an independent more generally.

The evaluation of the nominated independent reads as follows:

> Independent. He was not nominated on the Leading Party's slate. He has not been nominated previously for membership in the National Assembly. He depends on tribal support (*al-ʿashāʾiriyya*) and his personal relationships. He believes in God and the principles of the glorious 17–30 July revolution. He participated in the glorious battle of Saddam's *Qādisiyya* through his participation in the student military camps and by donating blood. He is earnest and carries responsibility. His reputation and that of his family is good.[38]

As evident from this and previous documents, the Baʿth evaluated a candidate for state office based upon his or her background and social standing. In this case, the nominee's reliance on his tribal background could have cut both ways. On the one hand, as the 1987 study that discussed *mukhtārīn* mentioned, the party liked to recruit independents with "social influence" into Baʿthist State institutions. The Baʿth wanted to co-opt tribal leaders who would be loyal to the Baʿthist cause and who would enlist their tribesmen to support the Baʿth. On the other hand, the Baʿth looked askance at tribalism for ideological reasons and considered it potentially dangerous if the regime ran afoul of the tribe in some fashion and triggered a dispute with it.[39] As a result, the party deemed other candidates "unsuitable" because of their overreliance on tribal connections. This independent's positives seem to have outweighed the negatives of his tribal support. Most notably, his "belief" in God and the Baʿth's legitimacy, the fact that he "carries responsibility" (one of the Baʿth's positive code phrases), and his participation in one of Hussein's wars made him a good candidate, as did the fact that the Baʿth did not have a record of him, or anybody in his family, committing a crime or participating in an opposition party. The Baʿth rated his personal character highly, and his level of education helped too; he held a master's degree in chemistry.[40]

In contrast, the assessment of the second independent, a teacher, read:

> Independent not on the party list. He has not been nominated for membership in the National Assembly previously. He does not have social influence. Previously, he was sentenced to three years for impersonating an officer. He is a shifty character (*shakhṣ mahzūz*) that is not suitable. Therefore we do not agree to nominate him.[41]

Hussein created the National Assembly and local People's Councils partially as a vehicle to draw non-Baʿthists with social followings into the regime's orbit. The evaluator in this case did not think that nominating the independent would buy the regime allegiance within a segment of society. The candidate's criminal past and socially disreputable character did not inspire confidence that the party could trust him. Nor did it fit with the regime's requirement that Baʿthist State officials present themselves as examples of appropriate conduct. The party thus did not allow his candidacy to proceed.

THE BAʿTHIFICATION OF STATE INSTITUTIONS

With its members ubiquitous throughout the Iraqi government, the Baʿth Party also extended its organizational apparatus into state institutions, "honeycombing" their hierarchical structures and implanting party committees and censors that both openly and covertly monitored the institutions they oversaw.[42] At times, the party took an active role in assisting the government to complete its tasks. In some cases, the Baʿth set up its own parallel capabilities that duplicated these institutions' functions.

Out of Iraq's state institutions, the Baʿth Party integrated the military most closely into its organizational structure. The Baʿth's Military Bureau existed as part of the party's regular organizational apparatus with its head office reporting to the Party Secretariat. Unlike the civilian bureaus, however, beginning at least in 1986, Hussein assumed the title of General-Secretary of the Military Bureau, giving him a direct line to the bureau within the party's chain of command.[43] A director and his deputies ran the day-to-day operations of the bureau underneath Hussein. In 1986, they oversaw an office staff of 287 officials working in twenty departments. The departments supervised everything related to military life and the armed forces from salaries to the officers' and enlisted men's restaurants to the commissaries and personnel transfers. The Military Bureau also contained departments of information (*qism al-maʿlūmāt*), security (*qism al-ʾamn*), and political guidance (*hayʾat al-tawjīh al-siyāsī*) as well as a "cultural committee" like those discussed in chapter 4. These four parts of the Military Bureau led the ideological indoctrination, surveillance, and enforcement of political directives in the armed services.[44]

Like its civilian brethren, the Military Bureau fanned out into branches, sections, divisions, and cells, which reached inside every military unit. Tables 6.1 and 6.2 provide a sense for how the Military Bureau expanded and contracted over the years, along with the size of the armed forces and the percentage of total soldiers in the party. Unsurprisingly, the Military Bureau seems to have reached its peak personnel size in the mid-1980s during the Iran–Iraq War. Similar to the personnel statistics of the entire party ap-

TABLE 6.1.
Party Organizations in the Military Bureau, Available Years

	1984	*1988*	*1990*	*2002*
Branches	5	11	11	Unavailable
Sections	40	69	54	82
Divisions	201	418	289	574
Cells	Unavailable	Unavailable	1,767	7,873 (total number of bureau organizations)

SOURCES: 098-5-3: 54–60; 023-4-4: 264; "Numerical Statistics for the Party Organization for the Second Part of the Year 1990," 134-4-3: 36; 108-4-6: 19–24.

TABLE 6.2.
Party Members in the Military Bureau, Available Years

	1986	*1988*	*1990*	*2002*
Full Members (all levels)	17,610	46,327	26,415	130,103
Members-in-Training	13,431	Not recorded	Not recorded	Not recorded
Nominees	Not recorded	Unavailable	6,601	6,046
Partisans	234,470	Unavailable	159,365	99,551
Supporters	332,595	Unavailable	334,928	195,983
Total	598,106	N/A	527,309	431,683

SOURCES: 164-3-1: 87; 023-4-4: 263; 134-4-3: 36; 108-4-6: 19–24.

paratus, the Military Bureau's membership fell around 1990 with the number of full members increasing markedly by 2002. Unlike the rest of the party, the Military Bureau never regained the number of partisans and supporters that it had in the 1980s.

Military Bureau organizations held their own meetings and filed reports showing that they conducted activities similar to their civilian counterparts. In 1988, the bureau claimed to have carried out 1,214 cultural sessions, 30,587 cultural discussions, and 25,852 research studies. Its respective organizations supposedly participated in 427,500 visits to other party units, and it claimed to have 407 party libraries filled with ideological material and Hussein's speeches, among other statistics.[45]

In addition to the Military Bureau's organizational structure, the party placed political commissars inside the regular army and the party's militia, the Popular Army (*al-jaysh al-Shaʿbī*), which fought alongside the regular army in the Iran–Iraq War.[46] A report by a section command member who lived with a Popular Army unit in 1985 at the war front on the Faw Peninsula, where some of the fiercest fighting in the war occurred, illustrates the kind of activities that commissars carried out.[47] The member, who characterized his duties as "cohabitation" (*muʿāyisha*), a requirement of party service among Baʿthists during the war, wrote that

> My daily activity generally focused on accompanying the commander of the unit (*qāṭiʿ*), comrade [name withheld], or the deputy commander of the unit, comrade [name withheld], on their daily rounds, inspection of the bases, and their oversight of the execution of the soldiers' daily obligations. . . . During these rounds I would add some instructions after the comrades spoke to the soldiers in order to arouse their ardor and deepen their awareness of the aspects of the Persian aggression against us and to clarify the positions of our wise leadership, steadfast against it.[48]

Commissars thus served to monitor the army and as founts of Husseini Baʿthist propaganda. They also provided an alternative channel of information to the party leadership from the war front. In an exasperated reproach of the conditions under which the Popular Army had to fight, and in a backhanded criticism of the Popular Army's command-and-control structure and leadership, this commissar described the phone lines of the unit he oversaw as inexcusably poor. The units could rarely communicate with headquarters in the rear yet still had to attain their permission to launch operations. Frequently the phone was broken altogether. "Is this acceptable?" he asked. "The region [these units] are responsible for is one of the most dangerous in this area. This is proved by the fact that I don't know who is responsible for it. I leave it to whomever is to take the necessary measures."[49]

Founded in 1970, the Popular Army was an example of a Baʿthist institution created to parallel and duplicate the functions of a traditional governmental body. A 1986 report from one of the Popular Army's installations in Baghdad described the Popular Army as "the strong arm of the party and the revolution," the purpose of which was, "to defend [the party and revolution's] existence and goals, and to be a second army that shares the national army's missions to defend national and pan-Arab sovereignty (*al-siyāda al-waṭaniyya wa-l-qawmiyya*) against external attack."[50] Before the Iran–Iraq War, the Popular Army protected strategic assets, acted as a rural security force, guarded the frontier, and stayed in and around Baghdad to protect the Baʿthist leadership.[51] During the war, it served on the front lines as much to keep an eye on the regular military as to fight Iran.[52] The Popular Army also allowed Baʿthists to perform their military service without joining the regular army with its longer service commitment and more rigorous training. Ironically, the Popular Army proved incredibly unpopular. It suffered large numbers of deserters, was a drain on state resources and private enterprise, and proved useless against the 1991 uprisings that followed the Gulf War.[53] As a result, Hussein dissolved it in 1991, creating in its wake two other paramilitary organizations that showed themselves equally as meddlesome and incompetent: the al-Quds (Jerusalem) Force and the Saddam's Fedayeen militia.[54] In contrast, the Republican and Special Republican guards counterbalanced the regular military more effectively.[55]

In addition to military party organizations, a document from a 1984 boxfile entitled "The Organizational Structure of the Bureaus of the Military Office" records the existence of a "National Security Branch Command" (*qiyādat furʿ al-ʾamn al-qawmī*) in the party. I did not find records of this branch in other Military Bureau documents, but if the command existed, it suggests the party apparatus integrated into the security services and police as well. In 1984 at least, the document lists twelve party police divisions split evenly into two sections along with one section each for the General Security Directorate (containing five divisions) and the General Directorate of Intelligence (*al-mukhābarāt*, seven divisions).[56]

In addition to the controls on the teaching academies, the Baʿthification of education (*tabʿīth al-taʿlīm*) included honeycombing schools as with the military. The Baʿth designated party organizations to supervise and work within schools in order to better organize, recruit, monitor, and indoctrinate students and teachers. At the end of 1989, for example, the Director of the Party Secretariat issued a set of instructions for how lower party organizations should establish cells within schools overseen by particularly competent divisional leaders. The divisions would then appoint one full member as part of a cell who would act as a full-time Baʿthist administrator within each school. This administrator was to coordinate with the school's representative of the National Union of Students and Youth of Iraq (*al-ʾittiḥād al-waṭanī li-ṭalaba wa-shabāb al-ʿirāq*), particularly with regard to activities planned on national occasions and celebrations, and in order to ensure the ideological purity of the "Thursday Word" (*kalimat yawm al-*

khamīs), a time each week when the principal or another school official gave a sermon to the students.[57] Upon execution of the plan, teachers were to immediately join the party. Otherwise, the Baʿth would "take fundamental measures" against them in conjunction with the Education Ministry. As with teachers found to have a relative in an opposition party, this probably meant transferring them to an administrative position or out of the Education Ministry entirely.[58] By organizing schools into the party apparatus, the director hoped to achieve a "direct influence in [students'] ideological and academic construction (*binā'ihim*)," "to improve the effectiveness of spreading revolutionary and struggling values into the souls of the students and the teaching corps," and "to recruit the entire school into the ranks of the party."[59]

To monitor the ministries, the Baʿth elected "party committees" (*al-lijān al-ḥizbiyya*) made up of party members employed in them. The Baʿth instructed the committees to report about and deal with "negative phenomena" present in the ministries, a phrase that could mean crime, corruption, inappropriate behavior, or inefficiency.[60] In one case of a minor offense thwarted, a member of the party committee within the Ministry of Higher Education and Scientific Research heard that somebody had stolen the answers to a nationwide accounting exam. He quickly rounded up other party members to investigate and, with the help of Baʿthist students, obtained a copy of the stolen questions, identified the culprit, and arrested him.[61]

The party committees assigned members to act as "internal control officials" (*mas'ūl al-raqāba al-dākhiliyya*) in companies that fell under the purview of their ministries. These officials kept in regular contact with both the companies' directors and the Baʿthists who worked in them. "A meeting with the director of the company occurred," a 2000 report from one such official reads:

> He is one of the good, cooperative, successful elements in his work and explained that in the company there is cooperation between him and the comrade party members for the sake of improving work and safeguarding the security and integrity of the company, and, indeed, everything is proceeding in a natural fashion and there is not a single problem.
>
> As for the security situation among [the company's] associates, the comrades who work in the enterprise are acquainted with, and have knowledge about, the associates who work in the company. No notable security situation exists.[62]

The control officials maintained an open relationship with the companies to heighten the awareness of the party's presence, spreading the seeds of deterrence among their directors and employees. At the same time, they used the Baʿthists also employed there to secretly verify the directors' information and to extend their surveillance deeper into the workforce.

According to a party report sent to Hussein in 1984, a model example of coordination between Baʿthist State institutions occurred in a campaign in the middle of the Iran–Iraq War. As the war's adverse economic effects began to bite, the regime decided to squeeze more productivity out of Iraqi workers. As a result, the report claimed that the party, the Baʿth's unions, and the state administration had come together as "one energy" (*ṭāqa wāḥida*) to push for the campaign's success.[63] The slogans attached to the campaign epitomized how Hussein and the Baʿth conflated loyalty to their regime with patriotism and personal honor. "No good comes to he who does not add extra energy to his daily work quantitatively and qualitatively for the sake of the great Iraq," read one. "Your work is your honor, and he who does not work has no honor," said another. And, finally, "All of the good workers are sons of the revolution whether they are Baʿthists or not."[64]

CORRUPTION

The BRCC records do not say whether or not the rosy claims like those from the 1984 report were true.[65] The documents indicate that the party, the PMOs, and the state administration cooperated on many occasions to execute Hussein's and the Baʿth's instructions. Numerous Baʿthist State officials clearly felt a sense of duty to serve the regime and regular citizens alike.

At various times, however, and most frequently during the 1990s when government salaries did not keep pace with inflation, the documents make clear that Baʿthist State officials lied to their superiors and exploited their positions of authority for personal gain at the expense of ordinary Iraqis. Corruption, inefficiency, and the propagation of exaggerated or misinformation were endemic in the Baʿthist State. As politicized entities that acted as an extension of Hussein's personal authority—an authority not subject to any institutional, legal, or other checks on its use—the Baʿthist State and its officials operated according to political considerations outside the rule of law. As long as officials did not cross their superiors or impede the implementation of Hussein's directives, they could act with relative impunity. The Baʿthist leadership pressured Baʿthist State officials to carry out unreasonable numbers of activities and achieve impossible results without sufficient time or resources. These officials could face severe physical, financial, and social consequences for failure, so they massaged the statistics. Hussein and the Baʿth routinely rotated party and state officials to different parts of the country. For officials in "locked" jobs, the indiscretions of a distant cousin could lead to being fired, retired, or transferred. Officials never knew how stable their positions were and thus attempted to extract as much personal benefit as possible while in their jobs. Lying to and bribing their superiors could buy them professional security. By making political loyalty the prime determinant for entry into a government-run academy or appointment to a state office, Hussein discouraged capability, competence, initiative, efficiency, and honesty. In exchange, the professional incentives inherent in the Baʿthist State apparatus fostered political reliability, allegiance, caution, inefficiency, and calculation.

One of the most difficult tasks of analyzing the BRCC is judging the accuracy of information presented in the archive's documents. The regime leadership suffered from the same problem. Recordings of Hussein's private conversations demonstrate that he voiced concern in 1984 about officials who kept bad news from him about Iraq's progress in the Iran–Iraq War. In March of 1991, his favorite son-in-law, Hussein Kamil, confirmed these fears in relation to the ongoing uprisings, saying, "we did not provide you with the true picture of the situation, for a variety of reasons: fear or giving the impression that we had been shaken or because it is normal to be cautious."[66] Although Kamil subsequently swore to Hussein that his top officials would be more honest with him, the BRCC shows that these officials continued to keep inconvenient facts to themselves. In August of 1991, the Director of the Party Secretariat told officials in the President's Office to erase an anti-Hussein slogan from the text of a report about a pro-American demonstration in the Kurdish territories, which by that time had fallen out of the regime's control. "Erase the underlined slogan for the high ranking readers," the director scribbled in the margin of the report, clearly referring to Hussein and his close inner circle of advisors. The slogan does not appear in the version of the report sent to Hussein.[67]

Along with redactions and padded statistics, Baʿthist State officials regularly provided excessively upbeat accounts of party activities and the reality of everyday life in internal party and government reports. In 1986, for example, in the midst of the Iran–Iraq War, the Baʿth's Karbala branch parroted back regime propaganda in its "Special Security Report" for June:

> The general opinion of the masses in the area is one of singing (*munshid*) for the party and the revolution and the struggling leader, Saddam Hussein (God save him). Citizens speak about the malevolent stance of the Iranian regime and its continuation of a war of aggression, just as they speak about the victories of our armed forces in all the sectors of operations against [the Iranians'] vanquished army, and they speak about the concern and care of Mr. President, the leader Saddam Hussein (God

save him), for the families of martyrs, prisoners, and those missing in action.[68]

Hussein and top regime officials repeatedly used phrases such as "malevolent stance," "war of aggression," "vanquished army," and "concern . . . for the families" when discussing the Iran–Iraq War. As a result, perhaps when speaking about the war in the company of a Baʿthist such as the one who wrote this report, the citizens of Karbala parroted these terms because they knew the regime expected them to use its politically correct phrases in public. Alternatively, the author of the report could have memorized these code words and then constructed his report around them. Whatever the truth, the author did not send an accurate account of wartime conditions in Karbala.

At various times, the party recognized problems such as these. In a 1990 memorandum sent by the Director of the Party Secretariat to a member of the party's Organizational Committee, the director included in his list of negative internal party phenomena, "the tendency not to provide a true picture of the organizational reality [of the party] in administrative reports, statistics, or studies, and, similarly, in symposia and meetings to try to please the high command."[69] Despite Hussein's attempt to construct channels of information in the Baʿthist State that allowed him to monitor its activities, the politicization of the information in those channels and Hussein's unrealistic expectations based upon the incorrect data that the channels fed him led to a gap between the information that Hussein received and reality.

The ability of Baʿthist State officials to manipulate the information they sent up the chain of command created space and opportunity for them to exploit their statuses as party members or government officials. One petition from 1996, for example, claimed that the Shatt al-Arab University had acquired a poor reputation because the administration required students to present bribes for admission and allowed failing pupils to buy better marks. A female student, meanwhile, could succeed at the university by "selling her honor to the dean."[70] Another petition from the same year told the story of a communications and post office in Dhi Qar where Iraqis had to bribe officials to fix their phone lines. Office employees stole office supplies and sold them in local markets. They also supposedly used official vehicles for personal business. The director of the office, the petitioner claimed, treated citizens poorly and boasted that he could do so because he gave presents to his superiors.[71] The BRCC contains numerous examples of small-scale corruption such as these.

The BRCC also provides a window into how local officials carved out pockets within the Baʿthist State bureaucracy where they created personal fiefdoms. In these pockets, they could act with relative impunity until a citizen's petition or an outraged official with access to the regime leadership exposed their operation, and the leadership decided to put a stop to it. Officials and party members created these pockets by scratching each other's backs, covering for one another, taking advantage of personal connections, and bribing their superiors.

Especially in small towns, villages, and cities far away from the central administration in Baghdad, families, officials related by marriage, and tribes could monopolize party and local government posts. In 1997, for example, a shopkeeper petitioned Hussein to save him from being expelled from Kirkuk Governorate (*al-Taʾmim*). The shopkeeper claimed that he bought a car from a customer who frequented his store. The customer subsequently asked the shopkeeper to return the car but refused to refund the purchase price. When the shopkeeper declined, the customer, whose brother was a divisional leader in the party, threatened to make things difficult for the shopkeeper, and, indeed, had the shopkeeper arrested five days later. Upon being released, the customer reportedly told the shopkeeper, "If you ask for the purchase price of the car to be returned, I'll have you expelled from Kirkuk Governorate." When the shopkeeper stood his ground and threatened to send an official complaint about the customer to the authorities, the customer scoffed, informing the shopkeeper that he was "the party official for Kirkuk Governorate, the director of security for Kirkuk, and the director of military intelligence for Kirkuk." The customer, in other words, *was* the authorities and, true to his word, summoned the shopkeeper to the local Baʿth Party headquarters and had the police arrest the shopkeeper with the intent to deport him. Unable to seek justice in Kirkuk, the shopkeeper petitioned Hussein to prevent his expulsion.[72]

Hussein must have known about the state of corruption in the Baʿthist State by reading citizen petitions such as this one. Petitioners had their own agendas, however, and did not always provide truthful information.[73] Local officials also sometimes fell under the protection of the people whom Hussein appointed to investigate petitioners' claims. While petitions were an important source of information for Hussein, they did not supply him or the party with enough information to eliminate corruption.

Hussein could not have eradicated corruption even if he wanted to—and it is not clear that he did. The BRCC records show that on at least two occasions Hussein acknowledged the existence of corruption and half-heartedly tried to stop it. In 1985, Hussein sent a letter to the ministries and state employees ordering officials not to favor their relatives in government transactions.[74] In 1996, he sent a directive to the heads of all ministries and governmental bodies asking them to reduce the opportunities for their employees to steal public monies.[75] Hussein never initiated a sustained program to enforce these directives, however. Hussein hired officials primarily for their loyalty and obedience, not, despite his claims, for their personal probity, innovation, and willingness to take responsibility. So long as officials demonstrated their fealty and worked within their institutions to carry out his policies, Hussein patronized them, which sometimes meant tolerating their corrupt or criminal dealings. The result was an inefficient and imperfect leviathan against which no Iraqi could win in the long run even if, at times, he or she succeeded in taking advantage of the Baʿthist State's dysfunction.

7. THE BAʿTHIFICATION OF SOCIETY

INTRODUCTION

As the two previous chapters indicated, the Baʿth "organized" civil society and the Iraqi state in order to Baʿthize the remainder of Iraqi society. The Baʿthification of society took place on two levels. On the first, the Baʿth Party apparatus, including the Professional and Mass Organizations (PMOs), targeted individual citizens for membership or participation in their organizations and activities, especially students and youth, women, the families of martyrs and those missing in action (MIA), and people with "social influence" such as men of religion and tribal sheikhs. On the second level, Saddam Hussein and the party Baʿthized Iraq's major social institutions by incorporating the institutions into the Baʿthist State. Hussein and the Baʿth did so by recruiting, co-opting, or replacing these institutions' leaders and bringing their appointment under the Baʿthist State's supervision. At the same time, they created organizational links, established administrative oversight, and promulgated regulations that effectively integrated the institutions into the Baʿthist State apparatus. Once in effective control of these institutions, Hussein patronized them in order to use them to support himself and mobilize their adherents behind his initiatives. In so doing, he sought to eliminate or blunt the alternative conceptions of normative political and social order that these institutions and their leaders propagated, and to imbue a Husseini Baʿthist worldview in their leaders and adherents.

THE BAʿTHIFICATION OF THE MASSES

Just as the Baʿthification of state institutions focused on installing faithful personnel in government positions, the Baʿthification of society was an attempt to turn as many Iraqis as possible into ideologically committed and politically loyal Baʿthists, whether they joined the party or not. To this end, Hussein instructed the Baʿth Party apparatus to not only recruit individuals into the party and the PMOs but also to establish direct personal connections with citizens that the Baʿth viewed as either inherently receptive to the party's message or potentially dangerous if left to their own devices. As a result, each party organization carried out a range of activities designed to simultaneously monitor the masses and draw them into the party's orbit.

Hussein used the Baʿth Party and PMOs' web-like structures to blanket the country with loyal officials who, as part of the "mass aspect" (*al-jānib al-jamāhīrī*) of their jobs, immersed themselves in local life. As one of Hussein's oft-quoted sayings went: "Work where the masses are."[1] This meant organizing public speeches, lectures, seminars, and symposia; conducting personal meetings with individual citizens and their families; attending local events and celebrations; and working with area officials to provide services to citizens. These vehicles for communication and connection between the party and the people served a variety of purposes. They allowed the regime to keep its finger on the pulse of area conditions in order to monitor them. They provided forums for the party to spread its propaganda. And they gave the Baʿth the opportunity to drum up support, foster trust with the people, and warn Iraqis to abstain from engaging in behavior that the regime wanted to eliminate. A 1991 study from the Baghdad Bureau, for instance, directed party members to urge the populace to refrain from carrying on tribal relationships and from dealing with "the other" (*al-ghayr*) through force. Instead, the study told members to encourage citizens to forge "national" and person-to-person bonds, and to follow existing laws and regulations to solve disputes. The study too suggested that Baʿthists attract (*'istiqṭāb*) local notables and the leaders of social groups in order to increase the party's influence among their supporters. Finally, it advocated including people who might have reason to oppose the Baʿthist State in its activities so as to block other political movements from influencing them.[2]

Baʿthist State officials used the "mass" activities they carried out as opportunities to monitor the population and the local political, social, and economic conditions where they worked. As the introduction to the aforementioned 1991 Baghdad Bureau study explained,

> The conditions for the success of party leadership include possessing a full conception of the social and economic reality of the area in which the leadership works . . . and with which the leadership can note the nature of society under its purview through the composition of [the area's] social strata, the nature of the problems that [the area] faces, the political and social tendencies found in [the area], and the role of the party organization in solving or overcoming these problems and obstacles. The leadership should similarly note the nature of the political powers, if

they exist, the places they are found, their influence, their size, and the means they use so that the [party's] desired plans [for the area] will be prepared precisely, which makes the leadership respond to and able to treat the nature of the local human conditions.[3]

Baʿth Party and PMO organizations kept files and statistics about individuals, families, political groups, and social trends within their geographic areas of responsibility. They used this information to create maps of their districts where, in one case in 1991, the Party Secretariat ordered them to plot the locations of the families of Baʿthists, independents, martyrs, POWs, those MIA, "Friends of the Comrade Leader," and political opposition movements.[4] In another case, as part of the Euphrates Bureau's 1985 "Plan for the Baʿthification of Society," the bureau instructed its organizations to use "field maps" (*al-kharāʾiṭ al-maydāniyya*), census data, party branch registers, and surveillance reports from family meetings to produce maps about the population.[5] The regime then used the maps to target individuals, families, and demographic groups for Baʿthification.

The most direct way for the regime to Baʿthize an individual was by recruiting the person into the party or PMOs. The Baʿth Party saw the success of its recruitment (*al-kasb*) as an indication of its broader ability to serve the people and to gain respect and legitimacy. According to a 1990 Northern Bureau report, "The subject of party recruitment remains, always, one of the main subjects in the life of the party and a yardstick of the verity of its relationship with the masses, on the one hand, and the organizational ability of the party to exert a positive influence on these masses and influence them organizationally, on the other hand."[6] A Baʿthist's record of recruitment served as a measurement of his "organizational" capabilities and dedication to party work; the Baʿth evaluated its members partially on the number of people that they recruited into the party.[7] This often led to an emphasis on quantity instead of quality, a fact bemoaned in many internal reports because it conflicted with the Baʿth's self-image as a "vanguard" party of elite individuals.[8] Indeed, the regime never intended to recruit all Iraqis into the Baʿth Party but rather to "identify the good and suitable elements for party recruitment in order to work on them and include them in the party apparatus":[9]

One of the main goals of the activity (*ḥaraka*) of the Baʿthification of society is to widen the party's base. However, that does not mean including all citizens, or even those that are suitable, in the party, because that conflicts with the concept of the revolutionary vanguard party. What is more, the party cannot absorb all of those who deserve inclusion because of the size of the existing cadre. Consequently, the Baʿthification

> of society means spreading the thought, values, and principles of the party in society and incorporating them into the daily behavior of its citizens.[10]

Even if Iraqis did not join the party, the Baʿth still sought to instill a Husseini Baʿthist worldview within them, which would influence them to act faithfully in their daily lives.

A "keep your friends close but your enemies closer" attitude characterized the Baʿth Party apparatus's strategy toward nonmembers. The "Work Plan for Coordination between the Party and Mass Organizations in the Field of the Baʿthification of Society" instructed each PMO branch to categorize its independents according to their suitability for different types of nonparty work. This included the PMOs themselves, party affiliated "National Activism" units (*al-nishāṭ al-waṭanī*) in the Kurdish territories, and the People's Councils. For people not suited to work in these capacities, the work plan told the PMOs to nonetheless "frame (*taʾṭīr*) and include (*ḍamm*)" them in its programs "in order to make the elements active, and to make them live the details of their daily lives within the atmosphere of the party and its general activity." Accordingly, the PMOs were to "identify and subdue (*taḥjīm*) the elements that either have previous connections to political movements or who have relatives that were executed or were members of opposition movements so as to monitor (*raṣd*) their activity and prevent any opposition force (*jiha*) from moving in on them, and to place them within the atmosphere of the party to make them feel assurance and trust."[11] Even if the PMOs did not include Iraqis as members in their organizations, the PMOs were still to subject the targets of their attention to intense propaganda in the hope of forming or reorienting Iraqis' political views to support the Baʿth, and to blind their targets from alternative avenues of thought and behavior. They would do this, as Aflaq believed, by manipulating the "atmosphere" in which Iraqis lived so that the only stimuli that Iraqis experienced caused them to develop into regime loyalists.

For this reason, Hussein placed special emphasis on "maintaining a connection" (*ʾidāmat al-ṣilla*) with the families of martyrs, POWs, those MIA, political criminals, and people executed by the regime.[12] For martyrs and those MIA, the Baʿth's patronage served as proof that the regime would provide for those who sacrificed for the sake of the Baʿthist Trinity. The Baʿth was more wary of POWs. Iran subjected Iraqi POWs to intensive indoctrination campaigns, which made the regime suspicious of returning POWs and their families.[13] The Party Secretariat issued a decree in 1987 stating that all returning POWs who were in the Baʿth Party should keep their rank but not be given any responsibilities for six months, during which they had to attend party symposia. In the meantime, the secretary of the local section would evaluate them regularly to determine whether or not to accept them back into the fold.[14] In the case of political criminals and those executed, meeting with the families showed that the Baʿth distinguished between the family and its deviant member, offering the family a chance to denounce their relative and prove their loyalty. The meetings also served as warnings to families not to lash out in anger at the Baʿthist State for its part in the loss or capture of their kin.

"Maintaining a connection" permitted the Baʿth to keep these families under surveillance. In 1985, the Euphrates Bureau ordered its local party organizations to regularly monitor families with relatives executed for joining the Shiʿi Daʿwa Party or for spying for a foreign country:

a) Continuously observe and monitor the families and whoever is in contact with them, and know the [political] orientation of whoever meets with them. Indicate this in the registry in the operations room and follow in a continuous fashion any changes in knowledge about them that occurs during the period of surveillance. Cooperate completely with the security apparatuses found in the area.

b) Carry out field visits to these families by good comrades who are equipped to find out about the family's situation and to know the extent of the family's proximity or distance from the revolution and the party according to the connection that they have to the executed person, whatever the degree of relation. These visits should be spaced three months apart according to the calendar prepared previously by the party division. These visits should be noted in special forms and registers at the division command in order to understand the family's development along with a full investigation. Facts and recommendations about the family should be sent up to the [Regional] Command for its review, and information should be elevated according to its importance.[15]

While the Baʿth manipulated familial loyalties for their own benefit, they also recognized that blood feuds could work against them. They thus tried to preempt any attempts at revenge by families that had members whom the regime killed or who died because of Hussein's decisions to go to war.

Students and Youth

While the Baʿthification of society targeted all Iraqis, the Baʿth focused in particular on students and youth (*al-ṭalaba wa-l-shabāb*), as explained by a party report from 1989:

> The leadership of the party takes a great interest in the youth, and the students especially, for the sake of their education and proper preparation and the development of their abilities in the patriotic, nationalist, educational, and scientific fields *because it considers them the tools capable of achieving the [party's] future aspirations* and carrying out [the party's] central goals in the process of construction (*al-bināʾ*).[16]

Hussein ordered that youth should be the largest demographic captured by the party because, as Hussein's famous dictum stated: "we recruit the youth to secure the future" (*naksib al-shabāb li-naḍman al-mustaqbal*).[17] The Baʿth considered young minds to be tabulae rasae that they could mold into a Baʿthist shape. In contrast, the Baʿth thought it harder to influence Iraqis with memories of the pre-Baʿthist era, who grew up exposed to other political systems and modes of thought. As an internal 1984 party report stated, "New recruitment should devote itself to the youth before anybody else because the youth have the ability to adapt according to what the party wants. As for those who are advanced in age, whatever the means of education (*tarbīya*), they will remain elements who are not in accord with the [party's] aspirations."[18] The Baʿth believed that recruiting youth into the party would ensure the maintenance of their power by creating true believers out of the generation that grew up in Baʿthist Iraq. These children would act as "the source of radiation within the family" to spread Baʿthist propaganda, monitor their relatives, and eventually raise their own future Baʿthists.[19] Toward these goals, the Baʿth directed its recruitment of youth particularly at the children of party members, martyrs, tribal notables, men of religion, other citizens with "social influence," and Iraqis who won awards and received special benefits for heroic acts or longtime faithful service.[20]

If the BRCC's admittedly spotty party statistics among students are any indication of the success of the Baʿthification of students and youth—and education in general—the Baʿth's emphasis in this area paid dividends. The percentage of students who joined the party was much higher than in the general population throughout Hussein's tenure, although the Baʿth's success rate varied widely in different schools and universities at different times. In 1984, for example, statistics show that 54 percent of students at Mustansiriyya University in Baghdad were Baʿthists, as were 55 percent in a party division that included the faculties of Islamic law, law and politics, and administration and economics at the University of Baghdad.[21] Three party divisions of university students from engineering and other technical fields in 2001 contained Baʿthists to the tune of 28, 30, and 61 percent.[22] In one party school division in Baghdad in 1990, the number of students and teachers in the party reached 95 percent.[23] All of these statistics outstripped the just under 7 to almost 16 percent of the general population that was in the Baʿth Party at any one time between 1986 and 2002.[24]

Why were so many students in the party? Relaxed admissions standards for Baʿthist students and the children of Baʿthists undoubtedly contributed to the elevated numbers of Baʿthists in universities; so too did the rules such as those for the teacher's colleges that contained quotas for Baʿthists and required students to join the party before graduation. Students may also have been more susceptible to recruitment and indoctrination because they were a young, captive audience without alternative sources of reference to rebut the claims of Husseini Baʿthist ideology. More than any other demographic, students and youth found themselves subject to the institutionalized rules, regulations, and overall organizational aspect of Baʿthification.

Women

Besides students and youth, the Baʿth singled out women for Baʿthification because the party's totalitarian ruling strategy required controlling both halves of society, and because the Baʿth saw women as a channel through which to enter Iraqis' homes and Baʿthize their families. As the aforementioned "Work Plan . . . in the Field of the Baʿthification of Society" put it,

> Women are half of society. There is not necessarily a worker or a peasant in each family, but there is a woman in each family. Due to the importance of working on the families in a direct fashion, that requires entrusting the General Federation of Iraqi Women (GFIW) with a great importance because it does not deal with defined professional sectors as is the case for the rest of the mass organizations but extends its activity to include all Iraqi families through the woman herself.[25]

Although the regular party apparatus contained some female-only organizations, Hussein commissioned the GFIW to lead his regime's ideological and political programs with women. Chapter 6 provides examples of how the GFIW at times genuinely pushed for women's rights and worked to improve their quality of life. The GFIW existed first and foremost, however, as an instrument of political control and mobilization.[26]

To take a typical example of how the regime employed the GFIW and female Baʿthists for public surveillance, in 1979 the Secretary of the High Council for the State Security Agency (*al-majlis al-ʾaʿlā li-l-ʾamn al-dawla wikāla*) sent a series of suggestions to Hussein about how to combat religious phenomena in society. He included among them the recommendation that female party members should attend prayer services and religious occasions in addition to visiting religious sites on a regular basis. The purpose, the secretary wrote, was for Baʿthist women to form relationships with regular Iraqi women who frequented these places and to attend religious events in order to benefit from the intelligence the women could provide. To facilitate the process, the secretary suggested bribing the women for information.[27] The BRCC contains many references to these types of activities carried out by female Baʿthists and the GFIW.

Much has been made in the secondary literature about a flurry of legal reforms in the late 1970s that improved women's rights, and the regime's backtrack on these reforms in the early 1990s. The BRCC documents, however, suggest that the regime's internal position on women stayed consistently paternalistic throughout Hussein's presidency, even if its public stance shifted to accommodate contemporary social trends. Thus, during more liberal times in the 1970s when many women did not cover their heads and wore miniskirts in Baghdad, the regime passed laws giving women more equal rights.[28] Most notably, the Personal Status Law of 1978 prevented forced marriages (with some loopholes) and gave women the right to split from or divorce their husbands under certain conditions. Other laws gave women more rights over the custody of their children, the right to seventy-two days of paid leave after giving birth (with free health care), and guaranteed monthly salaries for widows and divorcees.[29] These laws followed the Baʿth Party's official line in the 1970s that "One of the main aims of the Revolution of 17 July 1968 in building the new free society is the emancipation of women."[30]

In the 1980s, this message changed. As Achim Rohde has demonstrated, and the BRCC documents confirm, wartime conditions prompted the regime to stop publicly trumpeting women's rights and passing feminist legislation. Instead, the GFIW focused on mobilizing women for the war effort, as evidenced by a memorandum the secretary of the GFIW sent to Hussein in 1983.[31] In the memo, the secretary told Hussein that the GFIW had embarked on a new phase of activities over the last three years designed to shore up the domestic front. As such, the GFIW worked to strengthen the spirit of Iraqi soldiers. The GFIW also encouraged women to send their menfolk "to defend the nation," volunteer for the Popular Army, and take on "new missions inside the family previously held by men" while their fathers, husbands, brothers, and sons fought in the war.[32]

In the late 1980s and early 1990s, Iraqi women suffered setbacks in their legal and social statuses. Hit hard by the war's devastation and poor economic conditions, Iraqis fell back on tribal and religious mores. In the latter case, the rise of Islam as a powerful social and political force throughout the Muslim world contributed to a conservative trend in Iraqi society. It was no accident that the regime increased its own tribal and religious rhetoric and activities at this time. As a result, the regime "returned" to "traditional" values in order to burnish its regime's tribal and religious reputation, and as a way to eject women from the "men's" roles that the regime encouraged them to fill in the 1980s. This ostensibly allowed soldiers returning from the war front to find jobs, although the percentage of women in the workforce decreased only slightly from the 1980s to 1990s.[33] Emblematic of this public and legal about-face on women's issues was a February 1990 law that legalized honor crimes.[34] The law remained in force for just two months, but it epitomized the Baʿth's retreat from its progressive rhetoric of the 1970s to a more traditional stance designed to curry favor with tribal sheikhs and conservative religious elements in society.[35]

A study from the GFIW's Northern Bureau Office in 1990 captured the social atmosphere prevalent when the honor crimes law passed, claiming to provide the "real reasons" as to why women in the north tended to refrain from seeking full membership in the party. The study related that women had "lost their confidence in their personal abilities" and were convinced of their "second-class role," partially because society contained few examples of women in leadership positions. "Tribal and family influence" contributed to these problems and "did not pave the way for women (partisans)" to move forward in the party "because society still views women as incapable (*qāṣira*), and the prevailing view is that women are only found in the house." Husbands, the study said, frequently imposed conditions on their wives, including requiring them to leave the party in order to focus on housework. Women could not espouse their own political views but had to conform to those of their husbands or families. In religious families, the report said, families saw party work as antireligious and did not want women working with men they were not married to without the family's supervision. This likely contributed to rumors that Baʿthist women were not suitable for marriage, either because they were not chaste or because they were too strong willed. (Indeed, a 1982 party assessment of the GFIW issued the latter complaint about the Secretary of the GFIW herself.[36]) Thus the study concluded that some women refrained from pursuing full membership to increase their chances of marriage.[37]

The BRCC suggests that the Baʿthist leadership shared the paternalistic attitude reported by the 1990 study throughout Hussein's presidency despite the Baʿth's public rhetoric of egalitarianism in the late 1970s and early 1980s. In 1983, for example, a party report details an affair between a male full member in the party and a female partisan. When the party discovered the affair it expelled the man and suspended the woman "because she did not protect the reputation of her husband and her house and because she behaved in a manner incompatible with the morals of the party and its principles."[38] The "morals of the party," in other words, included not only refraining from committing adultery but also the prevailing view in Iraqi society that a woman's sexual behavior was tied to the reputation of her family—the reason why some families did not allow their womenfolk to join the party in the first place.[39]

The story of a female party member who petitioned Hussein for help in 1984 illustrates how the Baʿthist State treated even loyal Baʿthist women as second-class citizens. According to the woman's petition, and the documents left by an investigation that Hussein ordered into her case, the woman originally joined the Baʿth Party against her family's will. Consequently, her family excommunicated her. Unmarried, the woman did not have a husband or male relative to accompany her to make official requests for housing or for a visa to visit her brother in Kuwait in 1981. As a result, the party denied her requests, even though the woman originally turned her brother in when he fled the country to escape military service. The woman also claimed that her party superior sexually harassed her. When the investigators looked into her complaints, they suggested upholding the decisions about her housing and visa because the authorities who denied her requests had followed the law correctly and did not allow an unaccompanied woman to receive state benefits. The investigators also exonerated her superior, justifying their decision by saying that he had been "like a father" to the woman because she was a friend of his daughter. Despite demonstrating her allegiance to the party, therefore, by joining against her family's will and turning in a family member for dodging conscription, the party nonetheless trapped the woman in Iraq with no place to live and without protection from the unwanted advances of her party superior.[40] Showing that this was not an isolated case, Ala Bashir, one of Hussein's doctors, records a remarkably similar story in his memoirs. By Bashir's account, when the Iraqi husband of a Lebanese woman, who was a professor of Russian at Baghdad University, died suddenly in 1989, his death left the woman stranded in Iraq with no male relatives. When she tried to obtain an exit visa, the Iraqi authorities denied her. According to Bashir, she subsequently committed suicide with her two daughters, although one survived the attempt.[41]

Hussein clearly set the tone for the Baʿthist State's paternalism. In 1982, a memorandum to Hussein from Ali Hassan al-Majid, then the Director of the Party Secretariat, presented the case of a man who returned from the Iran–Iraq War front to find that his wife had committed adultery. His wife fled, but he tracked her down and killed her, "washing the stain" (*ghaslan li-l-ʿār*) from his reputation.[42] The courts convicted the man and sent him to prison, but al-Majid suggested pardoning him. "Yes," Hussein scribbled on the memorandum, "and pay him the right of adultery (*haqq al-ʿihr*) if he does not marry a second time."[43] This incident showcases what the BRCC documents suggest was Hussein's genuine attitude toward women, which derived more from his tribal background than classical Baʿthist ideology's egalitarian philosophy. In the above case, when state law against murder conflicted with tribal customs, Hussein decreed the latter should take precedence—long before the 1990 honor crimes law was enacted. While the Baʿth attracted women with promises of greater equality and women's rights, and the GFIW often genuinely championed those rights, the BRCC documents show Hussein and the Baʿth consistently manipulated Iraqi society's honor codes and paternalistic traditions in order to control women according to the regime's needs at a particular time. If the regime had allowed women to attain real equality with men, it could not have used them as a conduit to Baʿthize families, as it relied on women's roles as caregivers and homemakers to penetrate Iraqis' private lives.

How successfully did the regime control, or Baʿthize, Iraqi women? As the 1990 Northern Bureau report suggested, the number of women that the party recruited into its ranks fell far short of its stated goals. By June 2002, the party claimed to have 20,941 full female members, 35,261 members in training, 776 partisans, and 657,031 supporters for a total of 714,009 female adherents.[44] Women therefore constituted only 18 percent of party members at this time and just 4 percent of full members. Over 92 percent of Baʿthist women, moreover, were supporters, the lowest level of party membership, compared to the 58 percent of all members that were supporters in the total party population. The Baʿth Party did not recruit or promote women in the regular party apparatus as it did other demographics such as students and youth.

GFIW numbers tell a different story, however. Only two years of GFIW membership statistics were found for this study, but those numbers suggest that the GFIW had contact with a significant portion of Iraq's female population, at least in the 1980s. In 1983, the GFIW reported that it had 366,210 members.[45] By the end of 1989, that number increased to 1,167,017 members, which according to the federation included one out of every three women aged fifteen and older.[46] These women were not only expected to spread party propaganda and conduct surveillance in their homes but also to visit their friends and neighbors. If, as the Baʿth asserted, Baʿthification consisted of more than just recruiting people into the party but also immersing them in its "atmosphere," then the Baʿthification of women carried out by the GFIW succeeded to a greater extent than that executed by the regular party apparatus. Given the regime's demonstrated desire to benefit from yet control women's energies and retain male dominance, this may have been due to paternalistic design.

THE BAʿTHIFICATION OF SOCIAL INSTITUTIONS

In addition to individuals and demographic groups, the Baʿth regime attempted to transform all of Iraq's normally independent social institutions into Baʿthist organizations, drawing the institutions under the ideological and organizational umbrella of the Baʿthist State. The regime did this in order to control and monitor these institutions, mobilize their leaders and followers behind the Baʿth's policies, and reorient the institutions' political values and belief systems to support the Baʿthist Trinity. In 1962, John Kautsky described what this process looked like in the Soviet Union:

> all the new organizations profess the same ideology—the ideology of the regime. No matter how divergent the interests of their various memberships, all organizations serve primarily the interests of the regime. Thus, the individual member is led to believe that his own special interests, which he considers represented by his organization, coincide with the interests of the regime. The party and the ideology of the regime become the party and the ideology of both workers and managers, of peasants and professional men, of different nationality groups, and of different religious groups; the widely appealing notion of the general interest is triumphant under totalitarianism. In this fashion, the new organizations are not only organs of regimentation and supervision but also instruments of persuasion.[47]

In Baʿthist Iraq, former General Raad Hamdani described a similar but distinctly Iraqi process to journalist Wendell Steavenson:

> Arabs are not stupid, no, but our Eastern society is a society in which ideas are imposed, either on a tribal or a religious level. The sheikh imposes or the Imam imposes. It is a society formed by a shepherd into a flock of sheep. Our first thought is not like in the West, to judge for ourselves or to assess something, our first thought should be, as we are brought up to defer, "What would the religious leader think?" or "What will the tribal leader think?". . . that's what the Baath Party did. Instead of a tribal leader you were given a Baathie superior. The politicians came and took the role of the tribal elder and the religious leader. Saddam Hussein was very smart. But he didn't give others around him any chance to think. He believed he should think for everyone.[48]

Like the PMOs and pan-Arab organizations headquartered in Baghdad, the social institutions that Hussein's regime Baʿthized retained their notional independence so that their support for the Baʿth would carry the institution's traditional authority and the legitimacy that went with the blessings and support of the institution's leaders. In reality, however, the Baʿth either incorporated the institutions into the Baʿthist State or imposed so many bureaucratic and other controls on them that they could not function effectively without the regime's patronage and approval. This allowed the Baʿth control over the institutions' political positions, activities, and ideologies. As with the Baʿthification of individuals, the Baʿth harnessed the institutions' "social influence" for their own ends. To provide two concrete examples of this process, this section discusses the Baʿthification of Iraq's religious establishments and tribes.

Religion

Hussein made the Baʿthification of Iraq's religious establishments a priority because religion—and specifically Islam—presented a number of challenges to his regime's authority and legitimacy. In general, religious authorities threatened the Baʿth because they propagated comprehensive belief systems that competed with the Baʿth's "general philosophy in life." Part of this philosophy was the concept that national identity, both Iraqi and Arab, ought to constitute the defining characteristic of Iraqis' notions of self and community instead of religious or sectarian identities, which could divide the nation. The Baʿth's totalitarian strategy of rule did not tolerate independent institutions that pledged allegiance to powers higher than those contained in the Baʿthist Trinity and that espoused alternative ideas for Iraq's political and social orders.

After the Baʿth assumed power in 1968, they pursued expressly antireligious policies in line with the party's original national, socialist, secular ideology, which venerated the laws of history instead of a transcendental power. These policies included attacking the Shiʿi religious establishment, expelling foreign religious students and preachers, murdering Sunni and Shiʿi clerics who opposed the Baʿth's policies, and arresting the clerics' supporters. The Baʿth also purposefully antagonized religious Iraqis by banning the call to prayer, allowing the sale of alcohol in Shiʿi shrine cities, desecrating holy places, and erecting a statue of Abu Nuwas—the Abbasid-era poet of wine and Hedonism—in the heart of Baghdad. These policies backfired, however, as they angered men of religion and tread on the sensibilities of even secular Iraqis who nevertheless considered Islam a major part of their identities, culture, and value systems.[49]

In particular, the Baʿth's relationship with the Shiʿi establishment proved the most dangerous for their regime. The Baʿth found in their first decade in power that given their primarily Sunni leadership, bluntly attacking Shiʿi religious institutions, leaders, and popular rites was counter-productive, as it united the majority Shiʿi community against the Baʿth's minority government. During the annual Shiʿi holidays of Muharram, millions of Shiʿis from around the world congregate in the Iraqi shrine cities of Najaf and Karbala, during which they participate in mass processions and engage in highly emotional mourning rituals. From 1969 until 1977, a series of these processions and rituals turned into massive antigovernment demonstrations to protest both the Baʿth's policies toward the Shiʿi religious establishment and to voice general discontent toward the regime. On a few occasions, the government lost control of the demonstrations and had to bring in military units to quell them.[50]

Shiʿi religious leaders proved difficult to control because of their influence over the majority of Hussein's population and their institutional and financial independence from the Iraqi state. Until the Iranian Revolution and the Baʿth's repressive policies, most of Shiʿism's authoritative leaders, the "sources of emulation" (*marājiʿ al-taqlīd*, sing. *marjaʿ*), lived in Najaf and Karbala. Unlike their Sunni counterparts, many of whom had been connected to Iraq's political authority for centuries, the *marājiʿ* were, and are, independent of the Iraqi state. Political authorities do not generally decide who becomes a *marjaʿ*. The *marājiʿ* emerge as a result of their scholarship, the relevance of their religious rulings, and their abilities to gather "emulators" from around the world who choose to abide by a particular *marjaʿ*'s edicts. Some of the *marājiʿ* accepted government money in return for official support, but donations from their emulators constituted their main sources of funding.[51] Using these donations, the *marājiʿ* built up independent personal religious networks and institutions, including their own religious schools, which accepted students from many countries and were more authoritative and prestigious than state-run academies. Historically, the *marājiʿ*'s independence has allowed them to criticize the central government and has forced state authorities to seek their favor in order to attain their support for state policies. In the Baʿth's first decade, some of the *marājiʿ* helped to fuel the antiregime protests and supported a number of popular Shiʿi Islamist opposition groups, most notably the Daʿwa Party. During the Iran–Iraq War, Hussein felt particularly threatened by both the *marājiʿ* and the Daʿwa because the newly empowered clerical leaders of the Islamic Republic of Iran appealed to their Iraqi co-religionists to overthrow Hussein on religious grounds. Hussein relied on Shiʿis to man the rank-and-file of his army, and he did not want the *marājiʿ* or the Daʿwa Party to help Iran establish a fifth column within the Iraqi military or society at large.

In addition to the pressure that Hussein felt from Iran and the Iraqi

Shiʿi establishment, the 1980s and early 1990s saw a rise in the profile and influence of Sunni Islamist movements.[52] Sunni political Islam never posed an existential threat to Hussein. As Samuel Helfont and Amatzia Baram have shown, Hussein was willing from the early 1980s to ally with Sunni Islamist movements when it suited his foreign policy.[53] The BRCC clearly indicates, however, that Hussein and the Baʿth never trusted Sunni Islamists and pursued the same domestic Baʿthification strategy toward them as he did with regard to the Shiʿi religious establishment and the Daʿwa Party.

Indeed, to deal with the challenges that religious elements in Iraqi society posed to his regime, the BRCC records show that Hussein embraced Islam in order to suffocate it.[54] He did so by venerating religion in his and the party's rhetoric; patronizing cooperative religious leaders, institutions, and education systems; supporting unthreatening religious customs and rituals; and spreading his own Husseini Baʿthist version of Islam. The Baʿth combined these policies with intense surveillance of religious clerics, institutions, and rites, cracking down hard when they felt threatened by a preacher or practice.

The BRCC documents demonstrate that Hussein and the Baʿth maintained this general strategy toward religion from 1979 until 2003. As hinted at above, many scholars have pointed out that Hussein increased the consistency and frequency of his Islamic rhetoric during and after the Gulf War.[55] He also launched a national "Faith Campaign" in 1993, which provided overt state support for religious symbols, laws, practices, education, and institutions. For Baram, this constituted a tectonic shift for the Baʿth "From Militant Secularism to Islamism."[56] Evidence found for this study, however, suggests that Hussein's regime did not so much "Islamize" in the 1990s as expand its ongoing policy to Baʿthize religion; it changed its tactics as opposed to its strategy. The difference was that instead of focusing primarily on the Shiʿi religious establishment and Daʿwa Party during the Iran–Iraq War, Hussein now also concentrated on controlling and co-opting Sunni Islamists. Hussein did this in order to manipulate the increase in religious feeling throughout the Arab and Islamic world for domestic and international political purposes but also because his pan-Arab rhetoric rang hollow after invading Kuwait; it was no accident that Hussein added "God is Great" to the Iraqi flag days before the Gulf War began. As Helfont concluded about the Baʿth's use of religion in their international relations, "Islam did not guide Iraqi policy; rather, it was a tool to achieve policy goals."[57] The same can be said about Hussein's domestic policies. In the 1990s, Hussein more publicly trumpeted his veneration for Islam and used it to justify policies designed to help control the country at the weakest point in his regime. These policies included restrictions on alcohol that began in 1993 and the introduction of draconian punishments for theft in 1994.[58]

Correspondence from 1988 between the Director of the Party Secretariat and the Ministry of Endowments and Religious Affairs demonstrates the reasoning behind the Baʿthification of religion as a whole. In the memorandum, the director explained why the regime decided to establish an Islamic college:

1. To revive the original Arab and Islamic heritage.

2. To present the chance to Muslim students from all corners of the world to get to know that heritage and to understand religion outside of narrow sectarianism or doctrine (*al-madhhabiyya al-ḍayyiqa*).

3. To confirm that Arab-Islamic civilization is a humane civilization that interacts with other world civilizations in a positive way, and that this civilization has a large, well-known role in building world civilization.

4. To stand in the face of the popular [Islamic] tide that threatens the existence of the Arab nation, whatever its origin.

5. To thwart the hostile Khomeinist call and plans toward the Arab nation.

6. To create conviction among the students that the religious instructions deriving from Iran are nonreligious and hostile to the Arabs and the true Islamic religion, and that their aim is to split the Arabs and the Muslims in the Arab nation and around the globe.[59]

Going back as far as Aflaq, the Baʿth nationalized Islam, arguing that Islam was one glorious part of Arab history and, consequently, part and parcel of their larger attempt to resurrect Arab greatness in a unified nation-state. In the Baʿth's narrative, God chose to deliver his final message to an Arab prophet and to propagate that message to the world via the Arab people. No government that claimed to lead the Arab nation, such as the Baʿth's, could therefore possibly be anti-Islamic. To the contrary, because the Baʿth were the historically necessary leaders of the Arab nation, their version of Islam was the most pure and authentic. It was, as goal six stated, the "true Islamic religion" (*al-dīn al-ʾislāmī al-ḥanīf*) in contrast to what the Baʿth dubbed the "sectarian" (*ṭāʾifī*) teachings and practices of the *marājiʿ* and Daʿwa Party, the "religious extremism" (*al-taṭarruf al-dīnī*) of Sunni Salafists and Wahhabis, and the "Persian heresy" (*bidʿa fārsiyya*) of the Islamic Republic.[60] The Baʿth characterized all three of these "mistaken" versions of Islam as political movements backed by worldwide Zionism and imperialism dressed in Islamic garb. These movements, the Baʿth argued, aimed to sow the seeds of revolution by propagating their teachings within society until the movements had a large enough base of support to confront the government and take over the state. This would result not only in the triumph of heresy but also the end of Iraq as an Arab state, dealing a significant blow to the Iraqi and Arab national projects.

By claiming Islamic legitimacy and propagating a nonsectarian version of Islam, the Baʿth created an ideological framework that justified their crackdowns against religious opponents and their takeover of Iraq's religious establishments. It too offered an excuse for Iraqis of all religious stripes—devout and secular, Sunni and Shiʿi—to support them. No Baʿthist document read for this study ever characterized any Iraqi as Sunni or Shiʿi, and the Baʿth never recorded a person's sect, preferring to write only "Muslim" or "Christian" to describe a citizen's religion on an official form. Accordingly, in his religious policies Hussein often stuck to basic Islamic symbols that Sunnis and Shiʿis could agree upon: the centrality of universal Muslim faith, the *Qurʾān*, praise for the Prophet Muhammad and other commonly revered Islamic figures, and the importance of shrines and mosques.

This did not mean that sectarianism did not exist under the Baʿth, either emanating from the regime or the population. It did, particularly after the 1991 uprising, which came to be known as a "Shiʿi" revolt because the majority of the southern rebels were Shiʿi (in the north, they were Sunni Kurds), some of whom hoisted banners of Iraqi Shiʿi clerics and Imam Khomeini during the insurrection, stoking Sunni fears that the Shiʿi population wanted an Islamic state, as in Iran. While putting down the revolt, Hussein's mainly Sunni Republican Guard troops decimated Shiʿi shrines and cemeteries, fired indiscriminately at the Shiʿi population, and wrote "no more Shiʿis after today" on their tanks.[61] In the uprising's aftermath, the Baʿth Party's newspaper, *al-Thawra*, published three openly sectarian editorials, charging "a certain sect" with being "historically under the influence of the Persians."[62]

Overt sectarianism like this, however, rarely bubbled to the surface. More common was a latent tension that simmered underneath it. BRCC files containing rumors the Baʿth collected illustrate the types of sectarian anxieties that existed. One rumor, from 1993, reported that "If a Shiʿi enters the province of Tikrit and wants to pray in one of the mosques, he will be killed in the mosque and strung up on a pillar because he is Shiʿi and from one of the southern provinces which they (the Baʿth) consider rabble-rousing (*ghūghāʾiyya*) and which brought the Americans to Iraq."[63] The word "rabble-rousers" (*ghūghāʾiyīn*) appears suddenly in BRCC files from 1991 to refer to people who revolted against the Baʿth. It is most likely a euphemism for "Shiʿi."[64] Another rumor from 1996 claimed that the provinces of Najaf and Karbala, which contain the most important Shiʿi shrine cities, received electricity only 25 percent of the day compared to 75 percent in the rest of the country "because the Shiʿis live there."[65] As Fanar Haddad points out, Iraqis did not start killing and divorcing each other because of sect until after 2003.[66] Until then, Hasan Alawi's 1990 statement largely still applied. Iraqi sectarianism, Alawi argued, was "not sectarianism of the street but rather official political sectarianism connected to the ruling authority (*al-sulṭa*), which adopted for itself a ruling creed (*maẓhab*) and practiced sectarian discrimination from behind that creed (Sunnism) against the creed of those who are ruled (Shiʿism)."[67] Despite the Baʿth's mainly Sunni leadership and occasional sectarian outbursts, evidence from the BRCC indicates that the regime usually bent over backward to maintain an official egalitarianism.

Like the Baʿth's antisectarianism, their link between Arabism and Islam served to unite Iraqi Arabs, both Sunni and Shiʿi. Iraqi Shiʿis are not a monolithic bloc. Many are secular and evince greater loyalty to historically Arab, tribal values over religious ones, as the majority of Iraqi Shiʿis converted from Sunnism only in the late nineteenth and early twentieth centuries.[68] By connecting the patriotic and nationalist inclinations of tribal Shiʿis with Shiʿi religious sensibilities, the Baʿth hoped to cement their support among the tribal and secular Shiʿi demographics. The fact that many southern Shiʿi tribes did not revolt in 1991—and some even supported the regime—illustrates that this policy was at least partially successful when combined with the Baʿth's policy toward tribes and the other elements of Baʿthification.[69]

Relatedly, the Baʿth appealed to Arab solidarity and values to reinforce their anti-Iranian propaganda. As part of the instructions for how to deal with the Shiʿi rituals of Muharram in 1983, the Baʿth's Southern Bureau informed the Party Secretariat that it had directed its branches "to continuously mention that the elements who hate the nation (*al-ʾumma*), and especially the Persians, are working to try to distort the values of Islam and the values of Arabism and the characteristics of the Arab personality in their attempt to harm the Arabs by way of harming Islam and distorting it."[70] In this, Hussein played to popular Arab stereotypes against Iranians as hostile to Arab culture and its centrality within Islamic history. This, of course, supported the Baʿth's attempt to shore up domestic support against Iran and its leader, Ayatollah Khomeini, during the Iran–Iraq War. It also strengthened the Baʿth's attack on the Shiʿi religious establishment as an Iranian fifth column, as many of the *marājiʿ* in Najaf and Karbala originally hailed from Iran. In particular, BRCC documents single out as a Persian agent Abu al-Qasim al-Khoei, the most authoritative Shiʿi *marjaʿ* during Hussein's presidency until al-Khoei's death in 1992. According to the documents, al-Khoei, who was originally from Iranian Azerbaijan, spoke and often taught in Persian, as did his children and the junior clerics underneath him. This made the Baʿth paranoid about al-Khoei and gave them an excuse to crack down on his networks of supporters and the institutions he controlled.[71]

This said, the BRCC illustrates that unless a religious leader made his opposition to the Baʿth explicit, the regime rarely first used violence to induce him to cooperate. Especially if a religious leader had a large following within society, the Baʿth recognized that he would prove more useful if they could co-opt him instead of having to deal with the inevitable backlash that would ensue from the cleric's arrest or execution—as the Baʿth discovered in 1980 after they tortured and killed the popular Iraqi-born *marjaʿ* Muhammad Baqir al-Sadr. Hussein and the Baʿth recognized that religious support would be more effective if it came from a genuine source of religious leadership, which is why they usually tried to cultivate existing religious leaders before resorting to terror. Accordingly, the documents show that a Baʿthist delegation would first meet with a religious leader to explain the party's position on a particular matter and ask him for his public support in exchange for financial or other material backing, official recognition, and freedom of action in the leader's apolitical activities. The Baʿth tried to work with both Sunni and Shiʿi men of religion by encouraging them to appear on state television, to attend national occasions, to join the Ministry of Endowments and Religious Affairs' "religious propaganda committees" (*lijān al-tawʿiyya al-dīniyya*), and to issue official rulings (*fatāwā*, sing. *fatwa*) that conformed with the regime's wishes.[72] The Baʿth's meetings with religious leaders also served as warnings that if a leader did not cooperate, the Baʿth would remove him or employ sterner measures to elicit his blessing.

In addition to persuasion, the Baʿth took direct and indirect control over the appointment of clerics to their posts. The Baʿth allowed only officially sanctioned preachers to deliver the weekly sermon at midday Friday prayers, the main communal gathering for both Sunni and Shiʿi Muslims during the week. To determine whom to appoint, the Baʿth assessed a candidate according to three criteria: (1) "the integrity of his faith" (*salāmat ʿaqīdatihi*), or the extent to which his sermons and teachings conformed to the Baʿth's version of Islam; (2) "his position on the revolution and the party" (*mawqifuhu min al-thawra wa-l-ḥizb*); and (3) the degree to which he praised Hussein while giving the Friday sermon or reading the story of Imam Hussein in a *ḥusayniyya* (sing. of *ḥusayniyyāt*).[73] The Baʿth also censored the content of the Friday prayer leaders' sermons and supplied them with talking points.[74] If a religious leader did not heed the Baʿth's instructions, the party removed him, as it did a Baghdad preacher in 1986 "because he does not follow the instructions of the party to invoke our leader and the victory of our army over our enemies despite directing him to do so."[75] The ultimate criterion, in other words, was the man of religion's loyalty, which he exhibited by performing his traditional duties in a fashion supportive of the Baʿthist Trinity. The above criteria served as general guidelines for sanctioning the appointment of other religious officials as well.[76]

Besides exerting control over religious leaders, Hussein Baʿthized the institutions they served. While the BRCC contains many records detailing how the regime did this, one document in particular provides an excellent example of how Hussein and the Baʿth brought the Shiʿi religious establishment to heel. In the early 1980s, the Baʿth Party's Euphrates Bureau wrote a detailed study about the contemporary Shiʿi religious establishment. The study included profiles of the *marājiʿ* and other prominent leaders; sections about the Shiʿi educational establishment; explanations of Shiʿi religious doctrine; and descriptions of Shiʿi newspapers, publications, civil groups, mosques, and the *ḥusayniyyāt*. The steps the study prescribed to exert influence over Shiʿi religious schools—the "Hawza" of Najaf and Karbala—prove particularly instructive, especially considering the regime's emphasis on the Baʿthification of education.[77]

The document reveals that after the Shiʿi unrest of the 1970s and the murder of al-Sadr in 1980, the Baʿthist leadership discussed expelling the entire Hawza to Iran.[78] The regime had already expelled a number of the Hawza's students and teachers by this time, and expelling the remainder would have continued that policy. Instead, according to the Euphrates Bureau study, the leadership decided "to strengthen the role of the Hawza in order to serve the [Baʿth's] march (*masīra*) and the revolution."[79] Just as the Baʿth preferred to first try to work through men of religion instead of terrorizing them, the Baʿth would take control of the Hawza in order to play off of its historical and religious importance, making it into a tool of the regime.

The study noted that the Hawza's strength and vibrancy derived from its student body, which came from all over the Islamic world. It consequently suggested that the Baʿth focus its attention on regulating the conduct and admission of the Hawza's students, beginning with the foreign students who had to attain visas to enter Iraq to study. Once in Iraq, the foreign students had to renew their residency permits on a regular basis. The study thus advocated taking advantage of the visa and residency permit renewal processes to gather information about the foreign students and to force them to cooperate with the security services during their time at

امة عربية واحدة
ذات رسالة خالدة
حزب البعث العربي الاشتراكي
مكتب تنظيم الفرات
دراسة دينية
عن
المرجعية
الحوزة العلمية
طلاب ومدارس العلوم الدينية
المقترحات

FIGURE 7.1. ***The Cover Page to a Baʿthist Study about the Shiʿi Religious Establishment.*** The study is entitled "A Religious Study about the *marjaʿiyya* (the Institution of the *marājiʿ*), the Hawza, Students and Schools of the Religious Sciences, Recommendations." Source: BRCC, 023-4-7: 20. Courtesy of Hoover Institution Library & Archives, Stanford University.

the Hawza. The study additionally advocated providing financial assistance to the foreign students in exchange for their willingness to submit to the Baʿth's religious indoctrination and to propagate the Baʿth's Islamic teachings among the Hawza's student body. As the study put it, the security services should "influence [the foreign students] and feed them ideas of the Islamic religion, the essence of which is pure and far from the customary mistaken primitive practices with which these students' peers have been educated. As for those who deviate from [the Baʿth's religious] program, withdraw or revoke their residency permits and expel them to their countries."[80] Foreign students could attend the Hawza only if they became Baʿthist agents within it.

The study further advocated Iraqizing the Hawza's student body as part of its more general attempt to Iraqize and Arabize imams in the country. Consequently, the study recommended that the party and security services carefully select the Hawza's Iraqi students and give them scholarships and stipends in return for their agreement to act on the regime's behalf within the Hawza. These Iraqi students, the study said, would eventually become sympathetic Shiʿi religious leaders: "The final result of the application of [this] plan (*ṣīgha*) is to strengthen the existence of the Hawza in Iraq and its future administration by Iraqi men of religion themselves."[81] The Baʿth believed that increasing the number of Iraqi teachers in the Hawza would strengthen national security because Iraqi clerics would naturally be more nationalistic and less subject to Iranian influence. As another way to increase Iraqi influence in the Hawza, the study suggested selecting ripe students from the Islamic law faculties of Iraq's universities and subjecting them to intense indoctrination in Baʿthist ideology and the regime's version of Islam. The Ministry of Endowments and Religious Affairs would then appoint these students to religious positions throughout the country. The ministry would also support existing Iraqi men of religion, especially in Najaf and Karbala, in exchange for their attempts to influence the Hawza's students. Along with the culturalization and Iraqification of the Hawza's students, the study advocated taking over the Hawza's curriculum and censoring the books it assigned. It suggested doing this by removing from the Hawza's libraries and area bookshops all texts written by "Persian elements" and volumes that did not conform to "the principles of the true religion."[82]

Hussein's regime used the same tactics that they employed against the Shiʿi religious establishment to combat Sunni Islamists such as Wahhabis, other Salafis, and the Muslim Brotherhood. Of the documents read for this study, as far back as 1983 a memorandum that reached Hussein suggested that the army discharge a major and place him in a less sensitive civilian post because of his Salafist leanings. Hussein agreed with the recommendation.[83] Most references to Sunni Islamist tendencies occur beginning in 1990, however, when the BRCC shows that these movements began to gain followers. In that year, a committee consisting of high-ranking Baʿthists, the Minister of Charitable Endowments and Religious Affairs, and the head of the General Security Directorate put together a plan for combating Wahhabist influences seeping into society. Among other measures, the committee suggested arresting the most prominent Wahhabi men of religion in order to gain more information about the movement and to warn other Wahhabis of the consequences of crossing the Baʿth's religious red lines.[84] Throughout the 1990s, the Baʿth banned Sunni Islamists' books; removed Sunni Islamists as preachers and imams when they discovered the imams' Islamist leanings; did not allow Islamists to teach in religious schools; and disqualified them from entrance into the military, teaching, and other secular academies. In the Baʿth's opinion, Salafists did not evince the proper "intellectual integrity" (*al-salāma al-fikriyya*) for acceptance.[85]

While denying Islamists entry into state-run academies, the Baʿth built their own religious schools to compete with Iraq's independent religious educational establishments. Along with institutions such as the Islamic college, in 1985 a commission studying "the matter of treating the condition of the religious foundations in the country" suggested and received approval to found an institute to train imams and preachers in order "to treat the negative phenomenon of the graduates of religious faculties" who did not preach according to the Baʿth's desires. The commission recommended that the admissions committee for the institute include members of the ministries of Education, Higher Education and Scientific Research, and Endowments and Religious Affairs along with a Baʿth Party representative who would assess an applicant's "loyalty to the revolution." The institute's teachings, the commission said, should conform to the Baʿth's version of Islam for the purpose of indoctrination and should accept non-Iraqi and Iraqi students in order to propagate the Baʿth's religious ideas abroad and at home through appointments to government-controlled mosques and religious institutions.[86]

In addition to institutions, the Baʿth suppressed popular religious practices they did not like.[87] Shiʿi rituals surrounding the Muharram holidays came in for particular attention. These included mass processions to shrines, self-mutilation, emotional readings of the story of the martyrdom of Imam Hussein, the raising of banners and shouting of slogans in support of Shiʿi martyrs, and the providing of food and drinks to marchers. The Baʿth opposed these practices because, as in the 1970s, the processions had the potential to turn into protests, which the Baʿth feared Iran and Shiʿi opposition groups and preachers would exploit.[88] As a result, the Baʿth banned many popular religious practices and used force to stop them when necessary. During Shiʿi holidays the regime flooded the streets with security officials and Baʿth Party members. The regime maintained extensive surveillance of al-Khoei's network of supporters and sent spies on a regular basis to mosques, *ḥusayniyyāt*, and women's prayer circles to report on their activities and to try to steer the gatherings in a pro-Baʿthist direction. During holidays, the BRCC shows that the security apparatus used taxi drivers as informants, noted the license plates of out of town cars that came to the religious shrine cities, and worked with hoteliers to search pilgrims' bags. The Baʿth employed propaganda too, asking their members to personally talk to their families, relatives, friends, and tribesmen to explain the "uncivilized" character of popular rites. The Baʿth employed men of religion to preach the same message to their followers, and the Ministry of Culture and Media placed items in the press and put on programs to warn against mistaken practices and explain proper forms of faith.[89]

While simultaneously suppressing and exerting control over Iraq's religious leaders and establishments, Hussein attempted to take on the mantle of Islam. Although the Baʿth generally banned the distribution of food to Shiʿi marchers during Muharram, in 1995 the Director of the Party Secretariat congratulated the regime for inducing officials in the *ḥusayniyyāt* to hand out food during that year's festivities in the name of "the generosity of the Comrade Leader (God save him)."[90] Hussein too patronized Shiʿi shrine cities "because [patronization] has a large positive response among the simple people (*al-busaṭāʾ*) and foreign pilgrims."[91] Indeed, after the Republican Guard leveled the shrines of Najaf and Karbala during the 1991 uprising, the government rebuilt them, trumpeting its generosity along the way.[92] In a complete reversal of their initially antireligious policies, the Baʿth made Islamic holidays such as the Prophet's birthday into national occasions. In the 1990s, as part of the Faith Campaign, the regime shuttered shops that sold alcohol for the entire month of Ramadan and required that coffee shops, restaurants, and food stores be locked from sunup to sundown, among other measures designed to prove its Islamic credentials.[93] The content of these occasions served as platforms to spread Hussein's religious message that the Baʿth, the Arab and Iraqi nations, the leader, and Islam were all connected, and that Muslims of all sects were part of the same Baʿthized faith. The slogans for the Prophet's birthday in 2002, for example, included, "Life is a necessity for faith just as faith is necessary for life," "the Baʿth arose out of a basic spring, from a spiritual spring that is the great Islam," and "The principles of humane Islam and its values and civilized morals are the spirit of Arabism and the source of its perpetual renewed inspiration."[94]

The BRCC shows that Hussein's Baʿthification efforts toward religion did not always work. The regime never entirely ended the practice of popular religious rites; even some Baʿthists—both Sunni and Shiʿi—continued to practice them.[95] Salafist preachers and sentiments proliferated in the 1990s, and the Baʿth could not stop all of them from preaching openly.[96] The Daʿwa Party continued to operate underground throughout the Baʿth's tenure, occasionally carrying out successful attacks against regime officials. Until al-Khoei's death in 1992, the Baʿth spent considerable resources trying to control his network. The quality of the preachers and imams that graduated from state-run religious programs was not always high, which left the graduates with little influence in society.[97] And, as numerous rumors such as the two cited above demonstrate, a large portion of the Shiʿi community harbored negative impressions of the regime and did not succumb to the party's indoctrination.

Nonetheless, the preponderance of evidence from the BRCC suggests that the Baʿthification of religion was, on balance, successful. Party reports about the Shiʿi Muharram activities indicate that the regime succeeded in keeping them under control and even benefiting from them at times. By 1989, the practices had almost ceased completely, and although they saw a brief uptick in 1996 and at other points in the late 1990s, the practices never again seriously threatened the Baʿth as they did in the 1970s.[98] Without a doubt, Hussein and the Baʿth turned the Hawza into a shell of its former self, apparently going back on the above report's stated desire "to strengthen" it. By 1988, a report shows that the regime had eliminated Shiʿi religious schools entirely from Karbala and only two remained in Najaf, down from seven and twelve, respectively, in 1985.[99] The regime's statistics on men of religion reveal that it largely succeeded in filling religious posts throughout the country with loyalists and purging Islamists, both Shiʿi and Sunni. By 1995, only seventy out of the 1,501 imams in the country, or less than 5 percent, had any negative notations next to their names in the Baʿth's files.[100]

The Tribes

Tribal identity did not pose the same kind of direct threat to the Baʿth regime as did religious belief systems and groups. Tribal solidarities and values nevertheless played a major part in Iraqi society and culture, even in urban environments, and tribal sheikhs could command the loyalty of thousands of their tribesmen, which could work for or against the Baʿth. A tribal revolt against the government, or a blood feud with it, rarely, if ever, posed an existential threat to Hussein, but it could require him to expend significant resources to quell. In many rural areas where the state did not extend deep into the countryside, tribal relationships and mores governed daily life more than the local or central government. Until Hussein rehabilitated the tribes' image in 1991, the Baʿth portrayed tribes as part of a backward stage in Arab development because the tribes' intra- and, in some cases, interstate identities and tendencies to feud with other tribes could divide the Arab people and detract from the Baʿth's attempt to unite its citizens under the common umbrella of Iraqi patriotism and Arab nationalism.[101]

Yet even before 1991, the BRCC shows that Hussein recognized the need to curry favor with tribal leaders in order to control the tribes and mobilize them to support him. Hussein put less emphasis on the Baʿthification of tribal structures because the bonds between tribes were fluid and inexact, and because tribal identities did not necessarily conflict with intranational ties or constitute an Iraqi's main conception of self. Hussein consequently preferred to work through tribal sheikhs in order to influence their tribesmen.

As in the cases of women and religion, the BRCC indicates that the strategy behind Hussein's tribal policies stayed consistent throughout his presidency, although he made tribalism a more public part of Baʿthification after the 1991 uprisings. Unlike the Baʿthification of women and religion, however, evidence from the BRCC implies that the Baʿthification of the tribes was less successful in the sense that many tribes retained more independence from the Baʿthist State than other social groups or institutions. Disputes between tribes, and between tribes and the regime, bedeviled the central government from 1979 to 2003. Yet, overall, the tribes helped more than they hindered Hussein's attempt to control the country, which was in no small part due to the regime's attempt to Baʿthize them.

In 1991, Hussein famously met with delegations of sheikhs for the first time at the presidential palace, a signal that tribes now had a place in the Husseini Baʿthist ruling order. At this and subsequent meetings, tribal sheikhs publicly performed rituals demonstrating their loyalty and subservience to Hussein.[102] As Baram has pointed out, Hussein's public glorification of tribes, kinship ties, and honor codes in the early to mid-1990s ran contrary to traditional Baʿthist ideology, which caused rumblings within the party. The Baʿthist State took on certain practices that can be characterized as "neo-tribal" because it incorporated tribal customs and values into areas not normally influenced by tribal culture such as state and party laws and institutions. This, according to Baram, "was totally alien to the original Baʿthi socialist-revolutionary and egalitarian doctrine."[103]

As this study has argued, however, Hussein's regime did not operate according to purely Aflaqian principles but rather the logic of Husseini Baʿthism. The BRCC documents suggest that the Baʿth's "neo-tribalist" policies of the early 1990s were more an overt expansion of previous efforts to bring the tribes under central government control and use them for the regime's purposes than they were a departure from Baʿthification. The strategy that Hussein took toward the tribes followed the same logic as his policies toward the families of political criminals and POWs, state institutions, students and youth, women, and religion. He attempted to bring the tribes into his regime's fold by drawing tribal sheikhs and structures into the Baʿthist State, attaching tribal values to Hussein's person and the party, and eliminating antiregime tribal elements.

Hussein supported tribal sheikhs in exchange for their loyalty and ability to deliver their tribe or clan's allegiance. Tribal sheikhs oversaw social networks of thousands of individuals depending on their place within a tribe's hierarchy. Despite their antitribal rhetoric, the Baʿth began working with sheikhs after they came to power in 1968.[104] As far back as the early 1970s, Faleh A. Jabar shows that the Baʿth started engaging tribal sheikhs to improve security in border and rural areas.[105] During Hussein's presidency, the Baʿth tried to recruit sheikhs into the party, draft them into the army, and induce them to provide security in their tribal areas when Hussein's security and police forces were stretched with other tasks. A 1984 security service study, for example, discussed how to arm tribes near the Syrian border. It suggested doing so via the heads of tribes and their clans who would give out weapons to their followers and then collect them when their services were no longer needed.[106] The BRCC contains whole box-files about the weapons it handed out to tribesmen through their sheikhs, complete with the weapons' serial numbers and their assignees.[107] Hussein also used tribes to protect critical infrastructure installations such as oil wells.[108] Hussein leaned on tribes the most to police the country in the early to mid-1990s. At that time, the breakdown of the party and local security apparatuses during the 1991 uprisings, the economic effects of the international embargo following the Gulf War, the dissolution of the Popular Army, and the need to fill the void in his security regime left by hundreds of thousands of deserters, depleted Hussein's human and material resources.[109] As one party document from 1993 put it, "The support of the state and, at its head, Mr. President Leader (God save him), for the heads of the tribes (*ruʾasāʾ al-ʿashāʾir*), clans (*ʾafkhādh*, sing. *fakhdh*), and familial notables (*wujūh al-qawm*) aims to assemble all possible energies in the battle of righteousness that our nation fights against the nation of enmity (*qawm al-ʿadwān*)."[110]

Hussein entrusted the tribes with tasks like these on the theory that once he secured their support, their traditional codes of honor would require them to uphold their promises of allegiance to his regime. Oftentimes, this theory worked. The BRCC includes many reports of the Baʿth Party coordinating with sheikhs and the security services to track down "saboteurs" (*mukharribīn*), army deserters, and criminals. In one case, communication between members of a section (*shuʿba*) command and a member's brother, who was the sheikh of a tribe living in the marshlands, resulted in the capture of forty opposition movement members and deserters hiding in the area. Incorporating tribesmen into the Baʿthist State could strengthen the regime's reach by extending its authority through tribal sheikhs and their networks of tribesmen.

When push came to shove, Hussein insisted that sheikhs demonstrate more allegiance to the Baʿthist Trinity than to their tribes, and he demanded that they subordinate their tribal customs to the needs of his regime. The Baʿth ordered sheikhs not to seek revenge for their tribesmen that the government killed. Instead, just as with the families of deserters, Hussein held sheikhs responsible for turning in or killing their "criminal" or "agent" tribesmen. In 1988, three sheikhs wrote to Hussein after a few of their tribesmen committed an offense, exhibiting the type of loyalty the regime expected: "We pledged to you on our souls and our possessions and our honor, and on everything that is dear and precious, to be faithful to the revolution and its great leader. If it is proved that those mentioned are the ones who committed the event (*ḥādith*), we will soon execute them ourselves."[111] According to Baram, this type of action was a perversion of traditional tribal codes, as a tribe might excommunicate a member and allow another tribe to seek revenge upon him, but a tribe would never kill a member itself.[112] The Baʿth furthermore counted on the sheikhs' influence among their tribesmen to stop what the party considered "mistaken" or "uncivilized" religious and tribal practices such as the self-mutilation common in popular Shiʿi rites and the tendency to shoot off guns at celebratory occasions (*ẓāhirat ʾiṭlāq al-ʿiyārāt al-nāriyya*).[113]

The BRCC shows that the regime conditioned the extra publicity, social esteem, and tangible benefits it bestowed on sheikhs and tribes in the early 1990s on their willingness to come further under the umbrella of the Baʿthist State. Beginning in the early 1990s, the Baʿth required sheikhs to officially register with their local administrations as the heads of tribes and clans. Starting around 1999, an "Office of Tribal Affairs" (*maktab shuʾūn al-ʿashāʾir*) inside the President's Office had to recognize them as well. This brought the sheikhs under official government administration for the first time, at least as indicated in the BRCC.[114] For the Baʿthist State to recognize a sheikh, the sheikh had to demonstrate a record of personal service to the regime and show that his tribe supported the Baʿth and the sheikh as its leader. To do this, many sheikhs joined the Baʿth Party, attended national occasions with their tribesmen, and served in the army, playing up the medals and honors they received as proof of their qualifications. The sheikhs had the state certify the tribal elections that they won to obtain their positions, and they encouraged their tribesmen to volunteer in the Iraqi Army and Hussein's militias.[115] Just as the Baʿth rejected nominees with no "social influence" for the National Assembly, the Baʿthist State denied sanction to sheikhs who the party or security services considered "uninfluential" (*ghayr muʾaththir*), or incapable of ensuring their tribe's loyalty, and who did not actively support the regime's initiatives and participate in its events.[116] Tribes as a whole also had to register with the state, and the Office of Tribal Affairs kept statistics about them, noting their number of clans, the names of their sheikhs, the size of their memberships, and the number of people within their "fighting force" (*al-quwwa al-qutāliyya*).[117]

If the regime's tribal policies worked much of the time, the BRCC illustrates that sometimes the regime's attempt to exert control over tribes could backfire, especially in rural areas, where tribal honor codes played large roles in social interaction and tribes wanted to remain independent. Tribal sheikhs also did not always follow the Baʿthist State's directives. Security Committee reports from the mid-1990s in particular list tribal disputes and the protection that tribes afforded criminals and deserters from their ranks as regular occurrences, which the reports claim contributed to local insecurity.[118] The protection of deserters apparently occurred with enough frequency in the southern branches of Basra and Dhi Qar that in 1994 the regime made the sheikhs in those areas sign a pledge guaranteeing that no deserters or dodgers existed within their tribes and, if they did, the tribes would report them.[119] The Baʿth never regained many of the weapons it handed out to tribes. Although the tribes used the weapons to help maintain security, they also committed crimes with them and used them in intertribal disputes, and even in blood feuds with Baʿthist State officials who killed or injured fellow tribesmen. While incorporating tribal networks helped the Baʿthist State expand its reach, if an official triggered a feud, tribes could use those same networks to retaliate against the regime. This became such a problem that in 1997 the regime issued a resolution prohibiting tribes from taking any action against regime officials who had caused injury to a tribesman in the course of their official duties.[120] It was this type of leverage that the sheikh hinted at in chapter 4 when he asked Hussein to recognize him as the chief of his clan.

Despite these challenges, the preponderance of evidence in the BRCC indicates that Hussein at least partially transformed Iraq's tribes into Baʿthist support networks. He did this by making the sheikh of a tribe a state-sanctioned position and the Baʿth's decision to recognize a sheikh dependent on the sheikh's record of loyalty. He furthermore conditioned the legal existence of a tribe on government approval and redirected tribal honor codes to protect the Baʿthist State above and beyond the tribe itself. When Hussein called the Baʿth Party "the tribe of all the tribes" in 1992, therefore, he Baʿthized the tribes as much as he "tribalized" the party.[121] As a Baʿth Party symposium urged its participants in 1994, during the height of Hussein's "neo-tribalism," Baʿthists should always "prioritize Baʿthist principles and overcome all tribal, familial, and personal manifestations, and see to the welfare of the party, first and foremost."[122] While the need to give this instruction indicates that some Baʿthists still valued tribe and family over party, and that the Baʿthification of the tribes was imperfect, the statement sums up the regime's basic policy toward the tribes. It also summarizes the goal both of the "organization" of Iraqi state, society, and culture, and Hussein's overall totalitarian strategy.

PART IV. TERROR AND ENTICEMENT

To them it signifies nothing that this or that compatriot shouldered more than his share of the load in the long uphill struggle to establish Germany's prestige and means of existence in the black years after the military collapse, or that his German nationalism and patriotic devotion were, according to the lights of that day, beyond question. The measure of his right to any sort of present consideration is first of all whether or not he was a Nazi. If he was not, he is wiped out, usually even though he might now wish to swallow his past and accept Adolf Hitler's leadership.

Not merely is he wiped out, but the memory of him is wiped out. It is pretended that he never was. His name is not mentioned, even in scorn.

HAMILTON FISH ARMSTRONG, "HITLER'S REICH: THE FIRST PHASE"

The Stalinist era of the Soviet Union is known as one of the most murderous in history, a time when the fear sowed by the regime's terror prompted many of the regime's citizens to conform and obey. Yet, "while sanctioning mass violence, the Soviet regime never set the extermination of people as an objective in itself."[1] Rather, as Oleg Khlevnyuk argues about the "Great Terror" of 1937 to 1938, "the main aim . . . was the removal of all strata of the population, which in the opinion of the country's leaders were hostile or potentially hostile."[2] The stability of Stalin's regime did not rest solely on terror. Particularly after the "Cultural Revolution," from 1928 to 1931, and again after World War II, the Soviet regime added "inducements" as part of a "Big Deal" in which the Soviet government provided access to material goods in exchange for loyalty. These inducements facilitated the population's acceptance of the regime and, in so doing, helped to build a middle class that took on "Soviet manners, values, and attitudes."[3] Stalin's dual policy of stick and carrot reinforced the ideological indoctrination and organization of Russian society as part of his overall effort to transform that society into a communist utopia.[4]

In Saddam Hussein's Iraq, the BRCC documents show that the regime provided powerful negative *and* positive incentives for Hussein's citizens to accept the ideological and organizational aspects of Baʿthification. Chapter 8 deals with the negative side of this equation. It contends that, just as under Stalin, the Baʿth regime targeted its terror at Iraqis that it considered "traitors" (sing. *khāʾin*), "criminals" (*mujrimīn*), "enemies" (sing. *ʿadū*), and "saboteurs" (*mukharribīn*): people who proved themselves, or whom the Baʿth suspected to be, opponents of the ideological and political goals of the regime. Many innocents died at the hands of the Baʿthist State because of the extralegal, arbitrary power that Hussein and his organs of terror exercised, because of the structural incentives inherent in those organs, and because of the Baʿth's wide definition of its "enemies." But contrary to the Republic of Fear thesis, I did not find any evidence in the BRCC that the Baʿthist State ever purposefully meted out terror randomly in order to instill fear. The Baʿth's "means of violence" did not become "ends in themselves."[5] In fact, Husseini Baʿthist ideology precluded this possibility. In an oft-repeated quotation, Hussein said, "Iraq is the country of all and protecting its security and sovereignty is everybody's responsibility."[6] The regime worked on behalf of the people's security and, in the Baʿth's eyes, genuine Iraqis worked to protect the regime. By definition, anybody who showed his disloyalty to any part of the Baʿthist Trinity was a foreign "agent" or "traitor"; opponents of the regime were necessarily hostile to the Iraqi people because the regime and the people existed as one organic entity—the Iraqi nation.[7] Outside observers might find this reasoning absurd, but the BRCC documents demonstrate that this logic underlay the Baʿth's use of terror. From Hussein and the Baʿth's point of view, they employed violence under the moral authority of Husseini Baʿthism, the principles of which they codified in public laws and internal directives. "Cleansing" the country of their adversaries was one of many means they used to Baʿthize Iraq.

On the other side of the equation, chapter 9 explains how, if Iraq was a Republic of Fear, it was also a Republic of Rewards and Dependence. Complementing their violence and surveillance, Hussein and the Baʿth created an extensive regime of medals, awards, honors, and statuses that entitled their holders to financial, professional, academic, social, and other benefits. Iraqis won these rewards by demonstrating their allegiance to the Baʿthist Trinity. If an Iraqi's fealty ever wavered the regime would withdraw his perks and might mete out physical punishment. As long as an Iraqi remained loyal, however, he expected recompense for his service. This reciprocal relationship constituted the basic agreement between Hussein and the Iraqi people. Hussein ruled not merely through terror but also via enticement. He offered his citizens a stark choice designed to induce their consent: support me and prosper or, at least, live a normal life; oppose me and face the consequences. Once an Iraqi pulled a trigger on Hussein's behalf or accepted his bribes, he became complicit in the Baʿthist order, offering a further incentive to sustain it.

Hussein's system of terror and enticement, or *al-tarhīb wa-l-targhīb*, as Iraqis called it, worked particularly well because the consequences of a citizen's actions extended to their families, for better or worse. Individuals and families consequently had motivation to police one another so that all might prosper and neither would suffer for the other's transgressions. At stake was not just their physical or economic well being but also their dignity and self-worth. Within the Baʿthist system a person or family's honor depended, first and foremost, on the extent of their loyalty to the leader, the party, and the nation. When required to choose, Iraqis were expected to forsake their kin, co-religionists, or tribal members in favor of the Baʿthist Trinity.

Baʿthification simultaneously atomized individuals within families and manipulated familial solidarities to inculcate loyalty. Hannah Arendt characterized the predicament of people stuck within totalitarian systems as facing a choice between "murder and murder." To illustrate, she used the example of a Greek mother forced by the Nazis to choose which of her three children she wanted the Nazis to kill. The moral impossibility of this type of situation, Arendt argued, made "decisions of conscience absolutely questionable and equivocal."[8] In Baʿthist Iraq, however, terror and enticement succeeded to a large degree because the regime offered its citizens an *un*-equivocal choice. If families did not disown their deviant individual members, more family members might die or be tortured, and the entire extended family would thereafter fall under heightened suspicion with black marks in each relative's file. This would not only dishonor the family as a whole but also disadvantage the family's members in school, at work, and in any other type of interaction with the Baʿthist State. Instead of between "murder and murder," the Baʿth regime presented Iraqis with a choice analogous to that faced by somebody with a gangrenous limb who must decide whether or not to sever the arm or leg so that the infection does not spread to the rest of the body—or to try to save the limb and risk death. Like in Stalinist Russia, terror and enticement reinforced the ideological and organizational impetuses of Husseini Baʿthism.

8. TERROR

INTRODUCTION

In the preface to her 1970 edition of *The Origins of Totalitarianism*, Hannah Arendt wrote that the "most characteristic aspect of totalitarian terror" is that "it is let loose when all organized opposition has died down and the totalitarian ruler knows that he no longer need to be afraid." Accordingly, Arendt claimed that Stalin's purges in the Great Terror were not "motivated by a *raison d'etat* in the old sense of the term" but for their own sake, to atomize the population and instill loyalty through fear.[1] Kanan Makiya, whose *Republic of Fear* draws from Arendt's theories to analyze Baʿthist Iraq, made similar claims about the Baʿth regime. As noted in the introduction, Makiya argued that the Baʿth destroyed all "genuine opposition" and thus had to "invent their enemies" in order to justify their continued use of violence, upon which their authority rested. This, Makiya wrote, produced "a polity made up of citizens who positively expected to be tortured under certain circumstances."[2]

Evidence gathered for this study, however, suggests that the primary purpose behind Baʿthist terror was not to inculcate fear but rather to root out, destroy, and deter threats that the regime perceived to its security—"to purify" (*taṭhīr*) or "cleanse" (*tanẓīf*) the country of opposition.[3] Just as scholars of the Soviet and Nazi regimes have found that opposition to Stalin and Hitler never ceased—and that Stalin at least genuinely feared threats to himself[4]—the BRCC documents suggest that Saddam Hussein never eliminated resistance to the point where he no longer needed to be concerned about attacks against himself, his family, his inner circle, and his government.[5] Hussein survived a number of assassination attempts, notably in Dujayl, in 1982, and changed his location constantly "for security reasons" in the later 1990s. In December 1996, an unknown assailant shot and permanently disabled his son, Uday, an attack Amatzia Baram concluded must have been "at least in part an inside job." In 1980, one of Hussein's most trusted associates, Tariq Aziz, barely survived an assassination attempt at Mustansiriyya University in Baghdad.[6] Otherwise, the BRCC archive contains hundreds, if not thousands, of reports from all years of Hussein's presidency about assassination attempts and killings of party and state officials; assaults on Baʿthist State buildings and economic infrastructure; cases of smuggling that caused billions of dinars of currency, materials, and resources to leave the country; thefts; forgery; corruption; and extortion.[7] Many armed Baʿth Party security detachments (*mafāriz*, sing. *mafraza*), which acted as parallel police forces, saw members "martyred" or injured.[8] In 1987, an internal party report claimed that forty-seven party members had died in the line of duty thus far that year (the report is not dated); tens had been kidnapped; some fifty-five had sustained injuries; and a variety of "criminals," "saboteurs," and foreign "agents" had attacked various party headquarters and members' houses with bullets, RPGs, and Molotov cocktails.[9] When an individual decided to work for the Baʿthist State he became a representative of it and thus a target for antiregime acts, as did one *mukhtār* and security service agent from Basra killed by "saboteur elements" in 1995.[10] Other than the attempts on Hussein's life, these mostly isolated incidents did not constitute an existential threat to his regime. At times, Hussein undoubtedly exaggerated or perhaps even "invented" the threat of his opposition out of paranoia or political convenience. The BRCC records demonstrate, however, that throughout Hussein's presidency, the Baʿthist State, its leaders, and its officials faced a continuous series of attacks and plots from internal and external sources against which they legitimately felt the need to remain vigilant. Hussein's citizens were not the only ones who had reason to be afraid.

The BRCC offers little evidence, moreover, that Iraqis "expected to be tortured" indiscriminately. The purpose behind Baʿthification, and the stark contrast between terror and enticement, was to mobilize the populace behind the regime—to make Iraqis complicit in the regime's violence and shepherd them down the path of obedience. The Baʿth did not want to demobilize their citizens by making them *generally* afraid, or fearful of doing anything. If Iraqis expected to be tortured regardless of their actions, there was no reason to obey or refrain from resistance. They would endure violence regardless of their political stance. On the contrary, the way in which the Baʿth employed violence encouraged Iraqis to stay far away from the regime's blurry red lines and to consistently and actively demonstrate their allegiance so that the regime could not possibly conceive of them as the enemy. As one of Saddam Hussein's generals, Raad Hamdani, explained after the Baʿth's fall, "At the time it was a very bad system, a bad regime, but there were red lines. If you didn't cross the red lines you were OK."[11]

That being said, there is no denying that a degree of randomness governed Iraqi lives. No checks and balances outside of the disapproval of Hussein or another top official held the security services or Baʿth Party accountable for using violence excessively, and the Baʿth punished severely officials who failed to deal with a potential threat that proved real. Thus, if an Iraqi crossed a regime official or aroused the Baʿthist leadership's suspicions or jealousies—even if by accident, association, or doing one's job too well—the arbitrary power that the Baʿthist State held provided incentives for its employees to presume guilt and eliminate perceived threats in order to protect their lives and positions. Officials could also pursue personal vendettas with little fear of recrimination. Even if Hussein and the Baʿth never pursued a policy of indiscriminate terror toward the Iraqi population at large, the inherent structural and extralegal characteristics of the Baʿthist system could cause innocent civilians to be tortured through no fault of their own.

THE MEANS AND PURPOSES OF TERROR

In the history of totalitarian regimes, Hussein's Iraq does not rank among the most prolific killers of its citizens, although the full extent of its murder is still unknown. In its range of methods and willingness to use them, however, its terror was first rate. The files looked at for this study did not mention torture explicitly, but its existence has been detailed elsewhere, and the archive documents confessions of guilt, some of which probably occurred as a result of coercion.[12] Otherwise, the BRCC contains examples of the many types of punishments that Hussein's regime meted out against individuals, families, and entire populations: executions, killings, prison sentences, the destruction of homes, ethnic cleansing, deportation, the withholding of social and economic services, and the destruction of environments critical to Iraqis' livelihoods. In the surveillance category, the security services and Baʿth Party regularly monitored potential security threats through human and technological means, recruiting a large number of informants to spy on their friends, colleagues, neighbors, and kin. Why did the Baʿthist State use these means of terror? What purposes did they serve?

The most clear-cut use of terror occurred in instances when Hussein and the Baʿth Party could not first threaten, convince, cajole, or buy off Iraqis into supporting them—or when Hussein felt a loyalist had acquired too much of a personal power base. Hussein did not trust individuals, social groups, or political movements that did not support him explicitly, and if they voiced public opposition or used violence against the Baʿthist State, Hussein sought to eliminate or otherwise neutralize the threat he believed they posed. Hussein and his organs of terror thus used violence primarily to remove disloyal elements that they perceived to endanger the maintenance of their power, the regime's capacity to carry out Hussein's initiatives, and the population's sense of security, which could discredit the regime.

The regime also used violence as a deterrent against future acts of opposition and crime and as an incentive for resistance fighters and criminals to reform themselves into loyal citizens. The Baʿth offered a stark choice between the outcomes for enemies or lawbreakers who forced the Baʿth to hunt them down and committed repeated crimes versus those who turned themselves in quickly after a first offense. The regulations for army deserters, for example, stipulated that deserters who remained at large for more than a year or deserted for a second time should be executed. In contrast, first-time deserters who left for less than a year were sent back to their units for disciplining.[13] To drive home the message, the Baʿth made examples out of individuals or groups of deserters. In 1987, the Baghdad Bureau reported to Hussein that it had recently executed fifty-nine deserters who qualified for the death penalty in front of other runaways arrested for their first offenses as a means to prevent recidivism.[14] Similarly, when crime spiked, the Baʿth imposed harsh penalties to restore order, even for what normally did not constitute severe offenses. During the Gulf War, the Party Secretariat instructed its organizations to execute taxi drivers found exploiting wartime conditions to extort high fares from their riders. Following their execution, the Secretariat ordered the organizations to hang the drivers' bodies in public for three days accompanied by signs explaining the reason for their execution "in order for us to deter others."[15]

Hussein and the Baʿth employed terror against their enemies' families with the aim of convincing the families to inform on their relatives, and for the relatives to turn themselves in so as to spare their families punishment. When a party detachment in 2000 could not catch a deserter who fled to the marshes, for example, it destroyed his house. When that did not bring him in, the party arrested his father, his wife, and his children, which finally persuaded him to submit himself to the authorities.[16] To present a lesson to other security service personnel, in 1986 the Baʿth executed a man in the General Directorate of Intelligence (GDI) for failing to inform on his uncle and cousins who were Daʿwa Party members.[17] These cases not only served as effective means to capture criminals and weed out potential opposition sympathizers from sensitive state agencies but also to warn prospective offenders and their relatives to think twice before committing a crime or hiding their family members' transgressions. Extending terror to families widened its desired effect by inducing the population to police itself.

For these same reasons, the Baʿth conducted terror against groups of people within Iraqi society whom they failed to Baʿthize for one reason or another. As explained below, the genocide and ethnic cleansing of the Kurds was one case of this; another was the Baʿth's policy toward the marshes in the southeastern part of the country. Due to the difficult terrain in the marshes, their proximity to Iran, and the proliferation of hiding places for opposition fighters and criminals, the Baʿth took blunt measures against the entire area. In 1986, the head of the Southern Bureau reported to the Party Secretariat that government forces had shelled the marshes for three days and constructed an economic blockade whereby they did not allow in any foodstuffs or fuel. They also cut the electricity.[18] The following year, the Southern Bureau wrote in a letter to Hussein that it had a plan in place to "organize and purify" (*tanẓīm wa-taṭhīr*) the shoulders of the Tigris and Euphrates, as well as to continue the desiccation of their surrounding marshes, in order to "help control them and increase the agricultural lands it is possible to benefit from."[19] The state's benefit, however, destroyed the environment of the "Marsh Arabs," who were not opponents of the regime or criminals.[20]

Hussein's security apparatus conducted surveillance in two general ways: directly through its own technological monitoring and agents, and indirectly through informants. The party and security services sent agents to spy on mosques, markets, town squares, and other public spaces. The BRCC makes reference, for example, to "the commissioned spies" (*al-ʿuyūn al-mukallafa*) sent by the party to listen to and report about a Friday prayer sermon given by a preacher in Baghdad in 1986 who had drawn especially large crowds.[21] Whether through the party or security services, another document mentions a "town watchman" (*murāqib baladiyya*) who stumbled on anti-Saddam graffiti written on a wall during his normal rounds.[22] Also in 1986, the General Security Directorate wrote to the RCC's National Security Council (*majlis al-ʾamn al-qawmī*) suggesting that two women employed as the "deputy security officials" assigned to the al-Mustansiriyya and central al-Rashid markets in Baghdad be fired because of their flagging commitment to the Baʿth Party.[23]

The population monitored itself too because the Baʿth Party cultivated informants and obligated its members to report antiregime comments or criminal activity; otherwise it punished them. The party demoted a man who worked in the Central Workers Office in 1991, for instance, for failing to turn in another Baʿthist who made pro-Iranian and antiregime comments at a party meeting.[24] In a twist on this kind of case, a partisan being investigated for allegedly criticizing the regime's personal status law denied the charges, using the imperative for Baʿthists to inform the party about inappropriate comments as a defense. "First of all," he asked, "if the decisions [of the party] had really been criticized, shouldn't it have been incumbent upon comrades [name withheld] and [name withheld] to take the initiative to inform about it? Second, if the facts have been confirmed then why weren't these two comrades punished for covering up the criticism?"[25] Iraqis informed on their fellows for financial and personal reasons also. One Kurdish informant complained in a petition to Hussein that despite providing the GDI with good information, the GDI had mistreated him and did not compensate him properly.[26] People informed out of malice, using the skeletons they knew about from other Iraqis' closets to settle scores. A lawyer with a grudge against a recently elected National Assembly member, for example, told the party that the member had previously deserted from the army and been expelled from the party in the 1970s. The lawyer asserted that the National Assembly member returned to public life under an assumed name and forged identity, and eluded the party censors who vetted the candidates.[27] Families also frequently turned in individual members who ran afoul of the regime in order to save their collective reputations, lives, and benefits. The large number of Iraqis who cooperated with the regime and took the initiative to inform—even if just once—illustrates the degree to which the regime's overall system of control convinced and compelled Iraqis to support it for their own individual reasons.

In addition to eliminating enemies, Baʿthist terror served another purpose: it tied its perpetrators, and the populace at large, to the regime. The most egregious case of this occurred when Hussein forced Baʿth Party Regional Command members to kill their comrades when he assumed the presidency. Wafiq al-Samarrai, a former head of military intelligence until his defection in the early 1990s, claimed that his former organization used the same tactic on its officers. According to him, it regularly bussed the officers into the desert where large holes awaited them. The officers were then given Kalashnikovs and told to wait for another bus, this one containing men blindfolded with their hands tied. The men were led into the holes, and the officers were told to open fire. When they finished, they covered the dead bodies with dirt in mass graves. Describing the regime's intent behind these types of acts, al-Samarrai explained that:

> Saddam worked assiduously throughout his rule to generalize criminality, spread terror, and implicate (*tawrīṭ*) others. Frequently, Baʿthists were executed at the hands of Baʿthists in front of groups of Baʿthists in order to spread fear and terror, on the one hand, and implicate those who carried it out on the other because if they did not carry out the order others would carry it out against them and the people whom they wanted to execute in the first place![28]

Trapped between the choice of murder or suicide, those who chose the former could take comfort only in the moral universe that Husseini Baʿthism provided, that the people they killed were traitors and had to be eliminated for the sake of national security. Whether a person believed this or not, once he acted as if he did, he had a strong incentive to prolong the regime. If Hussein's government ever fell, the moral, political, and legal alibis that he killed under would disappear, and *he* could become the criminal subject to punishment and revenge. To a lesser extent, this same dynamic held among the general population, which had to buy into the Baʿthist system to prove their loyalty and gain access to the state benefits and opportunities required to prosper or live a normal life. As a result, regardless of an Iraqi's motives or degree of separation from the Baʿthist State's actual acts of terror, when he did not oppose those acts he tacitly countenanced them and, in the process, became implicated in the regime's survival.

BRCC statistics do not indicate how many Iraqis had a relative executed, disappeared, or imprisoned; underwent torture; or were subject to surveillance during Hussein's presidency. The number of memoranda, reports, petitions, and other correspondence that reference these types of cases, however, along with people who became involved in an affair that drew in the Baʿth Party or the security services, is immense. Their collective weight suggests that even if an Iraqi never personally suffered, he likely had some kind of brush with the political arms of the state and knew, or knew of, somebody affected in one of the above ways. Without a doubt, he heard rumors about them.[29] The violent and secretive arms of Hussein's Iraq did not touch every citizen, but they did not have to in order to instill fear of them in the populace. Fear might not have been the primary purpose behind Baʿthist terror, but it served as a useful consequence of the threat of violence and surveillance that underlay the Baʿthist State's interactions with society.

THE TARGETS AND JUSTIFICATIONS OF TERROR

Hussein and the Baʿth targeted their terror at four main categories of groups and individuals whom they perceived as threats to their security and the sources of their legitimacy: internal plotters and "weak" regime members, resistance movements, foreign countries, and criminals.

Internal Threats

Internal coup or assassination attempts constituted the most dangerous type of threat to Hussein and the Baʿth. Reports of uncovered plots within the archive confirm that conspirators infiltrated to the highest levels of Baʿthist State institutions despite the extensive background checks that the Baʿth conducted for officials working in security positions and their feeder academies. A party report from 1998, for example, details how the party received information from the GDI about the son of a Baʿthist sectional member who was a soldier in the Republican Guard (RG). The soldier, the report said, was part of a conspiratorial network within the RG that sought to assassinate Hussein, and the soldier's maternal uncle worked on the staff inside Hussein's home. The family connections between the father, his son, and the uncle created the potential for the RC conspiracy to spread into the party and, perhaps most dangerously, Hussein's personal core of servants. As a result, the GDI put the RG member under surveillance and wanted the party to know about the case so that it could take precautions as well.[30] This case shows that Hussein had good reason to develop multiple and overlapping security agencies—the Baʿth included—and illustrates one instance in which the services worked individually and as a unit to protect him. This, of course, was their primary duty, and the fact that Hussein never succumbed to internal intrigue justified the emphasis he placed on security from his perspective.

The Baʿth punished severely party members who exhibited cowardice or a lack of commitment in the face of danger to the party. This proved a particular problem in 1991, when many Baʿthists did not report for duty to defend party and government buildings, leaving their comrades who did to be "martyred."[31] Some even joined the uprisings. It must have been a shock to Hussein when his supposedly most loyal, ideologically committed institution melted in the face of the rebels. While the party granted regular Iraqis amnesty for their actions once the government recaptured control over the country, none of the amnesty decrees from 1991 found for this study mentioned *al-takhādhul*, or "weakness" in one's duties, as a pardonable offense. Instead, the BRCC records the execution of one party member from Basra who "fled from confronting the agent elements (*al-ʾanāṣir al-ʿamīla*)."[32] The Baʿth used the man's execution as an example to other Baʿthists of a "just punishment (*qiṣāṣan ʿādilan*) and an admonition to other weak ones (*mutakhādhilīn*)."[33] A rumor reported by the party in 1999 claimed that Ali Hassan al-Majid, an RCC member and the infamous commander who oversaw the genocide of the Kurds from 1987 to 1988, had put 260 Baʿthists to death in Basra and Amara "for accusations of weakness (*al-takhādhul*) and not performing their duties" during unrest in 1999.[34] Whether or not the rumor was true, it had to have some basis in its circulators' perceptions of the possible for it to gain traction. The Baʿth emphasized internal discipline precisely to forestall these types of lapses in allegiance, which damaged their attempt to present a united front to Iraqi society and the rest of the world.

Opposition Parties

Besides plots and "weakness" within the Baʿthist State, Hussein sought to eliminate all traces of resistance within society at large. Organized movements or antiregime political parties carried out most opposition activities. The Baʿth focused primarily on four main opposition parties: the Iraqi Communist Party, the Islamic Daʿwa Party (*ḥizb al-daʿwa al-ʾislāmiyya*), and the two main Kurdish parties, the Kurdistan Democratic Party (KDP) and the Patriotic Union of Kurdistan (PUK), which split off from the KDP in 1975.[35] A number of other smaller groups appear in the documents, mainly of the Islamist (both Sunni and Shiʿi) and Kurdish varieties, but statistics the party kept on each show that they had only token memberships.[36] A chart of "political movements" with numbers collected from all five party bureaus in 1986 and 1987 shows the "Agent Communist Party" (*al-ḥizb al-shuyūʿī al-ʿamīl*) with between 3,600 and 3,900 members, the KDP with almost 5,000, and the "Agent Daʿwa Party" with almost 2,200. In contrast, the "Muslim Brothers and other [Islamic] political groups" had only seventy-seven adherents and the pan-Arab and Nasserist movements sixteen.[37] The presence of Islamist parties other than the Daʿwa rose in the 1990s enough to concern the Baʿth, but they never produced the same level of anxiety as did the four main opposition parties. The existence of resistance movements throughout Hussein's presidency demonstrates that the Baʿth never succeeded entirely in "purifying" the country of opposition. Nonetheless, the relatively low numbers of regime opponents recorded in Baʿthist and security service records show that the regime weakened the opposition parties significantly.

THE COMMUNIST PARTY Of the four main opposition parties, the Baʿth succeeded in most thoroughly neutralizing the Communist Party. Once a major force in Iraqi politics in the 1950s and 1960s, a security report from al-Qadisiyya Governorate in 1986 claimed that the Baʿth had defeated the communists psychologically. As a result, their members suffered from "a condition of despair, hesitation, and a lack of trust in their leadership."[38] When the BRCC mentions Communist Party actions they are usually isolated affairs: assassination attempts of mid-level officials or acts of economic sabotage carried out by individuals or small cells that do not appear to have been in good contact with other communist groups.[39] With no significant foreign backers or natural places of refuge like the Kurdish parties had in the mountainous north, and the Daʿwa had in the marshes of the south, the Baʿth atomized the communists to the point of relative insignificance.[40]

THE DAʿWA PARTY The Baʿth Party feared the Shiʿi Daʿwa Party the most out of the four main opposition parties. The Daʿwa is the only political movement specifically named, for example, on a 1999 form found in a Military Bureau file for prospective Baʿth Party members. The form includes an oath the applicant had to sign promising under pain of death that he never had any connection to the Daʿwa.[41] The Baʿth's paranoia about the Daʿwa stemmed from its record of assassination attempts against Hussein, its attacks against Iraqi government installations at home and abroad, and the fact that it was an expressly Iraqi Shiʿi organization with a significant historical following among the religious Shiʿi population dating back to its founding in the late 1950s.[42] The Daʿwa received Iranian backing and sanctuary after the Iran–Iraq War started, but unlike other Shiʿi opposition movements created or sustained by Iran, the Daʿwa did not want to unite with Iran in a pan-Shiʿi state. Nor did the Daʿwa necessarily agree with Ayatollah Khomeini's notion of the "rule of the jurist" (*wilāyat al-faqih*), the ideological foundation on which the Islamic Republic rests. The Daʿwa also preached an inclusive Iraqi-Islamic nationalism that equated allegiance to both Sunni and Shiʿi Islam with Iraqi patriotism.[43] The Daʿwa therefore competed directly with the Baʿth for Iraqi hearts and minds from within Iraqi society's majority sectarian and ethnic groups, the Shiʿa and Arabs, respectively. As a result, the Baʿth feared that the Daʿwa could exploit its local knowledge and organic roots to turn the Shiʿi masses—which during the Iran–Iraq War comprised "the large majority" of the military's rank-and-file infantry—against it.[44] As a 1986 security report from al-Qadisiyya Governorate warned:

> The [Daʿwa] Party and its elements focus on exploiting the subject of the Iraq–Iran War and the mistaken religious practices (popular Shiʿi rites) to work on the simple citizens and recruit them. They similarly stir up the families of those executed and sentenced among them in order to recruit them or at least *alter their loyalty* and use them to broadcast opposition rumors. They also try to stir up discord (*fitna*) and sectarianism (*al-ṭāʾifiyya*) within the public.[45]

For a regime led mostly by Sunnis who tried to play down sectarian divisions in society and focus on Arab and Iraqi notions of identity, the Daʿwa's message represented a grave threat. Out of all of its enemies, the Baʿth offered the least amount of leniency to current or former Daʿwa members. In 1980, an RCC resolution made any past or present member of the Daʿwa subject to the death penalty. During the late 1970s and 1980s, the Baʿth killed hundreds of Daʿwa associates, driving the organization into the shadows and out of the country, significantly decreasing the Daʿwa's potential danger.[46]

THE KURDS While the Daʿwa presented a clear-cut case of an enemy, the Baʿth at various times allied with and clashed with both the KDP and PUK, which were the most organized and capable opposition groups.

In general, the Baʿth walked a fine line with the Kurds. The Iraqi constitution recognized the Kurds as one of two official "nationalities" but simultaneously claimed Iraq as part of the Arab nation.[47] Mirroring the Kurds' ambiguous legal situation, the Baʿth differentiated between "our Kurdish people" and the KDP and PUK, which they painted as traitorous groups controlled by foreign powers. The Baʿth referred to the KDP as the "band of the offspring of treachery" (*zumrat salīlī al-khiyāna*) and the PUK as the "band of Iranian agents" (*zumrat ʿumalāʾ ʾīrān*).[48] In negotiations that began in 1969 between the Kurds and the new Baʿthist government, the Baʿth officially recognized Kurdish national and cultural rights and set up a pathway for the Kurds to attain local autonomy. Yet the Baʿth refused to concede access to oil, its revenues, or the responsibility for defending Iraq's borders to the Kurds, and talks broke down. In 1974, the Baʿth unilaterally established an "autonomous region" in the three provinces of Suleimaniyya, Erbil, and Dohuk, governed by an elected assembly and executive council. The region was really only semiautonomous, however, as its borders excluded the oil fields, Baghdad appointed the head of the executive council, and the central government could dismiss the head of the executive council and dissolve parliament whenever it wished.[49]

For a variety of reasons, the Baʿth did not pursue a strategy of total control in the Kurdish regions. On the whole, the BRCC demonstrates that the Kurds did not support the Baʿth's policies, and the Baʿth treated the Kurdish areas as hostile territory. Due to cultural and linguistic differences as well as the northern region's relative lack of development, the population did not absorb party propaganda to the same extent as the rest of the country.[50] The Baʿth did not establish the same kind of organizational and bureaucratic control in Iraqi Kurdistan as they did in the remainder of Iraq, and their system of rewards and benefits did not reach the same number of Kurds as it did Arabs.

The Baʿth scaled back their aspirations in the Kurdish territories partly because they could not find members who wanted to work there. Few Baʿthists spoke Kurdish well, and the party had to offer a series of incentives for its members to agree to be transferred to the north and, if they desired, remain there for an extended period. These incentives included shorter than normal assignment times with offers of free housing and cars, accelerated party promotions, and bonuses upon signing up for and finishing tours of duty. During the Iran–Iraq War, working in the autonomous region fulfilled a Baʿthist's obligation to participate in the Popular Army and, if a Baʿthist died on duty, the state considered him a martyr in Saddam's *Qādisiyya* with all of the benefits for the member's family that accompanied that distinction.[51]

The BRCC gives the impression that the Kurds saw the Baʿthist State's presence in the Kurdish territories—consisting of the autonomous region and parts of the provinces of Diyala, Ninewa, and al-Ta'mim (Kirkuk)—as an occupying force instead of a legitimate authority. Throughout Hussein's tenure, Baʿthist and government installations in the north came under repeated attack, and the Kurds regularly assassinated, kidnapped, and threatened Baʿthist personnel.[52] In 1986, a memo circulating within the party's Central Organization Committee showed that, from about 1980 until 1986, of the 1,694 Baʿthists assigned to work in the "northern region," almost 30 percent (503) "had been martyred at the hands of saboteurs," a euphemism for members of the opposition.[53] Whenever the central government's control slackened or disappeared, demonstrations or acts of resistance broke out with the KDP and PUK taking over government buildings and Baʿth Party headquarters.[54] According to a DMI report, one such demonstration organized by the PUK in 1991 consisted of thirty people in al-Kalak, just east of Mosul, who chanted slogans against the Baʿth Party and Hussein while Kurdish children affixed papers to Arab houses urging them to leave the town.[55] The Baʿth always maintained that the Kurds' general opposition to their rule stemmed from the Kurds' "subjection to a campaign (*ʿamaliyya*) of psychological and intellectual sabotage" by the Kurdish opposition "to the extent that [the campaign] expunged any traces of feelings of belonging to the [Arab] nation and its sacred earth."[56] But fundamental differences over identity, land, and resources constituted the real reasons. Ultimately, the Baʿth wanted the Kurds to accept the Arab nationalist narrative and assimilate into Iraqi Arab culture. For the most part, however, the Kurds declined to do so. As a result, the Baʿth used a greater proportion of terror than enticement to maintain control in the Kurdish territories, and they took more collective measures against the population.

Hussein associated the level of security a particular area in the Kurdish regions enjoyed with its ethnic composition. The Baʿth Party kept statistics about the ethnic makeup of the population in Kurdish areas, where it recorded the numbers of Arabs, Kurds, and Turkmen who lived there.[57] The Baʿth did not keep statistics about ethnicity in other parts of the country. The Baʿth used these statistics as part of a strategic policy of Arabization (*taʿrīb*), which consisted of expelling (*tarḥīl*) Kurds from the north and replacing them with Arabs, primarily around the oil fields and along the border with Iran.[58]

In 1988, for example, most likely as part of the regime's al-Anfal campaign of genocide and ethnic cleansing, the BRCC documents a project to clear the Kifri district in Diyala Governorate of Kurds and to transfer the Kifri district's administrative center to a majority Arab location.[59] Accordingly, the head of the President's Office sent instructions to Ali Hassan al-Majid, Secretary of the Northern Bureau at the time, decreeing that "the percentage of Arabs in the administrative units [of a series of fourteen Kurdish villages] and the housing complexes (*mujamaʿāt*) connected to them should not be less than 80 percent of the total population." The instructions then laid out specific steps to Arabize the area, directing al-Majid "to carry out the operation of expelling the Kurds from the [administrative] units in a calm and gradual manner." This was to be done by "expelling the bad and disloyal families directly," "transferring [Kurdish] state workers to other areas in the autonomous region, or to the Arab depth (*al-ʿumq al-ʿarabī*) according to their wishes," and then transferring Arab families into the formerly majority Kurdish villages. As incentives for the Arab newcomers, the instructions ordered al-Majid to give each family a free piece of land on which to live, an advance payment from the Real Estate Bank, and a grant of either 5,000 or 3,000 Iraqi Dinars (ID) depending on where they resided. The instructions further dictated that the Arabs should be given employment either in the state, in the socialist or private sectors, on agricultural land, or in industrial programs set up and supported by the government.[60]

Further illustrating the link between ethnicity and security in the Baʿth's mind, after the central government regained control of the city of Khaniqin following the 1991 uprisings, the Baʿth's Diyala Branch suggested rebuilding the houses of the Arabs whom the Kurds expelled during the insurrection so the Arabs could return to live in them. The branch's report explained that "The return of the Arabs to their previous villages will constitute an addition to the armed forces and will return the city to its previous condition with an Arab majority, which will calm the security situation for the better and deny opportunities for enemies." The report also suggested arming the Arab tribes who returned to the area.[61]

In addition to Arabization, the Baʿth used a variety of means to weed out, deter, and monitor the Kurdish opposition. Hussein's forces eliminated Kurdish homes and entire villages (*ʾizālat al-duwar, ʾizālat al-qurā*) in order to "purify" them of KDP and PUK members as part of a counterinsurgency campaign.[62] A 1992 party study also advocated expelling the opposition members' families.[63] The BRCC contains tens of files with detailed information provided in the form of intelligence reports about the activities of the Kurdish opposition and foreign officials or intelligence agents in the north. The Baʿth maintained rigorous surveillance of the Kurdish regions even after some areas fell out of their control. The Baʿth could not have received the kind of detailed information about the KDP and PUK that they did unless they had agents inside the Kurdish parties, including their leaderships. In general, the Baʿth's various intelligence services had excellent information about opposition groups, which was a critical factor in the regime's largely successful campaigns against them.[64] (The loss of the Kurdish territories after 1991 was the major exception to this rule.) In the communist case, the BRCC contains a report from a GDI and General Security Directorate agent explicitly tasked with "infiltrating" (*al-taghalghul*) the Communist Party.[65]

In addition to opposition parties, Hussein and the Baʿth took exceptional interest in unorganized, isolated acts of resistance. The BRCC shows that individual acts or public proclamations of opposition occurred for reasons as varied as those for supporting the Baʿth, be they ideological; out of revenge or anguish after losing a loved one; as a paid agent on behalf of a foreign power; to protect or advance individual, familial, tribal, religious, or national honor and interests; to ameliorate the pressures of life in the Baʿthist system; or simply to exert a degree of self-autonomy and personal initiative which the Baʿth otherwise tried to destroy in their citizens. The exact causes of enmity mixed in different proportions on an individual basis. These kinds of actions, which did not directly threaten the regime's existence, could nevertheless turn into something greater if the Baʿth did not respond. As the Polish intellectual Leszek Kolakowski has argued, and Charles Kurzman's study of the 1979 Iranian Revolution has shown, nondemocratic regimes base their authority in large part on their ability to make their subjects, and those outside of the regime, believe that they cannot possibly be overthrown.[66] They do this by, over time, eliminating alternatives to their rule, giving the population something to lose if they fall, and maintaining the willingness to use violence when opposition arises. Ultimately, the people become convinced that resistance is futile, and the mental barrier to conceiving of a revolution becomes a closely guarded asset of the regimes. If left in front of Iraqis' eyes too long, graffiti reading "Death to Saddam—Death to Saddam—Wake up O' Iraqis!" as the party found written on a wall in a public square in Ramadi in 1991, could become a self-fulfilling prophecy, proof that the regime would not paint over such messages and that if a different person wrote a similar phrase on another wall the idea could spread, eventually coalescing in an organized movement.[67] Similarly, whenever the party found opposition pamphlets, it worked quickly to stop their circulation and punish their distributors.[68] For comparable reasons, the Baʿth banned the families of people they killed from carrying out burial rites, mourning rituals, or from publicizing their relatives' deaths. They did this because they expected families to condemn their criminal members instead of grieving for them but also so that the public rituals would not create opportunities for public displays of dissatisfaction that might coalesce into larger protests.[69]

Foreign Enemies

The Baʿth perceived Iran as its number one foreign enemy and depicted Iranians as inherently hostile toward Arabs and Iraq. Hussein and the Baʿth used this reasoning to galvanize support for and legitimize their Iran–Iraq War effort. Despite their appeals to Iraqi Shiʿis during the war, they did this primarily by drawing a distinction between Iran's claim to fight on behalf of Islam and Muslims and Iraq's position as the "Eastern Flank of the Arab World," the front line of Arab defenses against the onrushing Persian hordes. This characterization of the enemy contributed to the Baʿth's false claim that Iran initiated their war. A 1986 set of directives sent from the Southern Bureau to its branches directed the branches to carry out a mobilization and propaganda campaign in which they would explain to the public "the history of Iran and its malice (*ḥiqd*) toward the Arabs since ancient times." The people should not worry, however, since "the forces of evil and *shuʿūbiyya* (a historical term used to refer to Iranians who supposedly hated Arabs) could not achieve anything against our people in the past."[70]

The regime's depiction of Iranians as heretics and anti-Arab bigots provided cover to deport thousands of Iraqis "of Iranian origin" in the 1980s. The secondary literature has portrayed these deportations (*tasfīr*) as anti-Shiʿi acts whereby the Baʿth herded tens, if not hundreds of thousands, of southern Shiʿis over the border to Iran, en masse.[71] Evidence outside the Baʿth's internal documents suggests that Sunni regime officials harbored anti-Shiʿi feelings, and sectarianism may have been a motivation.[72] That is not the picture that the BRCC paints, however. In line with Hussein and the Baʿth's official nonsectarianism, none of the BRCC records about the deportation of "Iranians" contains the word "Shiʿi." The documents do not suggest, moreover, that the regime intended to randomly load Shiʿis onto trucks and dump them over the border. Whatever the character of their execution, the deportations were documented and planned and conformed to the general picture of how the Baʿth treated their enemies versus their supporters. This included deporting families for the acts of their individual members.

The documents show that the Baʿth Party and security services drew up lists of "Iranians" they recommended for deportation *and* lists of those they did *not* want to expel. People or families on the deportation lists had negative marks registered against them, much like the students not allowed into military or teaching academies. Hence, the Baʿth deported Iraqis that they deemed "disloyal" (*ghayr muwālī*), people who maintained "negative stances" (*mawāqif salbiyya*) toward the party, and "Iranians" who evinced support for "the racist Persian enemy" (*al-ʿadū al-fārisī al-ʿunṣurī*). The

Baʿth put a woman on their deportation list in 1982, for example, for reportedly saying during a blood drive that she would prefer "to donate poison to the Iraqi army." The regime deported criminals and deserters too, along with their families. In contrast, the Baʿth labeled individuals and families on the nondeportation lists as "loyal" (*muwālī*), often with notes stating that the loyalists had not committed any crimes, shown hatred toward the party, or evinced support for Iran. "Loyalists" also frequently had relatives who were martyrs or had volunteered for the army.[73]

An Iraqi's "Iranian origin" therefore did not automatically require their deportation if they had a record of faithful service. It is possible that being "of Iranian origin" made an Iraqi guilty until proven innocent in the Baʿth's eyes, and it is unlikely that many (if any) Sunnis had "of Iranian origin" attached to their names. It is also possible that "of Iranian origin" was a euphemism for "Shiʿi." Yet the organized character of the deportations, the reasons the Baʿth recorded for them, and the justifications *not* to deport somebody suggest that the loyalty of a person "of Iranian origin" was the Baʿth's primary concern, not his or her sectarian status. The assertion that Hussein's rank-and-file Shiʿi soldiers did not defect to Iran during the war because of their Iraqi patriotism and Arab solidarity is thus only partially correct.[74] The larger reason was because the Baʿth would have deported or otherwise punished them and their families if they did not fight for the regime.

The Baʿth tied Iran to their other foreign enemies in a vast conspiracy designed to produce a sense of solidarity between Iraqis in the face of external threats. Official regime statements linked Iran to America, Israel, the Kurds, Syria, and Iraqi resistance groups, sometimes all at the same time.[75] All of these countries and movements colluded, according to the Baʿth. Like all good propaganda, these claims contained kernels of truth and played off of popular prejudices.[76] Iran and Syria—themselves allies against Iraq—supported the opposition groups at varying levels, and a degree of racism against non-Arabs that preceded the Baʿth existed in Iraqi society. Exposed in 1986, the Iran-Contra affair gave credence to the American-Zionist-Iranian connection. Given Israel's bombing of Iraq's Osiraq nuclear reactor in 1982, and its conflicts with the Palestinians and its Arab neighbors, Hussein tapped into anti-Israel and anti-Semitic feelings within the population.

Nevertheless, the degree of paranoia depicted in the BRCC is not warranted based upon the often tenuous connections between these groups and the limited abilities of foreign countries to conduct operations inside Iraq. It is unlikely, for example, that "external entities" (*jihāt khārijiyya*)

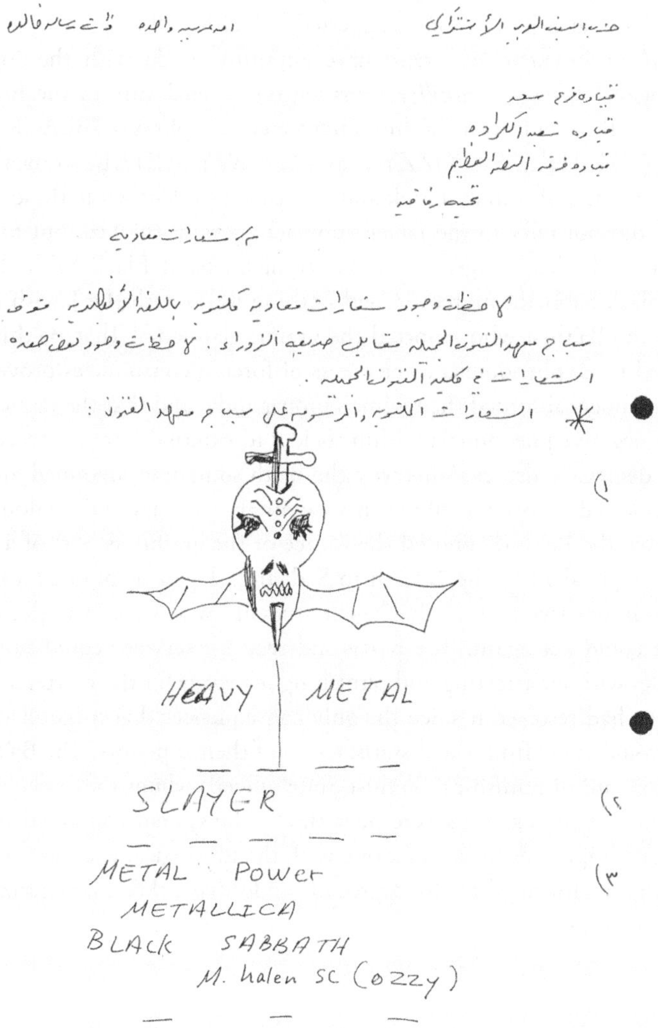
حزب البعث العربي الاشتراكي
أمة عربية واحدة ذات رسالة خالدة

قيادة فرع سعد
قيادة شعبة الكرادة
قيادة فرقة النضر العظام
تحية رفاقية

م/ شعارات معادية

لاحظنا وجود شعارات معادية مكتوبة باللغة الإنكليزية فوق سياج معهد الفنون الجميلة مقابل حديقة الزوراء. لاحظنا وجود نفس هذه الشعارات في كلية الفنون الجميلة.

* الشعارات المكتوبة والمرسومة على سياج معهد الفنون:

١)

٢) SLAYER

٣) METAL Power
METALLICA
BLACK SABBATH
M. halen SC (ozzy)

FIGURE 8.1. ***A Baʿthist Report about "Opposition" Slogans.*** The raw report appears as an attachment to a letter sent by the Official for the Baghdad Bureaus to the Office of the Party Secretariat. In the letter, the official claims that the Baʿthist who filed the initial report concluded that "the slogans originate from worldwide Zionism." Source: BRCC, 104-4-1: 112, 114. Courtesy of Hoover Institution Library & Archives, Stanford University.

were behind the profusion of narcotic pills in the Abi Ghrayb area of Baghdad in 2001, as a party report suggested.[77] Neither did "worldwide Zionism" (*al-ṣihyūniyya al-ʿālamiyya*) have anything to do with the "opposition slogans" (*shiʿārāt muʿādiyya*) written on an enclosure in the fine arts college in Baghdad, as a Baʿthist interpreted the phrases "BLACK SABBATH," "M. Halen SC (OZZY)," and "HEAVY METAL" to mean (figure 8.1). In fact, of course, a rock-and-roll loving student wrote these words. "Ozzy" did not refer to the Israeli submachine gun, the Uzi, but to Ozzy Osbourne, the lead singer in the heavy metal band Black Sabbath. The name Black Sabbath, moreover, had nothing to do with the Jewish day of rest, as the Baʿthist who reported the graffiti claimed.[78] That Baʿthists interpreted these phenomena as elements of foreign conspiracies proves that party members absorbed the regime's propaganda, and that the tactic of ascribing negative phenomena within society to external forces succeeded to a large degree. It also explains why the Baʿth sometimes detained and tortured or killed innocent civilians in a seemingly arbitrary and random fashion. Once the Baʿth diagnosed the source of the graffiti as part of a Zionist plot, equivalent to the "Death to Saddam" slogan mentioned above, it became imperative to find the "agent student" who wrote the slogan before he could act again. The party and security services could not close their files without arresting and punishing *somebody* for the matter as proof that they had resolved it since the only consequences that might accrue to them would come from the dissatisfaction of their superiors. The Baʿth had a track record of punishing Baʿthist State officials whom they believed did not mete out sufficiently severe penalties.[79] The system contained institutionalized impetuses for terror along with the ideological excuses for them, a fact that contributed to the degree of randomness that characterized life in Baʿthist Iraq.

"Crimes that Violate Honor"

In addition to obviously political offenses, the Baʿth justified the use of terror against Iraqis who committed "crimes that violate honor" (*jarāʾim mukhilla bi-l-sharf*), a legal category of misdeeds distinct from regular infractions. These included deserting or dodging military service (*al-hurūb wa-l-takhalluf*), leaving the country without permission, traveling without returning to Iraq in one's allotted time, quitting a government post without permission, stealing state property or resources, embezzlement of government funds, forgery, and giving or accepting bribes.[80] The Baʿth viewed all of these offenses as internal sabotage that impaired their ability to carry out their moral and political mission; they were crimes against the state.

Using this kind of reasoning, the Party Secretariat explained to its branch commands in 1993 that a rise in prostitution during the UN embargo resulted not just because of economic hardship but also because of foreign conspiracies. Catching the prostitutes thus constituted a national as well as a moral obligation. Similarly, because desertion decreased the military's manpower and evinced disloyalty to the country, the Party Secretariat described it as a negative phenomenon "nationally, morally, and legally" (*waṭaniyyan wa ʾakhlāqiyyan wa qānūniyyan*).[81] The regime likewise prescribed execution for the aforementioned extortionist taxi drivers during the Gulf War because the drivers were "traitor[s] to the nation and agent[s] for the foreigner."[82] "Crimes that violate honor" made the regime look weak, as if it could not police or provide for its employees or citizens and did not elicit their respect or allegiance. Just as with homosexual activity or rape in Iraqi society, both of which are crimes, the criminal does not necessarily violate his own honor. Instead, because he is seen as a powerful actor, he infringes upon the dignity of the weaker victim. The honor violated in cases of "crimes that violate honor" was the regime's and, by extension, Hussein and the country's. This logic gave the regime a reason—and imposed on it an obligation—to avenge itself against those who brought shame upon any element of the Baʿthist Trinity.[83]

The regime transferred this same logic to its citizens. In 1984, a long-time full Baʿth Party member turned in his nephews for joining the Daʿwa Party. The report detailing the affair claimed that the man said his nephews' treason made him feel like "his party loyalty (*ḥizbiyyatahu*) was lacking, and that the subject of his nephews brought shame (*ʿār*) upon him." Showing how Hussein expected Iraqis to subordinate their loyalties to the party, when he heard about the incident Hussein remarked, "I hope that his party loyalty is stronger than his familial allegiance (*ʾamal ʾan takūn ḥizbiyyatahu ʾaqwā min qarābatihi*)."[84] The word this account used for shame, *ʿār*, is the same as that employed by the letter from Ali Hassan al-Majid to Hussein described in chapter 7, about a man that Hussein pardoned after killing his wife for committing adultery. In an almost identical incident, al-Majid sent another letter to Hussein, also in 1982, in which al-Majid described a husband who returned from the Iran–Iraq warfront to find his wife having an affair. Feeling disrespected, the husband and his wife's father killed her, "washing the stain" (*ghaslan li-l-ʿār*) from their reputations. The husband then turned himself in and admitted the crime. "[The husband] mentions in his report," al-Majid wrote to Hussein, "that he became, in the end, imprisoned for no sin except the defense of his honor, which was defamed from behind while he was fighting in the battle of honor and nobility, defending the freedoms of Iraq." Clearly agreeing with this sentiment, al-Majid suggested to Hussein that the man be "included in your kindness for his bravery, for daring to sever the corrupt element of society. Releasing him will be a disciplinary lesson for everyone who lets himself be seduced—tackling his wife's perfidy is defending the honor and soil of this dear nation." "Yes," Hussein replied. "He is pardoned. Release him."[85] One of the keys to Hussein's system of control lay in his ability to refashion the rules of honor in Iraqi society so that the extent of an individual's personal and familial dignity tied into the level of loyalty that he demonstrated to the Baʿthist Trinity. A treasonous nephew equated to a wife's perfidy and an individual's disobedience; all were, essentially, "crimes that violate honor."

As the existence of a legal category of "crimes that violate honor" indicates, Hussein's regime employed the cover of legality to validate its terror, enshrining the difference between its enemies and supporters in law. A reference to a law in the form of an RCC decision, regulation, or internal directive accompanies almost every document about the regime's use of violence in the BRCC, and the Baʿth frequently put "criminals" through the motions of a legal process by parading them before the "Court of the Revolution" (*maḥkamat al-thawra*).[86] By the Baʿth's reasoning, their ends didn't merely justify their violent means; their means *were* justified because they used violence in order to enforce legislation enacted on behalf of the people. The Baʿth's laws sanctioned terror against the nation's "enemies," and thus the Baʿth could rationalize sending people whom they considered criminals "to receive their just punishments" (*li-yanālū jazāʾihim al-ʿādil*), as the BRCC's authors refer to the executions and prison sentences that the regime handed out.[87] Notice that in all of the cases presented in this study where family members killed their kin, or husbands killed their wives, the regime first arrested the killers before pardoning them. That was because killing or murder in and of itself was not permitted in Hussein's Iraq but killing or murder *for the right political purposes* was. The criminal justice system apprehended the killers, but in the process of adjudicating their cases either Hussein or Baʿthist judges acquitted them because political considerations sat above the law.

9. ENTICEMENT

INTRODUCTION

In *The Weight of a Mustard Seed*, Wendell Steavenson tells the story of Dr. Hassan al-Qadhani, a psychiatrist who joined the Iraqi military and, consequently, the Baʿth Party, in order to finance his medical studies. "By 1983," Steavenson writes,

> Dr. Hassan was a major in the army medical corps with a successful private practice. He dressed well and liked Italian shoes, he bought a new car every year and rented a house where he and his friends could gather for parties, a place to bring their girlfriends and drink and relax. He was comfortable, confident, proud of himself, he had rank and respect and money.[1]

Soon, however, Military Intelligence arrested Dr. Hassan on suspicion of his involvement with the Daʿwa Party. As part of his interrogation, he was beaten and forced to sign a statement admitting his relationship to two friends arrested for the same charge. Despite his proclaimed innocence, he spent months in prison before being released and allowed to resume his now more cautious, withdrawn life.[2]

As al-Qadhani's case shows, Iraqis joined the Baʿth Party or otherwise cast their lot with Hussein's regime for a variety of reasons, not least because the regime controlled access to academic, professional, economic, and social opportunity. A person who did the Baʿth's bidding and abided by their rules could lead a prosperous, good life. Yet there was always "the sense that whatever one has is a gift from the regime";[3] the Baʿth gave but they could also take away.[4] The BRCC documents demonstrate that Hussein used his ability to empower and emasculate, enrich and impoverish, as tools to entice Iraqis to support him, tying them to his regime in a web of complicity. Iraqis outside the political and socioeconomic elite had similar reasons to back Hussein. The stranglehold that he kept over both the public- and private-sector economies in addition to the state's social welfare net meant that many Iraqis depended on state programs and largesse to work, house, and feed their families.[5]

The relationship between Hussein and his citizens did not operate in only one direction, however. Hussein depended on Iraqis to sustain his regime. The Iran–Iraq and Gulf War years, and the time that Iraq spent under UN sanctions in the 1990s, caused many deaths and casualties, devastated Iraq's infrastructure, and destroyed the middle class built up during the 1970s, when oil revenues were plentiful. All of these factors created considerable resentment among the populace. Terror—a negative incentive—could not by itself secure Hussein's authority. Hussein needed to show that Iraqis who backed him in trying times would continue to thrive and that he would take care of people and their families who sacrificed in his name. Hussein needed positive incentives—or enticements—to complement terror.

In order to both manipulate and placate the population, therefore, Hussein tied the receipt of government benefits to service to the country, which he recognized by conferring awards, special statuses, and other official honors on their recipients. Obtaining and keeping these prizes became a key to survival and, if one was lucky, prosperity. In contrast, stepping over the Baʿth's red lines led to loss of benefits for both. As the BRCC documents illustrate, this twin mechanism of carrot and stick for individuals, combined with tying the consequences of personal action to communal welfare, constituted a key aspect of Baʿthification.

REWARDS AND BENEFITS

In Hussein's Iraq, citizens who received official recognition for their or their family members' efforts and sacrifices on behalf of the Baʿthist State could expect to lead a decent life. At the least, winning as many awards, honors, and statuses as possible, including party membership, afforded Iraqis a social safety net. At best, rewards opened the door to economic security and prosperity, housing assistance, superior medical care, luxury goods, professional and educational opportunity, the possibility for travel, privileged access to top regime officials, and leisure for themselves and their families. Put simply, the longer an Iraqi's record of loyal service, the better he and his family lived. In contrast, citizens with no special awards at all could find it difficult to make ends meet.[6]

The rewards and benefits doled out by the Baʿthist State served as a nationwide system of patronage from the top of Hussein's regime to the bottom. At the highest levels, Hussein used his system of awards and benefits as a cover for funneling largesse to his political inner circle and the top military brass, many of whom were his relatives. Instead of showing obvious favoritism, which might—and in the 1990s did—provoke popular discontent, Hussein simply gave them medals. In this spirit, Hussein created The Order of the Command (*shārat al-qiyāda*) in 1986, which he gave to Revolutionary Command Council and RC members.[7] On a wider scale, salary raises of up to 300 percent that Hussein distributed to Iraqis with at least two awards or honors in 1994 allowed him to keep loyal and longtime supporters on a firm financial footing during tough economic times when most Iraqis struggled to afford daily necessities.[8] Having categories of people with the same awards or combinations thereof made handing out patronage more efficient. Hussein could raise salaries or increase benefits for all the holders of a particular honor at once. Outside of the elite, even if an Iraqi hated the Baʿth, the receipt of a medal gave him or her a stake in perpetuating the system in order to hold onto its concomitant benefits.

One of the most common sources of benefits in Baʿthist Iraq came from having a family member officially declared a "martyr" (*shahīd*) and included in the pension rolls if the family member died during military, party, or other service to the regime. The Baʿthist State provided a certificate to the martyr's family as proof of his designation. In 1998, the official in charge of the Basra and Dhi Qar bureaus of the party asked Hussein's deputy to issue proclamations declaring a number of Baʿthist soldiers killed while pursuing "agents and traitors" as martyrs. "We are attaching two lists that include the names of the martyrs," the official wrote. "Please look at them and issue the individual decrees for their martyrdom so that the pension rights can be dispensed to their families in order to lighten the material burdens that they suffer from due to the unjust embargo imposed on our exalted Iraq."[9] As this quotation indicates, having a family member declared a martyr could make a big difference in a family's income, particularly during the terrible economic conditions of the 1990s. A woman in 1999 petitioned Hussein to name her husband a martyr, claiming that he was killed on a party mission looking for deserters in 1984. She never received his martyr's pension, however, and she wrote that, due to the high rate of inflation, the retirement fund she had as a teacher paid only for a portion of the school supplies for one of her three children, let alone the basic necessities of life.[10] The BRCC does not contain the answer that she received, but it does include many petitions like this from citizens asking that their relatives be added to the official rolls of martyrs in order to collect the benefits owed to martyrs' families.

For those who survived their patriotic duties, a plethora of medals, badges, honors, and other awards awaited. It is probably not a coincidence that in 1982—the same year the Iran–Iraq War turned against Iraq—the regime revamped the law dealing with four of the most common and prestigious state honors: the *Rāfidayn*, Revolution, and Saddam's *Qādisiyya* medals, as well as the Badge of Honor (*nawṭ al-shujāʿa*). The "Medal and Badge Law" (*qānūn al-ʾawsima wa-l-ʿanwāṭ*) from that year invalidated all previous regulations concerning these awards and stipulated that they be dispensed by Republican Decree (*marsūm jumhūrī*). Recipients wore the medals during holidays and other official occasions. When a recipient died, the person's eldest son carried it, and his wife and children continued to enjoy the related benefits.[11]

The *Rāfidayn* Medal (*wisām al-rāfidayn*) and Badge of Honor provide perfect examples of the types of financial, professional, academic, medical, and other benefits associated with the Baʿth regime's privileges. The regime awarded the *Rāfidayn* to people "who perform a general and venerable service to the Iraqi republic, or to the units of the armed forces that carry out honorable operations during active maneuvers, or war, and similarly to foreigners in appreciation of their stature."[12] The medal came in military and civilian versions and had five degrees depending, in the former case, on an officer or soldier's rank. A medal of the first degree carried a free 10,000 ID life insurance policy, the value of which the President's Office could raise. The recipient's children gained entrance into military and civilian universities, colleges, and institutes. The recipient, his spouse, and his children also received free perks, including medical treatment at home and abroad if, in the latter case, a health committee approved the need for travel; five dunams of agricultural land; membership in all state clubs; invitations to national celebrations; priority on the list for state housing if the recipient did not already own a residence; and, once per year, first-class tickets for the recipient, his wife, and his children on Iraqi Airways. Recipients of lower degrees received the same benefits but with reduced award amounts. In 2001, the government automatically awarded *Rāfidayn* medals to families with three or more martyrs in the Iran–Iraq and Gulf wars.[13] The Revolution and Saddam's *Qādisiyya* medals received benefits according to the same schedule as the *Rāfidayn*, with slight variations.[14] The regime awarded the Badge of Honor to "military personnel and civilians who show extraordinary bravery or carry out a heroic, honorable action, or who take pains to perform their obligation and service to the army and the nation during war, active maneuvers, or military clashes." Badge of Honor recipients received preference in their appointment to government positions, at least a 5,000 ID life insurance policy, and a free car exempt from customs duties.[15]

Multiple honors brought even more benefits than the sum total of one's individual awards. A 1994 RCC decision increased the salaries of the holders of one kind of award if they received a second.[16] Similarly, the Baʿth designated Iraqis who won two Badges of Honor and an Order of the Party (*shārat al-ḥizb*), or two Orders of the Mother of All Battles (*shārat ʾumm al-maʿārik*), as "Friends of Mr. President Leader, Saddam Hussein (God keep him)" (*ʾaṣdiqāʾ al-sayyid al-raʾīs al-qāʾid ṣaddām ḥusayn, ḥafẓuhu allāh*).[17] The BRCC contains photocopies of identification cards given to the "Friends of the President" by the Ministry of Interior. On the back, a card found in a boxfile from 1999 lists their benefits as:

1. The addition of five points onto the final grade point averages of the Friend, his wife, and his children for acceptance into schools, institutes, and universities during wartime and for five years subsequently.
2. The acceptance of the Friend's sons into military institutes and colleges regardless of the grade point average and age requirements during wartime and for five years subsequently.
3. The honor of meeting His Eminence (Hussein) at least one time per year.
4. The same reimbursement for holidays and official occasions that is granted to the members of the President's Office.
5. Having preference over the remainder of their fellow citizens with regard to meeting officials.
6. The right for himself and his family to personally communicate with the head of the President's Office, its secretary, the Director-General of the party, the Secretary of the Defense Ministry, and other important officials in order to request meetings with them, or for similar requests.
7. To receive two summer and two winter suits per year as a present from the President of the Republic.[18]

Friends of the President also received salary increases in addition to preferential political access.[19] In 1998, an RCC decision gave people handicapped or severely wounded in battle "Friends of the President" status along with the benefits that accrued to martyrs and a monthly salary of 10,000 ID for officers and 7,000 ID for enlisted men.[20] Toward the end of his reign, Hussein founded an even more exclusive club called the "Union of Saddamists" (*ʾiṭṭiḥād al-ṣaddāmiyīn*). A boxfile from 1999 contains an identity card handed out to the union's members. The card lists Hussein's oldest son, Uday, as the supervisor of the union and contains a symbol of an eagle on the back surrounded by the words "the nation," "God," and "Saddam."[21]

Aside from official honors that carried continuing benefits, Hussein's regime gave out one-time awards to Iraqis for specific acts of loyalty or in recognition of long records of exemplary service. The most common award of this nature was a commendation (*shukr wa taqdīr*), which the regime placed in a citizen's or Baʿthist's file, sometimes accompanied by a financial award.[22] The BRCC contains many letters from Baʿthists to party offices asking for confirmation of their commendations or their participation in a battle, the Popular Army, a mandatory drill session, one of the national occasions, or even the "Saddam's Cubs" (*ʾashbāl ṣaddām*) youth group.[23] Iraqis frequently referenced their commendations and evidence of their participation in Baʿthist organizations and initiatives when they petitioned Hussein or another high-ranking official for a favor.

The Baʿth regime also doled out rewards for extraordinary acts of unsolicited allegiance. Out of the blue and on a regular basis, Hussein received oaths of allegiance written in their authors' blood. Iraqis, and especially Baʿthists, also sent unsolicited "studies" about Baʿthist doctrine or Hussein's sayings and writings. One such report arrived at the party's Office of Culture and Media written by hand with ink-drawn lines straightened with a ruler and borders colored in with crayons. Entitled, "The Leader, the Party, and the Revolution," Hussein's face adorned the cover. The office's director suggested to the Party Secretariat that it remunerate the author.[24]

A final way that an Iraqi might obtain benefits was by volunteering to participate in a government initiative. The Baʿth gave out incentives such as free housing to Arabs willing to move to the north in order to shift the ethnic balance away from the Kurds. After the end of the Iran–Iraq War, Hussein decided to rebuild the Faw Peninsula, which the conflict destroyed completely, as a sign of Iraqi strength and to raise the population's spirits. To entice volunteers, Hussein offered families willing to live there a free piece of land, a loan, and a one-time payment of varying amounts. To be eligible for these benefits, the Director of the Party Secretariat wrote to the Baʿth's bureaus, a family had to "be completely loyal (*maḥsūma al-wilāʾ*) to the party, the revolution, and its principles." No family with a member who ever participated in an opposition group, acted as a foreign agent, or deserted or dodged army service could move to Faw.[25]

Being a Baʿthist carried its own special status and opened the door to awards and benefits not available to the regular population. David Baran reports that a sectional member received $250 per month in 2002 while the secretary-general of a branch took home $750 and a luxury car.[26] Hussein made sure to take care of long-time Baʿthists and those injured in national service. The Order of the Party went to Baʿthists who spent twenty-five years "struggling" in the party ranks. It carried its own salary and access to perks such as favorable loans. The exact benefits associated with it changed over the years, but they always ranked among the best.[27]

Hussein also established the prestigious Organization of the Strugglers (*munaẓẓamat al-munāḍilīn*), a Baʿthist retirement association. To be eligible, a Baʿthist had to spend twenty-five years in the party, amass an exemplary record of allegiance, and have served as a member of a branch command or in a higher office. Nobody could enroll who worked for another faction of the party (for example, in Syria), left the Baʿth for more than four months, studied outside the country and failed to keep in touch with the Iraqi government, or had been convicted of a felony or misdemeanor before rejoining the party. Only the party's General-Secretary (Hussein) or the Regional Command (RC) could make exceptions to these rules in cases of "people who exhibited heroism and courage in the battle of Saddam's Glorious *Qādisiyya* and who showed exceptional qualities in service to the party and the revolution."[28] This last caveat allowed Hussein to include not only those who clearly qualified under the regulations but also Baʿthists such as army generals or top party officials whom he wanted to purge peacefully.

In 1984, the Baʿth set up the Organization of Senior Citizens and the Ill (*munaẓẓamat kibār al-sinn wa-l-marḍā*). The organization served members regardless of title or party rank who could no longer work because they had reached retirement age, acquired a debilitating disease, or been wounded. Members of the organization received a free piece of land to live on, if they could not afford one themselves. Former government employees in the organization continued to enjoy salary promotions up to the maximum allowable for their position, and private-sector workers received a salary of 120–150 ID per month.[29]

Baʿthists and their children enjoyed professional and academic advantages above and beyond the rest of the population, especially if they carried honors. In addition to the perks listed above for the "Friends of the President," holding an Order of the Party, participating in the Popular Army or the Iran–Iraq and Gulf wars, having a father or brother martyred or wounded in battle, turning in a member of an opposition party or an army deserter, or volunteering for the Saddam's Fedayeen militia all officially gave Baʿthists preference over party members without these distinctions, and over independents.[30] Exceptionally, independents with these types of honors could receive preference too, especially in the Kurdish territories where Baʿthification proved less successful.[31] In a speech in 1979, Hussein mandated that all children of RCC members could attend any college or institute they liked regardless of the general criteria for acceptance. Meanwhile, the Baʿth added ten points to the averages of the children of RC members and members employed in the Party Secretariat's office and branch administrations "for purposes of acceptance and competition with their peers in the institutes, colleges, and schools of higher education." The Baʿth reduced this to five points in 1997, probably due to the public perception—correct, as it turned out—that high-ranking officials benefited from perks while the population floundered under terrible economic conditions.[32]

Baʿthists also benefited from free housing. Members employed full-time by the party often lived in Baʿthist-owned apartments, especially those serving away from their hometowns and in remote areas. Less fortunate members received free land on which they could build a house. In 1985, Hussein ordered that plots of party- or state-owned land should be given to Baʿthists who did not own a home or their own land, had put in at least twenty-five years of service (and were thus eligible for an Order of the Party), or were at least sectional command members. The First Deputy Prime Minister at the time, Taha Yasin Ramadan, suggested that the Baʿthist State should also give them a favorable loan since many of the people included in these categories had limited means with which to build a house.[33]

Since the perks associated with the Baʿthist State's awards touched on so many aspects of life critical to an honoree and his family's welfare, they facilitated an Iraqi's decision to serve the regime. As a soldier or officer involved in one of the Baʿth's bloody wars, a life insurance policy for his family was no small thing. Not only did a medal help an Iraqi's children get into good schools, which could lead to a desirable job, but without an award his children would compete at a disadvantage against other students whose fathers (or, rarer, mothers) had one.[34] The BRCC contains numerous requests from citizens who petitioned Hussein or other high party and state officials for permission to travel abroad for medical treatment in which the petitioners mention their awards and statuses in order to convince the officials to allow them to go and, possibly, for the Baʿthist State to pay for the treatment. Hussein granted many of these requests. The tacit agreement between the Husseini Baʿthist regime and its citizens stated that in exchange for the latter's loyalty, the former would see to its citizens' welfare. This agreement was fundamental to Hussein's retention of power and is a critical reason for why he survived for so long. Evidence for this comes not only in the sheer number of awards dispensed—173,823 just by the military during the Iran–Iraq War[35]—but also in the veiled outrage of petitioners who wrote to Hussein when they did not receive the benefits to which they felt entitled.[36]

THE WITHDRAWAL OF PRIVILEGES

Just as expressions of loyalty and service elicited official rewards and opportunities for Iraqis and their families, a series of public laws and internal Baʿth Party regulations found in the BRCC detail a developed legal and regulatory regime for removing awards and honors from political criminals. The BRCC records also show how a person's crime affected the benefits that his or her relatives enjoyed. The 1982 Medal and Badge Law, for example, stipulated that the *Rāfidayn* and Revolution medals should be taken away in the event of "deviation from the principles of the July 17–30 revolution."[37] Likewise, an internal Baʿth Party directive from 1984 stated that "In the case of the expulsion of a member from the party for reasons related to the security of the nation and the party, economic sabotage, or an absence of loyalty (*ʿadam al-wilāʾ*), all of the benefits that he has obtained are withdrawn." This contrasted with an expulsion from the party simply for disciplinary reasons, in which case the member could retain his or her benefits.[38] As in so many other areas of Baʿthist Iraq, the regime's conception of an Iraqi's political loyalty governed the process of dispensing and withdrawing privileges above all other considerations.

The 1984 directive quoted above provides insight into the types of infractions for which the Baʿth withdrew an award winner's advantages. Almost any crime in Hussein's Iraq could be interpreted as affecting "national security" or exhibiting "an absence of loyalty," including "crimes that violate honor." Activity in an opposition group, conspiring against the state and the party (*al-taʾammur*), or exhibiting "weakness" in one's Baʿthist duties all qualified as offenses under the 1984 guidelines. In 1996, a Baʿthist in the Kurdish territories had the gall to write "no" on his ballot card for the plebiscite on Hussein. For his "disgraceful stance" and "behavior that contradicts the principles of our great party and its eternal message," the party expelled him and took away all three of his Badges of Honor.[39] It is unclear whether or not the man in question lived in an area controlled by the Baʿthist State at this time, since central government authority no longer held sway over much of the Kurdish territories. Nevertheless, if he did, or if Hussein's forces ever reclaimed the area, his act of civil disobedience would have cost him and his family dearly, given that possessing three Badges of Honor would have entitled him to "Friends of the President" status.

Of course, political criminals had more to worry about than losing their benefits. Unless an individual had connections in the regime or received a pardon in one of Hussein's general amnesties, he would probably also lose his life or his freedom, be tortured, or be otherwise physically punished.[40] The calculus for political criminals was relatively straightforward. Unless the regime thought it could rehabilitate or use the criminal in some way, it eliminated, imprisoned, or otherwise neutralized him.

As a result, the largest impact of withdrawn benefits fell onto a criminal's relatives. On the one hand, the calculus for families was simple too. The benefits for most of the medals, badges, and statuses mentioned above either provided income to the winner's household or included advantages designated for his wife and children. If a person had a medal withdrawn, his family members also lost their perks. To illustrate, internal Baʿth Party regulations from 1979 stipulated that anybody who spied against the country participated in a political opposition movement, or sabotaged the party in some fashion could either not join the Baʿth Party or was to be expelled for a probationary period. This meant they lost the benefits and advantages associated with party membership and could have their state employment adversely affected too.[41] The criminals could not be accepted into any of the military colleges, security and intelligence academies, or other institutes reserved for party members and exceptionally loyal independents. They could not study abroad. And they could not work in the Media and Cultural Foundation, as pilots, or in the offices of the Party Secretariat, the RCC Secretariat, the Presidency of the Republic, or the Prime Minister. Women could also not work as fashion models outside of the country. These rules applied automatically to the wife of the criminal and any of his brothers and sisters, children, or fraternal nephews. If the regime executed the criminal, the criminal's grandchildren, sororal nephews, and uncles could also fall under the regulations if the execution had an emotional "effect" or "influence" (*taʾthīr*) on them as determined by a party assessment.[42] In other words, if the family member showed sorrow or resentment toward the regime because of the execution, the Baʿth treated the relative with more suspicion, and vice-versa.

On the other hand, as this last stipulation indicates, the calculus for families could be more complicated. As the years went on, the Baʿth made the rules for family members of criminals more lenient and subjective. In addition to the "effect" of a criminal's punishment on his family member, rules issued subsequent to those from 1979 also took more account of the degree of relation between a criminal and his family member, the individual family member's record of service to the regime, and the record of the family as a whole. If the criminal was an exception to the family's generally strong record of allegiance, the Baʿth might not impose a severe penalty or, in some cases, any penalty at all. Compared to the 1979 regulations, rules from 1994 about the relatives of political criminals focus more on a relative's record of loyalty instead of his family member's crimes. The 1994 regulations state that

> It should be taken into consideration in an evaluation [of a family of a criminal] whether or not the family has produced a martyr or their sons

> have risked their lives (*ʾistabsala*) and have been honored, regardless of the type [of honor], even if one of the family's sons showed a treasonous or oppositionist stance. I.e., employ the case of martyrdom and heroism and ignore the case of treachery and criminality.
>
> Similarly, in the case of a tribe, do not measure the tribe by the number of criminals or the cases of treason and opposition in it, but rather measure it by the number of martyrs, heroes, and honorees, lest enemies exploit that for their own interests.[43]

The Baʿth moderated their punishments for family members of criminals over the years perhaps because the type of blanket rules from 1979 denied too many qualified people the opportunity to work in Baʿthist State jobs for crimes that their relatives committed.

Relatives of political criminals could mitigate the severity of their punishments, or reverse them altogether, under at least one of two conditions: by turning a family member in and supporting their relative's punishment, or by highlighting their own records of loyal service.[44] Usually, the BRCC shows that relatives did both by loudly proclaiming their allegiance and conspicuously rushing to perform an act of fealty. In an effort to escape suspicion, for example, the nephew of a minister purged during Hussein's assumption of the presidency in 1979 sent a letter to the Baʿth extolling the party, promising to die for its principles, and denouncing his uncle as a "criminal." A party report attached to the letter described the nephew as previously close to the minister and greatly affected by his execution. The nephew nevertheless decided not to attend his uncle's wake or burial so as to prove his Baʿthist mettle.[45]

In less high-profile cases, the families of criminals often pretended that their deviant members did not exist in order to forestall collective punishment, prove their loyalty, save face, and retain their honors and benefits. When a Baʿthist discovered in 1981 that his son had been arrested for joining the Daʿwa Party, he quickly volunteered for the Popular Army, as told in a memorandum passed to members of the RC:

> Enclosed is the report of the fighter [name withheld], commander of a company in the section of al-Tuz . . . who urgently requests to participate in the battlefront, keeping in mind that his youngest son has a relationship with the agent (*ʿamīl*) Daʿwa party and is presently interned in the security directorate of Salah al-Din province.
>
> Please bring this subject to the attention of the comrade Secretary of the Country (Hussein), with the knowledge that we support accepting the volunteering of his father and not taking any party measures against the father in light of his volunteering and behavior.[46]

A letter from the father accompanied the memorandum in which he went on at length about what an honor it was to serve in the war effort without ever mentioning his son.[47] In another instance, when two male members of a non-Baʿthist family fled to Romania before the Iran–Iraq War, the government designated them as deserters from the army. Subsequently, when the young daughter of one of the men inquired about her father, her mother shushed her and told any nonrelatives that her daughter was psychotic and did not understand what she was saying.[48] Terror and enticement truly did "cleanse" the country of the regime's enemies when it eliminated "criminals" and induced Iraqis to pretend that their relatives did not exist.

CONCLUSION

A Total Strategy

In *Ordinary Men,* Christopher Browning attempted to explain why around five hundred German men in the Nazis' Reserve Police Battalion 101 killed some 38,000 Jews and deported 45,000 more to death camps while serving in Poland in the summer of 1942.[1] Browning explores a number of theories: "wartime brutalization, racism, segmentation and routinization of the task, special selection of the perpetrators, careerism, obedience to orders, deference to authority, ideological indoctrination, and conformity."[2] All of these factors contributed in varying degrees, Browning argues, "but none without qualification."[3] Each man in the battalion responded differently to the general conditions of the time depending on his personal psychology, emotional makeup, and background. "The behavior of any human being is, of course, a very complex phenomenon, and the historian who attempts to 'explain' it is indulging in a certain arrogance," Browning concluded. "When nearly 500 men are involved, to undertake any general explanation of their collective behavior is even more hazardous."[4]

It would be similarly arrogant and hazardous to proffer one explanation for why Iraqis individually and collectively supported—or, in lesser numbers, opposed—the Husseini Baʿthist State. Each person and group of people undoubtedly acted according to a different confluence of motivations, incentives, aspirations, fears, beliefs, pressures, circumstances, and communal dynamics. The genius, efficacy, and tragedy of Baʿthification lay in Saddam Hussein's total strategy of rule. Hussein and the Baʿth did not succeed in controlling every detail of each Iraqi's life, but as part of their aspiration to cement their authority and apply their utopian principles, Baʿthification targeted Iraqis at all levels of their individual and communal existence.[5] Regardless of the particular impetuses that drove each Iraqi to act, think, and believe, Baʿthification worked from all angles to coerce and elicit his, and his community's, loyalty. The Baʿth's controls affected who an Iraqi could marry; when, how, and where he traveled; where he could live; what he watched on television and in the theater; the artwork he viewed; the books he read; the poetry and music he listened to; the civil and professional organizations he joined; the schools he attended; the jobs he obtained; and the conversations he had in his home. The Baʿth tried to turn an Iraqi's religious faith into Baʿthist faith. They placed a regime loyalist at the head of his tribe. In all walks of life, the Baʿth subjected Iraqis to a constant stream of propaganda, forcing their citizens to repeat Baʿthist catchphrases on grammar school tests, at mass ceremonies, during public rallies, and in countless other everyday rituals. Baʿth Party and PMO officials, security service personnel, and *mukhtārīn* patrolled every town and neighborhood. The Baʿth placed spies and cultivated informants in the military, each business and bureaucracy, all of Iraq's tribes, and all of its religious establishments. The Baʿth used the intelligence they collected as a basis for accepting applicants into the military academies and teachers' colleges, for recruitment into the party and PMOs, for deportation, for naming sheikhs and imams, for staffing the top posts and most sensitive positions in the Baʿthist State, for targeting terror, and for awarding honors and benefits. The many forms that Iraqis had to fill out, the bureaucratic rules they had to follow, and the laws they had to obey were all based upon Hussein's decrees and the political considerations of his regime.

Hussein and the Baʿth designed their system of control to lead Iraqis down the path of obedience, and Baʿthification provided a moral, legal, and normative excuse for Iraqis to comply. Although Iraqis could make suggestions, critique government policy, and protest the decisions of their superiors, the petitions they sent to Hussein show that they could only do so after praising him, the revolution, and the country. In order to assert their rights, they first had to affirm the system. To become the sheikh of a tribe or clan, an Iraqi had to join the party, participate in the Baʿth's wars, and police his tribesmen. At the crucial moment, he had to demonstrate that his primary allegiance lay with the regime instead of his tribe. Most Iraqis did not engage in terror, but in order for them to maintain the regime's perception of their support, they had to back the Baʿth's use of violence, surveillance, and torture—or at least pretend that Baʿthist terror did not exist. During times of war or sanctions, which encompassed all but two years of Hussein's presidency, many Iraqis depended on the state for their welfare. To provide for their families, and to ensure their individual and collective futures, much of the population accepted the Baʿth's bribes. Hussein and the Baʿth hoped that the longer their system stood in place, and the more vigorously they asserted its legitimacy, the more ingrained it would become as the behaviors they forced Iraqis to take on became the normal state of affairs.[6] In this way, the Baʿth Party's original assertions of authority and legitimacy would find their ways into the Iraqi consciousness, in the process manifesting and justifying themselves in expressions of popular support. If, as Browning stated about Reserve Police Battalion 101, "killing was something one could get used to," so too was living in a Baʿthized society.[7]

Did Baʿthification work? There is no one answer. When faced with the combined pressures of Baʿthification's ideology, organization, terror, and enticement some Iraqis fled the country. Others joined opposition groups. The BRCC suggests that a critical mass, however, succumbed at some level to the boundaries placed on their thoughts and behaviors. At times and in places where the Baʿth succeeded in applying their four sets of controls, Iraqis tended to act as the regime desired.[8] This was not necessarily because the Baʿth converted Iraqis into believers but because Iraqis learned what the regime wanted them to say and do in specific situations. Regardless of whether or not Iraqis truly believed or agreed with Husseini Baʿthist values, the Baʿth's system of controls forced Iraqis to act according to the regime's wishes because the Baʿth injected political meaning into each action and thought in every sphere of life: public, civil, and private. A citizen's record of allegiance determined whether or not he and his family prospered, survived, or perished. The Baʿthist system treated every action—even normally private choices of whom to marry or how to mourn a loved one—as a test of an individual's loyalty. It then made the consequences for obedience or opposition so rewarding or severe, respectively, that it offered Iraqis little choice but to follow its rules. As a result, to succeed within the system a person had to constantly prove his allegiance by continuously proclaiming his loyalty and actively demonstrating the truth behind his words.

In the introduction, I related the stories of Iraqis who killed or turned in their family members to be executed in order to prove their loyalty to the regime. Neither the Baʿth Party nor the security services forced these people to murder or inform on their kin. They took the initiative, justifying their actions according to the ethical logic of Husseini Baʿthism. Whether these people truly believed what they said, or not, their behavior indicated that their loyalty to the Baʿthist Trinity trumped all other bonds—even to their own relatives. As the psychologist Stanley Milgram concluded about his experiments that tested why people tend to obey authority, even when doing so contradicts their normal beliefs and values, "subjective feelings are largely irrelevant to the moral issue at hand so long as they are not transformed into action. Political control is affected through action."[9] By this definition, Baʿthification proved an effective strategy of political control by, in the words of a party report, "spreading the thought, values, and principles of the party in society and incorporating them into the daily behavior of the party's citizens."[10] Baʿthification inspired what anthropologist, Clifford Geertz, called a "cultural system": a weltanschauung, or worldview, that Iraqis had to adopt if they wanted to orient themselves in and navigate the Baʿthist world in which they lived.[11]

Besides the total scope of its controls, Baʿthification's success as a cultural system—or "political culture"—derived from its basis in the notions of personal and familial honor and loyalty endemic in Iraqi society. Hussein both venerated and manipulated Iraq's "traditional" tribal and religious values and practices for his benefit, tying the conceptions of honor related to a family or tribe's womenfolk to each element in the Baʿthist Trinity. By instituting a legal category of "crimes that violate honor" and claiming that "Iraq is the country of all, and protecting its security and sovereignty is everybody's responsibility," Hussein extended the foundational principle of social allegiance in Iraqi society—"me and my brother are against my cousin, and me and my cousin are against a stranger"—to himself, the Baʿth Party, and the entire country.[12] In attempting to explain why the Partisan from Suwayra mentioned at the beginning of this book killed his son for deserting from the army, a police report found no impetus other than "a moral and patriotic motive. [The partisan] declined to betray the nation and the great leader, which would have polluted his and his family's reputation, because he decided that the defense of Iraq and his own dignity is the responsibility of all Iraqis. What is more, not performing this honor is a disgrace in and of itself."[13] Testifying in front of an investigatory commission, the father of the Special Republican Guard deserter similarly explained that he had to kill his son to preserve his personal and familial honor.[14] When asked about the reasons for their actions, all of the people cited in the introduction who killed or turned in their family members framed the issue in the same way. Baʿthification mirrored the strategies of other totalitarian regimes, but its effectiveness stemmed in large part from its roots in Iraq's political and social culture and history.

Despite its political success, Baʿthification failed if judged by the ideological standards of Husseini Baʿthism. Baʿthification established Hussein and the Baʿth's hegemony, but it did not cement their legitimacy; it rarely appears to have elicited genuine feelings of attachment or belief. This is evidenced by the fact that the degree to which Iraqis complied with the regime's wishes usually corresponded to the strength of the controls that the regime could enforce in a particular time and place, and how much Iraqis had to lose or gain by their demonstrations of fealty. To become an officer in the Iraqi army, a person had to join the Baʿth Party, but after the Iran–Iraq War hundreds of thousands of soldiers left the party when they left the military.[15] Iraqis under the Euphrates Bureau's jurisdiction similarly deserted their Baʿthist unions in the early 1990s when they no longer had to join them to keep their jobs.[16] When popular uprisings broke out following the Gulf War in 1991, the BRCC records show that few party members reported to their posts to defend Baʿthist and government installations in areas where the military and security services lost control.[17]

Overy has argued about Hitler's Germany and Stalin's Russia that "If repression is to work, a substantial section of society must identify with or even approve its activities."[18] Yet judging by their actions, a significant number of Iraqis publicly supported but did not really approve of the Baʿth's policies, even if many behaved "as if" they did.[19] "It was as if I was living two personalities," a Baʿthist doctor who served as an officer in the military, told the journalist Steavenson. "I would do my best as an officer with my duties and then I would come home and speak against the regime. All Iraqis have two or more characters. It was the only way to survive under pressure for such a long time."[20] Just as the Soviet scholar Sheila Fitzpatrick concluded about the lives of ordinary Soviet citizens, Iraqis who lived under Saddam Hussein and the Baʿth Party's rule sought, above all else, to survive.[21] Survival meant different things to different people depending on their unique personalities, backgrounds, values, and situations. Sometimes it meant killing a relative in order to preserve one's life and the lives of one's extended family. At others, it involved "joining the party out of self-interest" (*al-ʾintimāʾ al-maṣlaḥī li-l-ḥizb*), filching extra spending money from party coffers, or lying to superiors about the success of party initiatives.[22] At still others, it included joining an opposition group, running a smuggling ring, or, like the doctor from above, faithfully doing one's job in order to keep a privileged position and a clean file. Whatever a person or group's motivations, they chose their path within the context of living in a Baʿthized environment.

POSTSCRIPT

The Legacy of Baʿthification

> *[D]uring almost half a century of Communist rule, the possibilities for alternative institutional forms have been largely wiped out. Even were the will to democratic or pluralistic institutions substantially present—and it is not—it is highly doubtful that the resources currently available by way of formal structures, source philosophies, or practical experience would go very far. The Bolshevization of a society, if it goes on long enough, is an irreversible process, because it is so intense and so total that it indelibly alters not only earlier institutional forms but the entire pattern of a population's expectations of reasonable and workable alternative possibilities for social order.*
>
> ALLEN KASSOF, *THE ADMINISTERED SOCIETY*

The Baʿthist era left a legacy that today's Iraq is still struggling to overcome. Thirty-five years of Baʿthification made its mark on Iraq in the form of corrupt and dysfunctional political institutions; a disregard for the rule of law; a crony economy; communal mistrust; a culture of violence, paranoia, and revenge; the destruction of Iraq's civil society; the manipulation of and assault against Iraq's religious and tribal institutions and values; and the brain drain, death, and physical and economic destruction of Iraq's infrastructure and middle class brought on by war and UN sanctions. While Hussein and the Baʿth might have claimed that all of these phenomena resulted from the conspiracies of foreign agents, in fact they occurred because Baʿthification failed at its primary objective: to convert Iraqis from their traditional faiths and normative belief systems into genuine Baʿthists. Absent the regime's ability to do this, Baʿthification sowed the seeds of its own destruction. "The general point is this:" Herman Lübbe wrote, "totalitarian systems are either fortified within the inner being of their subjects, or they collapse. . . . no totalitarian system can support itself in the long run through sheer opportunism of the subject."[1] A political regime that claims to release the energies of its subjects but in reality shackles them to the desires of a dictator who casts suspicion upon anybody who exercises the very initiative that he claims to want to imbue in his citizens eventually cannibalizes itself. Pursuing a total strategy of rule is, in the end, unsustainable because it does not allow a totalitarian ruler's citizens enough oxygen to regenerate their energies—energies that the ruler needs to sustain his dictatorship. A ruler who denies this logic eventually smothers himself along with the society over which he rules.

This is not to say, however, that totalitarian rulers cannot hold on for a long time. So long as they have access to the resources with which to employ and equip their military, security services, party, and civilian forces of culturalization, organization, mobilization, surveillance, and terror, in addition to financing their elite and nationwide networks of patronage, totalitarian rulers can retain their all-encompassing strategies for control. While Hussein's oil revenues slowed to a trickle in the early to mid-1990s, by 2003 the oil-for-food program had begun to replenish his coffers and the Iraqi Baʿth Party enjoyed its largest ever membership. With the UN's sanctions regime crumbling and oil prices about to take off, the reconsolidation of Hussein's rule probably would have continued if the United States had not attacked him in 2003.

Given the inherent contradictions in any totalitarian strategy, however, Hussein would most likely have had to moderate his aspirations eventually. With the exception of North Korea, all forms of totalitarianism that have not ended as a result of war—such as Stalinism and the totalitarianisms in Eastern Europe at the beginning of the Cold War—have at some point devolved into an "administered society" or a "post-totalitarian" system in which the regime reached a détente with its citizens. In these instances, the regime generally reduced its reliance on violence but maintained its strict surveillance and the other three types of totalitarian controls.[2] At base, even totalitarianism rests upon an agreement between a ruler and the ruled as to what the latter will tolerate by way of terror in exchange for the regime's bribes and the relative predictability that accompanies life in a familiar political system. If any regime brutalizes its citizens too much and does not give them a stake in its perpetuation, the bar for revolution lowers.

That being said, even post-totalitarian regimes must retain their willingness to use violence if they want to survive. The Soviet satellites of Eastern Europe survived the upheavals of the 1950s because Soviet tanks crushed the popular demonstrations that threatened them. In contrast, Soviet leader Mikhail Gorbachev refused to send in his military in 1989, and the Berlin Wall fell. China's rulers had no such compunction in Tiananmen Square, and their political system survives to this day. While China's post-Mao leaders have gradually opened China up socially and economically, political dissent remains off limits and subject to quick and violent suppression. China's status as an economic powerhouse, moreover, induces other countries to look past its human rights record in order to stay on good terms. The BRCC documents do not provide any evidence that the severity or frequency of Hussein's terror had decreased by 2003. If Hussein had been able to reestablish and expand his oil production, the economic weight that he would have gained likely would have induced countries long opposed to his politics to reach an accommodation with him. If not for the 2003 war, Hussein probably would have continued to thrive as Iraq's leader even if his ruling strategy might have devolved into authoritarianism.

Part of the reason for this might have been because Hussein would have had to contend with the Internet and social media as competitors to his culturalization campaigns. The BRCC contains at least one boxfile with documents about the use of the Internet in Iraq. According to a pamphlet from the "State Company for Internet Services," Iraq first went online on September 22, 2001.[3] By the end of the noughts, Iraq would probably have had an increasing Internet population with cell phone usership in the millions. It would have been more difficult to prevent Iraqis from learning about the world, events inside their country, and from propagating rumors and circulating information. Outsiders would also have gained a better vantage point inside Iraq. If history is any guide, Hussein would have recognized the inevitability of these trends and tried to appropriate them for his own purposes—to Baʿthize the Internet. But he would also have undoubtedly lost some of the control he once had over the information, media, and culture that Iraqis consumed.

Would Hussein and the Baʿth have survived the Arab Spring of 2010–2011? It is impossible to say, of course, but the Syrian example proves most analogous and instructive. The revolutions in Tunisia, Egypt, and Libya allowed Syrians to imagine the possibility for political change, and Syrian president Bashar al-Assad did little at the beginning of the revolution to distinguish himself from the dictators in Tunis, Cairo, and Tripoli, who fell relatively quickly, in the last case with decisive Western and Arab military support. Unlike in Tunisia and Egypt, however, al-Assad eventually evinced a willingness to kill, detain, and torture in order to put down the protests, which morphed into an armed rebellion. In contrast to Libya, no foreign armies or air forces aided the Syrian revolutionaries. As minority rulers, the al-Assads and members of their Alawite sect, in addition to the other social and economic groups that support the al-Assad regime and the regime's international patrons, see al-Assad's potential loss of political power as a grave threat to their communities, businesses, ways of life, and national security. If anything, from the Syrian regime's point of view, al-

Assad's mistake lay in not suppressing the protests earlier with more force. How many of today's Syrian revolutionaries engaged in their own struggle against a Baʿthist regime would have begun their rebellion had they know that the Syrian uprising would result, at the time of writing, in over 200,000 deaths, the displacement of millions, the destruction of much of the country, and the loss of at least a third of Syria's territory to the Islamic State in Iraq and the Levant (ISIL)?[4]

Given his track record, it is doubtful that Hussein would have hesitated as al-Assad did. Many Iraqis revolted in 1991 only to be gunned down by Hussein's helicopter gunships. Iraqis, with the exception of the Kurds, had no illusions about the response that a revolutionary spark would bring, and they did not trust the West or other Arab countries to support them after the international community allowed Hussein to quash the southern part of the 1991 uprising. It is unlikely that Turkey or the Sunni Arab regimes of the Gulf would have backed what would have been a primarily Shiʿi revolt to topple a majority Sunni government. Who, moreover, would have led the revolution? As in the Syrian case, in 2003 the external Iraqi opposition did not present a united front. By 2011, Baʿthification would have had another eight years to further tighten Hussein's grip over Iraq's state, civil, and social institutions; to replace and co-opt Iraq's tribal and religious leaders; to expand the party, security services, and Hussein's paramilitary militias; to refinance Hussein's social welfare net of enticements; and to decimate and atomize his domestic opposition.

Even if Iraqis had overturned Hussein, with whom or what would they have replaced him? The BRCC documents show that Hussein and the Baʿth largely hollowed out Iraq's state, social, and cultural institutions and reconstructed them on Husseini Baʿthist foundations. When the United States and its allies removed Hussein and the Baʿth in 2003, first with a military campaign and then a "de-Baʿthification" policy, they not only dethroned a dictator and his ruling party; they also removed the structure of Iraq's political, cultural, and social order, built up over thirty-five years.[5] Hussein installed himself as the keystone of this structure from 1979 to 2003. As a result, when he fell, the order crumbled, leaving little amid the rubble with which to reconstruct the Iraqi nation.

Iraq will likely continue to suffer from the scars of the Husseini Baʿthist era for some time. "When we are through this difficult period for the country it will be easy to rebuild Iraq. But what to do with all the corrupt people is another and more complicated matter; to restore destroyed human beings is extremely demanding," Hussein's youngest son, Qusay, reportedly told Hussein's doctor, Ala Bashir, shortly before the regime fell.[6] Just as Hussein emphasized the Baʿthification of students and youth because his regime could more easily mold them into Husseini Baʿthists, it will probably take children with no memory of Baʿthist Iraq, or the sectarian strife that has followed in its wake, to recreate something resembling a unified nation. Each new generation will have its own vision, or visions, for Iraqi national identity and the country's proper political, cultural, and social configuration. As Allen Kassof's epigraph implies, and post-Soviet history suggests, this configuration might not be democratic. It might not also be unified. As history teaches, so long as a central authority in Baghdad imposes its will over Iraq's heterogeneous population without taking into account the interests of Iraq's many tribes, sects, ethnicities, and regions, Iraq will continue to suffer from the same types of conditions that made Husseini Baʿthism, and the country's reigning insecurity, possible.

APPENDIX 1. A WORK PLAN FOR COORDINATION BETWEEN THE PARTY AND MASS ORGANIZATIONS IN THE FIELD OF THE BAʿTHIFICATION OF SOCIETY

The following document appears in boxfile 025-5-5, pages 476–494. The boxfile is from 1988, but the document contains no date, so it is possible that it was written earlier. The pages of the document are mimeographed and the text appears faint, making some words illegible, particularly at the end of the introduction. The document likely refers to a specific party initiative called "The Baʿthification of Society," which might have begun sometime in the early to mid-1980s, as the language and style that its author uses conforms to documents related to other party initiatives throughout the years. Regardless of its provenance, the document's importance lies in the way it lays out the theory behind Saddam Hussein and the Baʿth Party's more general ruling strategy of Baʿthification, a logic that appears throughout the BRCC documents from 1979 to 2003.

..One Arab Nation..
..With an Eternal Message..

Arab Baʿth Socialist Party
((The Iraqi Region))

A WORK PLAN FOR COORDINATION BETWEEN THE PARTY AND MASS ORGANIZATIONS IN THE FIELD OF THE BAʿTHIFICATION OF SOCIETY

Introduction

The historical missions that our great party, the Arab Baʿth Socialist Party, which leads the Arab revolutionary movement in order to achieve its strategic goals, takes upon itself are to build a unified Arab socialist society and to foster the construction of a model [of that society] in the Iraqi region according to the principles and the goals of the party.[1] These principles and goals are unity, freedom, and socialism. Taking as a point of departure the characteristics of the theory of the Baʿth, which are interconnected with the authenticity of the nation and adhere to its principle of independence . . . [illegible]. . . the party has determined the spheres and premises for its distinctive, developed, organizational work.

What differentiates the Arab Baʿth Socialist Party from other parties and political movements is not only that which the Arab nation has witnessed in its national struggle (*al-waṭanī wa-l-qawmī*) but also what the revolutionary movement in the world has witnessed more generally, and the third-world in particular. That is, the Baʿth Party possesses two revolutionary experiences (*al-khibra wa-l-tajriba*) that produced an era of the accumulation of struggle within the framework of the total and bitter picture in which the Baʿth led the Arab revolutionary movement and the movement of the struggle of the Arab masses, which began with hope and optimism . . . [illegible] . . . and struggles under the banner of the Baʿth in order to achieve its hopes and aspirations of unity, freedom, and socialism.

Starting from the nature of the party as revolutionary and scientific, the party has utilized the experience that it has gained throughout its struggling journey in a systematic fashion in order to identify the nature of the new conditions and developments that have accompanied the journey. The party has examined its successes and failures in order to design new places and contexts for work, which accompany the party's progress and the new developments in the party's revolutionary journey in addition to the new conditions found in the Arab and international arenas. This confirms the depth of the party's revolutionary (*'inqilābiyya*) journey and the root of its organic and dialectical connection to the struggling movement of the masses. The connection between the party and the masses creates a firm block of woven cloth that is unified and homogenous in thought and practice.

The revolutionary experience of the party came . . . [illegible] . . . from the revolution of 17–30 July, 1968, . . . in the Iraqi region, from constructing a unified democratic socialist society and making it a resplendent example, and from the increasing and developing intellectual activity of the comrade struggling leader, Saddam Hussein (God keep him), with his peerless leadership of the party's journey and its pioneering revolution . . . [illegible] . . . [Saddam Hussein's] new additions and enrichments to the party's experience add to the accumulating stock of the party's revolutionary experiences . . . [illegible] . . . through which the party possesses the awesome ability to consolidate and deepen its revolutionary methods. The party insists, based on principle, that it must transform its intellectual and theoretical premises into an applied, active reality.

The comrade struggler Saddam Hussein (God keep him) has been able to produce great accomplishments during the party's journey and revolutionary experience in the Iraqi region. . .[illegible] . . . [Hussein's] exceptional and genius leadership has been confirmed by the comrade Founding Leader [Michel Aflaq] when the Founding Leader said, "The prominence of the great historical leader for this nation in the person of the comrade struggler, Saddam Hussein, . . . [illegible] . . . , is a great accomplishment of experience . . . [illegible]."[2] . . . [illegible] . . . for the masses through their loyalty and absolute [illegible] the condition of passion . . . [illegible] . . . and love . . . [illegible] . . . for the knight of the nation . . . [illegible] . . .

. . . Saddam and the Baʿth and Iraqis are unified in one body created by *al-Qādisiyya*.

Second / The Goals of the Plan

At the forefront of the goals of the process of the Baʿthification of society are the spreading and deepening of the thought of the party and its values and principles, and transforming them into revolutionary behavior within everyday practices by:

1) Sending the intellectual radiation of the party to all citizens, so that the principles of the party and its stances about economic, social, and political principles will be clear to all, and so that citizens will start to assess other intellectual currents and political positions in relation to the principles of the party, its positions, and its decisions. Indeed, deviating from them is national treason.

2) Strengthening revolutionary work and social practices according to Baʿthist principles by propagating and revealing Baʿthist values and practices embodied in the behavior of Baʿthists, by transferring them to all citizens in state and society, and by influencing and exposing values and practices that the Baʿth has condemned because they conflict with the party's values and ideas.

3) Employing the mass organizations' tremendous abilities and energies according to the ideological practices of the party so that they serve the party's goals and principles in a direct, central fashion. The mass organizations play an important and basic role in attracting the masses, mobilizing them, and investing their energies and capabilities in order to strengthen their progress. [The mass organizations] solidify and strengthen the mass base of the party and spread Baʿthist values within the sectors of the masses in which they work. They instill a revolutionary spirit and practices and enlist these sectors in an effective manner in the operation of revolutionary construction, in the defense of the nation, and in performing the national mission.

4) Transforming the mass organizations into basic foundations for party work within the varied sectors of the people by implementing the most preferable formulation of organization and interaction and finding an objective relationship between the main [party] organizations and the mass organizations in order to strengthen the continuation of party work in the "mass" category.[3] This relationship will give the party and mass organizations complete and detailed information about the social, cultural, and political aspects of the social sectors in which they work. The organizations will thus be more able to understand their sectors of work and, accordingly, will be better positioned to lead those sectors forward. Similarly, making the good party cadres available to lead the mass organizations will make the mass organizations more able to achieve the goals of the party through their activities. These activities attract the widest amount of the public and put the public under the influence of the thought of the party and its values and practices.

5) Having the party organizations achieve precise knowledge about all of the elements inside their geographic purviews, on the one hand, and, similarly, the state of the mass and professional organizations.[4] By coordinating with the party organizations, the mass organizations will possess detailed information about the sectors in which they work.

6) Identifying the good and suitable elements for party recruitment in order to work on them and include them in the party apparatus.

7) Raising the mass and professional organizations to work to frame (*li-ta'ṭīr*) and include the elements [in PMO activities] that are not suitable to be organized [into the party] in order to make the elements active, and to make them live the details of their daily lives within the atmosphere of the party and its general activity.

8) Identifying and subduing the elements that have previous connections to [alternative] political movements or who have relatives who were executed or were members of opposition movements so as to monitor their activity and prevent any opposition force from moving in on them, and to place the elements within the atmosphere of the party to make them feel assurance and trust.

9) Creating a state of awareness and mutual understanding between the party and the masses. This will lead the people to interact with the leading party in a way that produces accomplishments and will create a favorable reception for the party's initiatives and daily activity.

Third / The Party Leads the Mass Organizations

It is necessary to point, by means of introduction, to the fact that the recommended command made up of the main commands and the mass and professional organizations in order to Baʿthize society, forms a general framework. It is not necessary for each party branch to take the same organizational form. We leave flexibility to each main command to adopt the command shape that corresponds with the nature of the mass reality in which the command works. The recommended shape is:

Baʿthification Committee:

A Baʿthification Committee is to be formed in the main organizations in the governorates. It will be the responsibility of a member of the main organization. In Baghdad, the responsibility will be that of a member in the Office of the Baghdad Bureau—and as follows:

a) The head of the Baghdad Branch of the General Federation of Iraqi Women

b) A member of the Executive Office of the National Union of Students and Youth of Iraq

c) The head of the Union of Baghdad Peasants Associations

d) The head of the Union of Workers of Baghdad

e) The head of the Baghdad Bureau of the Teacher's Union

The Missions of the Baʿthification Committee

1) The work of these committees is not an alternative to the professional offices in the field of Baʿthification and professional work. Its work is, rather, defined by coordination and direction within the framework of the activity of the main organizations with regard to the Baʿthification of society.[5] The professional offices are special contexts for work, which correspond to the nature of their respective forms, goals, and the mediums in which they work, even though the results of their work, in the end, serve the goals of the party and its principles.

2) The Baʿthification Committee in the main region provides the professional offices with lists of the independent elements who cannot perform party work in the regions in order to involve them in the activities of the mass and professional organizations.

3) The Baʿthification Committee hosts the leadership cadre of the mass organizations at its regular meetings or invites them to attend a special meeting devoted to discussing the process of Baʿthification. At the meeting, the Baʿthification Committee discovers the nature of the mass organization's progress in executing its plans and programs in the field [of Baʿthification].

4) The Baʿthification Committee in the main organizations follows the activity of the mass organizations and their assignments for the purposes of Baʿthification in order to complete a survey and assessment of the work of the mass organizations and their accomplishments, which must correspond to the level of support that the mass organizations enjoy. The committee should recommend the level of support that it believes is appropriate.

5) The Baʿthification Committee in the main organizations studies the requests of the full-time employees attached to the mass and professional organizations for the purposes of their mission.

7) [*sic*] The mass organizations prepare the independent masses. They place them in the atmosphere of the party and recruit the good elements to join the party ranks. They send lists of these elements to the Baʿthification Committee in the main organizations . . . [illegible] . . . for the purpose of linking them with the party organizations.

8) The Baʿthification Committee presents a quarterly report about Baʿthification activities to the highest commands, indicating in the report which activities and events have been carried out on the path to the Baʿthification of society. The report identifies obstacles [to Baʿthification] and suggests solutions to treat them.

Fourth / Other Contexts for Work

1) The mass organizations represent a majority of the sectors of our people. They form, in truth, some of the party's most advanced and effective indirect organizational fronts (*wājihāt*) and are more capable of influence within the mediums that they represent. In light of that, it is necessary to ascribe a special and exceptional

importance to the work of the mass organizations and to benefit from their direct influence according to the individual abilities of each organization in the process of recruitment and the execution of the work plans of the main organizations in the field of the Baʿthification of society. It is also necessary to choose the party elements that are qualified and influential for work in the [mass] organizations.

2) The plans that the professional organizations possess are part of one unified framework, which makes them match the framework of the plan for the Baʿthification of society. This is so that no conflict or difficulty (*ʾijtihād*) arises as part of laying down and executing the plans while providing the professional organizations with flexibility to match their activities to the area of their work and the nature of the [geographic or social] sector in which these organizations work.

3) Women are half of society. There is not necessarily a worker or a peasant in each family, but there is a woman in each family. Due to the importance of working on the families in a direct fashion, that requires entrusting the General Federation of Iraqi Women (GFIW) with a great importance because it does not deal with defined professional sectors, as is the case for the rest of the mass organizations, but extends its activity to include all Iraqi families through the woman herself. Provide the material necessities and financial means that make the continuation of the GFIW's work possible and require the other mass organizations to interact and deal with the GFIW.[6]

4) The present stage requires that party activities take place in the party headquarters, just as the party's obligations in the mass organizations should take place in these organizations in order to advance the activities and necessities related to mass mobilization. It is difficult to take away full-time party employees who are assigned mass duties from their party duties because of the capacity of the size of the party apparatus and the importance for the employees to continue to do organizational work in the party. [7]

Therefore, we suggest the following:

a) Employ part-time the advanced workers and the heads of the branches of the mass organizations whose expertise is required in the mass framework and allocate them part-time to their party duties.

b) Reduce the party responsibilities of the members of the mass commands and give special flexibility to the party employees who have union responsibilities.

c) Employ professional branch officials part-time in the [professional] centers of governorates, counties, and municipalities so that they can check up on the responsibilities commissioned to the mass organizations [in these areas].

5) Place a special section in the party assessment form for the professional offices to use to assess the party employees who work in the mass organizations based upon their activities in these organizations. Use this assessment in the party's evaluation and promotion process. This will create an incentive to work in the mass and professional organizations.

6) Give special flexibility so that the party employees who have responsibilities in the unions within the mass organizations can be located in their organizations [in the same geographic area] when possible because mass work is an important and prominent form of party work. This will also form a big impetus to develop the work of the mass organizations and will govern the daily work of the unionist cadre. This might eliminate the excuse that doing party work requires cutting mass work short.

7) One of the main goals of the activity (*ḥaraka*) of the Baʿthification of society is to widen the party's base. However, that does not mean including all citizens, or even those that are suitable, in the party, because that conflicts with the concept of the revolutionary vanguard party. What is more, the party cannot absorb all of those who deserve inclusion because of the size of the existing cadre. Consequently, the Baʿthification of society means spreading the thought, values, and principles of the party in society and incorporating them into the daily behavior of its citizens.

8) The contexts of work of the party organizations or the mass and professional organizations in the field of the Baʿthification of society are as follows:

a) The party organization or the mass and professional organization carries out a field survey in their region of work, specifying in light of it the numbers of Baʿthists, independents, other political movements, and other information. It might be possible to take the format [of the survey] that the security committees have in the Baghdad office as a basis for these because of its comprehensiveness.

b) The existing information should be put in order in the field survey as it is in form number (1), attached.[8]

c) The existing information should be put in qualitative order in the field survey, and should record names, in form number (2), attached. I.e., mention the independents by their names and, among them, who is suitable for party recruitment, who is suitable for the National Activism units, who is suitable for the People's Councils, who is suitable for the activity of the National Union, who is suitable for professional activity, and who is suitable for women's activity and in other venues according to the nature of the organizational and mass reality.

d) Prepare a form with two fields. The first field should include the names of independents whereas the second field should include the names of the party members assigned to frame and Baʿthize the independents.

e) Each party organization should present its activity in the field of Baʿthification in form number (3) meant for keeping track of the activities. The organization should mention the numbers of what it has accomplished in the form.

f) Make the activity of Baʿthification one of the main parts of the party and mass and professional organizations' meetings, in which its members discuss the activity in the field of Baʿthification.

g) Each organization should prepare a quarterly report about its activity in the field of Baʿthification: what it has accomplished, what it has not, and the reasons for [the accomplishments and failures]. Each organization should also recommend solutions.

11) [*sic*] At an appropriate time after which the plan for the Baʿthification of society has been applied, it is necessary to carry out a careful study of Baʿthification activities in order to derive metrics through which it is possible to improve organizational and mass and professional work, and the activity of framing (*ḥarakat al-taʾṭīr*).[9] Some of these metrics should be:

a) A measurement of party effectiveness that gauges the relationship between the number of party members and the number of people who are framed (*muʾaṭṭarīn*) and recruited.

b) An assessment of the activity of an organization in the field of Baʿthification.

c) A measurement of the effectiveness of the comrade party member that gauges the relationship between a comrade and the number of people who he frames (*muʾaṭṭarīn*) and recruits.

d) The extent of knowledge about Baʿthification among minorities (Kurds, Turkmen . . .)

e) Better knowledge of what the best percentage is for the number of the party members under the responsibility of a party comrade, and the relationship between that and the effectiveness of the activity of the party organization in the field of Baʿthification, and other metrics.

12) Employ women party members full-time in the units of the GFIW and in its branches, and similarly employ women party members for work in the administrative divisions of the union sections. These women, however, should attend the main party meeting. Inform them that they will be appointed based upon their mass work and on the basis of the extent of their capabilities, the size of the efforts that they have expended in developing the women's work, exceptional activity, and the initiatives that they have carried out that have strengthened the advancement of society. Create a program to distribute the women party officials among the [GFIW] headquarters down to those who work on individual, daily missions.

13) Add a clause to the assessment form that indicates the extent of her success or development, and the party capability for those [women party members] who work with the unions . . . and assess her on this basis for purposes of demotion or promotion.

14) Program the party activity of the female comrade so that everyday her party work interacts with her union work. This should include not making her work later than 7 p.m. in winter and 8 p.m. in summer.

15) With the aim of supplying the necessities for the program of the Baʿthification of society, we suggest allocating a number of the empty houses that

belonged to the deported Iranians to be taken over as mass headquarters, and to widen the base of the GFIW by opening headquarters and centers for the GFIW's union activity in them. In addition, means of transportation should be made available that will safeguard women and ensure that they can carry out the activities suitable for executing the duties that fall on their shoulders.

16) It is necessary for the mass organizations, within the framework of the plan for Baʿthification, to prepare everything related to the practice of their organizational and cultural roles in order to make this plan succeed by employing particular cultural programs that govern the connection of the adherents of these organizations to the creed of the party, taking into consideration the nature of the social strata and their capability to absorb [the party's creed].

APPENDIX 2. SPECIAL REGULATIONS FOR HOW TO DEAL WITH THE RELATIVES OF CRIMINALS CONVICTED FOR POLITICAL CRIMES

This document appears in boxfile 042-5-5, pages 205–206, although the pages appear out of order, so the document begins on page 206 and ends on page 205. It is attached to a two-page cover letter on pages 203–204, dated May 28, 1994, and sent by the Director of the Party Secretariat to all of the party branch commands in the Military Office. According to the cover letter, the document details regulations drawn up by the party's Organizational Committee for how to deal with the relatives of people who were sentenced for political crimes. The document shows how the consequences for a political criminal's actions extended to his or her family members, a key aspect of Baʿthification.

SPECIAL REGULATIONS FOR HOW TO DEAL WITH THE RELATIVES OF CRIMINALS CONVICTED FOR POLITICAL CRIMES

1. The relatives of convicts are expelled from the Party if they are [full] members except in two instances:

a. If they had a role in exposing the aggression or turning the criminal in.

b. If they had an exceptional recognized fighting or struggling role in battle in Saddam's Glorious *Qādisiyya* and the Immortal Mother of All Battles and if [their relative] received a noncapital sentence. Then they are subject to the evaluation of the party organizations.

2. If the relatives of the convicted are not full members, and are of the first degree (parents and children), they are expelled from the party except if they are not affected [by their relative's punishment], according to the evaluation of their party organization.

3. If the relatives of the convicted are of the second degree (grandparents and siblings) then they are subject to the evaluation of the party, whether or not they are full members, partisans, or supporters. In light of the evaluation, a decision will be taken about whether or not to let them remain or remove them from the party. The party organizations will surveil the relatives and submit a regular report on them.

4. The relatives who are affected from the other degrees [of relation] are subject to the evaluation of the party organizations.

5. Included in these regulations are the family members up to the second degree of those convicted for being opposition members, criminals who cooperate with the West, and agents.

6. Relatives of the convicted are not accepted into the military academies and, similarly, cannot receive scholarships to study outside of the country.

7. Exclude relatives of the convicted up to the second degree from the vital intersections (*al-mafāṣil al-ḥayawiyya*) of the economy and politics.

8. The families of those executed and convicted to the first degree are barred from traveling outside the country for a period of three years. Afterward, they are allowed to travel on the condition that the party and security services give them a positive evaluation.

9. It should be taken into consideration in an evaluation if a family has produced a martyr or their sons have defied death (*ʾistabsala*) and have been honored, regardless of the type [of honor], even if one of the family's sons showed a treasonous or oppositionist stance. That is, employ the case of martyrdom and heroism and ignore the case of treachery and criminality.

10. Similarly, in the case of a tribe, do not measure the tribe by the number of criminals or the cases of treason and opposition in the tribe, but rather measure the tribe by the number of martyrs, heroes, and honorees, lest enemies exploit that for their own interests.

11. If any positive indication appears from the relatives of those condemned to execution that are included in these regulations who could be organized (*tanẓīmuhum*) into the party ranks, or for those who were expelled or re-admitted following a party evaluation, each case should be taken on its own merits. The evaluation should be carried out precisely, and the party organization will be responsible in the event of the appearance of any contrary information.

12. These regulations apply to the relatives of the first, second, and third degree (uncles, aunts, nephews, and nieces on both sides) of the elements of the Page of Treason and Treachery (the 1991 uprisings) who are still fugitives outside of the country or who have been convicted under these regulations.

13. There are elements that were lost during the events of the Page of Treason and Treachery, and nothing is known about their fate. An evaluation should be carried out for each individual case on the role of these individuals and the positions of their families during the events in order to determine their stances in light of the evaluation that will be undertaken by the party and the security services.

14. In the case of a re-evaluation, the main [party] commands should write convincing and warrantable suggestions about the elements who seek to remain in the party because they have not been influenced, and they should send them up to the [Regional] Command.

15. The party organizations should maintain a connection (*ʾidāmat al-ṣilla*) and monitor the families of people who have been executed in order to make those who would exploit the situation miss their chance (*li-tafwīt al-furṣa*).

16. Anyone at the level of full member and down who denounces the criminal activity that the executed criminal carried out and supports the decision of

the party and the revolution in relation to [the criminal] remains in the party and the state. Those who do not have membership from the second-degree [of relation] and down are subject to an evaluation. It is also possible to re-admit into the party those who were expelled or retired once they carry out exemplary work that confirms their complete allegiance to the party and the revolution.

17. Recruit into the party ranks the sons of the relatives of those convicted of crimes and people who have been executed, especially youth and students, in order to make the political opposition movements miss their chance to embrace [the sons].

18. Expel from the party anybody who has a relative of the first degree who has been proven to have committed treason or espionage in the case that the [Baʿthist] has been influenced by [his relative].

19. Those relatives of the convicted and executed who recorded exemplary positions in the immortal Mother of All Battles and confronted the Page of Treason and Treachery, are returned to their positions with the exception of military or security positions, which is for humanitarian considerations.

20. The members of the educational and teaching corps; the defense, interior, and foreign ministries; intelligence (*mukhābarāt*); and atomic energy agency of the first-degree are included in these regulations.

NOTES

PREFACE

1. The MoU is confidential, but according to Richard Sousa, the former director of the Hoover Institution Library and Archives, it states that both sides acknowledge that the IMF materials are the property of the Iraqi people with Hoover serving as a remote repository for them. Richard Sousa e-mail, message to the author, March 13, 2012.

Taking the BRCC and its sister archives out of Iraq has engendered controversy. In 2008, the director of the Iraqi National Library and Archive, Saad Eskander, wrote to the Hoover Institution demanding the documents' return and calling the agreement between Hoover and the IMF illegal. The Society of American Archivists and the Association of Canadian Archivists supported him in a joint statement, characterizing the removal of the IMF collections from Iraq and the US government's seizure of millions of pages of Iraqi records as "an act of pillage, which is specifically forbidden by the 1907 Hague Convention." Bruce Montgomery, Professor and Faculty Director of Archives and Special Materials at the University of Colorado, presents a much more nuanced and detailed legal analysis of the Iraqi and Baʿth Party records held by both the US government and Hoover. He concludes that taking the documents occupies a gray area under international law, and that "There are no clear answers as to when the United States should return the hundred million pages of captured intelligence files to authorities in Baghdad . . . or when the IMF should return the Ba'ath Party documents under its control." For the statement by the American and Canadian archivists associations see Society of American Archivists and Association of Canadian Archivists, "SAA/ACA Joint Statement on Iraqi Records," April 22, 2008, http://www.archivists.org/statements/IraqiRecords.asp [accessed March 14, 2012]; Bruce P. Montgomery, "Saddam Hussein's Records of Atrocity: Seizure, Removal, and Restitution," *The American Archivist* 75 (Fall/Winter 2012): 326–370. For more on the controversy see Dina Rizk Khoury, *Iraq in Wartime: Soldiering, Martyrdom, and Remembrance* (Cambridge: Cambridge University Press, 2013), 12–17; and Hugh Eakin, "Iraqi Files in US: Plunder or Rescue?" *New York Times*, July 1, 2008, http://www.nytimes.com/2008/07/01/books/01hoov.html [accessed March 8, 2012].

2. Hoover Institution Archives, "Register of the Hizb al-Baʿth al-ʿArabi al-Ishtiraki [Baʿth Party] Records, 1968–2003," (Stanford: Hoover Institution Archives, 2010), http://cdn.calisphere.org/data/13030/g3/c84j0cg3/files/c84j0cg3.pdf [accessed March 28, 2012].

3. I am indebted to the Iraq Memory Foundation's Hassan Mneimneh for the characterization of the Baʿth Party as a form of "meta-control."

4. As an Arab nationalist organization, the Baʿth Party originally aimed to set up a unified nation-state encompassing all Arab lands. As such, the party's "National Command," which it hoped would one day govern the pan-Arab country, had jurisdiction over the various "Regional Commands," which ran the Baʿth's branches in each state. From 1966 on, however, the only two major Baʿthist branches, in Iraq and Syria, feuded. Each set up its own National Command, but in each case the National Command served primarily propagandistic and ceremonial functions. The Regional Commands in each state thus served as their de facto national leaderships with no authority above them. Hanna Batatu, *The Old Social Classes and the Revolutionary Movements of Iraq: A Study of Iraq's Old Landed and Commercial Classes and of its Communists, Baʿthists, and Free Officers* (Princeton: Princeton University Press, 1978), 1085.

5. Khoury, 180.

6. The best effort to date is the incomplete annotation index compiled by the Iraq Memory Foundation at the Hoover Institution.

7. For more information on the CRRC see its website: http://crrc.dodlive.mil/ [accessed Jan. 23, 2015]. Due to funding constraints, at the time of writing the long-term viability of the CRRC was uncertain. A book with many translated passages of the audio tapes has also been published: Kevin M. Woods, David D. Palkki, and Mark E. Stout, eds., *The Saddam Tapes: The Inner Workings of a Tyrant's Regime, 1978–2001* (Cambridge: Cambridge University Press, 2011). The CRRC holdings consist of declassified documents taken from the over one hundred million pages of records captured by the US government (Montgomery, 326).

8. Marion Farouk-Sluglett and Peter Sluglett, "The Historiography of Modern Iraq," *The American Historical Review* 96 (December 1991): 1408–1409.

9. Joseph Sassoon, *Saddam Hussein's Baʿth Party: Inside an Authoritarian Regime* (Oxford: Oxford University Press, 2012); Khoury. Yitzhak Nakash, e.g., concludes *The Shiʿis of Iraq* in 1958, "not only because of the change in regime but also due to the different source material and issues that one can fruitfully explore thereafter" (Princeton: Princeton University Press), 3. Even Batatu's monumental *The Old Social Classes and the Revolutionary Movements of Iraq* contains just four references to government documents in the post-1958 period, only one collection of which has records up to 1970.

10. Makiya, *Republic of Fear: The Politics of Modern Iraq* (Berkeley: University of California Press, 1998), xxxvi. The original edition, published under the pseudonym Samir al-Khalil, appeared in 1989.

11. Marion Farouk-Sluglett and Peter Sluglett, *Iraq since 1958: From Revolution to Dictatorship*, rev. ed. (London: I.B. Tauris, 2001), 308.

12. Merle Fainsod, *Smolensk under Soviet Rule* (Cambridge, MA: Harvard University Press, 1958), 5. For a view on methodological issues related to the archival "gold rush" on Joseph Stalin in the Soviet archives see Kevin McDermott, "Archives, Power and the 'Cultural Turn': Reflections on Stalin and Stalinism," *Totalitarian Movements and Political Religions* 5 (Summer 2004): 5–24.

13. Fainsod, 447.

14. Khoury, 17.

PART I

No notes

CHAPTER ONE

Hizb al-Baʿth al-ʿArabi al-ʾIshtiraki. *Hizb al-Baʿth al-ʿArabi al-ʾIshtiraki [in Iraq] Records, 1968–2003*. Baʿth Arab Socialist Party Regional Command Collection (BRCC). Boxfiles Dataset. Hoover Institution Archives. "Report," Director of the Party Secretariat to the Presidency of the Republic/Secretary of the President of the Republic for Party Affairs, Dec. 15, 1984, 025–1–2: 42. From here on out, all BRCC Boxfiles Dataset documents are cited individually with as much of the following information as is available in this order: "Title of document," sender, recipient, date, boxfile number: document pages.

1. The original battle of *Qādisiyya* (as opposed to "Saddam's *Qādisiyya*," the Iran–Iraq War), in which the prophet Muhammad's grandson, Hussein, a Shiʿi patron saint, was martyred, took place in 637 AD on the Iraqi plain, southwest of where Kufa was later founded, between the Arab Muslim invading armies and the Sassanian Persians. M. Streck and L. Veccia Vaglieri, "al- Ḳādisiyya," in *Encyclopaedia of Islam*, 2nd ed., ed. P. Bearman, Th. Bianquis, C. E. Bosworth, E. van Donzel, and W. P. Heinrichs, in *Brill Online*, http://www.brillonline.nl/subscriber/entry?entry=islam_COM–0412 [accessed Oct. 13, 2010].

2. "Information," [Name withheld] Secretary of the Wasit Branch Command/President of the Committee for Deserters and Draft Dodgers to the President of the High Committee for Deserters and Draft Dodgers, the Struggler Comrade, the Honorable, Ali Hassan al-Majid, March 4, 1984, 021–2–3: 446; "Information," The Director of General Security to the Comrade Secretary of the President of the Republic for Party Affairs, April 8, 1984, 021–2–3: 449–450.

3. "Deserters from Military Service," Secretary of the Middle Bureau Command to the Office of the Party Secretariat, Jan. 8, 1985, 069–1–3: 44–47.

4. "Information," Director of the Office of the Party Secretariat to the Presidential Diwan, Aug. 25, 1993, 023–4–2: 103.

5. "A Patriotic Stance," Director of the Office of the Party Secretariat to the Presidential Diwan, June 7, 1995, 030–2–4: 14.

6. See the previous section for examples of fathers killing their sons. For a case of tribal sheikhs who promised to execute three of their own tribesmen who com-

mitted crimes, see their petition to Saddam Hussein, 041–2–1: 725; "The Deportation of Iranians," Secretary of the Office of the Southern Bureau Command, March 22, 1982, 028–1–1: 446.

7. See, e.g., "Oath of Allegiance in Blood," Secretary of the Office of the Southern Bureau Command to the Office of the Party Secretariat, Dec. 4, 1986, 022–1–5: 41; Secretary of the President of the Republic for Party Affairs to the Presidential Diwan, June 29, 1985, 001–5–1: 1; "Oath of Allegiance," Director of the Office of the Party Secretariat to the Presidential Diwan, Sept. 25, 1991, 021–2–5: 10; 040–3–1: 601–604.

8. According to Hanna Batatu's interviews of Baʿthists, in 1976 the party had around 500,000 people at all levels of membership, including in the Popular Army and the Professional and Mass Organizations (PMOs). Of these, he reports that "scarcely more than 10,000" were "active" members, which this study refers to as "full members." Batatu does not record the numbers of other levels of party membership (partisans, supporters, etc.), and he does not say how many members there were in the regular party apparatus versus the PMOs and Popular Army. Batatu, 1078.

9. Unlike Batatu's numbers, these numbers do not include the PMOs and the Popular Army. See table 5.1, chapter 5.

10. To cite just one example (chapter 8 contains many more), in 2000 the head of the Baʿth Party's Basra, Dhi Qar, and Muthanna bureaus reported that two "agents of the racist Persian regime" had tried to carry out separate suicide bombings against a section and division headquarters. Both bombers were blocked from entering the buildings and detonated their explosive belts outside of them, killing one person and injuring eleven in total. "Assault," the Official for the Basra, Dhi Qar, and Muthanna bureaus to the Attendant to the President Leader (God save him and keep him), Comrade General [name withheld], Sept. 1, 2000, 028–1–7: 592–593.

11. Ofra Bengio, "Iraq," in *Middle East Contemporary Survey, Vol. 5, 1980–1981*, ed. Haim Shaked, Colin Legum, and Daniel Dishon (New York: Holmes & Meier Publishers, 1982), 585; RCC Decision No. 860, Nov. 30, 1988, 021–5–6: 46; RCC Decision No. 770, Dec. 2, 1989, 029–4–2: 97; "Iraq President Extends Amnesty for Kurds," *BBC Summary of World Broadcasts*, May 14, 1990; "Order," Director of the Office of the Party Secretariat to the Honorable Comrade Secretary of the Office of the Euphrates Bureau, July 1, 1991, 039–1–6: 267; Director of the Office of the Party Secretariat to the Comrade Deputy Secretary of the Regional Command of Iraq, July 4, 1993, 120–4–1: 389; Director of General Military Intelligence to the Office of the Party Secretariat, July 22, 2000, 029–1–3: 153, references an amnesty from July 22, 1995; "Information," Assistant to the Director of the Office of the Party Secretariat to the Basra Branch Command, July 29, 2001, 157–3–2: 261, references a general amnesty offered on Oct. 20, 1999.

12. "Study," Director of the Office of the Party Secretariat to The Honorable Member of the Organizational Committee, Oct. 25, 1990, 076–2–4: 39–57; "Meeting," Office of the Secretariat to the Military Office of All of the Party Branch

Commands, Jan. 4, 1993, 004–1–4: 162–163; "The Methods for Circulating Party Mail," Director of the Administration of the Military Office to All of the Military Branch Commands, April 4, 1982, 034–2–1: 146–147; "Practicing Responsibility from the Lowest Position," Arab Baʿth Socialist Party—Office of the Northern Bureau Command, 029–2–3: 95; "The Final Report for the Fourth Round of Central Cultural Meetings for the Year 1987/86," Office of Culture and Media, 037–3–5: 26–39; "The City of Kufa," Secretary of the President of the Republic to the Office of the Party Secretariat, May 25, 1986, 088–5–3: 231–232; "The Occasion of the Tenth of Muharram," Secretary of the Office of the Southern Branch Command to the Office of the Party Secretariat, Nov. 22, 1983, 023–4–7: 566.

13. "Study," Director of the Office of the Party Secretariat to the Presidency of the Republic/Secretary of the President of the Republic for Party Affairs, Aug. 31, 1990, 104–3–1: 276–277.

14. This can be seen in many party reports from the 1991 uprisings, including 024–5–2: 96.

15. "Honoraria for Religious and National Occasions," Director of the Office of the Party Secretariat to the Military Office Commands of the Party Branches, July 4, 1995, 171–3–1: 64.

16. Farouk-Sluglett and Sluglett, *Iraq since 1958*, 134.

17. Amatzia Baram, "The Ruling Political Elite in Bathi Iraq, 1968–1986: The Changing Features of a Collective Profile," *International Journal of Middle East Studies* 21 (Nov. 1989): 447–493; Amatzia Baram, *Building toward Crisis: Saddam Husayn's Strategy for Survival*, Policy Paper No. 47 (Washington, DC: Washington Institute for Near East Policy, 1998), 7–38. For Ofra Bengio's contributions, see her entries under "Iraq" in the *Middle East Contemporary Survey*, Vols. 4–22, covering the years 1979–1998.

18. Charles Tripp, *A History*, 3rd ed. (Cambridge: Cambridge University Press, 2007), 259–264.

19. Sassoon, *Saddam Hussein's Baʿth Party*, 105–106. For more on the use of tribalism to solidify the SSO and other elite units see Amatzia Baram, "The Missing Link: 'Badu' and 'Tribal' Honor as Components in the Iraqi Decision to Invade Kuwait," in *Changing Nomads in a Changing World*, ed. Joseph Ginat and Anatoly M. Khazanov (Brighton: Sussex Academic Press, 1998), 157.

20. 021–2–3: 446–450; "A National Defense Regiment Section," Director of the Office of the Party Secretariat to The Office of the Northern Bureau, July 1, 1989, 073–3–4: 86; "Practices," Director of the Office of the Party Secretariat to The Honorable Comrade Officials of the Party Bureaus, March 29, 1997, 123–5–5: 213. For a description of the National Defense Regiments see Khoury, 100.

21. Makiya, *Republic of Fear*, 129.

22. Makiya, *Republic of Fear*, 206–209. Aflaq was one of three founders of the Baʿth Party in the mid-1940s along with Salah al-Din Bitar and Zaki al-Arsuzi. Aflaq lived in Iraq during Saddam Hussein's presidency where the Iraqi Baʿth venerated and protected him during their tenure.

23. Makiya, *Republic of Fear*, 129.

24. Makiya, *Republic of Fear*, xii.

25. Hannah Arendt, *The Origins of Totalitarianism* (New York: Harcourt, Brace, Jovanovich, 1973), 344.

26. Richard Overy, *The Dictators: Hitler's Germany, Stalin's Russia* (London: Allen Lane, 2004), 73.

27. As Overy writes, "A more historically sophisticated definition of totalitarianism has been developed, one that highlights the extent to which the [Nazi and Soviet] systems were driven by a positive vision of an exclusive social and cultural utopia (often described with the term 'political religion'), while recognizing that the political and social practices of the regime were often very different from the utopian aspirations." Overy, xxxii. See also Peter Grieder, "In Defence of Totalitarianism: Theory as a Tool of Historical Scholarship," *Totalitarian Movements and Political Religions* 8 (Sept.–Dec. 2007): 565; and Geoff Eley, "History with the Politics Left out Again?" *Russian Review* 45 (Oct. 1986): 385–394; Allen Kassof, "The Administered Society: Totalitarianism without Terror," *World Politics* 16 (July 1964): 560–561.

28. As quoted in Gerald R. Hughes, "Of Revelatory Histories and Hatchet Jobs: Propaganda and Method in Intelligence History," *Intelligence and National Security* 23, no. 6 (Dec. 2008): 845.

29. The first part of this sentence is a paraphrase from John Kautsky, who sees totalitarianism in the Soviet case "as a way of having one's cake and eating it, too—of having industrialization and yet retaining or establishing authoritarian government." John H. Kautsky, *Political Change in Underdeveloped Countries* (New York: John Wiley and Sons, 1962), 93; Juan Linz, *Totalitarian and Authoritarian Regimes* (Boulder: Lynne Rienner, 2000), 66.

30. As Peter Grieder writes, "As a tool of scholarly analysis, [totalitarianism] will be posited not just as a concept but as a theory, on the grounds that it can help *explain* as well as *describe* certain polities." Grieder, 565.

31. Kamaludin Gadshiiev, "Reflections on Russian Totalitarianism," *Totalitarianism and Political Religions: Concepts for the Comparisons of Dictatorships*, vol. 1, ed. Hans Maier, trans. Jodi Bruhn (London: Routledge, 1996), 55.

32. Linz, *Totalitarian and Authoritarian Regimes*, 66.

33. Arendt, xxxiv–xl.

34. As Baram wrote about Hussein in 1980: "The system he has developed to execute and implement his rule is itself a hybrid between a Stalinist-style dictatorship, and a traditional Middle Eastern society, where family, tribe, religious sect, and ethnic group play leading roles." Amatzia Baram, "The Future of Baʿthist Iraq: Power Structure, Challenges, and Prospects," in *The Politics of Change in the Middle East*, ed. R. B. Satloff (Boulder: Westview, in cooperation with the Washington Institute for Near East Policy, 1993), 38.

35. "((A Study on Mass Mobilization)) and How to Develop It [double brackets appear as in the documents]," The Office of the Baghdad Bureau Command, 038–2–4: 157; "An Executive Plan to Consecrate the Values and Principles Included in the Speech that the Comrade Leader Struggler, Saddam Hussein (God save

him), Gave to the Comrades Who Were Honored with the Order of the Party on the Evening of 3/5/1989," the Office of the Southern Bureau, 071–1–7: 66.

The Nazis, Soviets, and Italian Fascists all used these same terms when spelling out the goals behind their ideologies. See Timothy S. Brown, *Weimar Radicals: Nazis and Communists between Authenticity and Performance* (New York: Berghahn Books, 2009), 133; Czeslaw Milosz, *The Captive Mind*, trans. Jane Zielonko (New York: Octagon Books, 1981), 77; Emilio Gentile, "Fascism, Totalitarianism and Political Religion: Definitions and Critical Reflections on Criticism of an Interpretation," *Totalitarian Movements and Political Religions* 5 (Winter 2004): 328.

36. "A Work Plan for Coordination between the Party and Mass Organizations in the Field of the Baʿthification of Society," 025–5–5: 481. This document is likely from 1988 as it is preceded by a cover letter dated from the latter part of that year: "The Committee on Framing (*taʾṭīr*) and Baʿthification," Secretary of the Office of the Baghdad Bureau to the Office of the Party Secretariat, Dec. 1, 1988, 025–5–5: 475.

37. "Cultural Report," The Official for the Central Cultural Committee to the Office of the Baghdad Bureau Command, Aug. 6, 1984, 041–1–5: 255; "The Assumption of Lower Responsibility," Secretary of the Diyala Branch Command from a lower position to the Office of the Party Secretariat, Nov. 18, 1985, 029–2–3: 412. "Practicing responsibility from the lowest position" was a Baʿth Party initiative begun in the mid-1980s in which party members of organizational commands (divisions, sections, branches, and bureaus) spent a period of time running the affairs of lower level organizations so as to impart their experience to those further down the chain of command, and so higher Baʿthist officials could get a sense for life in the lower-level cadre.

38. "What We Do and How We Work," Sept. 23, 1995, 025–1–7: 40. The title refers to a set of remarks that Saddam Hussein gave at a meeting of the RCC on Sept. 23, 1995, which became party doctrine.

39. That the Baʿth did not tolerate neutrality was a frequent theme of the Culture Minister under Saddam, Latif Nisayyif al-Jasim, who said in relation to Iraqi writers in 1989, "We cannot understand why some have kept silent for the past eight years of the Iraq–Iran war. Our memory holds some names of those in our society who have been waiting, like snakes hiding in their holes, for the right moment to show their teeth and tongues while we hear their breath." And in the same paper on the same day: "whoever is reluctant to commit himself to a clear position, a question mark will be raised against what he writes." *Al-Jumhurriya*, April 30, 1989, quoted in Fatima Mohsen, "Cultural Totalitarianism," in *Iraq Since the Gulf War: Prospects for Democracy*, ed. Fran Hazelton for CARDRI (London: Zed Books, 1994), 14, 18.

40. Batatu, *Old Social Classes*, 730.

41. The Slugletts describe Baʿthist ideology as "couched in extremely wide and vague terms" and as lacking "both an analytical framework and clearly defined objectives. As a result, the mere reiteration of pious nostrums about, for example, 'Arab unity,' was and occasionally still is thought sufficient to confirm the gener-

ally erroneous impression that Baʿthist parties or governments were or are actually working actively towards this end." Farouk-Sluglett and Sluglett, *Iraq since 1958*, 109, 134, 334 n76; Majid Khadduri, *Socialist Iraq: A Study in Iraqi Politics since 1968* (Washington, DC: The Middle East Institute, 1978).

42. Makiya, *Republic of Fear*, 208.

43. Woods, et al., *The Saddam Tapes*, 328–329.

44. Ofra Bengio, *Saddam's Word: Political Discourse in Iraq* (Studies in Middle Eastern History. New York: Oxford University Press, 1998), 71.

45. Giovanni Gentile, "The Philosophic Basis of Fascism," *Foreign Affairs* 6 (Jan. 1928): 300.

46. Eric Davis, *Memories of State: Politics, History, and Collective Identity in Modern Iraq* (Berkeley: University of California Press, 2005), 22.

47. Leszek Kolakowski, "Hope and Hopelessness," 45–46.

48. "A Plan for the Baʿthification of Society," The Arab Baʿth Socialist Party Office of the Euphrates Bureau, 111-3-2: 16.

49. 111-3-2: 27.

50. Michel Aflaq, *"al-Haraka al-Fikriyya al-shamila," Fi Sabil al-Baʿth – al-Juzʾ al-ʾAwwal*, http://albaath.online.fr/Volume%20I-Chapters/Fi%20Sabil%20al%20Baal-Vol%201-Ch11.htm [accessed Feb. 2, 2012].

51. Karl Dietrich Bracher, "Stages of Totalitarian 'Integration' (Gleichschaltung): The Consolidation of National Socialist Rule in 1933 and 1944," in *Republic to Reich: The Making of the Nazi Revolution*, trans. Ralph Manheim (New York: Pantheon Books, 1972), 109–128; Brown, 123; Anthony Giddens, *The Nation-State and Violence: Volume Two of a Contemporary Critique of Historical Materialism* (Berkeley: University of California Press, 1985), 9; Michael Mann, "The Autonomous Power of the State: Its Origins, Mechanisms and Results," in *States, War, and Capitalism: Studies in Political Sociology*, ed. Michael Mann (Oxford: Basil Blackwell, 1988), 5–8.

52. Ronald Grigor Suny, "Stalin and His Stalinism: Power and Authority in the Soviet Union, 1930–1953," in *Stalinism*, ed. David L. Hoffman (Cornwall: Blackwell Publishing, 2003), 34.

53. There is no exact, one-word translation of *targhīb* in English. A more accurate, multiword translation might be "arousing an interest in" or "awakening one's desire for." Baram translates the entire phrase as "tremendous terror" and "considerable enticement." Another way of translating the expression is "sticks and carrots." Baram, *Building toward Crisis*, 67; Wafiq al-Samarrai, *Huttam al-Bawwaba al-Sharqiyya wa-Haqaʾiq ʿan al-Zaman al-Sayiʾ fi al-ʿIraq: Qiraʾa Jadida fi Harbay al-Khalij al-ʾUwwla wa-l-Thaniyya* (Kuwait: Sharikat Dar al-Qubs li-l-Sahafa wa-l-Nashr, 1997), 190–195.

54. See Vaclav Havel for an excellent explanation of the type of fear referred to here: Havel, "Letter to Dr. Gustav Husak," in *Vaclav Havel: Living in Truth*, ed. Jan Vladislav, (London: Faber and Faber, 1990), 4–7.

55. Baram, *Building toward Crisis*, 37–38; Baram, "Neo-Tribalism in Iraq: Saddam Hussein's Tribal Policies 1991–1996," *International Journal of Middle East Stud-*

ies 29 (Feb. 1997): 1–31; Baram, "Re-Inventing Nationalism, in Ba'thi Iraq 1968–1994: Supra-Territorial and Territorial Identities and What Lies Below," *Princeton Papers: Interdisciplinary Journal of Middle Eastern Studies* 5 (Fall 1996): 29–56; Ofra Bengio, "Iraq," in *Middle East Contemporary Survey, Vol. 16, 1992*, ed. Ami Ayalon (Boulder: Westview Press, 1995), 456–458; Farouk-Sluglett and Sluglett, *Iraq since 1958*, 307–308; Faleh A. Jabar, "Clerics, Tribes, Ideologues and Urban Dwellers in the South of Iraq: The Potential for Rebellion," *The Adelphi Papers* 354 (Jan. 2003), 172–174; Jabar, "Shaykhs and Ideologues: Detribalization and Retribalization in Iraq, 1968–1998," *Middle East Report* 215 (summer 2000): 31; Achim Rohde, *State-Society Relations in Ba'thist Iraq: Facing Dictatorship* (London: Routledge, 2010), 57–64: Toby Dodge, *Inventing Iraq: the Failure of Nation-Building and a History Denied* (New York: Columbia University Press, 2003), 162. Also Baram, "Re-Thinking."

56. Makiya, *Republic of Fear*, xv.

57. Makiya, *Republic of Fear*, xxx–xxxi.

58. Jabar, "Shaykhs and Ideologues," 31; Bengio, "Iraq," in *Middle East Contemporary Survey, Vol. 17, 1993*, ed. Ami Ayalon (Boulder: Westview Press, 1995), 391–393. The exams anecdote comes from Hussein's son-in-law, Hussein Kamel, in his debrief with UNSCOM after his defection in 1995: Campaign against Sanctions on Iraq, http://www.casi.org.uk/info/unscom950822.pdf [accessed August 19, 2014].

59. See Baram's "Neo-Tribalism," "Re-Inventing," and *From Militant Secularism to Islamism: The Iraqi Ba'th Regime 1968–2003*, History and Public Policy Program Occasional Paper (Washington, DC: Woodrow Wilson International Center for Scholars, October 2011).

60. As chapter 6 explains in greater detail, I define the "Baʿthist State" as the Baʿth Party in addition to Iraq's regular state institutions.

61. Khoury, 8; David Baran, *Vivre la tyrannie et lui survivre: L'Irak en transition* (Paris: Mille et Une Nuits, 2004), 91–112.

62. Linz, *Totalitarian and Authoritarian Regimes*, 177; Baram, *Building toward Crisis*, 65.

63. This statement follows Edward N. Peterson in *The Limits of Hitler's Power* when he says that "the assumption during my research was that most men will resist power to some extent and for many varied reasons. Human reaction is complex, rarely a full support or full rejection of any group action; it is rather a wavering between support and rejection, an acceptance of one part, a rejection of another." (Princeton: Princeton University Press, 1969), xvii–xviii.

CHAPTER TWO

1. Leonard Schapiro argues that one of the five critical "contours" of totalitarianism is the emergence of a single "Leader" who turns the party and state into vehicles for him to assume supreme power. By this logic, Baʿthist Iraq did not become truly totalitarian until Hussein became president. Other totalitarian theo-

rists, such as Linz, do not believe that one leader's supremacy is essential, although Linz does argue that power must be monopolized by a "monistic but not monolithic" group of rulers. Leonard Schapiro, *Totalitarianism* (New York: Praeger, 1972), 21–29; Linz, "Fascism and Non-Democratic Regimes," *Totalitarianism and Political Religions: Concepts for the Comparisons of Dictatorships: Theory and History of Interpretation*, vol. 3, ed. Hans Maier, trans. Jodi Bruhn (London: Routledge, 1996)," 66–71, quote 70.

2. There are at least two boxfiles from 1978 (031-3-4 and 119-4-6) in the BRCC labeled as containing records related to the Baʿth Party's professional associations and the Presidential Diwan, respectively. There are also a handful of boxfiles from 1979. See, e.g., boxfile 044-2-1 that has information about internal security officers from 1979, and a boxfile labeled "1979 Mr. President" (*1979 al-sayyid al-raʾīs*), which contains memoranda and reports handed to Saddam Hussein. The latter boxfile in particular shows that the way Hussein did business in 1979 did not differ greatly from the end of his regime. Boxfile 003-1-1, labeled "Decisions of the Regional Command" (*qarārāt al-qiyāda al-quṭriyya*), is from 1980 but has many documents from 1979. A number of the BRCC boxfiles from the early 1980s have documents from the late 1970s because the years listed on the outside of the boxfiles do not always correlate to the documents inside, and because Baʿthist bureaucrats attached relevant documents from the late 1970s as background for many of the matters dealt with in the early 1980s.

3. David Pool, "From Elite to Class: The Transformation of Iraqi Political Leadership," in *The Integration of Modern Iraq*, ed. Abbas Kelidar (London: Croom Helm, 1979), 63–87.

4. In 1932, the year that Iraq gained nominal independence from Great Britain, Arabs made up about three-quarters of the population with Shiʿi Arabs 53 percent and Sunnis 21 percent. The Kurds (overwhelmingly Sunni but also with a small Shiʿi contingent, known as Faylī Kurds) consisted of between 15 to 20 percent. Gabriel Baer, *Population and Society in the Arab East*, trans. Hanna Szoke (New York: Frederick A. Praeger, 1964), 105–108.

5. Mohammad Tarbush, *The Role of the Military in Politics: a Case Study of Iraq to 1941* (London: KPI, 1982); Phebe Marr, *The Modern History of Iraq*, 2nd ed. (Boulder: Westview Press, 2004), 40. For more on the political history of the monarchy and Great Britain's role in creating it, see Elie Kedourie, "The Kingdom of Iraq: A Retrospect," in *The Chatham House Version and Other Middle Eastern Studies* (Chicago: Ivan R. Dee, 2004), 236–282; Dodge, *Inventing Iraq*; Khadduri, *Socialist Iraq*; Tripp, 30–142.

6. Batatu, *Old Social Classes*, 182–183, 300.

7. This pattern reoccurred ad nauseam. After General Bakr Sidqi allied with Hikmat Sulaiman and members of the left-leaning *Ahālī* group to carry out Iraq's first coup d'état in 1936, installing Sulaiman as prime minister, Sidqi and Sulaiman arranged for the *Ahālī* group's ministers to lose the next election. In 1937, Sidqi was assassinated, causing the fall of Sulaiman's government. From 1937 to 1941, Nuri al-Said, the most powerful civilian and master manipulator of Iraqi pol-

itics during the British mandate and monarchical periods, variously allied with and betrayed allies within the army in an effort to retain the prime ministership. In 1958, Abd al-Karim Qasim joined with Abd al-Salam Arif to overthrow the monarchy before Qasim imprisoned Arif. Arif then entered a coalition with the Baʿth Party and Nasserist officers in 1963 to depose Qasim but purged his two allies shortly thereafter. For their part, the Baʿth dispensed with their military allies after pulling off the 1968 coup. Saddam Hussein subsequently eased out Ahmad Hasan al-Bakr as president in 1979. Batatu, *Old Social Classes*, 182–183, 300; Marr, 73–74; Tripp, 132–139.

8. Arif, for instance, after shunting aside the Baʿthists and Nasserists in 1963, fell back on his Sunni tribe from Ramadi, the Jumaila, placing tribe members into top military offices. The Baʿth followed this example. Fuad al-Rikabi, a Shiʿi, led the Baʿth Party in Iraq in the 1950s and its leadership consisted mostly of his family members. By the time of the 1968 coup, however, the Baʿth Party was led by Ahmad Hassan al-Bakr and Saddam Hussein's group of Tikriti Sunnis of the Albu Nasr tribe. From 1968 to 1977, not a single Shiʿi and only one Kurd served in Iraq's top political body, the Revolutionary Command Council (RCC). Marr, 124–127; Farouk-Sluglett and Sluglett, *Iraq since 1958*, 194; Yitzhak Nakash, *The Shiʿis of Iraq* (Princeton: Princeton University Press, 1994), 136; Batatu, *Old Social Classes*, 1090–1091.

9. As Lisa Wedeen remarked about Hafez al-Assad's regime in Syria, "It is the historical predicament of the Syrian regime that in order to survive it must negotiate between the conflicting imperatives of state- and nation-building, between exclusive practices to consolidate political power and enforce the regime's dominance, and inclusive policies to generate collective, national identification." This statement describes the predicament of Iraq's rulers as well. Lisa Wedeen, *Ambiguities of Domination: Politics, Rhetoric, and Symbols in Contemporary Syria* (Chicago: University of Chicago Press, 1999), 15.

10. The political report of the party's Eighth Regional Conference, held in 1974, contains an entire chapter on the history of the Iraqi military and the important roles it played in sparking coups in 1936, 1941, 1958, 1963, and 1968. It says explicitly that Baʿth Party leaders kept their experience from 1963 in the back of their minds when planning and executing the 1968 coup. Hizb al-Baʿth al-ʿArabi al-ʾIshtiraki, *Revolutionary Iraq, 1968–1973: The Political Report Adopted by the Eighth Regional Congress of the Arab Baʿth Socialist Party—Iraq, January, 1974* (Baghdad: The Arab Ba'th Socialist Party, Jan. 1974), 13–14, 57, 166. See also James T. Quinlivan, "Coup-Proofing: Its Practices and Consequences in the Middle East," *International Security* 24 (Autumn 1999): 131–165.

11. Al-Bakr was one of an initial crop of poor, young Tikrit-area men with no other career prospects who managed to enroll in the Iraqi officer academy under the monarchy, taking advantage of the connections of Muhammad Mukhlis, a Tikriti who fought alongside King Faysal in the Great Arab Revolt and then joined Faysal's patronage network after Faysal became king. For a good account of the background and failure of the 1963 coup and its aftermath, including the Baʿth's

internal struggles and consolidation by Sunni Tikriti military officers, see Batatu, *Old Social Classes*, 966–973, 1003–1026, and 1071–1089. See also Amatzia Baram, "Saddam's Power Structure: The Tikritis Before, During, and After the War," *The Adelphi Papers* (Jan. 2003), 94–97; Marr, 117–122; Ibrahim al-Marashi and Sammy Salama, *Iraq's Armed Forces: an Analytical History* (London: Routledge, 2008), 110–111.

12. Khadduri, 25–30; Tripp, 184.

13. In June 1969, e.g., Baʿth Party leaders executed two northern commanders for supposedly conspiring with Iran to oust the government. Seven months later, they sentenced over thirty current and retired officers to death for a plot revealed by the security services. Ahmed S. Hashim, "Saddam Husayn and Civil-Military Relations in Iraq: The Quest for Legitimacy and Power," *Middle East Journal* 57 (Winter 2003): 16–21; al-Marashi and Salama, 114–120. For more examples, see Batatu, *Old Social Classes*, 1093–1094.

14. Hizb al-Baʿth, *Revolutionary Iraq*, 169; Bengio, *Saddam's Word*, 149; Hashim, "Saddam Husayn and Civil-Military Relations in Iraq," 22–23; Baram, "Future of Baʿthist Iraq," 35.

15. Hashim, "Saddam Husayn and Civil-Military Relations in Iraq," 18–25.

16. Tripp, 189, 200–202; Marr, 171.

17. Al-Samarrai, 134, 201.

18. Al-Samarrai, 202–207.

19. Baram, "Saddam's Power Structure," 94–97.

20. Jawad Hashim, *Mudhakkarat Wazir maʿa al-Bakr wa Saddam* (Beirut: Dar al-Saqi, 2003), 251–255.

21. Baram, "Saddam's Power Structure," 95–96; Tripp, 215–216.

22. Farouk-Sluglett and Sluglett, *Iraq since 1958*, 208.

23. Jawad Hashim, 256–257.

24. Farouk-Sluglett and Sluglett, *Iraq since 1958*, 120. The main tribes that Hussein relied on from this area were the *ʾalbū nāṣir* (Hussein and al-Bakr's tribe), *al-ʿizza*, *al-ʿubayd*, and *al-jubūr*. Al-Samarrai, 187.

25. Baram, "Neo-Tribalism in Iraq," 5–6.

26. Toby Dodge, "Cake Walk, Coup, or Urban Warfare: The Battle for Iraq," *The Adelphi Papers* 354 (Jan. 2003): 66.

27. Jabar, "Clerics, Tribes," 175.

28. Marr, 161–168.

29. Quote from Juman Kubba, *The First Evidence: A Memoir of Life in Iraq under Saddam Hussein* (Jefferson, NC: McFarland, 2003), 1–2. See also Ala Bashir, *The Insider: Trapped in Saddam's Brutal Regime* (London: Abacus, 2005), 46.

30. Diya al-Din al-Majmai, *Hurub Saddam: Shahid ʿAyyan li-ʾAhdath Thalatha ʿUqud min Tarikh al-ʿIrāq al-Hadīth* (London: Dar al-Hikma, 2006), 14; Bashir, 43, 63; Jawad Hashim, 50–51.

31. Jawad Hashim, 292.

32. Hussein's ruthlessness and paranoia are encapsulated in statements such as this, as told to Efraim Karsh and Inari Rautsi: "I know that there are scores of people plotting to kill me . . . and this is not difficult to understand. After all, did we

not seize power by plotting against our predecessors? However . . . I am far cleverer than they are. I know they are conspiring to kill me long before they actually start planning to do it. This enables me to get them before they have the faintest chance of striking at me." Karsh and Rautsi, *Saddam Hussein: A Political Biography* (New York: Grove Press, 2002), 3.

33. Isaiah Berlin, "Political Ideas in the Twentieth Century," *Foreign Affairs* 28 (April 1950): 366.

34. For accounts of Hussein's childhood see Karsh and Rautsi; Said K. Aburish, *Saddam Hussein: The Politics of Revenge* (New York: Bloomsbury, 2000), 9–35; Con Coughlin, *Saddam: His Rise and Fall* (New York: Harper Perennial, 2004), 1–22.

35. Jerrold M. Post and Amatzia Baram, *Saddam Is Iraq: Iraq is Saddam* (Maxwell Air Force Base, AL: USAF Counterproliferation Center Maxwell Air Force Base Air University, 2002), 9–12.

36. Batatu, *Old Social Classes*, 1084–1085.

37. It is possible that this organization, about which little information exists, was the aforementioned Office of Public Relations. Mustafa Alani, "Saddam's Support Structure," in *Gulf Security: Opportunities and Challenges for the New Generation*, ed. Patrick and Toase McKnight (London: Royal United Services Institute, 2001), 42.

38. Marr, 144–146; Batatu, *Old Social Classes*, 1079, 1082–1085; Khadduri, 71–76.

39. See, e.g., Khalidah Abd al-Qahhar, *Sikritirat Saddam Tatakallam* (Cairo: al-Zahrā' li-l-Iʿlam al-ʿArabi, 1990), 21–25; and Talib al-Hassan, *Hukumat al-Quriyya: Fusul min Sulta Nazihin min Rif Tikrit* (Beirut: UR Press, 2004).

40. Linz, "Fascism," 252–253, quote 253.

41. The Baʿth Party constitution can be found in Kamel Abu Jaber, *The Arab Baʿth Socialist Party: History, Ideology, and Organization* (Syracuse: Syracuse University Press, 1966), 167–174, quotes 167, 170. Abu Jaber takes the constitution word for word from Sylvia Haim, *Arab Nationalism: An Anthology* (Berkeley: University of California Press, 1962), 233–241. For more on the constitution and the Baʿth Party's genesis see Amatzia Baram, *Culture, History, and Ideology in the Formation of Baʿthist Iraq, 1968–1989* (New York: St. Martin's Press, 1991), 9–10.

42. Adeed Dawisha, "Identity and Political Survival in Hussein's Iraq," *The Middle East Journal* 53 (Autumn 1999): 563.

43. There are countless examples of these forms in the BRCC. See, e.g., two forms that the SSO and the Baʿth Party's Baghdad Bureau filled out about individuals in boxfile 005-3-6: 109, 146–147. In his interviews with Saddam after the Iraqi president's capture by American forces, FBI agent George L. Piro wrote in his report that "Hussein explained that the selection or dismissal of individuals for particular military or governmental positions often involves consideration of the perception of one's family or tribe." "Saddam Hussein Talks to the FBI," Interview Session 14, March 13, 2004, http://www.gwu.edu/~nsarchiv/NSAEBB/NSAEBB279/15.pdf [accessed Aug. 27, 2012].

44. Emphasis added. Article 41, clause 2 says something similar: "The state is

responsible for the protection of the liberty of speech, of publication, of assembly, of protest, and of the press, within the limits of the higher Arab national interest. It is for the state to facilitate all the means and the modalities which tend to realize this liberty." Abu Jaber, 167–168, 173.

45. I. L. Kandel, "Education in Nazi Germany," *Annals of the American Academy of Political and Social Science* (Nov. 1935): 158.

46. 025-1-7: 38.

47. Abu Jaber, 126.

48. Michel Aflaq, "Nationalism and Revolution," in *Arab Nationalism: An Anthology*, ed. Sylvia Haim (Berkeley: University of California Press, 1962), 242–243.

49. Haim, 70.

50. Abu Jaber, 172.

51. Abu Jaber, 169.

52. Abu Jaber, 126.

53. Abu Jaber, 169–172.

54. M. Farouk-Sluglett and P. Sluglett, "Iraqi Baʿthism: Nationalism, Socialism and National Socialism," in *Saddam's Iraq, Revolution or Reaction* (Avon, UK: Zed Books and CARDRI, 1986), 89–107.

55. Farouk-Sluglett and Sluglett, *Iraq since 1958*, 228.

56. Abu Jaber, 169.

57. Hizb al-Baʿth al-ʿArabi al-ʾIshtiraki, *Al-Taqrir Al-Markazi Li-l-Muʾtamar Al-Qutri at-Tasiʿ* (Baghdad: Dar al-Hurriya li-l-Tabaʿa, 1983), 89–148, but especially 114–115.

58. Hizb al-Baʿth, *Revolutionary Iraq*, 51.

59. Saddam Hussein, *On History, Heritage and Religion*, trans. Naji al-Hadithi (Baghdad: Translation & Foreign Languages Publishing House, 1981), 5.

PART II

1. 040-4-7: 149.

2. "Jihad . . . and Revolutionary Work—A Draft Party Working Paper," Office of the Baghdad Bureau, Dec. 29, 1990, 051-1-2: 609.

3. Boxfiles 023-2-6 and 027-4-1, e.g., contain many such reports.

4. See, e.g., a petition by a sheikh asking to be officially recognized as the head of his clan (*fakhdh*) in which he included an original poem praising Hussein. June 14, 2000, 049-5-7: 168–169.

CHAPTER THREE

The epigraph for this chapter is from the epigraph of a report from the al-Rashid Branch of the Baʿth Party. "Report of Responsibility," Member of the Office of the Baghdad Bureau to the Honorable Struggling Comrade Secretary of the Office, Dec. 4, 1985, 035-2-3: 262.

1. Suny, 19.

2. The Iraqi Baʿth adopted Aflaq as their patron saint after Aflaq fell out with his Baʿthist compatriots in Syria.

3. Baram, *Culture*, xiii; Bengio, *Middle East Contemporary Survey, Vol. 7, 1982–1983*, 561.

4. This quotation comes from David L. Hoffman's editor's introduction to Suny in *Stalinism*, 14–15.

5. Vaclav Havel, "The Power of the Powerless," in *Vaclav Havel: Living in Truth*, ed. Jan Vladislav (London: Faber and Faber, 1990), 39.

6. Hizb al-Baʿth al-ʿArabi al-ʾIshtiraki, *Niḍal al-Baʿth* (Syria, 1963).

7. "The Cultural Program for Members," Deputy Official of the Office of Culture and Media to the Honorable Comrade Struggler Saddam Hussein, Deputy Secretary-General of the Party (God save him), June 2, 1986, 087-1-1: 87–114, quote 88.

8. 087-1-1: 89, 90, 92–94.

9. al-Majmai, 14. Similar sentiments are expressed or discussed in Bashir, 43, 63; and Jawad Hashim, 50–51.

10. al-Majmai, 15–17.

11. The phrase "preservation of the revolution" comes from the party's 1974 conference report (Hizb al-Baʿth, *Revolutionary Iraq*, 240–241).

12. Gaetano Mosca, *The Ruling Class (Elementi Di Scienza Politica)*, trans. Hannah D. Kahn (New York: McGraw Hill Book Company Inc., 1939), 71.

13. Overy, 265.

14. Amatzia Baram, "Saddam Hussein: A Political Profile," *Jerusalem Quarterly* 17 (Autumn 1980): 139.

15. Tripp, 207.

16. Quote from Abu Islam Ahmad Abd Allah, *Saddam Husayn: al-Nashaʾa.. al-Tarikh..al-Jarima* (Cairo: Bayt al-Hikma), 82; Neil MacFarquhar, "Saddam Hussein, Defiant Dictator Who Ruled Iraq With Violence and Fear, Dies," *New York Times*, Dec. 30, 2006, http://www.nytimes.com/2006/12/30/world/middleeast/30saddam.html?pagewanted=print [accessed Aug. 24, 2011]; Makiya, *Republic of Fear*, 70–72; Walid Hilli, *al-ʾIraq: al-Waqiʾ wa-ʾAfaq al-Mustaqbal* (Beirut: Dar al-Furat, 1992), 43–44.

17. Jawad Hashim, 345.

18. See, e.g., boxfile 040-3-6, entitled "*al-Sayyid al-Raʾīs*"; Jawad Hashim, 347–348.

19. 071-1-7: 66.

20. Hizb al-Baʿth, *Revolutionary Iraq*, 11–12.

21. Hussein, *On History*, 9.

22. Hizb al-Baʿth, *Revolutionary Iraq*, 7.

23. Jawad Hashim, 347–348.

24. Hizb al-Baʿth, *al-Taqrir al-Markazi*, 28–40.

25. Hizb al-Baʿth, *al-Taqrir al-Markazi*, 40.

26. Hizb al-Baʿth, *al-Taqrir al-Markazi*, 9.

27. Hizb al-Baʿth, *al-Taqrir al-Markazi*, 28.

28. See, e.g., a letter from a party cell member to the director of his division, which repeats many of these same historical assertions: "Cultural Report," [name withheld] the First Cell/the Qaʿqa Division to the Comrade Official of the Division, 026-4-4: 65.

29. A citizen petition to Saddam Hussein, June 17, 2000, 029-1-3: 118.

30. See, e.g., "A Work Program Recommended to Transform the Directives of Mr. President Leader, Saddam Hussein (God save him and keep him), During His Eminence's Heading of the Thirteenth Meeting of the Council of Ministers on 28/3/2000, into Active, Applied Behavior," 050-5-5: 177–180; 031-2-1: 7–9; "Being Attentive to the Cleanliness of the Party's Headquarters," Director of the Office of the Party Secretariat to All of the Bureau Offices in the Country, Oct. 19, 1989, 022-1-4: 28; "Reducing the Phenomenon of Smoking," The Head of the Presidential Diwan to the Secretariat of the Council of Ministers, Sept. 13, 2000, 053-4-1: 319–320.

31. A citizen petition to Saddam Hussein, 022-1-3: 387–388.

32. "Amendment to the Law of the Flag of Iraq Number 33 for the Year 1986," RCC Decision #25, Jan. 22, 1991, 168-4-1: 418–419.

33. "Initiative," The Director of the Party Secretariat to the Presidency of the Republic, Sept. 1, 2002, 026-3-3: 1.

34. According to Abu Islam Ahmad Abd Allah, Iraqis were supposed to repeat this phrase after each time that they spoke or referred to Hussein in conversation as well. Abd Allah, 78.

35. "The Occasion of the 10 of Muharram," Director of the Office of the Party Secretariat to the Comrade Brigadier General Abd al-Ghafour/Aid to the Honorable Mr. President of the Republic, July 1, 1995, 046-5-4: 299.

36. Amir Iskandar, *Saddam Husayn Munadilan wa-Mufakkiran wa-Insanan* (Casablanca: Tansift, 2000), 21.

37. According to Schapiro, "Theocracy, or fusion of church and state in one ruler or ruling elite, is, of course, a salient feature of the totalitarian regime." Schapiro, 93.

38. 023-5-4. The boxfile is entitled "Placards of the Comrade Leader (God save him)," [*Jadāriyāt al-rafīq al-qāʾid (ḥafẓuhu allah)*].

39. In 2000, the Saʿad bin Abi Waqas branch of the party, for instance, suggested putting "recommendations" from a speech Hussein had given recently onto posters, "Posters of the Commandments of the Comrade Leader," Secretariat of the Saʿad bin Abi Waqas Branch Command to the Office of the Party Secretariat, Sept. 19, 2000, 183-4-1: 482–501.

40. For a discussion of the most potent example of this, the "Victory Arch" erected in Baghdad in 1989, see Kanan Makiya, *The Monument: Art and Vulgarity in Saddam Hussein's Iraq* (New York: Palgrave Macmillan, 2004).

41. 079-5-1: 422; 028-1-7: 41, 47.

42. Secretary of Mr. President of the Republic for Party Affairs to the Military Office, 23 April, 1983, 035-1-4: 62.

43. RCC Decision No. 840, Nov. 4, 1986, http://www.iraq-ild.org/LoadLaw

Book.aspx?SP=FREE&SC=1301200128993302&Year=1986&PageNum=1 [accessed March 24, 2013].

44. "Answer," Director of General Security to the Arab Baʿth Socialist Party—Office of the Party Secretariat, Oct. 21, 1987, 038-5-4: 123.

45. See, e.g., 025-1-7: 125; "Speech of Mr. President Leader (God save him)," Minister of Culture to the Office of the Party Secretariat, March 7, 1994, 031-2-1: 1.

46. "Publications of the Comrade Leader," Secretary of the Command of the Office of the Southern Bureau to the Commands of the Branches Subordinate to the Office, Aug. 13, 1985, 038-3-7: 286.

47. Marion Farouk-Sluglett and Peter Sluglett make this point in "Iraqi Baʿthism," 105.

48. From a 1996 Baʿth Party member petition to Hussein, 119-4-8: 308–309.

49. 018-5-2: 32. In Arabic, the vowels for words are generally not written in normal texts and must be read based on knowledge of grammar and the pronunciation of Modern Standard Arabic.

50. 040-4-7: 149.

51. See, e.g., 022-1-5: 41; 001-5-1: 1; 021-2-5: 10.

52. Secretary of Mr. President of the Republic for Party Affairs to the Honorable Mr. President Leader, April 10, 1983, 044-5-1: 298.

53. "[Name withheld]," Director of the Office of the Party Secretariat to the Presidential Diwan, Aug. 13, 2002, 028-1-7: 131.

54. As told to Haddad during an interview of a young woman from Shomali. Fanar Haddad, *Sectarianism in Iraq: Antagonistic Visions of Unity* (New York: Columbia University Press, 2011), 64.

CHAPTER FOUR

1. William Henry Chamberlin, "Making the Collective Man in Soviet Russia," *Foreign Affairs* (Jan. 1932): 280.

2. Brown, 133.

3. Kandel, 157.

4. Clifford Geertz, "Ideology as a Cultural System," in *The Interpretation of Cultures: Selected Essays by Clifford Geertz* (New York: Basic Books, Inc., 1973), 216. Geertz uses the term "cultural patterns" and lists a few of these cultural sources as examples.

5. Boris Souvarine, *Stalin: A Critical Survey of Bolshevism* (New York: Octagon Books, 1972), 575; Kandel, 162.

6. Emilio Gentile, "Fascism," 363–364; Emilio Gentile, "The Sacralisation of Politics: Definitions, Interpretations and Reflections on the Question of Secular Religion and Totalitarianism," *Totalitarian Movements and Political Religions* 1 (Summer 2000): 25; Hans Maier, "Political Religion: A Concept and Its Limitations," *Totalitarian Movements and Political Religions* 8 (March 2007): 11; Philippe Burrin, "Political Religion: The Relevance of a Concept," *History and Memory* 9 (Fall 1997): 321–349; Overy, xxxii.

7. George L. Mosse, *The Nationalization of the Masses: Political Symbolism and Mass Movements in Germany from the Napoleonic Wars through the Third Reich* (New York: Howard Fertig, 1975), 81; Jiping Zuo, "Political Religion: The Case of the Cultural Revolution in China," *Sociological Analysis* 52 (Spring 1991): 104.

8. 041-1-5: 256.

9. After 1991, the Baʿth eliminated these committees and designated the party's Office of Culture and Media as the primary source of cultural programming. The Office of Culture and Media then tasked party organizations to implement its directives. A ministry of the same name also existed. The two were technically separate offices—one for the state, the other for the party—but they carried out the same activities and served the same functions. For the abolishment of the branch cultural committees and empowerment of the central office, see "Eliminate the Cultural Committees," Director of the Office of the Party Secretariat to the Commands of all of the Party Branches, Sept. 24, 1991, 162-1-4: 170.

10. 041-1-5: 255.

11. As chapter 5 will show, each party organization throughout the party apparatus had to send in reports about a variety of subjects at regular intervals.

12. 041-1-5: 255–258.

13. "Decision," Secretary of the Organizational Committee to the Organizational Committees in the Entire Country, Dec. 31, 1985, 046-5-4: 183–185.

14. Director of the Office of the Party Secretariat to the Comrade Official of the Organizational Committee, May 21, 1989, 021-1-4: 368. This question appeared on an evaluation from 1989. Similar ones appear on other forms throughout the BRCC.

15. 025-1-7: 46.

16. This was the title of a speech that Hussein gave at the Baʿth Party's Baghdad Branch on July 28, 1979. 087-1-1: 93. For an extended passage that lays out the entire logic behind putting Hussein's words into practice see 071-1-7: 66.

17. My analysis here was heavily influenced by Clifford Geertz, "Religion as a Cultural System," in *Anthropological Approaches to the Study of Religion*, ed. Michael Banton (New York: Frederick A. Praeger, 1966), 9.

18. 038-2-4: 159.

19. 025-5-5: 481.

20. Berlin, 372.

21. Stephen H. Roberts, *The House That Hitler Built* (New York: Gordon Press, 1975), 254.

22. Carl J. Friedrich and Zbigniew K. Brzezinski, *Totalitarian Dictatorship and Autocracy* (New York: Frederick A. Praeger, 1956), 115.

23. "Study Number ((1)): Ways to Culturalize the Masses ((Mass Mobilization)) The Office of the Euphrates Bureau Command (the Cultural Committee), 021-1-5: 645–649. Double and single parentheses appear as in the documents.

24. 021-1-5: 645–649. For an analysis of the Baʿthification of popular culture see Mohsen.

25. C. K. Ogden and I. A. Richards, *The Meaning of Meaning* (London: Routledge, 2001), 30.

26. Bengio, *Saddam's Word*, 9; Ogden and Richards, 30, 59.

27. The "Saddam River" was a huge drainage canal inaugurated in 1992 that Hussein claimed to be Iraq's third great river next to the Tigris and Euphrates. The Ba'th used it, among other things, to drain the marshes. A list of "Central Slogans for the Celebration of the River Saddam," 028-3-4: 2.

28. Marr, 207.

29. There are many examples of this. See, e.g., boxfile 029-5-3.

30. See, e.g., Khoury's interviews of soldiers who served on the frontlines. Khoury, 207–211.

31. Milosz in *Captive Mind* discusses the process by which intellectuals living behind the Iron Curtain eventually succumbed to their environments and began to parrot the ideological viewpoint of the regimes under which they lived.

32. It should be noted that although the overwhelming majority of the uses of "phenomenon" found for this study in the BRCC are negative, this was not an absolute rule. In a report about the Ashura events of 1989, e.g., a report lists the "Positive Phenomenon" observed that year. "A Report about the Occasion of the 10 of Muharram and the Visit of Arbain 20 Safar," Office of the Baghdad Bureau, 001-5-4: 7.

33. "The Day of the Big March," Director of the Office of the Party Secretariat to the Presidency of the Republic, Dec. 7, 1995, 072-5-4: 325.

34. "Notable Activities During the Year/1983," al-Taamim Branch Command to the Office of the Northern Bureau, Feb. 26, 1984, 065-4-3: 434.

35. Geertz, "Religion as a Cultural System," 3–4.

36. See, e.g., with regard to the Ba'th's view of the Kurdish region in "The Expectations of the Office about what Will Result from the Elections of the National Assembly in the Autonomous Region," Office of the Northern Bureau, 031-3-5: 12; and, in relation to Shi'i rituals, "Information," Director of the Office of the Party Secretariat to the Comrade Official of the Baghdad-al-Karkh Bureau and the Comrade Official of the Baghdad-al-Rasafa Bureau, Dec. 5, 1996, 046-5-4: 82.

37. 029-2-3: 88, 92, 93; "The Phenomenon of Beggary," Head of the Secretariat of the Council of Ministers to the Ministry of Labor and Social Affairs—the Office of the Minister, May 24, 1999, 021-2-7: 233–236.

38. "Celebration on the Birthday of the Noble Prophet," Head of the Presidential Diwan to the Secretariat of the Council of Ministers, etc., April 27, 2002, 063-2-4: 52.

39. Some of the Shi'i rituals performed on the anniversaries of the deaths of Shi'i martyrs that the Ba'th refer to as "phenomena" are "the phenomenon of the processions" (*ẓāhirat al-mashī*), "the phenomenon of the banquets" (*ẓāhirat ʾiqāmat al-walāʾim*), and "the phenomenon of banner burning" (*ẓāhirat ʾiḥrāq al-ʾiṭārāt*).

40. Michel Aflaq, "*Nazaratna ʾila al-din*" *Fi Sabil al-Baʿth – al-Juzʾ al-ʾAwwal*, http://albaath.online.fr/Volume%20I-Chapters/Fi%20Sabil%20al%20Baal-Vol

%201-Ch28.htm [accessed Aug. 2, 2011]. The ninth regional congress too appropriated Islam by calling it "a great revolution" (*thawra ʿuẓmā*). Hizb al-Baʿth, *al-Taqrir al-Markazi*, 264–265.

41. Nils B. Kvastad, "Semantics in the Methodology of the History of Ideas," *Journal of the History of Ideas* 38 (Jan.–Mar. 1977): 163.

42. Emphasis added. 063-2-4: 50, 52.

43. For more on the Baʿthist idiom see Baran, 40–55.

44. In a survey of Soviet scholarship, Fitzpatrick came to this same conclusion. Sheila Fitzpatrick, "New Perspectives on Stalinism," *Russian Review* 45 (Oct. 1986): 367–372.

45. A petition from a tribal sheikh to Hussein, June 14, 2000, 049-5-7: 168–169.

46. Bengio, *Saddam's Word*, 156.

47. See, e.g., "Minutes of the Session of the Supplementary Electoral Conference of the Buldruz Section Command," June 15, 2000, 043-1-4: 49–50.

48. 041-2-1: 725.

49. "Martyr's Day," Head of the Presidential Diwan to All of the Ministries—the Special Office, et al., Nov. 12, 1984, 035-3-4: 216–217.

50. "Funeral Procession," Director of the Party Secretariat to the Honorable Comrade Secretary of the Khalid bin Walid Branch Command and the Honorable Comrade Secretary of the Adhamiyya Branch Command, 052-1-6: 125.

51. Director of General Security to Honorable Mr. Secretary of the President of the Republic, Dec. 1, 1997, 076-1-6: 145.

52. 076-1-6: 145–151.

53. The BRCC documents are replete with references to the democratic character of the party and the regime as a whole. See, e.g., "The Main Special Slogans for the Elections," Director of the Party Secretariat to the Offices of the Bureaus in the Entire Country, Feb. 20, 1989, 022-1-7: 245–248. For more on Nazi and Soviet "democratic" traditions and rituals see Overy, 54–97.

54. 072-5-4: 323.

55. "No Surprise in Iraqi Vote," *New York Times*, Oct. 17, 1995, http://www.nytimes.com/1995/10/17/world/no-surprise-in-iraqi-vote.html [accessed April 7, 2013].

56. "The Day of the Iraqi Child," Director of the Office of the Party Secretariat to All of the Party Branch Commands, 036-3-5: 293–297.

57. "The Day of the Glorious Victory," Secretary of the Babil Branch Command to the Office of the Party Secretariat, Dec. 23, 1999, 029-2-2: 277–282. The translation of the term *yawm al-fatḥ al-mubīn* is N. J. Dawood's from his translation of the *Qurʾān*. *The Koran*, trans. N. J. Dawood (London: Penguin Books, 2003), 359. See note 2 on the same page for his interpretation that the term might instead refer to the conquest of the Jewish oasis of Khaybar a year before the Muslims took Mecca.

58. 036-3-5: 295.

59. For other examples of official programs for Baʿthist "occasions" see "The Celebrations of the Holidays of July," Secretary of the Central Office of the Profes-

sional and Popular Bureau to the Office of the Party Secretariat, July 10, 1988, 029-2-4: 349–351; "The Celebrations of the Great Victory," Director of the Office of the Party Secretariat to the Military Office and All of the Party Branch Commands, July 4, 1999, 020-1-5: 290–291; and boxfile 028-3-4: 1–24, which contains a number of documents about the preparations for the opening of "The River Saddam." David Baran also analyzes "The Mechanics of 'Spontaneous' Parades" in *Vivre la tyrannie*, 70–78.

60. For an excellent exposition of the excusatory aspect of totalitarian ideology see Havel, "Power of the Powerless," 42–43.

61. General discussion of the role of ritual in political ceremonies guided the analysis in this paragraph and this section more generally. See Geertz, "Religion as a Cultural System," 28–32; Christel Lane, *The Rites of Rulers: Ritual in Industrial Society—the Soviet Case* (Cambridge: Cambridge University Press, 1981), 11, 24, 33, 61, 64; Sally F. Moore and Barbara G. Myerhoff, "Introduction: Secular Ritual: Forms and Meanings," in *Secular Ritual*, ed. Sally F. Moore and Barbara G. Myerhoff (Assen/Amsterdam: Van Gorcum, 1977), 3–8; Mosse, 74.

PART III

1. "Integration" is Bracher's definition, 117–118; "synchronization" is Brown's, 123.

2. Hamilton Fish Armstrong, "Hitler's Reich: The First Phase," *Foreign Affairs* (July 1933): 591–592, quote 591; Richard J. Evans, *The Coming of the Third Reich* (New York: The Penguin Press, 2003), 381–389, quote 389, 441–442, 461; Bracher, 117–125; Brown, 123–148.

3. Evans, 389, quote 461.

4. Arendt, 364.

5. Brown, 123.

6. Giddens, 9.

7. The BRCC documents list Iraq's traditional government institutions and agencies as the Revolutionary Command Council, the Office of the President, the ministries, the security and intelligence services, the army, the National Assembly, the judiciary, and "agencies unconnected to a ministry" (*al-dawā'ir ghayr al-murtabiṭa bi-wizāra*) such as the Atomic Energy Agency and the Iraqi Central Bank. In short, these bodies were all those commonly considered governmental bodies or parts of the "public sector" in any country. See, e.g., "The Day of the Glorious Victory," The Head of the Presidential Diwan to the Secretariat of the Council of Ministers, et al., Dec. 13, 1999, 029-2-2: 285.

CHAPTER 5

Epigraph from Northern Bureau, "Practicing Responsibility from the Lowest Position," 1985, 029-2-3: 88.

1. Jawad Hashim, 284.

2. For an example of the Baʿth Party's attempt to instill "creativity" in its members see a series of documents exploring ways to increase worker productivity in boxfile 023-2-6: 3–93. The admonition to "carry responsibility" for one's actions, and for carrying out party duties properly, was a significant concept within the Baʿth Party. Hussein harped on it frequently. See, e.g., the admonishment by an investigatory committee of a party member who stood accused of disparaging an official tourism policy: Director of the Party Secretariat to The Presidency of the Republic—the Secretary, Aug. 2, 2000, 029-1-3: 26.

3. The Party Secretariat repeatedly scolded lower-level Baʿthist organizations for not responding quickly to its correspondence, as required by party rules. The Secretariat also complained that lower-level organizations did not take enough care to maintain the secrecy and integrity of the contents of party correspondence. See, e.g., 004-1-4: 162–163; 034-2-1: 146–147.

4. Director of the Office of the Party Secretariat to the Honorable Comrade Deputy General-Secretary, Aug. 30, 1989, 156-4-4: 485.

5. Director of the Office of the Party Secretariat, the Special Secretary for Party Affairs to the Honorable Mr. President Leader, May 24, 1989, 022-1-7: 152–163.

6. See, e.g., a petition to Hussein about a neighborly dispute in which the petitioner charged that another family he was feuding with contained enemies of the party. 025-4-5: 399.

7. The BRCC contains tens of boxfiles from the President's Office that contain only correspondence related to personnel appointments, and which seek information from the security services and the Baʿth Party about the candidates for jobs so that Hussein could make a decision. Until 1991, Hussein signed off on all party appointments and transfers from the district level and higher. In that year, he gave the Organization Committee carte blanche to appoint members to branch-level commands and to move members between branch commands and regional bureau offices. At this time, the regional bureaus also received other new powers including the ability to order punishments for members at the district command level and below. "The Expansion of Authority," Director of the Office of the Party Secretariat to the Honorable Comrade Secretaries of the Organizational Offices, Feb. 5, 1991, 024-5-2: 86–87. See also, e.g., boxfiles 026-3-7, 071-4-2, and 091-5-4. On Hussein's appointing district heads, see 027-5-2: 407.

8. Head of the Presidential Diwan to the Honorable Mr. President Leader, Jan. 14, 1987, 045-3-5: 549–550.

9. "The Responsibility of State Departments to Solve the Issues of Citizens," Director of the Party Secretariat to All of the Party Branch Commands, Sept. 12, 1991, 004-1-4: 259.

10. 004-1-4: 259.

11. For more on Hussein's ever-changing inner circle and the drama within it see Ofra Bengio, "A Republican Turning Royalist? Saddam Husayn and the Dilemmas of Succession," *Journal of Contemporary History* 35 (Oct. 2000): 641–653, and her *Middle East Contemporary Survey* entries, especially 1992 and 1998; Baram, *Building toward Crisis*, 7–44, and "Ruling Political Elite"; and Tripp, 259.

12. Hussein's family began to fall out of favor in the early to mid-1990s as arguments between them began to embarrass him and threatened the coherence of his inner circle, culminating in the defection to Jordan of two of his sons-in-law, the Kamil brothers, with their families. The BRCC contains the internal letter that Hussein sent to the party to explain their defection: "Party Bulletin," to the Honorable Comrade Officials of the Party Bureaus, Feb. 21, 1996, 133-1-3: 407–410.

13. David Baran characterizes these people as the "mass of subordinate employees" who were "in reality the strength of the regime." Baran, 128.

14. See, e.g., "Competition," Director of the Party Secretariat to the Bureau Offices in the Entire Country, Jan. 16, 1991, 024-5-2: 195–208; and, "What Has Been Accomplished from the Organizational Plan for the Year 2000," Secretary of the Maysan Branch Command to the Office of the Party Secretariat, Oct. 7, 2000, 037-1-3: 13–15.

15. See, e.g., a petition from a party member who worked in the security services: "Connection to the Party," 023-2-8: 118–119.

16. "Regulations," Director of the Office of the Party Secretariat to The Military Bureau, All Party Branch Commands, May 28, 1994, 042-5-5: 206.

17. Fadil Abbas Azzawi, *al-Buniyya al-Tanzimiyya li-l-Hizb al-Baʿth al-ʿArabi al-ʾIshtiraki* (Baghdad: Dar al-Shuun al-Thaqafiya al-ʿAmma Wizarat al-Thaqafah wa-l-Iʿlam, al-Dar al-Wataniyya li-l-Tawziʿ wa-l-Iʿlan, 1986), 73.

18. See, e.g., the structure given in "Schedule of the Vacancies of Main Branch Personnel in the Organizational Offices in the Entire Country up until Dec. 4, 1988," 077-3-1: 251.

19. For all of the branches in 2002 see "Statistical Register for the Party Apparatus throughout the Country until the Date of Sept. 9, 2002," 108-4-6: 19–23.

20. There are hundreds of examples of these reports in the BRCC. See, e.g., a quarterly administrative report from the Wasit Bureau from 1986: "The First Quarterly Administrative Report for the Year 1986," Arab Baʿth Socialist Party Office of the Southern Bureau, Wasit Branch Command, 045-5-7: 23–52.

21. For local organization statistics see boxfiles: 150-2-5; 118-2-6; 088-3-1; 080-3-6; 077-2-3; 098-5-3; 169-4-6; 134-4-3; 158-2-1; 133-2-7; 062-4-7; 165-1-7; 027-1-4; 043-1-4; 182-4-2; 044-2-4; 087-4-3; and 044-2-4.

22. It does not necessarily follow, for example, that the organizations from the Tikrit and Mosul areas, from which many of the regime's top leaders were drawn, contained the highest percentage of party members, although it is possible that a statistical analysis could reveal such a pattern.

23. Christine Moss Helms, *Iraq: Eastern Flank of the Arab World* (Washington, DC: The Brookings Institution, 1984), 87.

24. "A Report about Why I Do Not Want to Receive the Honor of [Full] Membership," A member of the Shumer Division to the Comrade Official, Oct. 16, 1989, 003-3-2: 49.

25. Director of the Division of Information and Documentation to the Honorable Comrade Director of the Office of the Party Secretariat, 003-3-2: 34.

26. 104-3-1: 276–277.

27. This mass exodus of military men after the Iran–Iraq War is one of the reasons why party membership numbers dipped between 1986 and 1997 (see table 5.1). "Study," Director of the Office of the Party Secretariat to the Presidency of the Republic/Secretary of the President for Party Affairs, Oct. 4, 1990, 104-3-1: 271.

28. Emphasis added. "How to Deal with Partisans and Supporters Who Ask to be Retired from the Party," Comrade [name withheld] to the Honorable Comrade Party Secretary, Nov. 10, 1990, 104-3-1: 297–298.

29. The Director of the Office of the Party Secretariat to the Honorable Comrade Deputy Secretary-General of the Region of Iraq, Oct. 4, 1992, 119-2-7: 282.

30. It is not clear whether the official was referring to the Revolutionary Command Council or the Baʿth's Regional Command. "Study," Official of the Middle Euphrates Bureau to the Office of the Party Secretariat, March 8, 1992, 120-2-3: 321–323.

31. See, e.g., a Baʿth Party memorandum about the party's inability to pay its full-time employees salaries that kept up with the rate of inflation in 1993. As a result, many did not come in to work, and the party had to hire temporary employees. Director of the Office of the Party Secretariat to the Comrade Deputy Secretary-General of the Command of the Region of Iraq, May 20, 1993, 027-1-2: 29. See also RCC Decision No. 55, May 27, 1997, 028-5-1: 443, which reduced the salaries and expenditures for the President, the Deputy of the RCC, all of the RCC's members, the Vice Presidents, the President of the National Assembly, and the Head of the Council of Ministers by 10 percent. Additionally, the decision cut the budgets for national and religious holidays and slashed salaries and expenditures for the GDI by 30 percent. According to the RCC decision, all of the reduced expenditures went to the treasury in light of the UN embargo. See also Baran, 94–104.

32. See notes 60–62 in chapter one.

33. Baram, *Building toward Crisis*, 43; Khoury, 157.

34. "Jihad and Revolutionary Work—A Party Work Paper Plan," Office of the Baghdad Bureau, Dec. 29, 1990, 051-1-2: 609.

35. 025-1-7: 37–38.

36. 034-2-1: 146–147. For how much people had to pay in dues in 1978 see Director of the Office of the Party Secretariat to the Main Commands in the Entire Country, May 28, 1978, 003-1-1: 202–203. For regulations for being appointed as a head of an office or a secretary see "Regulations for the Appointment of Directors of the Offices and the Secretaries," Head of the Presidential Diwan to the Council of Ministers, April 12, 1994, 113-3-3: 39–40.

37. *Yawm al-nakhwa* was a national occasion celebrated on April 18, 1998, when Baʿthists gave nonmembers a taste of military training for which both received a certificate and notation in their files.

38. Not all of the requests for information are found on the assessment form exactly as they are depicted here. The questions are paraphrases. I have turned some of them into questions where, e.g., on the form they merely said, "the extent of the manifestation of principles in daily behavior." "Annual Evaluation Forms from 1/1/1999 to 31/12/1999," 043-1-4: 282.

39. "Ta'amim (Kirkuk)," Director of the Office of the Party Secretariat to All of the Organizational Offices in the Country, Nov. 14, 1983, 003-3-5: 24.

40. See, e.g., Secretary of the Office of the Southern Bureau Command to the Party Secretariat, Feb. 11, 1985, 002-4-4: 279.

41. See, e.g., boxfile 022-4-4, which has tens of examples of this phenomenon, including Secretary of the Office of the Southern Bureau Command to the Party Secretariat, Feb. 9, 1985, 022-4-4: 192; and Comrade Ali Hassan al-Majid, Director of the Office of the Party Secretariat to the Honorable Comrade Head of the Organizational Committee, Aug. 20, 1982: 251–252.

42. A 1978 letter about purging suspect elements from the party includes a directive to expel any member who marries a foreigner or who has a wife that is related in the first or second degree with "agents" of foreign intelligence agencies, embassies, or "sensitive centers of the state." Director of the Office of the Party Secretariat to All of the Main Commands in the Country, June 25, 1978, 003-1-1: 418. A directive about rules for party members to marry puts the onus on local party commands to "investigate the Arabness (*ʿurūbat*) of the family of the wife and not to give agreement for [party] members [to marry] families of non-Arab origins." 003-3-5: 24.

43. RCC decision No. 1529, Dec. 21, 1985, 036-1-2: 1.

44. See, e.g., "Comrade (name withheld)," Secretary to Mr. President of the Republic for Party Affairs to the Regional Command—Office of the Party Secretariat, Nov. 16, 1983, 027-5-2: 1–5; 003-1-1: 418.

45. 003-3-5: 24.

46. Secretary of the Office of the Southern Bureau to the Office of the Party Secretariat, 002-4-4: 424.

47. Security Director for Maysan Governorate to the Honorable Comrade Secretary of the Maysan Branch Command, Jan. 23, 1985, 002-4-4: 325.

48. It is unclear how long the weigh-ins continued after 1989. "Report," Secretary of the Office of the Central Bureau Command to the Regional Command—the Organizational Committee, Dec. 18, 1985, 029-2-3: 427; boxfile 060-2-3; "Decision," Director of the Office of the Party Secretariat to the Deputy Secretary-General of the Region, Feb. 28, 1989, 022-1-7: 243; Director of the Office of the Party Secretariat to the Comrade Deputy Secretary-General of the Region, June 18, 1989, 021-1-4: 166.

49. 037-1-3: 13–15.

50. For regulations restricting the length and frequency of meetings by party membership level see "Decision," Director of the Office of the Party Secretariat to All of the Organizational Offices in the Country, April 11, 1984, 146-2-4: 364–366; 003-3-2: 34.

51. For the definitions of the "three spheres" of society, including civil society, see Caroline Hodges Persell, Adam Green, and Liena Gurevich, "Civil Society, Economic Distress, and Social Tolerance," *Sociological Forum* 16 (June 2001): 204–207.

52. The Baʿth originally created the Central Office out of the first three specialized offices listed in 1987. In 1988, the National Union of Students and Youth of

Iraq joined the original three offices in the Central Office after the Baʿth abolished the Central Office for Students and Youth. At the same time, the party gave the responsibility for supervising student and youth activities to regular party organizations as well. "Decision," Director of the Office of the Party Secretariat to All of the Organizational Offices in the Country, June 13, 1988, 037-3-5: 403; "Summary of the Work of the Central Office from its Formation until Now," Secretary of the Central Office for the Professional and Popular Bureau to the Honorable Comrade Deputy Secretary-General of the Region/the Honorable Official of the Organizational Committee, July 23, 1987, 038-2-4: 183–189.

53. 025-5-5: 476–494.

54. 025-5-5: 487.

55. "Work Plan," Secretary of the Office of the Southern Bureau to the Office of the Party Secretariat, Oct. 24, 1990, 104-1-2: 190–198.

56. A Memorandum to Hussein from the Secretary of Party Affairs for Mr. President of the Republic, Oct. 9, 1983, 027-5-2: 457–459.

57. 025-5-5: 484–486.

58. See the report entitled, "A Report on the Activities of the General Federation of Iraqi Women for the period 1980–1983, Presented to the Meeting of the Council of the World Democratic Union for Women," attached to The President of the General Federation of Iraqi Women to the Central Professional Office, Sept. 11, 1983, 027-5-2: 462, quote 464. The entire report begins on 463.

59. "The Semi-Annual Administrative Report of 1995," The Central Office of Workers, 089-3-6: 374.

60. 025-5-5: 483.

61. President of the General Federation of Iraqi Women to the Venerable Professional Office, Dec. 11, 1994, 131-4-7: 28.

62. 104-1-2: 191–192.

63. For a good discussion of gender politics and the situation of Iraqi women under Hussein and the Baʿth see chapter 4, "Gender Politics in Baʿthist Iraq," in Rohde, 75–118.

64. 027-5-2: 457–459.

65. "An Analytical Report about the Family and Legal Problems for the Period from 2/1 until 30/6/1993," General Federation of Iraqi Women, 040-3-4: 734–739.

66. "Study," Secretary of the Office of the Northern Bureau Command to the Office of the Party Secretariat, March 24, 1990, 028-3-6: 601–610; "The Cultural Center for Women to Face the Challenges of the Present Phase," 029-2-6: 78–84.

67. "Text of the Letter that the President Leader Saddam Hussein Received from the Baʿth Party Command on 9/1/1992 by Way of the (name withheld) the Director of the Party Secretariat," 101-1-1: 100.

68. "A Report about the Visit of a Delegation of the General Federation of Iraqi Women to the Socialist Republic of Cuba for the period from 5/6 until 12/6/88," General Federation of Iraqi Women, 029-2-4: 20–34, quote 29.

69. "Regulations for Putting on Scientific Conferences and Special Exhibitions," 049-5-7: 296.

70. See, e.g., the letters of support from Arab organizations in 029-2-6: 670–834.

71. "The Arab Organizations that have Headquarters in Baghdad," Secretary of the Central Office of the Professional and Popular Bureau to the Presidency of the Republic, April 22, 1990, 029-2-6: 452.

CHAPTER 6

1. Director of the Party Secretariat to All of the Main Commands in the Country, March 23, 1978, 003-1-1: 419.

2. Director of Correspondence and Organizational Affairs to the Comrade Director of the Party Secretariat, May 23, 1991, 085-2-4: 633.

3. 029-2-3: 88.

4. Southern Bureau ((Contexts of Work from the Party and Mass Standpoints)), 023-2-8: 25. Double parentheses appear in the document.

5. See, e.g., Director of the Office of the Party Secretariat to the Honorable Comrade General-Secretary of the Party, Oct. 13, 1979, 040-3-6: 97.

6. A series of documents from a boxfile in 1979 shows that the process of weeding out independents from the security services was still ongoing at that time. The boxfile lists the "officers of the internal security forces" within governorates and party bureaus and branches throughout the country. In a few areas, such as al-Muthanna Governorate and the Kirkuk branch, the officials who compiled the boxfile's statistics recorded all security personnel as Baʿthists. In the Baghdad branch, however, the officials listed 23 percent of the officers as "independent" (*mustaqill*) or did not indicate their political affiliation. In the Southern Bureau, they logged 4 percent of the officers as independent. In the Salah al-Din and al-Anbar branches, they recorded 12 and 11 percent of officers as independents, respectively. 044-2-1: 2–9, 151–157, 164–166, 167–170, 255–259, 261–266.

7. The GSD officer's petition has no date but comes from a boxfile containing documents from 1983 and 1984. 023-2-8: 118–119.

8. Office of the Party Secretariat to the Honorable Comrade Deputy Secretary-General of the Region, 003-1-1: 70.

9. "Report," Secretary of the Central Professional Office to the Office of the Party Secretariat, July 23, 1978, 040-3-6: 472.

10. "Military academies" (*al-kulliyāt al-ʿaskariyya*) was the general rubric for all national-security-related preparatory and officer institutes. In addition to those related to the security services, a document from 1990 provides a complete list of the academies as including "the first, second, and third military academies" (*al-kulliya al-ʿaskariyya al-ʾūlā wa-l-thāniyya wa-l-thālitha*); the Air Force and Naval academies; the Academy of Military Engineering; the Police Academy; the Police Preparatory School; the Center for Naval Training (*markaz al-tadrīb al-baḥrī*); the Judicial Institute (*al-maʿahad al-quḍāʾī*); the Sessions for Judicial Clerics (*dawrāt li-kuttāb al-ʿudūl fī wizārat al-ʿadal*); and the appointments of stewardesses on Iraqi Airlines (*taʿyīn al-muḍīfāt fī al-khuṭūṭ al-jawiyya al-ʿirāqiyya*). "Authorities,"

Director of the Office of the Party Secretariat to the Presidency of the Republic—the Secretary, Jan. 10, 1990, 056-4-4: 7.

11. "The Central Admissions Plan for the Teachers Institutes," Head of the Presidential Diwan to the Ministry of Higher Education and Scientific Research/the Special Office, April 12, 1986, 088-5-3: 590–591.

12. There are tens if not hundreds of files on acceptances and rejections into military academies in the BRCC. See, e.g., in relation to admissions into the "First Military Academy": Director of the Division of Military Sessions to the Honorable Comrade Struggler Lieutenant General Ali Hassan al-Majid/Member of the Regional Command/the Supervisor of the Division of Military Sessions, Dec. 28, 1999, 020-3-5: 21; and, with regard to admission into "The High Institute for Officers of the Internal Security Forces" (*al-maʿahad al-ʿālī li-ḍubāṭ qiwā al-ʾamn al-dākhilī*): Director of the Division of Military Sessions to the Honorable Comrade Member of the Regional Command of Iraq—the Supervisor of the Division of Military Sessions, Oct. 26, 1993, 056-1-4: 6–7.

13. See, e.g., "Acceptance into the Military Colleges," Deputy Secretary of the Military Office to the Office of the Party Secretariat, Jan. 14, 1992, 056-4-4: 1; "The Regulations for Acceptance in the Universities," Head of the Presidential Diwan to the Regional Command—Office of the Party Secretariat, Oct. 17, 1985, 056-4-4: 29–30.

14. "Student Inventory," Director of the Office of the Party Secretariat to the Honorable Comrade Director of General Security, Jan. 10, 2001, 068-1-2: 97–100. See chapter 9 for more on "Friend of the Leader President" status.

15. These forty-one were picked out of a summary list of all of the nominees for acceptance into the police academy. "A List of the Names of Students Nominated for Acceptance into the Police Preparatory School for the Session (47) of the Year 2002," 020-4-3: 2–9.

16. Makiya, *Republic of Fear*, 135–136.

17. These forms are ubiquitous in the BRCC. See, e.g., boxfile 133-2-1, which contains a large party pamphlet published by the Northern Bureau in 1985. Pages 129 to 184 in the pamphlet are all appendices of various types of party forms.

18. Isam al-Khafaji, "State Terror and the Degradation of Politics in Iraq," *Middle East Report*, No. 176, Iraq in the Aftermath (May-June 1992): 17.

19. Director of the Office of the Party Secretariat to the Honorable Comrade Secretary-General of the Region, June 19, 1980, 088-5-3: 603; "Agreement about the Acceptance of the Students," Secretary for Party Affairs of Mr. President of the Republic to the Presidency of the Republic, Oct. 11, 1983, 027-5-2: 439.

20. "Regulations for Acceptance into the Colleges of Education and the Exempted Colleges and Institutes and Departments," Head of the Presidential Diwan to the Ministry of Higher Education and Scientific Research/the Special Office, July 27, 1986, 087-1-1: 30–31.

21. See 113-3-3: 48–79, for a series of regulations enacted from 1981 to 1992 regarding teacher conduct and requirements that the teachers be Baʿthists or transferred outside the teaching corps under different conditions.

22. Baʿthist Iraq had separate ministries for "Education" (*wizārat al-tarbiyya*) and "Higher Education and Scientific Research" (*wizārat al-taʿlīm al-ʿālī wa-l-baḥth al-ʿilmī*).

23. "The Special Regulations about How to Deal with the Relatives of Convicted Criminals from the Agent Daʿwa Party," Director of the Office of the Party Secretariat to the Main Commands in the Entire Country, July 15, 1981, 041-1-5: 467; "The Special Regulations about How to Deal with the Relatives of Convicted Criminals from Opposition Parties," Head of the Presidential Diwan to the Ministry of Defense—the Office of the Minister, et al., June 10, 1987, 047-1-7: 420–422; "Regulations," Director of the Office of the Party Secretariat to the Military Office, All of the Party Branch Commands, May 28, 1994, 042-5-5: 203–206; "Degree of Relation," 041-1-5: 441. This last document, which defines levels of relation, was found inside a boxfile from 1990. The same regulations, frequently carbon copies appended to an assessment of the relative of a political criminal, were also discovered as far back as 1982 (001-5-1: 271), although their origin likely preceded that date.

24. "Removal from the Teaching Corps," Secretary of the Office of the Euphrates Bureau to the Office of the Party Secretariat, Dec. 25, 1983, 021-1-5: 510; "Removal from the Police Corps," Director of the Office of the Party Secretariat to the Interior Ministry/the Special Office, April 19, 1984, 021-1-5: 532.

25. "Retired," Director of the Office of the Party Secretariat to the Presidential Diwan, Dec. 19, 1984, 001-5-1: 614.

26. "Removal from the Teaching Corps," Director of the Office of the Party Secretariat to the Presidential Diwan, Feb. 9, 1985, 024-1-6: 498.

27. Ali Hasan Majid, Director of the Office of the Party Secretariat to Saddam Hussein, 030-4-2: 363. This document is from a boxfile dated 1983.

28. "Statement of Opinion," Secretary of the Office of the Euphrates Bureau to the Office of the Party Secretariat, Dec. 6, 1988, 038-5-2: 215–216.

29. Raymond A. Hinnebusch, *Authoritarian Power and State Formation in Baʿthist Syria: Army, Party, and Peasant* (Boulder: Westview Press, 1990), 159–160.

30. There are many examples of this process in the BRCC. See, e.g., files that the Ministry of Endowments and Religious Affairs (*wizārat al-ʾawqāf wa-l-shuʾūn al-dīniyya*) sent to ask for permission to appoint various people as prayer leaders, *muʾaḏhḏhins* (those who call to prayer), or religious school teachers in boxfile 038-5-5. See also letters from the Council of Ministers asking for party opinions about ministerial appointments in 028-4-2.

31. "Information," The Minister of Education to the Office of the Party Secretariat, April 21, 2001, 045-3-1: 174–176.

32. "Information," Director of the Office of the Party Secretariat to the Ministry of Education—the Office of the Minister, June 2, 2001, 045-3-1: 164–170.

33. Technically, county and municipal chiefs could also be appointed, demoted, or transferred by decision of the Council of Ministers and by recommendation from the Interior Ministry. In reality, however, Hussein often personally made the decisions and almost always signed off on them. See 125-5-2: 148–165 for drafts

of what became the "Governorates Law" (*qānūn al-muḥāfaẓāt*). For the nomination process for governors and the heads of counties and municipalities see 148-4-1: 1–317.

34. 029-2-3: 414.

35. The government paid *mukhtārīn* to watch and report about their immediate surroundings, be it the families in the apartment building in which a *mukhtār* lived, a city block, small village, or other limited area. The *mukhtār* worked under the head of his *nāḥiya*, or neighborhood. The position predated the Baʿth, but after 1968, the Baʿth had to approve all local government appointments, including the *mukhtārīn*. For more, see the section on "The Baʿthification of State Personnel."

36. "(A Study about Mass Mobilization) and How to Improve It," 038-2-4: 162. Parentheses appear as in the document.

37. "The Appointment of Two *Mukhtārs*," Director of the Office of the Party Secretariat to the Baghdad Governorate/*Mukhtār* Affairs, May 17, 1999, 042-4-5: 280.

38. From a nomination assessment form found in 115-5-1: 4.

39. Although Hussein depended on tribes for support in key positions in his regime, he had to weather a series of organized coup attempts and local revolts by tribes beginning in 1990. Baram, *Building toward Crisis*, 25–31.

40. 115-5-1: 4.

41. 115-5-1: 6.

42. The word "honeycombing" is borrowed from Marr, 149.

43. For all other party bureaus, the bureau reported to him through the Party Secretariat or the Secretary for Party Affairs in the President's Office.

44. "Personnel of the Military Office," Comrade Ali Hassan al-Majid of the Military Office to the Comrade Secretary-General of the Regional Command—the Honorable Secretary of the Military Office, Oct. 1, 1986, 025-4-2: 154–164. For more on the Directorate of Political Guidance see Khoury, 86–94.

45. "Summary of the Activity of the Military Office from 1/1/1988 until 31/12/1988," 023-4-4: 264. For more on the Baʿthification of the army see Khoury, 84.

46. For a good summary of the role of commissars see Khoury, 86.

47. Although the Popular Army was a party militia and parallel army to the regular army, party commissars exercised the same oversight and political control over regular military units.

48. "A Report of Cohabitation within the Advanced Area of al-Rashid, Faw 19/2/1985–20/4/1985," The Fighting Comrade [name withheld], 040-1-6: 565. According to Khoury, "cohabiting" constituted a larger range of activities than just living with military units during the Iran–Iraq War: "Cohabiting consisted of living with the affected sectors of society to study the repercussions of the war, report on them to the local regional offices, and identify ways to ensure that complaints were heard and needs met." Khoury, 69.

49. 040-1-6: 569.

50. "Operational Training Plan for the Year 1986," Command of the Baghdad Region for the Popular Army, 089-4-4: 128.

51. Helms, 99–100.

52. Ofra Bengio, "Iraq," in *Middle East Contemporary Survey, Volume Five 1980–1981*, ed. Haim Shaked, Colin Legum, and Daniel Dishon (New York: Holmes & Meier Publishers, 1982), 584–585.

53. For an example of a report (there are many) including information about deserters from the Popular Army see 026-3-6: 133. As an example of the army's drain on resources, see a report that owners of private companies were both firing and threatening to fire workers who volunteered for the Popular Army: "Volunteering," Secretary of the Office of the Northern Bureau Command to the Office of the Party Secretariat, Sept. 26, 1990, 041-3-7: 54. The RCC decision dissolving the Popular Army can be found in 041-3-7: 60.

54. For more on these two militias see Kevin M. Woods, et al. Michael R. Pease, Mark E. Stout, Williamson Murray, and James G. Lacey, *Iraqi Perspectives Project: A View of Operation Iraqi Freedom from Saddam's Senior Leadership* (Joint Center for Operational Analysis, 2006), 48–55; Sassoon, *Saddam Hussein's Baʿth Party*, 147–150.

55. The relationships between the Republican and Special Republican guards and the army has been covered extensively in the secondary literature. Nothing read in the BRCC for this study seems to contradict or add to what has already been written, so I will not elaborate here. See Woods, et al., *Iraqi Perspectives Project*, 25, 27, 46, 56, 58; Ahmed S. Hashim, "Saddam Hussein," 23–25; Alani, 44–45; Faleh A. Jabar, "The Iraqi Army and Anti-Army: Some Reflections on the Role of the Military," *The Adelphi Papers* 354 (Jan. 2003): 123; and al-Marashi and Salama, 156–157, 167–168.

56. 098-5-3: 60.

57. "Organizational Unity," Director of the Office of the Party Secretariat to All of the Organizational Offices in the Country, Dec. 21, 1989, 073-3-4: 76–78.

58. 073-3-4: 76–80.

59. 073-3-4: 75–80.

60. "Party Committees," Director of the Office of the Party Secretariat to All of the Party Branch Commands in the Country, Oct. 25, 1997, 042-4-6: 577.

61. "The Leaking of Examination Questions," Secretary of the Party Committees to the Office of the Party Secretariat, June 27, 2000, 042-4-6: 263–264.

62. "Information," Director of the Office of the Party Secretariat to the Secretariat of the Party Committees, May 13, 2000, 042-4-6: 352.

63. "A Report about the Mobilization Process, Especially Stopping the Dispersal of the Additional Wages of the Workers," to the Honorable Mr. President Leader Struggler Saddam Hussein, Feb. 7, 1984, 023-2-6: 112.

64. "The General Framework for the Plan for Raising the Ability of the Individual," President of the General Union of Labor Syndicates to the Union Syndicates in All of the Governorates/All of the General Syndicates, 023-2-6: 92–93.

65. For how I have tried to deal with these issues, see the preface.

66. Woods et al., *The Saddam Tapes*, 146, 203.

67. "Information," Director of the Office of the Party Secretariat to the Presidency of the Republic—the Presidency of the Republic—the Secretary, Aug. 11, 1991, 021-2-5: 114–116; "Information," Director of the Office of the Party Secretariat to the Presidency of the Republic, Aug. 11, 1991: 116.

68. "The Special Security Report by the Karbala Branch Command for the Month/June/1986," 039-3-7: 78.

69. "Study," Director of the Office of the Party Secretariat to the Honorable Member of the Organizational Committee, Feb. 15, 1990, 076-2-4: 52.

70. 021-1-2: 342–343.

71. 021-1-2: 152–153.

72. A citizen petition to Hussein dated August 17, 1997, 076-1-6: 555–556.

73. See, e.g., two citizen petitions to Hussein, both of which have information contradicting the petitions attached to them, Feb. 3, 1984, 023-2-8: 149–150; 2001, 025-4-5: 488–489.

74. "Letter," Head of the Presidential Diwan to All of the Ministries, et al., Sept. 28, 1985, 118-3-4: 141–144.

75. Head of the Presidential Diwan to the Secretariat of the Council of Ministers, Dec. 19, 1996, 021-1-2: 161–162.

CHAPTER SEVEN

1. 025-1-7: 40.

2. "An Analysis of the Social Reality of the City of Baghdad and the Role of the Party Apparatus," Office of the Baghdad Bureau, Feb. 1989, 070-5-5: 403–404.

3. 070-5-5: 390.

4. See also chapter 9. The actual maps that this and the previous document referred to were not found for this study. It is not known whether or not they exist in the BRCC or other open Baʿthist archives, if they still exist anywhere at all. 024-5-2: 199.

5. 111-3-2: 14–15.

6. 076-2-4: 49–50.

7. Secretary of Party Affairs for Mr. President of the Republic to the Honorable Mr. President Leader, March 26, 1983, 023-2-8: 28.

8. See, e.g., 029-2-3: 95. In the case of women recruits see 028-3-6: 607, 609.

9. 025-5-5: 483.

10. 025-5-5: 480.

11. 025-5-5: 483.

12. Khoury refers to "maintaining a connection" as "perpetuating of ties." Khoury, 69.

13. Khoury, 106–110.

14. "Decision," Director of the Office of the Party Secretariat to the Organizational Offices throughout the Country, October 5, 1987, 024-3-3: 336.

15. 111-3-2: 25–26.

16. Emphasis added. The phrase "proper preparation" (*al-ʾiʿdād al-salīm*) has the connotation of proper ideological preparation. 073-3-4: 76.

17. The Arabic root "*kasaba*" can also be translated as "to win" or "to gain" in a more general sense than "to recruit."

18. 023-2-8: 25.

19. "A Study about the Phenomenon of Processions (*al-mashi*)," Official of the Baghdad Bureau—al-Rasafa, Secretary of the Branch Command to the Office of the Party Secretariat, Nov. 11, 1996, 046-5-4: 90.

20. See, e.g., 025-1-7: 34.

21. "Decision," Secretary of the Office of the Baghdad Bureau to the al-Rashid Branch Command, Oct. 15, 1984, 098-5-3: 368, 370.

22. "Creation (*ʾIstiḥdāth*) of a Division," Member of the Regional Command of Iraq, Official of the Baghdad Bureau al-Rasafa to the Office of the Party Secretariat, June 12, 2001, 044-2-4: 9–13.

23. "Decision," Secretary of the Office of the Baghdad Bureau to the al-Rashid Branch Command, Feb. 12, 1990, 134-4-3: 162–164.

24. See table 5.1.

25. 025-5-5: 487–488.

26. This conclusion corresponds to those of Rohde, 90, 108–109; Suha Omar, "Women: Honour, Shame and Dictatorship," in *Iraq Since the Gulf War: Prospects for Democracy*, ed. Fran Hazelton for CARDRI (London: Zed Books, 1994)," 65; and Marion Farouk-Sluglett, "Liberation or Repression? Pan-Arab Nationalism and the Women's Movement in Iraq," in *Iraq: Power and Society*, ed. Derek Hopwood, Habib Ishow, and Thomas Koszinowski (Reading: Ithaca Press, 1993), 67.

27. Secretary of the High Council for National Security Agency to the Leader President, Dec. 29, 1979, 003-1-1: 410–411.

28. Wendell Steavenson, *The Weight of a Mustard Seed* (New York: Harper, 2009), 19, 23.

29. See the Personal Status Law at: www.iraq-ild.org/LoadLawBook.aspx?SP=ALL&SC=010320061162736 [accessed May 5, 2013]; 027-5-2: 457–459.

30. Found in the editor's introduction to a compilation of speeches by Hussein about women's issues. Saddam Hussein, *The Revolution and Woman in Iraq*, ed. Naji al-Hadithi, trans. Khalid Kishtainy (Baghdad: Translation & Foreign Language Publishing House, 1981), 5.

31. Rohde, 88–90.

32. 027-5-2: 457–459.

33. Women's share in the work force decreased from just 11.6 percent in 1987 to 10.4 percent in 1997. Rohde, 101.

34. Omar, 64.

35. Rohde, 102.

36. "Evaluation of the Members of the Executive Office of the General Federation of Iraqi Women," Secretary of the Professional Office Command, Dec. 30, 1982, 030-4-2: 325–327.

37. 028-3-6: 601–610.

38. "Comrade [Name Withheld]," Secretary for Party Affairs of Mr. President of the Republic to the Regional Command—the Office of the Party Secretariat, Nov. 16, 1983, 027-5-2: 5.

39. Omar, 61; Steavenson, 209; Sana al-Khayyat, *Honour and Shame: Women in Modern Iraq* (London: Saqi Books, 1990), 201; Bashir, 236.

40. Citizen petition to Hussein, May 28, 1984, 028-1-1: 360–361; "Report," Secretary of the Office of the Southern Bureau to the Office of the Party Secretariat, Nov. 14, 1984, 028-1-1: 358–359; "Inquiry," Director of General Security to the Presidency of the Republic/Secretary for Party Affairs of Mr. President of the Republic, Dec. 30, 1984, 028-1-1: 352.

41. Bashir, 144–145.

42. For more on this phrase in a political and legal context, see chapter 8.

43. A memorandum sent to Hussein by Ali Hassan al-Majid, Director of the Office of the Party Secretariat, 030-4-2: 292. The document appears in a boxfile from 1983 but is found among files that date to 1982.

44. "Census for the Women's Organizations in the Women's Apparatus," June 25, 2002, 108-4-6: 40–43.

45. 027-5-2: 457–459.

46. Head of the Central Council of the General Federation of Iraqi women to Mr. President Leader, Saddam Hussein, Builder of Renaissance and Glory of Iraq (God save him and keep him), May 15, 1990, 029-2-6: 70.

47. Kautsky, 94–95.

48. Wendell Steavenson, 61.

49. Pierre-Jean Luizard, "The Nature of the Confrontation between the State and *Marjaʿism*: Grand Ayatollah Muhsin al-Hakim and the Baʿth," in *Ayatollahs, Sufis and Ideologues: State, Religion and Social Movements in Iraq*, ed. Faleh Abdul-Jabar (London: Saqi Books, 2002), 90–91, 98–99; Rodger Shanahan, "The Islamic Daʿwa Party: Past Development and Future Prospects," *Middle East Review of International Affairs* 8 (June 2004): 18; T. M. Aziz, "The Role of Muhammad Baqr al-Sadr in Shii Political Activism in Iraq," *International Journal of Middle East Studies* 25 (May 1993): 212; Faleh A. Jabar, *The Shiʿite Movement in Iraq* (London: Saqi Books, 2003), 203–206; Nakash, *The Shiʿis of Iraq*, 100–105; Tripp, 202–203; Chibli Mallat, "Religious Militancy in Contemporary Iraq: Muhammad Baqer as-Sadr and the Sunni-Shia paradigm," *Third World Quarterly* 10 (April 1988): 719; Joyce N. Wiley, *The Islamic Movement of Iraqi Shiʿas* (Boulder: Lynne Rienner Publishers, 1992), 46; Robert Soeterik, "The Islamic Movement of Iraq (1958–1980)," *Occasional Paper No. 12* (Amsterdam: Middle East Research Associates (MERA), Dec. 1991), 16; D. Kehat, "Iraq," in *Middle East Record, Volume 5*, ed. Daniel Dishon (Jerusalem: Israel Universities Press, 1977), 728; Basim al-Azami, "The Muslim Brotherhood: Genesis and Development," in *Ayatollahs, Sufis and Ideologues: State, Religion and Social Movements in Iraq*, ed. Faleh Abdul-Jabar (London: Saqi Books, 2002), 172–175; "The Islamic Party and the Political Future of Iraq: An Interview with Dr. Osama Takriti," *Middle East Affairs Journal* 3 (Winter/Spring 1997): 159;

Sami Shourush, "Islamist Fundamentalist Movements among the Kurds," in *Ayatollahs, Sufis and Ideologues: State, Religion and Social Movements in Iraq*, ed. Faleh Abdul-Jabar (London: Saqi Books, 2002), 177–182; "Exclusive Interview: Muhammad Baqir al-Hakim: Head of the Supreme Islamic Revolutionary Council of Iraq," *Middle East Insight* 5 (1987), 18–24; Baram, *Culture*, 77, plate 13.

50. Nakash, *The Shiʿis of Iraq*, 144–145; Jabar, *The Shiʿite Movement*, 208–213; Shanahan, 18; Wiley, 51–52; Hannah Batatu, "Shiʿi Organizations in Iraq: Al-Daʿwah al-Islamiyah, and al-Mujahidin," *Shiʿism and Social Protest*, Nikki R. Keddie (New Haven: Yale University Press), 724; Amatzia Baram, "Two Roads," 557; Tripp, 216–217; and Farouk-Sluglett and Sluglett, *Iraq since 1958*, 198.

51. A. K. S. Lambton, "A Reconsideration of the Position of the Marja ʾal-Taqlid and the Religious Institution," *Studia Islamica* 20 (1964): 115–135.

52. In 1979, the *mujāhidīn* began their ultimately successful quest to expel Russia from Afghanistan. In the same year, Sunni extremists seized the grand mosque in Mecca. Islamic Jihad assassinated Egyptian President Anwar Sadat in 1981, and the Muslim Brotherhood became increasingly active in Jordan and Syria where, in the latter case, Hafez al-Assad's forces killed some 20,000 civilians in an effort to wipe out the Muslim Brothers in Hama in 1982 for revolting against his regime. In 1987, Shaykh Ahmed Yassin formed Hamas in Gaza. Influential Islamist thinkers such as Hassan al-Turabi in Sudan and Rashid al-Ghannoushi in Tunisia gained prominence, with al-Turabi seizing power in 1989. In Algeria, the Islamic Salvation Front won local and national elections in 1990 and 1992, respectively, before the army brutally deposed it. When the Berlin Wall fell, so too did the major patron of many socialist Arab regimes, including Hussein's, leaving not only a military but ideological vacuum that Sunni Islamists rushed to fill. Aaron Faust, "The Evolution of Islam's Role under the Socialist Arab Baʿth Party in Iraq" (master's thesis, Tel Aviv University, 2006), 68–69.

53. Samuel Helfont, "The Baʿthist Regime's Instrumentalization of Religion in Foreign Affairs," *Middle East Journal* 68 (Summer 2014): 352–366, especially 355. See also Baram, "From Militant Secularism to Islamism," 1–3.

54. The phrase "embrace Islam in order to suffocate it" is a paraphrase of Leonid Luks's comment about the Nazis' similar policies toward churches in Germany. Leonid Luks in "Concluding Discussion," *Totalitarianism and Political Religions: Concepts for the Comparison of Dictatorships*, Vol. II, ed. Hans Maier and Michael Schäfer, trans. Jodi Bruhn (London: Routledge, 1997), 187.

55. See the introduction, 64n.

56. Baram, "From Militant Secularism to Islamism."

57. Helfont, 353.

58. "*Iraq/pirsum tsvaim b'dvar sgirat mikomot bidur v'onshei gnavim-tochnim, hityahasut lahem v'ofen y'shumam*," *Hatsav*. 843/50/Oct. 10, 1994, 7–11; "Iraq Forbids Moslems to Sell Alcohol," *Agence France Presse*, Sept. 23, 1993; "Iraq Restricts Alcohol Sale, Shuts Down Bars," *Associated Press*, Sept. 26, 1993; "*Iraq/pirsum tsvaim*," *Hatsav*, 843/50/Oct. 10, 1994, 1–6; Baram, "Re-Inventing," 40–42; Baram, "From Militant Secularism to Islamism," 10, 18–19.

59. "The Islamic College University," Director of the Office of the Party Secretariat to the Comrade Minister of Higher Education and Scientific Research, Aug. 11, 1988, 029-1-6: 74–75.

60. See, e.g., "The Phenomenon of Extremism in Rituals of Worship," Member of the al-Gharis Section Command, Secretary of the First Tarimiyya Division, March 27, 1993, 023-4-2: 207; "Instructions," Official of the Baghdad al-Karkh Bureau to the Branch Commands of the Baghdad al-Karkh Bureau, May 22, 1997, 046-5-4: 8.

61. Nakash, *Shi'is of Iraq*, 278–279; Haddad, 73–86.

62. Quoted in al-Khafaji, "State Terror and the Degradation of Politics in Iraq," 4.

63. "Rumor," March 13, 1993, 005-3-3: 274.

64. See, e.g., a fascinating petition to Hussein from a Ba'thist detailing the events of the 1991 uprising in the town of al-Khudur in Muthanna Province. May 24, 1991, 039-1-6: 237–241. The word *ghūghā'iyīn* appears on p. 237. I am indebted to Kanan Makiya for pointing out the sudden appearance of this word.

65. "Rumors," July 28, 1996, 148-4-5: 985.

66. Haddad, 53–55.

67. Hasan Alawi, *al-Shi'a wa-l-Dawla al-Qawmiyya fi al-'Iraq, 1914-1990* (London: Dar al-Zura, 1990), 12.

68. Most Shi'is in Iraq outside of the Najaf and Karbala area are relatively secular and place more emphasis on their Arabness and tribal identities than their religion. Nakash, *Shi'is of Iraq*, 138.

69. Baram, "Neo-Tribalism," 8.

70. 023-4-7: 569.

71. 023-4-2: 205. See the al-Khoei foundation website for a short biography: al-Khoei Islamic Institute. "*Wiladatuhu wa-Hijratuhu 'ilā al-Najaf (His Birth and His Emigration to Najaf)*," http://www.alkhoei.net/arabic/?p=page&id=10 [accessed Nov. 29, 2012].

72. For a fascinating account of a Ba'thist delegation's discussions with the Shi'i religious establishment's leaders in 1997 see Minister of Endowments and Religious Affairs to the Presidency of the Republic—Office of the Secretary of the National Security Council, May 18, 1997, 028-5-1: 583–585. In this case, the delegation visited the leaders to ask them to issue rulings against the display of pictures of Shi'i saints in public places. For other examples of attempts to use men of religion in order to benefit from their influence in different media see: "A Report about the Occasion of the 10 of Muharram and the Visits of Arbain on the 20 of Safar," Office of the Baghdad Bureau, Oct. 17, 1989, 001-5-4: 9; "Report," Head of the Presidential Diwan to the Ministry of Endowments and Religious Affairs—the Special Office, Sept. 9, 1984, 046-3-6: 620; "Follow the Plan," Director of the Office of the Party Secretariat to All of the Party Branch Commands, 123-4-7: 446.

73. "Evaluation," Director of the Office of the Party Secretariat to the Honorable Comrade Secretaries of the Party Branch Commands, Sept. 2, 1995, 103-1-5: 374.

74. "The Important and Special Suggestions about the Condition of the Men of Religion which were Approved at the Meeting of the Comrade Secretaries of the Branch Commands in the Bureaus of the Middle Governorates," The Bureaus of the Middle Governorates, 089-1-3: 163.

75. "The Preacher of Abi Ubayda Mosque," Official of the Office of the Baghdad Bureau, the Security Committee to the Office of the Baghdad Bureau Command, April 19, 1986, 029-2-7: 497.

76. See, e.g., a party report from 1983 about the 10 of Muharram that claimed that all of the Shiʿi religious leaders who read the story of Imam Hussein were officially licensed and each praised the party, the revolution, and the leader during their remarks: "The Occasion of the 10 of Muharram," Secretary of the Office of the Southern Bureau Command to the Office of the Party Secretariat, Nov. 22, 1983, 023-4-7: 566.

77. "A Religious Study about the *marjaʿiyya* (the Institution of the *marājiʿ*), the Hawza, Students and Schools, the Religious Sciences, Recommendations," Office of the Euphrates Bureau, 023-4-7: 20–59. This study was found in a boxfile from 1984 but was undated and could have been written earlier.

78. The term "Hawza," short for *al-ḥawza al-ʿilmiyya*, refers to the series of Shiʿi religious schools connected to the *marājiʿ* who lived in Najaf and Karbala.

79. 023-4-7: 52.

80. 023-4-7: 54.

81. 023-4-7: 55.

82. 023-4-7: 56.

83. Secretary of the President of the Republic for Party Affairs to the Honorable Mr. President Leader, May 3, 1983, 035-1-4: 96–97.

84. "The Wahhabi Movement," Director of the Office of the Party Secretariat to the Honorable Comrade Secretary of Mr. President of the Republic, Aug. 21, 1990, 056-4-4: 100–102.

85. Director of the Office of the Party Secretariat to the Honorable Comrade Deputy Secretary-General, Aug. 24, 1990, 056-4-4: 93; Director of the Office of the Party Secretariat to the Honorable Comrade Deputy Secretary-General, Jan. 2, 1994, 123-4-7: 721; "Imam of a Mosque," Director of the Office of the Party Secretariat to the Ministry of Endowments and Religious Affairs—the Office of the Minister, May 9, 2002, 040-3-1: 421.

86. "The Job of the Secretariat," Head of the Presidential Diwan to the Ministry of Endowments and Religious Affairs—the Special Office, June 29, 1985, 088-5-3: 608.

87. See, e.g., a report about the phenomenon of Shiʿi processions from 1996, which theorized that they were part of an "Imperialist-Zionist" plot: "A Study about the Phenomenon of [Shiʿi] Processions," The Official of the Baghdad Bureau—al-Rasafa, Secretary of the Branch Command to the Office of the Party Secretariat, Nov. 11, 1996, 046-5-4: 89–91. See also a report on the events of Muharram in 1983 which claimed that the "mistaken practices" (*al-mumārasāt al-khāṭiʾa*) of the faithful had Persian roots: "The Measures and the Observations and

the Suggestions about the Occasions of the Month of Muharram," Official of the Committee for National Activism and Security in the Baghdad Bureau Command to the Honorable Comrade Struggler Secretary of the Office, Oct. 27, 1983, 023-4-7: 584–587.

88. 023-4-7: 566–570.

89. 046-5-4: 89–91. For lists of the men of religion in al-Khoei's network that the regime considered loyal and disloyal, see "Study," Director of the Office of the Party Secretariat to the Comrade Deputy Secretary-General, Feb. 27, 1985, 023-4-7: 64–72; Director of the Office of the Party Secretariat to the Comrade Deputy Secretary-General of the Regional Command of Iraq, Aug. 1, 1996, 046-5-4: 120–123; 046-5-4: 8–9; 123-5-5: 213.

90. 046-5-4: 298.

91. 023-4-7: 57.

92. Meir Litvak, "Iraq," in *Middle East Contemporary Survey, vol. 15, 1991*, ed. Ami Ayalon (Boulder: Westview Press, 1993), 424.

93. See, e.g., Head of the Presidential Diwan to the Secretariat of the Council of Ministers, et al., Dec. 29, 1996, 021-1-2: 47–49.

94. 063-2-4: 43–52.

95. See, e.g., "Report," Secretary of the Command of the Office of the Middle Bureau to the Regional Command—the Organizational Committee, December 18, 1985, 029-2-3: 429.

96. See, e.g., a party report about the preachers in mosques in Salah al-Din governorate in 1998, most of whom were labeled "independent" and a few of which the party considered "Wahhabi." "Answer," Secretary of the Salah al-Din Branch Command to the Office of the Party Secretariat, July 18, 1998, 093-4-4: 23–26.

97. "Statement of Opinion," Director of the Office of the Party Secretariat to the Presidential Diwan, April 6, 1985, 023-4-7: 165–166.

98. 001-5-4: 6–9; Director of the Office of the Party Secretariat to the Honorable comrade Deputy Secretary-General of the Regional Command of Iraq, Aug. 14, 1995, 025-5-7: 187; "The Visit of the Middle of Sha'ban," Official of the Bureau of the Governorates of Babil/Karbala to the Office of the Party Secretariat, Dec. 30, 1996, 046-5-4: 77; 123-5-5: 212–214.

99. "The Religious Schools," Director of the Office of the Party Secretariat to the Comrade Deputy Secretary-General and the Comrade Members of the Organizational Committee, March 15, 1988, 023-4-7: 89–90.

100. "Men of Religion," 148-1-4: 289–554.

101. Baram, "Neo-tribalism," 1–2.

102. Faleh A. Jabar, "Sheikhs and Ideologues: Deconstruction and Reconstruction of Tribes under Patrimonial Totalitarianism in Iraq, 1968–1998," in *Tribes and Power: Nationalism and Ethnicity in the Middle East*, ed. Faleh Abdul-Jabar and Hosham Dawood (London: Saqi, 2003), 93; Baram, "Neo-Tribalism," 10–13.

103. Baram, "Neo-Tribalism," 10–14, quote 13.

104. Baram, "Neo-Tribalism," 4.

105. Baram, "Neo-Tribalism," 82.

106. "A Study of the Subject of Arming a Portion of the Arab Tribes on the

Borderline and the Recommendations in Relation to It," Dec. 29, 1984, 080-2-6: 82–85; 031-1-4. See also Jabar, "Sheikhs and Ideologues," 90–91, 95–96.

107. See, e.g., 097-1-6.

108. "Suggestion," Director of the Office of the Party Secretariat to the Comrade Minister of the Interior, Nov. 5, 1991, 059-4-6: 356.

109. Jabar, "Shaykhs and Ideologues," 31.

110. "Meetings," Director of the Office of the Party Secretariat to the Party Branch Commands, Dec. 21, 1993, 123-4-7: 425.

111. 041-2-1: 725.

112. Baram, "Neo-Tribalism," 12.

113. "The Convention of a Symposium," Official of the Bureau of Maysan and Wasit to the Office of the Party Secretariat, June 15, 1995, 037-4-6: 169–170; "Practices," Director of the Office of the Party Secretariat to the Honorable Comrade Officials of the Party Bureaus, March 29, 1997, 123-5-5: 212.

114. The BRCC does not indicate when sheikhs had to start registering. The earliest document found for this study that refers to the registration of a sheikh with a county government occurs in 1992: 039-4-3: 236. Beginning in 1999, files from the President's Office contain tens, if not hundreds, of petitions from sheikhs throughout the country asking the Office of Tribal Affairs to officially recognize them, suggesting that they all had to comply with a new regulation. Jabar believes this happened earlier, in 1996. Jabar, "Sheikhs and Ideologues," 94.

115. See, e.g., a petition from one sheikh to the head of the Office of Tribal Affairs, 039-4-3: 236.

116. E.g., "[name withheld]," Director of the Office of the Party Secretariat to the Presidential Diwan, May 31, 1999, 039-2-5: 15.

117. "The Request of [name withheld]," Secretary of the al-Anbar Branch Command to the Office of the Party Secretariat, June 19, 1999, 045-3-6: 265–266. For an example of a table of tribal statistics see "The Organizational Structure and the General Force and the Fighting Force of the Tribe [name withheld]," 045-3-6: 279.

118. See, e.g., 123-4-7: 421–425.

119. Director of the Office of the Party Secretariat to the Comrade Deputy Secretary-General of the Regional Command of Iraq, March 26, 1994, 123-4-7: 220.

120. Jabar, "Sheikhs and Ideologues," 99.

121. Baram, "Neo-Tribalism," 18.

122. Director of the Office of the Party Secretariat to the Comrade Deputy Secretary-General of the Regional Command of Iraq, Jan. 2, 1994, 123-4-7: 723.

PART IV

Epigraph from Armstrong, "Hitler's Reich: The First Phase," 589. Reprinted by permission of *Foreign Affairs* (July 1933). Copyright (1933) by the Council on Foreign Relations, Inc.

1. Peter Holquist, "State Violence as Technique: The Logic of Violence in So-

viet Totalitarianism," in *Stalinism*, ed. David L. Hoffman (Cornwall: Blackwell Publishing, 2003), 156.

2. Khlevnyuk claims that this policy conformed to the Soviet leadership's earlier policies of repression as well. Oleg Khlevnyuk, "The Objectives of the Great Terror, 1937–1938," in *Stalinism*, ed. David L. Hoffman (Cornwall: Blackwell Publishing, 2003), 97.

3. James van Geldern, "The Centre and the Periphery: Cultural and Social Geography in the Mass Culture of the 1930s," in *New Directions in Soviet History*, ed. Stephen White (Cambridge: Cambridge University Press, 1992), 62; quote from Vera Dunham, *In Stalin's Time: Middleclass Values in Soviet Fiction* (Durham, NC: Duke University Press, 1990), 4; Suny, 28.

4. As Peter Holquist writes with regard to the logic behind Soviet violence: "Soviet state violence was not simply repressive. It was employed as a tool for fashioning an idealized image of a better, purer society." Holquist, 134.

5. Makiya, *Republic of Fear*, xii.

6. This phrase occurs many times in the BRCC. See, e.g., 123-4-7: 220.

7. John Kautsky describes this same type of logic with regard to the Soviet regime and to totalitarian governments more generally: "All failures of the regime are blamed on the outside enemy, implying that the regime, of itself, can do no wrong. And all domestic opposition is identified with the outside enemy, implying (by a definitional trick) that there is complete domestic unity behind the regime—since anyone opposing the regime is, by definition, no longer a good member of the society but an agent, subjectively or objectively, of the outside enemy." Kautsky, 96.

8. Arendt, 452.

CHAPTER 8

1. Arendt, xxx, 321–323.

2. Makiya, *Republic of Fear*, 129, xii.

3. The Soviets used similar language. Holquist, 140.

4. John L. Stanley, "Is Totalitarianism a New Phenomenon?: Reflections on Hannah Arendt's *Origins of Totalitarianism*," *The Review of Politics* 49 (Spring 1987): 186.

5. For an excellent discussion of the meaning and character of resistance, dissent, and opposition to Stalin and Hitler's regimes see Overy, 304–348. For a list of works on this issue from the Soviet perspective, see David L. Hoffman, "Introduction: Interpretations of Stalinism," *Stalinism*, ed. David L. Hoffman (Cornwall: Blackwell Publishing, 2003), 6, 14n.

6. Baram says that in the early 1990s, Hussein unearthed "one coup plot after another" by three tribes that he had relied on: the *al-ʿubayd*, *al-jubūr*, and *al-dulaym*. Baram, *Building Toward Crisis*, 17–18, 37; Ofra Bengio, "Iraq," in *Middle East Contemporary Survey, vol. 7, 1982–1983*, ed. Haim Shaked, Colin Legum, and Daniel Dishon (New York: Holmes & Meier Publishers, 1985), 564–565; Bashir,

206; Ali Babakhan, "The Deportation of Shi'is During the Iran-Iraq War: Causes and Consequences," in *Ayatollahs, Sufis and Ideologues: State, Religion and Social Movements in Iraq*, ed. Faleh Abdul-Jabar (London: Saqi, 2002), 193.

7. See, e.g., Petition from a citizen [name withheld] to Saddam Hussein, Aug. 27, 2001, 038-2-8: 305; Director of the Office of the Party Secretariat to the Honorable Comrade Deputy Secretary-General, Jan. 12, 1988, 039-2-2: 182; The Kirkuk (*al-Ta'mīm*) Branch Command to the Office of the Party Secretariat, Dec. 20, 1994, 029-1-3: 559–560; "The Regime and Regulations for Safeguarding the Places for Cars on Public Roads," Minister of the Interior to the Minister of Justice, May 22, 1996, 062-3-5: 573; "Citizen [name withheld]," Director of General Military Intelligence to the Presidency of the Republic—the Secretary, Oct. 8, 1998, 030-3-3: 72–73. Boxfile 051-4-4, labeled as relating to correspondence with the President's Office (*dīwān al-ri'āsa*) from 1995, contains many reports about antiregime attacks on the security forces, the police, the party, and the army, as does boxfile 110-4-7 from 1998. No systematic effort was undertaken to determine exactly which time periods between 1979 and 2003 contained more of these types of incidents than others, but the heaviest concentration appeared to occur in the 1990s. Exploiting criminal statistics for further study is an area of potentially fruitful research.

8. See, e.g., a petition from a woman to Saddam Hussein explaining how her husband was martyred while looking for deserters in a party detachment: Aug. 27, 1999, 036-3-5: 131. In another petition to Hussein, a man explained how he was hit over the head with the butt of a rifle and cut with a knife while searching for army deserters: Oct. 23, 1999, 029-2-2: 266–267. On Ba'thist detachments acting like police see Baran, 31–32.

9. Secretary of the Organizational Committee to the Honorable Comrade Official of the Organizational Committee, 029-4-4: 3–12. The report is not dated, but the introduction mentions "this year/1987."

10. "Assassination Event," Official of the Basra and Dhi Qar Bureau to Mr. Aid to the Mr. President Leader (God save him), Nov. 6, 1995, 036-4-7: 79.

11. Steavenson, 87.

12. For stories of torture and the conditions within prisons under the Ba'th, see Amir Hayder, "A Personal Testimony," in *The Iraqi Marshlands: a Human and Environmental Study*, ed. Emma Nicholson and Peter Clark (London: Politico's, 2002), 307–313; An Iraqi Mother and Su'ad Khairi, "Ba'th terror—Two Personal Accounts," in *Saddam's Iraq: Revolution or Reaction*, Committee Against Repression and for Democratic Rights in Iraq (CARDRI) (London: Zed Books, 1986), 108–119; Chapter 3, "Omar: Inside a Baghdad Prison," in Kanan Makiya, *Cruelty and Silence: War, Tyranny, Uprising and the Arab World* (New York: W. W. Norton, 1993), 105–134; Abd al-Qahhar, 104–105; and Qasim al-Buraysim, *al-Sharara wa-l-Ramad: Shahada Hayya 'an 'Intifadat al-Sha'b al-'Iraqi wa-'Adhab al-Muntafidin fi Sujun al-Ridwaniyya* (Beirut: Dar al-Kunuz al-'Adabiyya, 2004). For an example of a confession see "Relating Initial Information," The Investigator, Jan. 1986, 035-4-6: 86–87. This document details the case of seven men who supposedly were

part of an Iranian-backed opposition group. According to the confessions of three of the men, they planned to assassinate a divisional Baʿth Party member. All seven men were Baʿthists.

13. "Monitoring Deserters from Military Service," General Secretary for the General Command of the Armed Forces to the Office of the Party Secretariat, Dec. 4, 1987, 027-1-1: 229–231.

14. Secretary of the Office of the Baghdad Bureau to Mr. President Leader—God save him and keep you, June 20, 1987, 027-1-1: 234–243.

15. "Convening of Symposia," Director of the Office of the Party Secretariat to All of the Party Offices, Feb. 7, 1991, 024-5-2: 226.

16. "Information," Secretary of the al-Nasiriyya Branch Command to the Office of the Party Secretariat, July 3, 2000, 049-5-7: 69.

17. "Reply," Director of the Intelligence Apparatus (*jihāz al-mukhābarāt*) to the Regional Command/the Office of the Party Secretariat, Jan. 7, 1986, 038-4-1: 565–566.

18. "The Deserters and Dodgers in the Marsh Areas," Secretary of the Office of the Southern Branch Command to the Office of the Party Secretariat, June 7, 1986, 052-1-3: 48–49.

19. Secretary of the Office of the Southern Bureau Command to Mr. President Leader, May 20, 1987, 038-5-2: 542–543.

20. Tripp, 264–265.

21. "Information," Official of the Committee of the Office (the Security Committee in the Office of the Baghdad Bureau) to the Office of the Baghdad Bureau Command, Jan. 27, 1986, 035-2-3: 99.

22. "Information," Secretary of the Office of the Euphrates Bureau to the Office of the Party Secretariat, Sept. 12, 1990, 047-1-7: 67–68.

23. "Two Assistants to Two Security Officials," Director of General Security to the Revolutionary Command Council—National Security Council—the Office of the Secretariat, Oct. 19, 1986, 026-1-3: 65.

24. "Closed Report," Director of the Office of the Party Secretariat to the Presidency of the Republic/Secretary of the Republic for Party Affairs, Jan. 14, 1991, 024-5-2: 133.

25. Director of the Office of the Party Secretariat to the Honorable Comrade General-Secretary, 034-2-1: 150–151.

26. Citizen petition to Saddam Hussein, 050-5-2: 130–132.

27. [Name withheld] to the Honorable Mr. President of the National Council in Baghdad, 021-1-2: 169. The letter contains no date but comes from a boxfile from 1996.

28. Al-Samarrai, 193–194. Al-Samarrai claims to have heard about and witnessed these mass executions but never participated.

29. The Baʿth Party tracked rumors assiduously and kept large files of reports about them. There was an official form for reporting rumors that asked for the text of the rumor, the medium in which it circulated, the date of its circulation, an opinion about it from the security official (*al-masʾūl al-ʾamanī*) in the area, and

the opinion of the person who reported the rumor about whether or not the rumor was true. For an example of a form see "Form for Reporting a Rumor," April 18, 1993, 005-3-3: 9. Many of the reported rumors dealt with things the security services supposedly either did or were planning to do. See, e.g., a number of rumors reported by the party's Najaf branch in 1993: "Rumors," Director of the Office of the Party Secretariat to the Presidency of the Republic/the Office of the Secretariat of the National Security Council, April 24, 1993, 005-3-3: 1. Other boxfiles besides 005-3-3 that contain rumors include: 148-4-5, 162-2-2, 087-5-3, 133-5-7, and 040-4-2.

30. "Information," Official of the Bureaus to the Office of the Party Secretariat, March 16, 1998, 129-3-7: 555.

31. See, e.g., the story of a woman whose husband was supposedly martyred during the fighting in 1991: Petition from a citizen to Saddam Hussein, May 10, 1991, 039-1-6: 296.

32. 024-5-2: 96.

33. 024-5-2: 96.

34. "Two Rumors," Director of the Office of the Party Secretariat to the Presidency of the Republic/The Office of the Secretariat of the National Security Council, May 8, 1999, 087-5-3: 206.

35. Marr, 171–172.

36. A DMI report from 1986, e.g., claimed that the agency had uncovered a new group called The Organization of the Awaited Imam Mahdi (*munaẓẓamat al-ʾimām mahdī al-muntaẓar*), named after the twelfth Shiʿi imam who Shiʿis believe went into occultation in 873 AD. The group was supposedly funded and armed by Iran and came into the country to conduct "sabotage" operations. The report contains an organizational map of the group listing thirty-two total members. "Exposure of an Opposition Organization," Director of the DMI to the Presidency of the Republic—the Secretary, May 22, 1986, 026-1-3: 272–278. For a representative list of smaller opposition parties in addition to the four main ones see "Activities of the Opposition Movements," Secretary of the Office of the Northern Bureau Command to the Office of the Party Secretariat, Aug. 13, 1990, 030-5-5: 1–38.

37. The table does not list the PUK for some reason. "Inventory of the Political Movements in the Entire Country," 132-2-6: 390–397.

38. "Security Report for the Month of October/1986, for Qadisiyya Governorate," 039-3-7: 132.

39. See, e.g., "Information," Secretary of the Office of the Euphrates Bureau Command to the Office of the Party Secretariat, June 10, 1985, 001-5-1: 30.

40. The BRCC records limited contacts between the Communist Party and Syria in boxfile 031-4-1: 65, 132, 143, 222–223. The communists also had a presence in the north, and the same security report (039-3-7: 132) that claims the communists were psychologically beaten also says that the Communist Party took Iran's side in the Iran–Iraq War (039-3-7: 132). These two pieces of information together suggest that the Communist Party had links to Iran, even if tenuous.

41. 026-4-4: 66.

42. Nakash, *Shiʿis of Iraq*, 138.

43. The Daʿwa was responsible for a series of assassinations of top Baʿthist officials and ideologues in the late 1970s and a number of terrorist attacks against Iraqi government installations in Iraq and abroad in the 1980s. They also famously tried to assassinate Hussein in Dujayl in 1982 (and again in Mosul in 1987), after which Hussein's forces responded with a massacre of residents; Hussein was ultimately sentenced to death and hanged for these murders on December 30, 2006. For more about the origins and early activities of the Daʿwa, see Amatzia Baram, "The Radical Shiʿite Opposition Movements in Iraq," in *Religious Radicalism and Politics in the Middle East*, ed. Emmanuel Sivan and Menachem Friedman (Albany: State University of New York Press, 1990), 104–105; Amatzia Baram, "The Impact of Khomeini's Revolution on the Radical Shi'i Movement of Iraq," *The Iranian Revolution and the Muslim World*, ed. David Menashri (Boulder: Westview Press, 1990), 132; Yitzhak Nakash, "The Nature of Shiʾism in Iraq," in *Ayatollahs, Sufis and Ideologues: State, Religion and Social Movements in Iraq*, ed. Faleh Abdul-Jabar (London: Saqi Books, 2002), 31–32; Jabar, *Shiʾite Movement*, 75–142, 201–215.

44. Nakash, *Shiʿis of Iraq*, 138.

45. 039-3-7: 132. Emphasis added.

46. Jabar, *Shiʾite Movement*, 228–231; Baram, "Impact of Khomeini's Revolution," 142; Wiley, 55, 62–63.

47. Al-Jumhuriyya al-Iraqiyya. *Wizarat al-ʾIʿlam al-Dustur al-muʾaqqat wa-taʿadilatuhu*, 2nd ed. (Baghdad: Dar al-Huriyya li-l-Tabaʿa, 1976), 6.

48. 030-5-5: 2–5.

49. Marr, 157; Tripp, 192–194.

50. For propaganda to be effective the people targeted by it must be able to read it and understand it. Linz, *Totalitarian and Authoritarian Regimes*, 71; Hitler, 33–34.

51. See also chapter 9. "Decision," Director of the Office of the Party Secretariat to All of the Main Commands in the Country, April 27, 1980, 024-1-7: 605–606; "Suggestions," Head of the Presidential Diwan to the Office of the Party Secretariat, April 9, 1987, 072-1-5: 98–101.

52. See, e.g., "Information," Director of the Office of the Party Secretariat to the Presidency of the Republic—the Secretary, Sept. 3, 1991, 021-2-5: 50–52; "Information," Director of the Office of the Party Secretariat to the Presidency of the Republic—the Secretary, Aug. 12, 1991, 021-2-5: 109; "Information," Office of the Secretariat to the Director of the Office of the Northern Bureau, Sept. 15, 1991, 038-4-5: 56–57.

53. Secretary of the Organizational Committee to the Comrade Official of the Organizational Committee, July 16, 1986, 029-2-3: 209.

54. 029-2-3: 209.

55. "Information," Directorate of General Military Intelligence/the Room of Joint Information, Sept. 22, 1991, 038-4-5: 13.

56. 031-3-5: 12; 030-5-5: 3–5.

57. See, e.g., "A Study about Dividing the *Taʾmīm* (Kirkuk) Branch," The *Taʾmīm* (Kirkuk) Branch Command, 027-1-4: 44–51.

58. The phrase, "the Arabization of Kurdistan" shows up, for example, in a 2002 letter from the Democratic National Union of Kurdistan (*al-ʾitiḥād al-qawmī al-dīmuqrāṭī al-kūrdistānī*), a smaller Kurdish party, addressed to Arab tribes that the Baʿth resettled in the north, encouraging them not to remain pawns in "the conspiracy of the Arabization of Kurdistan," and to go back to their prior homes. The letter, written in the run-up to the American invasion in 2003, when the Kurds expected to capture the north, contained the not-so-subtle hint that if the Arab tribes did not leave the Kurdish region this "would reflect in a negative fashion on the future of relations between the Kurds and the Arabs." "Bulletins," Official of the Bureaus of Ninewa to the Office of the Party Secretariat, March 17, 2002, 006-4-1: 595–596.

59. "A Study about the Situation in the Counties of Kifri," Director of the Office of the Middle Bureau to the Office of the Party Secretariat, Feb. 27, 1988, 025-2-2: 205.

60. "The Counties of Kifri," Head of the Presidential Diwan to Comrade Ali Hassan al-Majid—the Honorable Secretary of the Office of the Northern Bureau, June 22, 1988, 025-2-2: 189–193.

61. "A Study about Khaniqin," The Diyala Branch Command, July 13, 1992, 119-2-7: 507–508.

62. Khoury, 115–121.

63. "Study," Director of the Office of the Party Secretariat to the Presidential Diwan, Nov. 7, 1992, 089-1-3: 33.

64. See, e.g., boxfiles 026-2-2 and 006-4-1. The Kurds also benefited from a no-fly zone.

65. "Report," May 18, 1986, 042-2-7: 375–376.

66. Kolakowski, 51; Charles Kurzman, *The Unthinkable Revolution in Iran* (Cambridge, MA: Harvard University Press, 2004), 1–11.

67. "A Pamphlet and Opposition Slogans," Director of the Office of the Party Secretariat to the Presidency of the Republic—the Secretary—Directorate of General Security, June 4, 1991, 021-2-5: 159; "The Slogans Written on the Walls in the Square for Celebrations in al-Ramadi," 021-2-5: 170.

68. For a case of pamphlets see "Opposition Slogans," Secretary of the Office of the Southern Bureau Command to the Office of the Party Secretariat, Dec. 11, 1986, 022-1-5: 64–77.

69. Director of the Office of the Party Secretariat to the Honorable Comrade Deputy Secretary-General of the Region of Iraq, July 2, 1995, 089-3-6: 775.

70. "Instructions," Secretary of the Office of the Southern Bureau to the Branch Commands Attached to the Office, Dec. 13, 1986, 022-1-5: 149–150. As Roy Mottahedeh has shown, the *shuʿūbiyya* was not a political group but "primarily a literary controversy" whose advocates staked an intellectual claim to a place for non-Arab culture in Islamic history. Yet, as far back as the Abbasid era, Arabs used

the term to charge Persian scribes with corrupting the government from within. Roy P. Mottahedeh, "The Shuʿubiyah Controversy and the Social History of Early Islamic Iran," *International Journal of Middle Eastern Studies* 7 (April 1976), 161–182. For more on the *shuʿūbiyya* issue see Davis, 184–188; Makiya, *Republic of Fear*, 216–220; Fouad Ajami, *The Dream Palace of the Arabs: A Generation's Odyssey* (New York: Vintage Books, 1998), 157; and Nakash, *Shiʾis of Iraq*, 47, 113.

71. Pursuant to Interior Ministry directive 2884, on April 10, 1980, the Baʿth declared, "All Iranians in the country, as well as those who do not have Iraqi citizenship and those whose naturalization applications are being processed, shall be deported." Babakhan, 200.

72. See, e.g., Babakhan, 186–187, 193, 195, 198–200; Isam al-Khafaji, "Not Quite an Arab Prussia: Revisiting Some Myths on Iraqi Exceptionalism," in *Iraq: The Human Cost of History*, ed. Tareq Y. Ismael and William W. Haddad (London: Pluto Press, 2004), 223–226; and Alawi, *al-Shiʿa wa-l-Dawla al-Qawmiyya*, 12, 46–47. See also chapter 7.

73. 028-1-1: 445–459; "The Deportation of Iranians," Secretary of the Wasit Branch Command to the Office of the Party Secretariat, July 31, 1983, 028-1-1: 419–424; "The Deportation of Iranians," Director of the Office of the Party Secretariat to the Wasit Branch Command, Sept. 25, 1983, 028-1-1: 412–413; "The Deportation of the Families of Iranian Origin," Secretary of the Wasit Branch Command to the Office of the Party Secretariat, Dec. 13, 1984, 028-1-1: 371–386; "The Deportation of Families," Secretary of the Office of the Southern Bureau Command to the Office of the Party Secretariat, July 25, 1986, 022-1-5: 257–258.

74. See, e.g., Yitzhak Nakash, "The Shiʾites and the Future of Iraq," *Foreign Affairs* 82 (July/August 2003), http://www.foreignaffairs.com/articles/58994/yitzhak-nakash/the-shiites-and-the-future-of-iraq?page=show [accessed Feb. 29,2012] and Adeed Dawisha, "The Assembled State: Communal Conflicts and Governmental Control in Iraq," in *Ethnic conflict and International Politics in the Middle East*, ed. Leonard Binder (Gainesville: University Press of Florida, 1999), 74.

75. See, e.g., 022-1-5: 149–150.

76. Overy, 212–214.

77. "The Phenomenon of the Entry of Narcotic Pills into the Departments of Social Rehabilitation in Abi Ghrayb: A Study Diagnosing the Reasons and Describing the Cures," 038-2-8: 69–75. Interestingly, this is almost exactly the same argument that Muammar al-Qaddafi used to explain the protests that enveloped his regime during the Arab Spring in 2011. "Gaddafi says protesters are on hallucinogenic drugs," *Reuters*, Feb. 24, 2011, http://www.reuters.com/article/2011/02/24/us-libya-protests-gaddafi-idUSTRE71N4NI20110224 [accessed 28 Jan., 2012].

78. "Information," Official of the Baghdad Bureaus to the Office of the Party Secretariat, Aug. 2, 1992, 104-4-1: 112–119.

79. See, e.g., the case of Ali Hassan al-Majid, who expelled from the party a group of five Baʿthists on a committee that suggested leniency in punishing a military deserter: "Statement of Opinion," Secretary of the Office of the Northern Bu-

reau to the Presidential Diwan—Secretary of Mr. President of the Republic for Party Affairs, Aug. 9, 1989, 029-5-6: 85–88.

80. 035-3-4: 1; 113-4-5: 4; RCC Decision No. 267, Law No. 21, 1992, "Amendment of the Medal and Badge Law," Oct. 15, 1992, 113-4-5: 302; "Consideration of the Crime of Desertion from Military Service as One of the Crimes that Violate Honor," http://iraqilaws.doral-aliraq.net/?p=7477 [accessed Jan. 5, 2012].

81. 123-4-7: 421–427.

82. 024-5-2: 226.

83. Ali Wardi, *Understanding Iraq: Society, Culture, and Personality* (Lewiston, NY: Edwin Mellen Press, 2008), 21, 100.

84. 025-1-2: 42.

85. Memorandum to Hussein from Ali Hassan Majid, Director of the Office of the Party Secretariat, Dec. 25, 1982, 030-4-2: 342–343.

86. See, e.g., 038-4-1: 565–566.

87. Versions of this phrase are ubiquitous in the BRCC. See, e.g., its use in a petition to Hussein in 1996, 021-1-2: 187–188.

CHAPTER NINE

1. Steavenson, 47.

2. Steavenson, 47–57.

3. Quinlivan, 154.

4. As David Baran put it, the regime "locked political personnel and the population in a relationship of dependence and precarity." Baran, 87, 104–112.

5. In this sense, the BRCC supports the work of Baran, 29–33. For more on the various phases of Iraq's economy under the Baʿth and during Hussein's presidency see Farouk-Sluglett and Sluglett, *Iraq since 1958*, 215–254; Marr, 161–168; Kiren Aziz Chaudhry, "Economic Liberalization and the Lineages of the Rentier State," *Comparative Politics* (Oct. 1994): 1–25, and "On the Way to Market: Economic Liberalization and Iraq's Invasion of Kuwait," *Middle East Report* No. 170, Power, Poverty and Petrodollars (May–June 1991): 14–23; Joseph Sassoon, "Management of Iraq's Economy Pre and Post the 2003 War: An Assessment," in *Iraq Between Occupations: Perspectives from 1920 to the Present*, ed. Amatzia Baram, Achim Rohde, and Ronen Zeidel (New York: Palgrave Macmillan, 2010), 189–208; Abbas Alnasrawi, "Iraq: Economic Sanctions and Consequences, 1990–2000," *Third World Quarterly* 22 (April 2001): 205–218; Denis J. Halliday, "The Impact of the U.N. Sanctions on the People of Iraq," *Journal of Palestine Studies* 28 (Winter 1999): 29–37.

6. See, e.g., the story of a party branch leader who claimed that his father died defending a local Baʿth Party headquarters building during the 1991 uprisings but claims that his family can nonetheless not make ends meet: 044-4-6: 98.

7. "Order of the Command," Law No. 23, Feb. 18, 1986, http://www.iraq-ild.org/LoadLawBook.aspx?SP=REF&SC=091220054959474&Year=1986&PageNum=1 [accessed Feb. 27, 2012].

8. RCC decision No. 101, Aug. 1, 1994, 004-1-4: 46–49.

9. "Martyrdom Decrees," Official of the Basra and Dhi Qar Bureaus to the Honorable Aid to Mr. President Leader (God save him and keep him), Comrade Brigadier General Abd al-Ghafour Suleiman, Oct. 17, 1998, 110-4-7: 11.

10. Citizen petition to Saddam Hussein. Aug. 27, 1999, 036-3-5: 131.

11. Law No. 95, The Medal and Badge Law, Oct. 6, 1982, 026-2-7: 229.

12. 026-2-7: 230.

13. 026-2-7: 230–236; Republican Decree No. 285, Sept. 15, 2001, 038-2-8: 62.

14. The Revolution Medal (*wisām al-thawra*) was given "to those who participated actively in the outbreak of the great July 17–30 revolution." The Saddam's *Qādisiyya* Medal (*wisām qādisiyyat ṣaddām*) went "to military personnel and civilians who carried out venerable operations in service to the battles entered into by the country on the regional and national levels during the Iran–Iraq War." 026-2-7: 236–241.

15. 026-2-7: 241–242, quote 241.

16. 004-1-4: 46–49.

17. Director of the Office of the Party Secretariat to the Honorable Deputy Secretary-General of the Regional Command of Iraq, May 7, 1996, 117-4-5: 695; Baran, 33.

18. 002-2-3: 733–734.

19. 004-1-4: 47–49.

20. RCC Decision No. 208, April 14, 1998, 018-3-4: 293.

21. 010-1-3: 101–102; Sassoon, *Saddam Hussein's Baʿth Party*, 211.

22. See, e.g., "Commendation," The Muʿatasim Sections of the Popular Army to the Fighter [name withheld], Feb. 16, 1984, 001-5-4: 542.

23. See, e.g., 041-3-7: 1–24. For copies of the certificates Baʿthists received for participating in the *yawm al-nakhwa* drills, for "volunteering to liberate Palestine," and for graduating from Saddam's Cubs, respectively, see 020-4-3: 177–179.

24. "Research," Director of the Office of Culture and Media to the Office of the Party Secretariat, June 21, 1998, 054-2-6: 579. The actual report is in the same boxfile, 586–604.

25. Quote from "The City of Faw (the City of Sacrifice and the Doors of the Great Victory)," Director of the Office of the Party Secretariat to All of the Organizational Offices in the Country, June 18, 1989, 026-3-5: 30; "The City of Faw (the City of Sacrifice and the Doors of the Great Victory)," Director of the Office of the Party Secretariat to All of the Organizational Offices in the Country, June 14, 1989, 026-3-5: 31–32.

26. Baran, 32.

27. The text of the Order of the Party read: "In appreciation of the struggling role of comrade (name) who spent more than twenty-five struggling years in the ranks of the Arab Baʿth Socialist Party for the sake of achieving the goals of the outstanding Arab nation: unity, freedom, and socialism. In appreciation for his struggling journey, the Regional Command presents him with the Order of the Party on (date)." Photocopies of the Order of the Party can be found throughout

the BRCC, including in boxfile 183-4-1: 92. The Order of the Party was originally given to people who had spent twenty-five continuous years in the party, but this was changed in 1984 to twenty-five total years. See the letter from Hussein to the members of the Regional Command, July 28, 1984, 029-1-6: 2–13.

28. "Decision," Director of the Office of the Party Secretariat to All of the Organizational Offices in the Country, May 14, 1985, 158-3-2: 537–538.

29. "Decision," Director of the Office of the Party Secretariat to the Honorable Comrade Deputy Secretary-General and the Honorable Comrade Member of the Regional Command, Jan. 19, 1984, 088-2-4: 7–8.

30. 027-5-2: 39; "A List of the Names of the Students Nominated for Acceptance into the Police Academy for the Session (52) of the Year 1998," 019-1-5: 147–245; Director of the Department of Military Sessions to the Honorable Comrade Struggler Member of the Regional Command of Iraq/the Supervisor over the Department of Military Sessions, Oct. 25, 1997, 014-5-4: 20.

31. See, e.g., Director of the Department of Military Sessions to the Honorable Comrade Member of the Regional Command of Iraq, the Supervisor over the Department of Military Sessions, Dec. 13, 1992, 066-4-1: 44–45.

32. "Acceptance of the Children of Members of the Revolutionary Command Council and the Members of the Regional Command," Head of the Presidential Diwan to the Ministry of Higher Education and Scientific Research/the Special Office, Oct. 23, 1984, 113-3-3: 10; Director of the Office of the Party Secretariat to the Honorable Comrade Members of the Regional Command, June 9, 1980, 003-1-1: 482; "Acceptance of the Sons of the Members of the Revolutionary Command Council and the Members of the Regional Command of Iraq," Director of the Office of the Party Secretariat to the Honorable Members of the Regional Command of Iraq, Sept. 22, 1997, 113-3-3: 1.

33. Taha Yasin Ramadan, the First Deputy to the Prime Minister to the Honorable Mr. President Leader, May 25, 1985, 087-1-1: 3–5.

34. In addition to the evidence from the BRCC, see Baran, 33.

35. This number comes from a memorandum by the Military Bureau, which reported that 173,823 people had been honored during the Iran–Iraq War. Among them, 2,675 were declared "Friends of the President"; 88,049 were promoted to a higher rank; 44,979 Badges of Honor were dispensed; 2,568 people received a car, money, watch, or other gifts; and 10,028 were given commendations (*kitāb shukr*). It is not clear if these numbers comprised just Baʿthists or not. 023-4-4: 265.

36. There are hundreds of petitions in the BRCC requesting missing benefits for one reason or another. See, e.g., the case of a man whose son was hurt as a result of an American bombing raid but claimed that his son did not receive any honors as the other injured children did. Citizen petition to Hussein, Aug. 9, 2001, 028-5-7: 204.

37. 026-2-7: 236. The quote relates specifically to the Revolution Medal, 238. The law does not explicitly say that the Saddam's *Qādisiyya* Medal and Badge of Honor could be taken away in these instances but that seems to be implied by the way the law is written.

38. "Sanctions," The Secretary of Mr. President of the Republic for Party Affairs to the Presidency of the Presidential Diwan, Nov. 20, 1984, 035-3-4: 1.

39. "Recalling Medals and Badges," Director of the Office of the Party Secretariat to the Presidential Diwan, Feb. 15, 1996, 113-4-5: 527.

40. In 1988, e.g., after the conclusion of the Iran–Iraq War, Hussein pardoned all military deserters and political criminals so long as they turned themselves in within one month for Iraqis inside the country and within three months for those outside of it. Every few years, Hussein proclaimed a similar amnesty if the sheer number of people who had committed crimes against the state reached large proportions, making it difficult to prosecute them and affecting the ability of the party and state to take in or retain new members and employees. 021-5-6: 46.

41. 025-1-7: 46; 003-1-1: 419–426. See chapter 1, n11, for a list of Hussein's amnesties.

42. Director of the Office of the Party Secretariat to the Main Commands in the Entire Country, Aug. 13, 1979, 003-1-1: 288–290.

43. 042-5-5: 206.

44. 042-5-5: 206.

45. Comrade [name withheld] to Mr. President of the Republic, the Comrade Leader Struggler Saddam Hussein, Aug. 24, 1979, 003-1-1: 295–299; Director of the Autonomous Administration to the Honorable Comrade Director of the Office of the Party Secretariat, Sept. 12, 1980, 003-1-1: 281.

46. "The Volunteering of a Fighter," Taha Yasin Ramadan, the General Leader of the Popular Army to the Regional Command—the Office of the Party Secretariat, Dec. 4, 1981, 034-2-1: 12.

47. "Report," the Fighter [name withheld] to the Comrade Leader of the Popular Army in the Area of Salah al-Din by Way of the Comrade Commander of the Area in the Possession of the Popular Army, Nov. 28, 1981, 034-2-1: 13.

48. "Information," Assistant Director of the Office of the Party Secretariat to the Intelligence Apparatus (*jihāz al-mukhābarāt*), Sept. 30, 1989, 001-5-4: 366–367.

CONCLUSION

1. Christopher R. Browning, *Ordinary Men: Reserve Police Battalion 101 and the Final Solution in Poland* (New York: HarperCollins, 1998), 142.

2. Browning, 159–189.

3. Browning, 159.

4. Browning, 188.

5. As Richard Overy has written about totalitarianism in relation to the Nazi and Soviet parties, "'Totalitarian' does not mean that they were 'total' parties, either all-inclusive or wielding complete power; it means that they were parties concerned with the 'totality' of the societies in which they worked. In this narrower sense both movements did have totalitarian aspirations, and never were simply parliamentary parties. There were few areas of public life that did not come under party review, or had to be co-ordinated with the party, or eliminated. The pub-

lic was subjected, willingly and unwillingly, to permanent party surveillance." Overy, 173.

6. As Gaetano Mosca wrote: "When there is a more or less masked antagonism between a doctrine, or a creed, that aspires to universality, and the sentiments and traditions that support the particularism of a state, what is really essential is that those sentiments and traditions should be really vigorous, that they should also be bound up with many material interests and that a considerable portion of the ruling class should be strongly imbued with them and should propagate and keep them alive in the masses. If, in addition, this element in the ruling class is soundly organized, it can resist all the religious or doctrinary currents that are exerting an influence in the society that it rules." Mosca, 80.

7. Browning, 85.

8. See the preface for the origins, general contents, and character of the Baʿthist documents on which this study is based.

9. Stanley Milgram, "The Dilemma of Obedience," *The Phi Delta Kappan* 55 (May 1974): 606.

10. 025-5-5: 489.

11. See Geertz, "Religion as a Cultural System" and "Ideology as a Cultural System."

12. Wardi, 54.

13. 021-2-3: 449–450.

14. 023-4-2: 103.

15. 104-3-1: 276–277.

16. 120-2-3: 321–323.

17. This can be seen in many party reports from the 1991 uprisings, including 024-5-2: 96.

18. Overy, 208.

19. Wedeen, 6.

20. Steavenson, 132.

21. Fitzpatrick, 162–163.

22. 029-2-3: 95.

POSTSCRIPT

1. Herman Lübbe, "The Historicity of Totalitarianism," in *Totalitarianism and Political Religions: Concepts for the Comparisons of Dictatorships*, Vol. 1, ed. Hans Maier, trans. Jodi Bruhn (London: Routledge, 1996), 237.

2. Kassof, 558–575; Havel, "Power of the Powerless," 42–95.

3. The pamphlet can be found in 151-2-4: 29–30. The September 2001 date may not be accurate. A document from August 1999 claimed that each ministry was to receive one computer hooked up to the World Wide Web, suggesting the Baʿthist State, at least, may have gained Internet access earlier. Director of the Office of the Party Secretariat to the Comrade Deputy Secretary-General of the Region of Iraq, June 8, 1999, 151-2-4: 69.

4. According to the Syrian Observatory for Human Rights. "*200,000 dead? Why Syria's rising death toll is so divisive*," http://syriahr.com/en/2015/01/200000-dead-why-syrias-rising-death-toll-is-so-divisive/ [accessed January 18, 2015].

5. For the decree see http://www.iraqcoalition.org/regulations/20030516_CPA ORD_1_De-Ba_athification_of_Iraqi_Society.pdf [accessed January 18, 2015].

6. Bashir, 276.

APPENDIX I

1. In their more ideological tracts, and in official titles, the Baʿth referred to the country of Iraq as the "Iraqi region," just as they called their highest authoritative body the "Regional Command," because the Baʿth believed that one day all of the Arab "regions" would coalesce into one unified nation.

2. The remainder of this paragraph contains too many illegible words to translate. The gist of the passage seems to be that the public has "total loyalty" for Hussein and exists in a state of "passion" and "love" for "the knight of the nation" (Hussein).

3. As opposed to the "organizational," "security," or "cultural" categories of party work. "Main" organizations in the document refer to regular Baʿth Party branches, sections, divisions, and cells. "Mass" organizations refer to the PMOs.

4. The word "elements" could refer to people, groups, or both depending on the context. It often carried a negative connotation.

5. "Professional offices" refers to those offices and unions among the PMOs that dealt with professional associations such as doctors or engineers as opposed to demographics such as women or students and youth.

6. The intent here was to provide the GFIW with basic necessities and sums of money for the federation to hand out to Iraqi women in order to attract the women to the federation and the party as part of their Baʿthification.

7. By "mass duties," the author of the work plan meant the responsibilities assigned to regular party members that they discharged while working with, or in, the PMOs.

8. None of the three forms referenced here, in c), or e), were found attached to the work plan.

9. To "frame" somebody meant to place him within the atmosphere of the Baʿth Party by including him in Baʿthist activities—to culturalize him without having him join the regular party apparatus.

GLOSSARY OF ARABIC TERMS

ʿadū An enemy
al-ʿadū al-fārisī al-ʿunṣurī The racist Persian enemy
ʾafwāj al-difāʿ al-waṭanī National Defense Regiments
ʿāʾila maʿarūfa A known family
ʾakram minna jamīʿan "Those who are nobler than us all" (a euphemism for Baʿthist martyrs)
al-ʾanāṣir al-ʿamīla "Agent elements"
ʾaṣdiqāʾ al-sayyid al-raʾīs al-qāʾid ṣaddām ḥusayn (ḥafẓuhu allāh) Friends of Mr. President Leader, Saddam Hussein (God keep him) (an honored status the Baʿth conferred on regime loyalists)
al-ʿashāʾiriyya Tribalism
ʾashbāl ṣaddām Saddam's Cubs (a youth group)
bidʿa fārsiyya "Persian heresy"
bināʾ Construction (in the ideological sense of reconstruction and revival)
dawlat al-ḥizb The Party State
al-dīn al-ʾislāmī al-ḥanīf "The True Islamic Religion" (the Baʿth's term for their version of Islam)
dīwān al-riʾāsa Office of the President
dumtum li-l-niḍāl "Keep struggling" (the closing salutation in Baʿthist correspondence)
faḥaṣ A survey
fakhdh, pl. ʾafkhādh A clan
falsafa ʿāma fi-l-ḥayāt "A general philosophy in life" (the purpose of Baʿthism according to party founder Michel Aflaq)
farʿ, pl. *furūʿ* A party branch
fāris al-ʾumma "The Knight of the Nation" (a moniker for Saddam Hussein)
fatwa, pl. *fatāwā* A religious decree
firqa, pl. *furuq* A party division
ghaslan li-l-ʿār "Washing the stain" (from one's reputation)
ghayr muʾaththir Uninfluential (in society and thus an unimportant person to the Baʿth)
ghayr multazim Uncommitted (to party work)

ghayr mushajjiʿa Unencouraging (information about a person under investigation)
ghayr muwālī Disloyal (an official classification for a person)
ḥafẓuhu allāh wa raʿāhu "God save him and keep him"
al-ḥamla al-ʾīmāniyya The Faith Campaign
ḥaml al-masʾūliyya "Taking responsibility" (a trait Hussein tried to imbue in the Baʿthist cadres)
al-hayʾa al-tadrīsiyya, or, *silk al-taʿlīm wa-l-tadrīs* The teaching corps
Ḥizb al-Baʿth al-ʿArabī al-ʾIshtirākī The Arab Baʿth Socialist Party
ḥizb al-daʿwa al-ʾislāmiyya The Islamic Daʿwa Party
al-ḥizb al-qāʾid "The leading party" (a Baʿth Party self-description)
al-ḥizb al-shuyūʿī al-ʿamīl "The Agent Communist Party" (the Baʿth's name for the Iraqi Communist Party)
al-hurūb wa-l-takhalluf Desertion and dodging military service
ḥusayniyya, pl. *ḥusayniyyāt* A Shiʿi religious center
ʿibdāʾ Creativity (a personal characteristic the Baʿth valued)
ʾiʿdādiyyat al-shurṭa Police Preparatory School
ʾidāmat al-ṣilla "Maintaining a connection" (to families or individuals the Baʿth wanted to recruit from or monitor)
ʾījābiyyāt Positives
ʾīmān Faith
ʾinḍibāṭ Discipline
al-ʾinsān al-jadīd "The new man"
ʾistīʿāb To absorb
ʾistiḍāfāt Receptions, to host other party organizations or delegations
ʾistiftāʾ Plebiscite
ʾistishhād The act of martyrdom
al-ʾittiḥād al-ʿām li-l-nisāʾ al-ʿirāq The General Federation of Iraqi Women
ʾittiḥād al-ṣaddāmiyīn The Union of Saddamists
al-ʾittiḥād al-waṭanī li-ṭalaba wa-shabāb al-ʿirāq The National Union of Students and Youth
ʾizālat al-duwar The demolition of houses
ʾizālat al-qurā The demolition of villages
al-jamāhīr The masses
al-jānib al-ʾamanī The security aspect (of party work)
al-jānib al-jamāhīrī The mass (public) aspect (of party work)
al-jānib al-tanẓīmī The organizational aspect (of party work)
al-jānib al-thaqāfī The cultural aspect (of party work)
jarāʾim mukhilla bi-l-sharf "Crimes that violate honor"
jaysh ʿaqāʾidī An ideological army
al-jaysh al-Shaʿbī The Popular Army
jihāz al-ʾamn al-khāṣṣ Special Security Organization
jihāz al-himāya al-khāṣa Special Protection Apparatus
al-jihāz al-ḥizbī The party apparatus
kādir Cadre

kalimat yawm al-khamīs The Thursday Word (a weekly speech given at Baʿthist schools about ideological topics)
al-kasb Recruitment
khāʾin Traitor
khaliya, pl. *khalāyā* A party cell
al-kharāʾiṭ al-maydāniyya Field maps (on which the Baʿth recorded information about the population)
khibra Experience
al-kulliyāt al-ʿaskariyya The Military Academies
lā yaṣluḥ "Unsuitable" (a negative notation the Baʿth placed in an individual's file)
al-lajna al-tanẓīmiyya Organization Committee
lajna thaqāfiyya Cultural Committee
lajnat al-jadāriyyāt Poster Committee
lajnat tabʿīth Baʿthification Committee
al-lijān al-ḥizbiyya Party committees
lijān al-tawʿiyya al-dīniyya Religious propaganda committees
madāris al-ʾiʿdād al-ḥizbī Party preparatory schools
mafraza, pl. *mafāriz* An armed party detachment
al-majlis al-waṭanī The National Assembly
al-munaẓẓamāt al-mihniyya wa-l-jamāhīriyya Professional and Mass Organizations
maḥkamat al-thawra Court of the Revolution
majālis al-shaʿb People's Councils
majlis al-ʾamn al-qawmī National Security Council
majlis qiyādat al-thawra Revolutionary Command Council
al-makātib al-ʾistishāriyya Advisory offices
al-maktab al-filāḥī al-markazī The Central Office of Peasants (a PMO)
maktab al-ʿalāqāt al-ʿāma Office of Public Relations
al-maktab al-ʿaskarī The Military Bureau
maktab ʾimānat sirr al-quṭr Office of the Party Secretariat
al-maktab al-markazī li-l-tanẓīm al-mihnī wa-l-shaʿbī The Central Office of the Professional and Popular Bureau (the office that oversaw all of the PMOs)
al-maktab al-mihnī al-markazī The Central Professional Office (a PMO)
maktab shuʾūn al-ʿashāʾir Office of Tribal Affairs
maktab al-ṭalaba wa-l-shabāb al-markazī The Central Office of Students and Youth (a PMO)
maktab al-thaqāfa wa-l-ʾiʿlām Office of Culture and Media
maktab al-ʿumāl al-markazī The Central Office of Workers (a PMO)
mantaqat al-ḥukm al-dhātī The Autonomous Region
marākiz ʾitiḥādiyya Union Centers
marḥala jadīda "A new stage"
marjaʿ al-taqlīd, pl. *marājiʿ* Source of Emulation (a leading Shiʿi cleric)
marsūm jumhūrī A Republican Decree

masīra March, journey (the Baʿth's march through history)
mas'ūl al-raqāba al-dākhiliyya Internal Control Official
mawāqif salbiyya "Negative stances" (a reference to current or past resistance to the Baʿth's policies)
muʿāyisha Cohabitation (acting as a political commissar)
mu'ayyid Supporter (the lowest level of party membership)
mudīr al-nāḥiya Municipal Director, Mayor
mudīriyyat al-ʾamn al-ʿāma General Security Directorate
mudīriyyat al-ʾistikhbārāt al-ʿaskariyya Directorate of Military Intelligence
mudīriyyat al-mukhābarāt al-ʿāma General Directorate of Intelligence
mudīriyyat al-tawjih al-siyāsī Directorate of Political Guidance
mughlaq li-ṣāliḥ al-ḥizb "Locked for the party" (state positions open only to Baʿth Party members)
muḥāfiẓ Governor
mujrim A criminal
mukharribīn Saboteurs
mukhtār, pl. *mukhtārīn* A local watchman
al-mujtamaʿ al-jadīd "The new society"
mumārasa Practice (the concept of putting Baʿthist ideology into practice)
al-munāḍil The struggler (one of Hussein's monikers)
al-munāsabāt al-waṭaniyya wa-l-qawmiyya National Occasions (Arab and Iraqi)
munaẓẓam Organized (into the party ranks)
munaẓẓama, pl. *munaẓẓamāt* A party organization (bureau, branch, section, division, or cell)
munaẓẓamat kibār al-sinn wa-l-marḍā The Organization of Senior Citizens and the Ill
munaẓẓamat al-munāḍilīn The Organization of the Strugglers
murāqib baladiyya A town watchman
murashshaḥ A "nominee" for full party membership
mustaqill Independent
al-mutasarribīn Those who shirk their party obligations
muwālī "Loyal" (an official notation included in a person's file)
nadwa Symposium (a Baʿth Party event)
nāḥiya, pl. *nawāḥī* Municipality
naql Transfer (of Baʿthist values to the masses, or from one post in the Baʿthist State to another)
naṣīr, pl. *ʾanṣār* Partisan (second lowest party membership level)
naṣīr mutaqadam Advanced Partisan (party level above partisan and below a "nominee" for full membership)
nawṭ al-shujāʿa Badge of Honor
qādisiyyat ṣaddām al-majīda Saddam's Glorious *Qādisiyya* (the Iran–Iraq War)
qaḍāʾ, pl. *ʾaqḍiyya* County
al-qāʾid "The leader" (Saddam Hussein)

al-qāʾid – al-ḍarūra "The Leader—The Necessity" (a moniker given to Hussein at the Baʿth's Ninth Regional Congress in 1982)
al-qāʾid al-muʾassis "The Founding Leader" (Michel Aflaq)
qāʾimmaqām The chief officer of a county
qānūn al-ʾawsima wa-l-ʿanwāṭ The Medal and Badge Law
qawmiyya Nationalism
qiyāda Command (the leadership of a party organization)
al-qiyāda al-jamāʿiyya Collective leadership
al-qiyāda al-qawmiyya The National Command
qiyādat furʿ al-ʾamn al-qawmī National Security Branch Command
al-quwwa al-qutāliyya "Fighting force" (the number of fighters present in a tribe)
riʾāsat al-jumhūriyya The Presidency of the Republic
ṣafḥat al-khiyāna wa-l-ghadr The Page of Treason and Treachery (the 1991 uprisings)
al-salāma al-fikriyya wa-l-ʾamaniyya "Intellectual and security-related integrity" (a criterion for acceptance into Baʿthist academies and for appointment to sensitive state positions)
salbiyyāt Negatives
sāqiṭa khalqiyan Morally disreputable
al-shaʿb The people
shahīd Martyr
shārat al-ḥizb The Order of the Party
shārat al-qiyāda The Order of the Leadership
shārat ʾumm al-maʿārik The Order of the Mother of All Battles
al-shaṭr wa-l-ʾistiḥdāth Fusing and splitting up party organizations
shiʿārāt muʿādiyya Opposition slogans
shuʿba, pl. *shuʿab* A party section
shukr wa taqdīr A commendation
al-ṣihyūniyya al-ʿālamiyya Worldwide Zionism
al-taʾammur To conspire
taʿayīn To appoint
tabaʿiyya ʾīrāniyya Of Iranian origin
taʿbiʾa To mobilize
al-taʿbiʾa al-jamāhīriyya Mass mobilization
tabʿīth Baʿthification
tabʿīth al-taʿlīm The Baʿthification of education
al-taghalghul Infiltration
taḥiyya rifāqiyya "Comradely greetings" (a salutation included at the start of most Baʿth Party correspondence)
al-ṭāʾifiyya Sectarianism
tajriba Experience
al-takhādhul Evincing weakness or cowardice in one's party obligations
al-ṭalaba wa-l-shabāb Students and Youth

ṭalīʿa Vanguard
al-Taʾmīm What the Baʿth called Kirkuk
tanfīdh The concept of "executing" or "carrying out" Baʿthist principles
tanẓīf To cleanse (an area of opposition)
tanẓīm, pl. *tanẓīmāt* A party bureau
al-tarhīb wa-l-targhīb Terror and enticement
tarḥīl To expel
taʿrīb Arabization
tasfīr To deport
al-taṭarruf al-dīnī Religious extremism
taṭbīq To apply (Baʿthist principles in practice)
taṭhīr To purify (a place of opposition)
taʾthīr Influence or effect (a metric the Baʿth used to assess the suitability of family members of political criminals to gauge whether or not they could remain in sensitive posts)
tathqīf To culturalize
al-tathqīf al-dhātī Self-culturalization
taʾṭīr To frame (to Baʿthize somebody without actually including them in the party; to place somebody within the "atmosphere" of the party)
tawḍīḥ To explain
tawʿiyya To indoctrinate
thaqāfa Culture
thawrat 17–30 tamūz July 17–30 revolution
ʿuḍū mutadarrab A member in training
al-ʿudwān al-ʿaskarī al-thalāthīnī The Thirtieth Military Aggression (The Persian Gulf War)
ʾumma Nation (Arab or Iraqi), the Muslim community
ʾumma ʿarabiyya wāḥida dhāt risāla khālida "One Arab nation with an eternal message" (an original Baʿth Party slogan)
ʾumm al-maʿārik al-khālida The Eternal Mother of All Battles (The Persian Gulf War)
ʿunṣūr jayyid "A good element," somebody who is loyal to Hussein and the Baʿth
waḥda, ḥurriyya, wa-l-ʾishtirākiyya "Unity, freedom, and socialism" (an original Baʿth Party slogan)
wathīqat ʿahd bi-l-damm An oath of loyalty written in blood
wilāyat al-faqih The rule of the jurist (the ideological foundation of the political system of the Islamic Republic of Iran)
wisām qādisiyyat ṣaddām The Saddam's *Qādisiyya* Medal
wisām al-rāfidayn The *Rāfidayn* (Tigris and Euphrates) Medal
wisām al-thawra The Revolution Medal
wizārat al-thaqāfa wa-l-ʾiʿlām Ministry of Culture and Media
li-yanālū jazāʾihim al-ʿādil "To receive their just punishment" (the Baʿth's phrase to refer to the punishments or sentences they meted out)
yawm al-fatḥ al-mubīn The Day of the Glorious Victory

yawm al-ṭifl al-ʿirāqī The Day of the Iraqi Child
yawm al-zaḥf al-kabīr The Day of the Big March
ẓāhira Phenomenon
ẓāhirat ʾiṭlāq al-ʿiyārāt al-nāriyya The practice of shooting off guns at celebratory occasions
ziyārāt Visits (to families, other party organizations, etc.)
zumrat salīlī al-khiyāna The Band of the Offspring of Treachery (the Baʿth's euphemism for the KDP)
zumrat ʿumalāʾ ʾīrān The Band of Iranian Agents (the Baʿth's euphemism for the PUK)

BIBLIOGRAPHY

ARCHIVE

The main documentary collection used for this study is *Hizb al-Baʿth al-ʿArabi al-ʾIshtiraki [in Iraq] Records, 1968–2003*. Baʿth Arab Socialist Party Regional Command Collection (BRCC). Boxfiles Dataset. Hoover Institution Archives. All documents are cited individually in the endnotes with as much of the following information as possible: "Title of document," sender to (*ʾilā*) recipient, date, boxfile number: document pages.

SOURCES

Abd Allah, Abu Islam Ahmad. *Saddam Husayn: al-Nashaʾa..al-Tarikh..al-Jarima.* Cairo: Bayt al-Hikma, 1990.

Abd al-Qahhar, Khalida. *Sikritirat Saddam Tatakallam.* Cairo: al-Zahraʾ li-l-ʾIʿlam al-ʿArabi, 1990.

Abu Jaber, Kamel. *The Arab Baʿth Socialist Party: History, Ideology, and Organization.* Syracuse: Syracuse University Press, 1966.

Aburish, Said K. *Saddam Hussein: The Politics of Revenge.* New York: Bloomsbury, 2000.

Aflaq, Michel. "*al-Haraka al-Fikriyya al-Shamila*," *fi Sabil al-Baʿth – al-Juzʾ al-ʾAwwal*, http://albaath.online.fr/Volume%20I-Chapters/Fi%20Sabil%20al%20Baal-Vol%201-Ch11.htm [accessed Feb. 2, 2012].

———. "Nationalism and Revolution," in *Arab Nationalism: An Anthology*, ed. Sylvia Haim, 242–246. Berkeley: University of California Press, 1962.

———. "*Nazaratna ʾila al-din*," *fi Sabil al-Baʿth – al-Juzʾ al-ʾAwwal*, http://albaath.online.fr/Volume%20I-Chapters/Fi%20Sabil%20al%20Baal-Vol%201-Ch28.htm [accessed Aug. 2, 2011].

Ajami, Fouad. *The Dream Palace of the Arabs: A Generation's Odyssey.* New York: Vintage Books, 1998.

Alani, Mustafa. "Saddam's Support Structure." In *Gulf Security: Opportunities and Challenges for the New Generation*, edited by Patrick and Toase McKnight, 42–46. London: Royal United Services Institute, 2001.

Alawi, Hasan. *Dawlat al-ʾIstiʿara al-Qawmiyya: min Faysal al-ʾAwwal ʾila Saddam Husayn*. London: Dar al-Zura, 1993.

———. *al-Shiʿa wa-l-Dawla al-Qawmiyya fi al-ʿIraq, 1914–1990*. London: Dar al-Zura, 1990.

Alnasrawi, Abbas. "Iraq: Economic Sanctions and Consequences, 1990–2000." *Third World Quarterly* 22 (April 2001): 205–218.

An Iraqi Mother and Suʿad Khairi. "Baʿth Terror—Two Personal Accounts." In *Saddam's Iraq: Revolution or Reaction*, edited by Committee against Repression and for Democratic Rights in Iraq (CARDRI), 108–119. London: Zed Books, 1986.

Arendt, Hannah. *The Origins of Totalitarianism*. New York: Harcourt, Brace, Jovanovich, 1973.

Armstrong, Hamilton Fish. "Hitler's Reich: The First Phase." *Foreign Affairs* (July 1933): 589–608.

Al-Azami, Basim. "The Muslim Brotherhood: Genesis and Development." In *Ayatollahs, Sufis and Ideologues: State, Religion and Social Movements in Iraq*, edited by Faleh Abdul-Jabar, 162–176. London: Saqi Books, 2002.

Aziz, T. M. "The Role of Muhammad Baqr al-Sadr in Shii Political Activism in Iraq." *International Journal of Middle East Studies* 25 (May 1993): 207–222.

Azzawi, Fadil Abbas. *al-Buniyya al-Tanzimiyya li-l-Hizb al-Baʿth al-ʾArabi al-ʾIshtiraki*. Baghdad: Dar al-Shuun al-Thaqafiya al-ʿAmma Wizarat al-Thaqafah wa-l-Iʿlam, al-Dar al-Wataniyya li-l-Tawziʿ wa-l-Iʿlan, 1986.

Babakhan, Ali. "The Deportation of Shiʿis during the Iran–Iraq War: Causes and Consequences." In *Ayatollahs, Sufis and Ideologues: State, Religion and Social Movements in Iraq*, edited by Faleh Abdul-Jabar, 183–210. London: Saqi, 2002.

Baer, Gabriel. *Population and Society in the Arab East*, translated by Hanna Szoke. New York: Frederick A. Praeger, 1964.

Baram, Amatzia. *Building toward Crisis: Saddam Husayn's Strategy for Survival*. Policy Paper No. 47. Washington, DC: Washington Institute for Near East Policy, 1998.

———. *Culture, History, and Ideology in the Formation of Baʿthist Iraq, 1968-89*. New York: St. Martin's Press, 1991.

———. *From Militant Secularism to Islamism: The Iraqi Baʾth Regime 1968–2003*. History and Public Policy Program Occasional Paper. Washington, DC: Woodrow Wilson International Center for Scholars, October 2011.

———. "The Future of Baʿthist Iraq: Power Structure, Challenges, and Prospects." In *The Politics of Change in the Middle East*, edited by R. B. Satloff. Boulder: Westview in cooperation with the Washington Institute for Near East Policy, 1993.

———. "The Impact of Khomeini's Revolution on the Radical Shiʿi Movement of Iraq." In *The Iranian Revolution and the Muslim World*, edited by David Menashri, 131–151. Boulder: Westview, 1990.

———."The Missing Link: 'Badu' and 'Tribal' Honor as Components in the Iraqi Decision to Invade Kuwait." In *Changing Nomads in a Changing World*, edited by Joseph Ginat and Anatoly M. Khazanov, 155–170. Brighton: Sussex Academic Press, 1998.

———. "Neo-Tribalism in Iraq: Saddam Hussein's Tribal Policies 1991–1996." *International Journal of Middle East Studies* 29 (Feb. 1997): 1–31.

———. "The Radical Shiʿite Opposition Movements in Iraq." In *Religious Radicalism and Politics in the Middle East*, edited by Emmanuel Sivan and Menachem Friedman, 95–125, notes 210–219. Albany: State University of New York Press, 1990.

———. "Re-Inventing Nationalism in Ba'thi Iraq 1968–1994: Supra-Territorial and Territorial Identities and What Lies Below." *Princeton Papers: Interdisciplinary Journal of Middle Eastern Studies* 5 (Fall 1996): 29–56.

———. "The Ruling Political Elite in Bathi Iraq, 1968–1986: The Changing Features of a Collective Profile." *International Journal of Middle East Studies* 21 (Nov. 1989): 447–493.

———. "Saddam Husayn, the Baʿth Regime and the Iraqi Officer Corps." In *Armed Forces in the Middle East: Politics and Strategy*, edited by Barry Rubin and Thomas A. Keaney, 206–230. London: Cass, 2002.

———. "Saddam Hussein: A Political Profile." *Jerusalem Quarterly* 17 (Autumn 1980): 115–144.

———. "Saddam's Power Structure: The Tikritis before, during and after the War." *The Adelphi Papers* 354 (Jan. 1997): 93–114.

———. "Two Roads to Revolutionary Shiʿite Fundamentalism in Iraq." In *Accounting for Fundamentalisms: The Dynamic Character of Movements*, edited by Martin E. Marty and R. Scott Appleby, 531–588. Chicago: University of Chicago Press, 1994.

Baran, David. *Vivre la tyrannie et lui survivre: L'Irak en transition*. Paris: Mille et Une Nuits, 2004.

Bashir, Ala. *The Insider: Trapped in Saddam's Brutal Regime*. London: Abacus, 2005.

Batatu, Hannah. *The Old Social Classes and the Revolutionary Movements of Iraq: A Study of Iraq's Old Landed and Commercial Classes and of its Communists, Baʿthists, and Free Officers*. Princeton: Princeton University Press, 1978.

———. "Shiʿi Organizations in Iraq: Al-Daʿwah al-Islamiyah, and al-Mujahidin." In *Shiʿism and Social Protest*, edited by Juan R. I. Cole and Nikki R. Keddie, 179–200. New Haven: Yale University Press, 1986.

Bengio, Ofra. "How Does Saddam Hold On?" *Foreign Affairs* 79, (July–Aug. 2000): 90–103.

———. "Iraq." In *Middle East Contemporary Survey, Vol. 4, 1979-80*, edited by Haim Shaked, Colin Legum, and Daniel Dishon, 501–536. New York: Holmes & Meier, 1981.

———. "Iraq." In *Middle East Contemporary Survey, Vol. 5 1980–1981*, edited by Haim Shaked, Colin Legum, and Daniel Dishon, 578–604. New York: Holmes & Meier, 1982.

———. "Iraq." In *Middle East Contemporary Survey, Vol. 6, 1981–1982*, edited by

Haim Shaked, Colin Legum, and Daniel Dishon, 582–630. New York: Holmes & Meier, 1984.

———. "Iraq." In *Middle East Contemporary Survey. Vol. 7, 1982–1983*, edited by Haim Shaked, Colin Legum, and Daniel Dishon, 560–594. New York: Holmes & Meier, 1985.

———. "Iraq." In *Middle East Contemporary Survey, Vol. 8, 1983–1984*, edited by Haim Shaked and Daniel Dishon, 465–496. Boulder: Westview, 1986.

———. "Iraq." In *Middle East Contemporary Survey, Vol. 9, 1984–1985*, edited by Itamar Rabinovich and Haim Shaked, 460–486. Boulder: Westview, 1987.

———. "Iraq." In *Middle East Contemporary Survey, Vol. 10, 1986*, edited by Itamar Rabinovich and Haim Shaked, 361–396. Boulder: Westview, 1988.

———. "Iraq." In *Middle East Contemporary Survey, Vol. 11, 1987*, edited by Itamar Rabinovich and Haim Shaked, 423–459. Boulder: Westview, 1989.

———. "Iraq." In *Middle East Contemporary Survey, Vol. 12, 1988*, edited by Ami Ayalon and Haim Shaked, 500–542. Boulder: Westview, 1990.

———. "Iraq." In *Middle East Contemporary Survey, Vol. 13, 1989*, edited by Ami Ayalon, 372–418. Boulder: Westview, 1991.

———. "Iraq." In *Middle East Contemporary Survey, Vol. 14, 1990*, edited by Ami Ayalon, 379–423. Boulder: Westview, 1992.

———. "Iraq." In *Middle East Contemporary Survey, Vol. 16, 1992*, edited by Ami Ayalon, 447–498. Boulder: Westview, 1995.

———. "Iraq." In *Middle East Contemporary Survey, Vol. 17, 1993*, edited by Ami Ayalon, 364–414. Boulder: Westview, 1995.

———. "Iraq." In *Middle East Contemporary Survey, Vol. 18, 1994*, edited by Ami Ayalon and Bruce Maddy-Weitzman, 320–368. Boulder: Westview, 1996.

———. "Iraq." In *Middle East Contemporary Survey, Vol. 19, 1995*, edited by Bruce Maddy-Weizman, 310–349. Boulder: Westview, 1997.

———. "Iraq." In *Middle East Contemporary Survey, Vol. 20, 1996*, edited by Bruce Maddy-Weitzman, 323–359. Boulder: Westview, 1998.

———. "Iraq." In *Middle East Contemporary Survey, Vol. 21, 1997*, edited by Bruce Maddy-Weitzman, 372–409. Boulder: Westview, 2000.

———. "Iraq." In *Middle East Contemporary Survey, Vol. 22, 1998*, edited by Bruce Maddy-Weitzman, 286–320. Boulder: Westview, 2001.

———. "A Republican Turning Royalist? Saddam Husayn and the Dilemmas of Succession." *Journal of Contemporary History* 35 (Oct. 2000): 641–653.

———. *Saddam's Word: Political Discourse in Iraq*. New York: Oxford University Press, 1998.

Berlin, Isaiah. "Political Ideas in the Twentieth Century." *Foreign Affairs* 28 (April 1950): 351–385.

Bracher, Karl Dietrich. "Stages of Totalitarian 'Integration' (*Gleichschaltung*): The Consolidation of National Socialist Rule in 1933 and 1944." In *Republic to Reich: The Making of the Nazi Revolution*, edited by Hajo Holborn, translated by Ralph Manheim, 109–128. New York: Pantheon, 1972.

Brown, Timothy S. *Weimar Radicals: Nazis and Communists between Authenticity and Performance*. New York: Berghahn, 2009.

Browning, Christopher R. *Ordinary Men: Reserve Police Battalion 101 and the Final Solution in Poland.* New York: HarperCollins, 1998.

al-Buraysim, Qasim. *al-Sharara wa-l-Ramad: Shahada Hayya ʿan ʾIntifadat al-Shaʿb al-ʿIraqi wa-ʿAdhab al-Muntafidin fi Sujun al-Ridwaniyya.* Beirut: Dar al-Kunuz al-ʾAdabiyya, 2004.

Burrin, Philippe. "Political Religion: The Relevance of a Concept." *History and Memory* 9 (Fall 1997): 321–349.

Chamberlin, William Henry. "Making the Collective Man in Soviet Russia." *Foreign Affairs* (Jan. 1932): 280–292.

Chaudhry, Kiren Aziz. "Economic Liberalization and the Lineages of the Rentier State." *Comparative Politics* (Oct. 1994): 1–25.

———. "On the Way to Market: Economic Liberalization and Iraq's Invasion of Kuwait," *Middle East Report* no. 170, Power, Poverty and Petrodollars (May–June 1991): 14–23.

Coughlin, Con. *Saddam: His Rise and Fall.* New York: Harper Perennial, 2004.

Davis, Eric. *Memories of State: Politics, History, and Collective Identity in Modern Iraq.* Berkeley: University of California Press, 2005.

Dawisha, Adeed. "The Assembled State: Communal Conflicts and Governmental Control in Iraq." In *Ethnic Conflict and International Politics in the Middle East,* edited by Leonard Binder, 61–76. Gainesville: University Press of Florida, 1999.

———. "'Identity' and Political Survival in Saddam's Iraq." *Middle East Journal* 53 (Autumn 1999): 553–567.

Dawood, N. J., trans. *The Koran.* London: Penguin, 2003.

Dodge, Toby. "Cake Walk, Coup, or Urban Warfare: The Battle for Iraq." *The Adelphi Papers* 354 (Jan. 2003): 59–76.

———. *Inventing Iraq: The Failure of Nation-Building and a History Denied.* New York: Columbia University Press, 2003.

Dunham, Vera. *In Stalin's Time: Middleclass Values in Soviet Fiction.* Durham: Duke University Press, 1990.

Eley, Geoff. "History with the Politics Left out Again?" *Russian Review* 45 (Oct. 1986): 385–394.

Evans, Richard J. *The Coming of the Third Reich.* New York: Penguin, 2003.

"Exclusive Interview: Muhammad Baqir al-Hakim: Head of the Supreme Islamic Revolutionary Council of Iraq," *Middle East Insight* 5 (1987): 18–24.

Fainsod, Merle. *Smolensk under Soviet Rule.* Cambridge, MA: Harvard University Press, 1958.

Farouk-Sluglett, Marion. "Liberation or Repression? Pan-Arab Nationalism and the Women's Movement in Iraq." In *Iraq: Power and Society,* edited by Derek Hopwood, Habib Ishow, and Thomas Koszinowski, 51–73. Reading: Ithaca Press, 1993.

Farouk-Sluglett, Marion, and Peter Sluglett. "The Historiography of Modern Iraq." *The American Historical Review* 96 (Dec. 1991): 1408–1421.

———. *Iraq since 1958: From Revolution to Dictatorship,* Rev. ed. London: IB Tauris, 2001.

———. "Iraqi Baʿthism: Nationalism, Socialism and National Socialism." In *Sad-*

dam's Iraq, Revolution or Reaction, edited by Committee against Repression and for Democratic Rights in Iraq (CARDRI), 89–107. London: Zed Books, 1986.

Faust, Aaron. "The Evolution of Islam's Role under the Socialist Arab Baʿth Party in Iraq." MA Thesis, Tel Aviv University, 2006.

Fitzpatrick, Sheila. "New Perspectives on Stalinism." *Russian Review* 45 (Oct. 1986): 357–373.

Fraenkel, Ernst. *The Dual State: A Contribution on the Theory of Dictatorship*, translated by E. A. Shils. New York: Oxford University Press, 1941.

Friedrich, Carl J., and Zbigniew K. Brzezinski. *Totalitarian Dictatorship and Autocracy*. New York: Frederick A. Praeger, 1956.

Gadshiiev, Kamaludin. "Reflections on Russian Totalitarianism." In *Totalitarianism and Political Religions: Concepts for the Comparisons of Dictatorships, Vol. 1*, edited by Hans Maier, translated by Jodi Bruhn, 53–57. London: Routledge, 1996.

Geertz, Clifford. "Ideology as a Cultural System." In *The Interpretation of Cultures: Selected Essays by Clifford Geertz*, 193–223. New York: Basic Books, 1973.

———. "Religion as a Cultural System." In *Anthropological Approaches to the Study of Religion*, edited by Michael Banton, 1–46. New York: Frederick A. Praeger, 1966.

———. "Thick Description: Toward an Interpretive Theory of Culture." In *The Interpretation of Cultures: Selected Essays by Clifford Geertz*, 3–30. New York: Basic Books, 1973.

Gelvin, James L. *Divided Loyalties: Nationalism and Mass Politics in Syria at the Close of Empire*. Berkeley: University of California Press, 1998.

Gentile, Emilio. "Fascism, Totalitarianism and Political Religion: Definitions and Critical Reflections on Criticism of an Interpretation." *Totalitarian Movements and Political Religions* 5 (Winter 2004): 326–375.

———. "The Sacralisation of Politics: Definitions, Interpretations and Reflections on the Question of Secular Religion and Totalitarianism." *Totalitarian Movements and Political Religions* 1 (Summer 2000): 18–55.

Gentile, Giovanni. "The Philosophic Basis of Fascism." *Foreign Affairs* 6 (Jan. 1928): 290–304.

Giddens, Anthony. *The Nation-State and Violence: Vol. 2 of a Contemporary Critique of Historical Materialism*. Berkeley: University of California Press, 1985.

Gramsci, Antonio. *Selections from the Prison Notebooks of Antonio Gramsci*. New York: International, 1973.

Grieder, Peter. "In Defence of Totalitarianism Theory as a Tool of Historical Scholarship." *Totalitarian Movements and Political Religions* 8 (Sept.–Dec. 2007): 563–589.

Haddad, Fanar. *Sectarianism in Iraq: Antagonistic Visions of Unity*. New York: Columbia University Press, 2011.

Haim, Sylvia. *Arab Nationalism: An Anthology*. Berkeley: University of California Press, 1962.

Halliday, Denis J. "The Impact of UN Sanctions on the People of Iraq." *Journal of Palestine Studies* 28 (Winter 1999): 29–37.

Hashim, Ahmed S. "Military Power and State Formation in Modern Iraq." *Middle East Policy* 10 (Dec. 2003): 29–47.

———. "Saddam Husayn and Civil-Military Relations in Iraq: The Quest for Legitimacy and Power." *Middle East Journal* 57 (Winter 2003): 9–41.

Hashim, Jawad. *Mudhakkarat Wazir ʿIraqi maʿa al-Bakr wa-Saddam*. Beirut: Dar al-Saqi, 2003.

al-Hassan, Talib. *Hukumat al-Quriyya: Fusul min Sulta Nazihin min Rif Tikrit*. Beirut: UR Press, 2004.

Havel, Vaclav. "Letter to Dr. Gustav Husak." In *Vaclav Havel: Living in Truth*, edited by Jan Vladislav, 3–35. London: Faber and Faber, 1990.

———. "The Power of the Powerless." In *Vaclav Havel: Living in Truth*, edited by Jan Vladislav, 36–122. London: Faber and Faber, 1990.

Hayder, Amir. "A Personal Testimony." In *The Iraqi Marshlands: A Human and Environmental Study*, edited by Emma Nicholson and Peter Clark, 307–313. London: Politico's, 2002.

Helfont, Samuel. "The Baʿthist Regime's Instrumentalization of Religion in Foreign Affairs." *Middle East Journal* 68 (Summer 2014): 352–366.

Helms, Christine Moss. *Iraq: Eastern Flank of the Arab World*. Washington, DC: The Brookings Institution, 1984.

Hilli, Walid. *al-ʿIraq: al-Waqiʿ wa-ʾAfaq al-Mustaqbal*. Beirut: Dar al-Furat, 1992.

Hiltermann, J. R. *Bureaucracy of Repression: The Iraqi Government in Its Own Words*. New York: Human Rights Watch, 1994.

Hinnebusch, Raymond A. *Authoritarian Power and State Formation in Baʿthist Syria: Army, Party, and Peasant*. Boulder: Westview, 1990.

Hitler, Adolf. *Mein Kampf*, translated by Ralph Manheim. Boston: Houghton Mifflin, 1943.

Hizb al-Baʿth al-ʿArabi al-ʾIshtiraki. *Revolutionary Iraq, 1968–1973: The Political Report Adopted by the Eighth Regional Congress of the Arab Baʿth Socialist Party—Iraq, January, 1974*. Baghdad: The Arab Baʿth Socialist Party, Jan. 1974.

———. *al-Taqrir al-Markazi li-l-Muʾtamar al-Qutri al-Tasiʿ*. Baghdad: Dar al-Hurriya li-l-Tabaʿa, 1983.

Hoffman, David L. "Introduction: Interpretations of Stalinism." In *Stalinism*, edited by David L. Hoffman, 1–7. Cornwall: Blackwell, 2003.

Holquist, Peter. "State Violence as Technique: The Logic of Violence in Soviet Totalitarianism." In *Stalinism*, edited by David L. Hoffman, 133–156. Cornwall: Blackwell, 2003.

Hughes, R. Gerald. "Of Revelatory Histories and Hatchet Jobs: Propaganda and Method in Intelligence History." *Intelligence and National Security* 23 (Dec. 2008): 842–877.

Humadi, Zuhair. "Civil Society under the Baʿth in Iraq." In *Toward Civil Society in the Middle East? A Primer*, edited by J. Schwedler, 50–52. Boulder: Rienner, 1995.

Hussein, Saddam. *On History, Heritage and Religion*, translated by Naji al-Hadithi. Baghdad: Translation & Foreign Languages Publishing House, 1981.

———. *The Revolution and Woman in Iraq*, edited by Naji al-Hadithi, translated by Khalid Kishtainy. Baghdad: Translation & Foreign Language Publishing House, 1981.

Iskandar, Amir. *Saddam Husayn Munadilan wa-Mufakkiran wa-Insanan*. Casablanca: Tansift, 2000.

"The Islamic Party and the Political Future of Iraq: An Interview with Dr. Osama Takriti." *Middle East Affairs Journal* 3 (Winter/Spring 1997): 159.

Jabar, Faleh A. "Clerics, Tribes, Ideologues and Urban Dwellers in the South of Iraq: The Potential for Rebellion." *The Adelphi Papers* 354 (Jan. 2003): 161–178.

———. *al-Dawla, al-Mujtamaʿ al-Madani wa-l-Tahawwul al-Dimuqrati fi al-ʿIraq*. Cairo: Ibn Khaldun Center, 1995.

———. "The Iraqi Army and Anti-Army: Some Reflections on the Role of the Military," *The Adelphi Papers* 354 (Jan. 2003): 115–130.

———. "Shaykhs and Ideologues: Detribalization and Retribalization in Iraq, 1968–1998," *Middle East Report* 215 (Summer 2000): 28–48.

———. "Sheikhs and Ideologues: Deconstruction and Reconstruction of Tribes under Patrimonial Totalitarianism in Iraq, 1968–1998." In *Tribes and Power: Nationalism and Ethnicity in the Middle East,* edited by Faleh Abdul-Jabar and Hosham Dawood, 69–109. London: Saqi, 2003.

———. *The Shiʿite Movement in Iraq*. London: Saqi, 2003.

Al-Jumhuriyya al-ʿIraqiyya, Wizarat al-ʾIʿlam. In *al-Dustur al-Muʾaqqat wa-Taʿadilatuhu*. 2nd ed. Baghdad: Dar al-Huriyya li-l-Tabaʿa, 1976.

Kandel, I. L. "Education in Nazi Germany." *Annals of the American Academy of Political and Social Science* (Nov. 1935): 153–163.

Karsh, Efraim, and Inari Rautsi. *Saddam Hussein: A Political Biography*. New York: Grove, 2002.

Kassof, Allen. "The Administered Society: Totalitarianism without Terror." *World Politics* 16 (July 1964): 558–575.

Kautsky, John H. *Political Change in Underdeveloped Countries*. New York: John Wiley, 1962.

Kedourie, Elie. "The Kingdom of Iraq: A Retrospect." In *The Chatham House Version and Other Middle Eastern Studies*, 236–282. Chicago: Ivan R. Dee, 2004.

Kehat. D. "Iraq." In *Middle East Record,* Vol. 5, edited by Daniel Dishon, 701–740. Jerusalem: Israel Universities Press, 1977.

Khadduri, Majid. *Socialist Iraq: A Study in Iraqi Politics since 1968*. Washington, DC: The Middle East Institute, 1978.

Al-Khafaji, Isam. "A Few Days After: State and Society in a Post-Saddam Iraq." *The Adelphi Papers* 354 (Jan. 2003): 77–92

———. "Not Quite an Arab Prussia: Revisiting Some Myths on Iraqi Exceptionalism." In *Iraq: The Human Cost of History*, edited by Tareq Y. Ismael and William W. Haddad, 213–257. London: Pluto, 2004.

———. "The Parasitic Base of the Baʿthist Regime." In *Saddam's Iraq: Revolution or Reaction*, edited by Committee against Repression and for Democratic Rights in Iraq (CARDRI), 73–88. London: Zed Books, 1986.

———. "State Terror and the Degradation of Politics in Iraq." *Middle East Report* No. 176, Iraq in the Aftermath (May–June 1992): 15–21.

al-Khayyat, Sana. *Honour and Shame: Women in Modern Iraq*. London: Saqi, 1990.

Khlevnyuk, Oleg. "The Objectives of the Great Terror, 1937–1938." In *Stalinism*, edited by David L. Hoffman, 87–104. Cornwall: Blackwell, 2003.

Khoury, Dina Rizk. *Iraq in Wartime: Soldiering, Martyrdom, and Remembrance*. Cambridge: Cambridge University Press, 2013.

Kluckhohn, Clyde. *Mirror for Man: The Relation of Anthropology to Modern Life*. Tucson: University of Arizona Press, 1985.

Kolakowski, Leszek. "Hope and Hopelessness." *Survey* 17 (Summer 1971): 37–52.

Kubba, Juman. *The First Evidence: A Memoir of Life in Iraq under Saddam Hussein*. Jefferson, NC: McFarland, 2003.

Kurzman, Charles. *The Unthinkable Revolution in Iran*. Cambridge, MA: Harvard University Press, 2004.

Kvastad, Nils B. "Semantics in the Methodology of the History of Ideas." *Journal of the History of Ideas* 38 (Jan.–Mar. 1977): 157–174.

Lambton, A. K. S. "A Reconsideration of the Position of the Marja ʾal-Taqlid and the Religious Institution." *Studia Islamica* 20 (1964): 115–135.

Lane, Christel. *The Rites of Rulers: Ritual in Industrial Society—the Soviet Case*. Cambridge: Cambridge University Press, 1981.

Linz, Juan. "Fascism and Non-Democratic Regimes." In *Totalitarianism and Political Religions: Concepts for the Comparisons of Dictatorships; Theory and History of Interpretation*, Vol. 3, edited by Hans Maier, translated by Jodi Bruhn, 225–291. London: Routledge, 1996.

———. *Totalitarian and Authoritarian Regimes*. Boulder: Lynne Rienner, 2000.

Litvak, Meir. "Iraq." In *Middle East Contemporary Survey, Vol. 15, 1991*, edited by Ami Ayalon, 416–448. Boulder, San Francisco, and Oxford: Westview, 1993.

Lübbe, Herman. "The Historicity of Totalitarianism." In *Totalitarianism and Political Religions: Concepts for the Comparisons of Dictatorships*, Vol. 1, edited by Hans Maier, translated by Jodi Bruhn, 235–259. London: Routledge, 1996.

Luizard, Pierre-Jean. "The Nature of the Confrontation between the State and *Marjaʿism*: Grand Ayatollah Muhsin al-Hakim and the Baʿth." In *Ayatollahs, Sufis and Ideologues: State, Religion and Social Movements in Iraq*, edited by Faleh Abdul-Jabar, 90–100. London: Saqi, 2002.

Luks, Leonid. "Concluding Discussion." In *Totalitarianism and Political Religions: Concepts for the Comparison of Dictatorships*, Vol. 2, edited by Hans Maier and Michael Schäfer, translated by Jodi Bruhn, 187. London: Routledge, 1997.

Maier, Hans. "Political Religion: A Concept and Its Limitations." *Totalitarian Movements and Political Religions* 8 (March 2007): 5–16.

Makiya, Kanan. *Cruelty and Silence: War, Tyranny, Uprising and the Arab World*. New York: W. W. Norton, 1993.

———. *The Monument: Art and Vulgarity in Saddam Hussein's Iraq*. New York: Palgrave Macmillan, 2004.

———. *Republic of Fear: The Politics of Modern Iraq*. Berkeley: University of California Press, 1998.

al-Majmai, Diya al-Din. *Hurub Saddam: Shahid ʿAyyan li-ʾAhdath Thalatha ʿUqud min Tarikh al-ʿIrāq al-Hadīth*. London: Dar al-Hikma, 2006.

Mallat, Chibli. "Religious Militancy in Contemporary Iraq: Muhammad Baqer as-Sadr and the Sunni-Shia Paradigm." *Third World Quarterly* 10 (April 1988): 699–729.

Mann, Michael. "The Autonomous Power of the State: Its Origins, Mechanisms and Results." In *States, War, and Capitalism: Studies in Political Sociology*, edited by Michael Mann, 1–32. Oxford: Basil Blackwell, 1988.

al-Marashi, Ibrahim. "An Insight into the Mindset of Iraq's Security Apparatus." *Intelligence and National Security* 18 (Autumn 2003): 1–23.

al-Marashi, Ibrahim, and Sammy Salama. *Iraq's Armed Forces: An Analytical History*. London: Routledge, 2008.

Marr, Phebe. *The Modern History of Iraq*. 2nd ed. Boulder: Westview, 2004.

McDermott, Kevin. "Archives, Power and the 'Cultural Turn': Reflections on Stalin and Stalinism." *Totalitarian Movements and Political Religions* 5 (Summer 2004): 5–24.

Milgram, Stanley. "The Dilemma of Obedience." *The Phi Delta Kappan* 55 (May 1974): 603–606.

Milosz, Czeslaw. *The Captive Mind*, translated by Jane Zielonko. New York: Octagon Books, 1981.

Mohsen, Fatima. "Cultural Totalitarianism." In *Iraq since the Gulf War: Prospects for Democracy*, edited by Fran Hazelton for CARDRI, 7–19. London: Zed Books, 1994.

Montgomery, Bruce P. "Saddam Hussein's Records of Atrocity: Seizure, Removal and Restitution." *The American Archivist* 75 (Fall/Winter 2012): 326–370.

Moore, Sally F., and Barbara G. Myerhoff. "Introduction: Secular Ritual; Forms and Meanings." In *Secular Ritual*, edited by Sally F. Moore and Barbara G. Myerhoff, 3–24. Assen/Amsterdam: Van Gorcum, 1977.

Mosca, Gaetano. *The Ruling Class (Elementi Di Scienza Politica)*, translated by Hannah D. Kahn. New York: McGraw Hill, 1939.

Mosse, George L. *The Nationalization of the Masses: Political Symbolism and Mass Movements in Germany from the Napoleonic Wars through the Third Reich*. New York: Howard Fertig, 1975.

Mottahedeh, Roy P. "The Shuʿubiyah Controversy and the Social History of Early Islamic Iran." *International Journal of Middle East Studies* 7 (April 1976), 161–182.

Nakash, Yitzhak. "The Nature of Shiʿism in Iraq." In *Ayatollahs, Sufis and Ideologues: State, Religion and Social Movements in Iraq*, edited by Faleh Abdul-Jabar, 23–35. London: Saqi, 2002.

———. *The Shiʿis of Iraq*. Princeton: Princeton University Press, 1994.

———. "The Shiʾites and the Future of Iraq." *Foreign Affairs* 82 (July/August 2003). http://www.foreignaffairs.com/articles/58994/yitzhak-nakash/the-shiites-and-the-future-of-iraq?page=show [accessed Feb. 29, 2012].

Ogden, C. K., and I. A. Richards. *The Meaning of Meaning*. London: Routledge, 2001.

Omar, Suha. "Women: Honour, Shame and Dictatorship." In *Iraq since the Gulf*

War: Prospects for Democracy, edited by Fran Hazelton for CARDRI, 60–71. London: Zed Books, 1994.
Overy, Richard. *The Dictators: Hitler's Germany, Stalin's Russia*. London: Allen Lane, 2004.
Persell, Caroline Hodges, Adam Green, and Liena Gurevich. "Civil Society, Economic Distress, and Social Tolerance." *Sociological Forum* 16 (June 2001): 203–230.
Peterson, Edward N. *The Limits of Hitler's Power*. Princeton: Princeton University Press, 1969.
Pool, David. "From Elite to Class: The Transformation of Iraqi Political Leadership." In *The Integration of Modern Iraq*, edited by Abbas Kelidar, 63–87. London: Croom Helm, 1979.
Post, Jerrold M., and Amatzia Baram. *Saddam Is Iraq: Iraq Is Saddam*. Counterproliferation Papers. Future Warfare Series no. 17. Maxwell Air Force Base, AL: USAF Counterproliferation Center, Maxwell Air Force Base Air University, 2002.
Qadduri, Fakhri. *Hakadha ʿAraftu al-Bakr wa-Saddam: Rihla 35 ʿAm fi Hizb al-Baʿth*. London: Dar al-Hikma, 2006.
Quinlivan, James T. "Coup-Proofing: Its Practices and Consequences in the Middle East." *International Security* 24 (Autumn 1999): 131–165.
Roberts, Stephen H. *The House That Hitler Built*. New York: Gordon Press, 1975.
Rohde, Achim. *State-Society Relations in Baʿthist Iraq: Facing Dictatorship*. London: Routledge, 2010.
Al-Samarrai, Wafiq. *Huttam al-Bawwaba al-Sharqiyya wa-Haqaʾiq ʿan al-Zaman al-Sayiʾ fi al-ʿIraq: Qiraʾa Jadida fi Harbay al-Khalij al-ʾUwwla wa-l-Thaniyya*. Kuwait: Sharikat Dar al-Qubs li-l-Sahafa wa-l-Nashr, 1997.
"Saddam Hussein Talks to the FBI: Twenty Interviews and Five Conversations with 'High Value Detainee #1' in 2004." http://www.gwu.edu/~nsarchiv/NSAEBB/NSAEBB279/ [accessed Aug. 27, 2012].
Sassoon, Joseph. "Management of Iraq's Economy Pre and Post the 2003 War: An Assessment." In *Iraq Between Occupations: Perspectives from 1920 to the Present*, edited by Amatzia Baram, Achim Rohde, and Ronen Zeidel, 189–208. New York: Palgrave Macmillan, 2010.
———. *Saddam Hussein's Baʿth Party: Inside an Authoritarian Regime*. Oxford: Oxford University Press, 2012.
Schapiro, Leonard. *Totalitarianism*. New York: Praeger, 1972.
Shanahan, Rodger. "The Islamic Daʿwa Party: Past Development and Future Prospects." *Middle East Review of International Affairs* 8 (June 2004): 16–25.
Shourush, Sami. "Islamist Fundamentalist Movements among the Kurds." In *Ayatollahs, Sufis and Ideologues: State, Religion and Social Movements in Iraq*, edited by Faleh Abdul-Jabar, 177–182. London: Saqi, 2002.
Soeterik, Robert. "The Islamic Movement of Iraq (1958–1980)." *Occasional Paper no. 12*. Amsterdam: Middle East Research Associates (MERA), Dec. 1991.
Souvarine, Boris. *Stalin: A Critical Survey of Bolshevism*. New York: Octagon, 1972.

Stanley, John L. "Is Totalitarianism a New Phenomenon?: Reflections on Hannah Arendt's *Origins of Totalitarianism*," *The Review of Politics* 49 (Spring 1987): 177–207.

Steavenson, Wendell. *The Weight of a Mustard Seed*. New York: Harper, 2009.

Suny, Ronald Grigor. "Stalin and His Stalinism: Power and Authority in the Soviet Union, 1930–1953." In *Stalinism*, edited by David L. Hoffman, 16–35. Cornwall: Blackwell, 2003.

Tarbush, Mohammad. *The Role of the Military in Politics: A Case Study of Iraq to 1941*. London: KPI, 1982.

Tripp, Charles. *A History of Iraq*. 3rd ed. Cambridge: Cambridge University Press, 2007.

van Geldern, James. "The Centre and the Periphery: Cultural and Social Geography in the Mass Culture of the 1930s." In *New Directions in Soviet History*, edited by Stephen White, 62–80. Cambridge: Cambridge University Press, 1992.

Wandawi, Hisham. *al-'Idara w-l-Siyasa: Dirasa ʿan Dawr al-'Idara wa-Ahdafiha fi Nazariyyat al-Nizam al-Siyasi fi al-ʿIraq*. Baghdad: Baghdad University Press, 1980.

Wardi, Ali. *Understanding Iraq: Society, Culture, and Personality*. Lewiston, NY: Edwin Mellen, 2008.

Wedeen, Lisa. *Ambiguities of Domination: Politics, Rhetoric, and Symbols in Contemporary Syria*. Chicago: University of Chicago Press, 1999.

Wiley, Joyce N. *The Islamic Movement of Iraqi Shiʿas*. Boulder: Lynne Rienner, 1992.

Woods, Kevin, James Lacey, and Williamson Murray. "Saddam's Delusions: The View from the Inside." *Foreign Affairs* 85 (May/June 2006): 2–26.

Woods, Kevin M., David D. Palkki, and Mark E. Stout, eds. *The Saddam Tapes: The Inner Workings of a Tyrant's Regime, 1978–2001*. Cambridge: Cambridge University Press, 2011.

Woods, Kevin M., Michael R. Pease, Mark E. Stout, Williamson Murray, and James G. Lacey. *Iraqi Perspectives Project: A View of Operation Iraqi Freedom from Saddam's Senior Leadership*. Joint Center for Operational Analysis, 2006.

Zuo, Jiping. "Political Religion: The Case of the Cultural Revolution in China." *Sociological Analysis* 52 (Spring 1991): 99–110.

INDEX

Page references followed by n or *t* indicate notes or tables, respectively. Page numbers in *italics* indicate figures and maps.

absolute loyalty (*al-wilāʾ al-muṭlaq*), 12–13
Abu Jaber, Kamel, 219n41
Abu Nuwas, 129
administered society, 189
adultery, 90, 126, 167, 169
advisory offices (*al-makātib al-ʾistishāriyya*), 22
Afghanistan, 241n52
Aflaq, Michel, 6–7, 10, 25, 28, 35–37, 60, 211n22, 259; as "the Founding Leader" (*al-qāʾid al-muʾassis*), 37–38; as patron saint, 221n2
Aflaqian Baʿthism, 38–39
Agent Communist Party (*al-ḥizb al-shuyūʿī al-ʿamīl*), 155, 260
Agent Daʿwa Party, 159, 181
agent(s): Baʿthist, 137, 163; enemy, 246n7; foreign, 89, 134, 152, 158, 164, 169, 173, 176, 188–189, 204, 231n42; intelligence or security service, 155, 204n5; Iranian, 161, 265; student, 168; tribesmen, 144
agent elements (*al-ʾanāṣir al-ʿamīla*), 155
Ahālī, 216n7
al-Anfal campaign, 162–163
Alawi, Hasan, 134
Alawites, 104, 190–191
Albu Nasr tribe, 217n8, 218n24
Algeria, 241n52
al-Khudur, Iraq, 241n52
allegiance, tests of, 90, 101
al-Quds (Jerusalem) Force, 109–110
al-Rasafa Bureau (Baʿth Party), 81–82
al-ʿUja, Iraq, 25
Al-Wathba, xi
al-Zubayr Branch (Baʿth Party), 50
amnesty, 256n40
Arab Baʿth Socialist Party (*Ḥizb al-Baʿth al-ʿArabī al-ʾIshtirākī*): organizational structure, 69; in Syria, 208n4; Wasit Bureau, 3, 229n20. *See also* Baʿth Party
Arabic, 223n49
Arabism, 134
Arabization (*taʿrīb*), 162–163, 251n58
Arab nationalism, 27–28, 60, 208n4
Arab Revolution, The, 36–37
Arabs, 101; history of, 41; Iraqi population, 216n4; Marsh Arabs, 155
Arab Spring, 190–191
Arendt, Hannah, 7, 9, 70, 149, 151
Arif, Abd al-Rahman, xi, 19–20
Arif, Abd al-Salam, xi, 19–20, 39, 217nn7–8
Armstrong, Hamilton Fish, 69, 147
Arsuzi, Zaki al-, 211n22
Assad, Bashar al-, 190–191

Assad, Hafez al-, 103–104, 217n9, 241n52
assassinations, 162, 250n43; attempted, 25, 151–152, 157–158, 246n6, 250n43
Association of Canadian Archivists, 207n1
associations, professional, 95–96
Atomic Energy Agency, 103, 227n7
authoritarianism, 8–9
awards, 175–176
Aziz, Tariq, 80, 151–152
Azzawi, Fadil Abbas, 81
Azzawi, Saadun Shakir al-, 22

Badge of Honor (*nawṭ al-shujāʿa*), 174–175, 179, 254n35, 255n37
Baghdad Branch (Baʿth Party), 54, 224n16, 233n6
Baghdad Bureau (Baʿth Party), 54–56, 77, 105, 118, 219n43
Baghdad Cultural Committee, 54–55
Bakr, Ahmad Hassan al-, xii, 11, 18–24, 35–36, 40, 73, 217nn7–8, 217n11
Baram, Amatzia, 6, 40, 142, 144, 151
Baran, David, 176, 253n4
Bashir, Ala, 126, 191
Basra, Dhi Qar, and Muthanna Bureau (Baʿth Party), 210n10
Basra, Iraq, 145
Batatu, Hanna, 10, 208n9
Baʿth Arab Socialist Party Regional Command Collection (BRCC), xv, xvi–xvii, xviii–xxi, 207n1
Baʿthification (*tabʿīth*), 5–12, 70; of civil society, 91–97; as cultural system, 185–186; de-Baʿthification, 191; of education (*tabʿīth al-taʿlīm*), 110–111, 136; failure of, 186–189; historical trends behind, 18–24; impetus for, 24; of individuals, 119–120; key elements of, 53; legacy of, 188–192; levels of, 117; of masses, 117–128; measures and methods, 12–16, 117; "A Plan for the Baʿthification of Society," 12–13, *13*, 119; of religion, 129–141; as ruling strategy, 18; of social institutions, 128–146; of society, 117–146; of state institutions, 107–112; of state personnel, 77, 98–107; strategy and tactics, 16–18, 117, 183–187; of students and youth, 121–123; as total strategy, 183–187, 189; of tribes, 141–146; of women, 123–128; "A Work Plan for Coordination between the Party and Mass Organizations in the Field of the Baʿthification of Society," 92, 120, 123, 193–201 (text)
Baʿthification Committee (*lajnat tabʿīth*), 93
Baʿthism, 29; Aflaqian, 38–39; classical, 38–39; Husseini, 9–30, 35–50, 53, 55–56, 73; ideology, 10, 213n41; loyalty to, 97–98; *Nidal al-Baʿth*, 37; purpose of, 259; as worldview, 55
Baʿthist agents, 137, 163
Baʿthists, 82
Baʿthist State, 14, 71, 97–115; centralization of power, 77–78; communications structure, 76–77; definition of, 215n60; institutions, 107–112; personnel appointments, 77, 98–107; rewards and benefits doled out by, 148–149, 172–178
Baʿthist Syria, 104
Baʿthist Trinity. *See* Husseini Baʿthist Trinity
Baʿth Party (*Ḥizb al-Baʿth al-ʿArabī al-ʾIshtirākī* in Iraq), 26–30; activities, 91; anti-religious policies, 129; apparatus (*al-jihāz al-ḥizbī*), 73, 80–91; Arabization (*taʿrīb*), 162–163, 251n58; as Arab nationalist organization, 208n4; authority, 5, 31; Baghdad Branch, 54, 224n16, 233n6; Baghdad Bureau, 54–56, 77, 105, 118, 219n43; Baghdad Cultural Committee, 54–55; Basra, Dhi Qar, and Muthanna Bureau, 210n10; benefits,

176–177; Central Office (*al-maktab al-markazī li-l-tanẓīm al-mihnī wa-l-shaʿbī*), 91–92, 96, 224n9, 231–232n52; Central Organization Committee, 162; Central Workers Office, 155–156; chronology, xi–xii; collaboration with, 6; committees (*al-lijān al-ḥizbiyya*), 53–55, 76–77, 111; constitution, 27–29, 219n41; controls on individual behavior, 90; cultural aspect of work, 56, 91; cultural committees, 53–55; culturalization (*tathqīf*), 30, 32–33, 51–67; cultural training, 36–37; definition of freedom, 27–29; definition of marriage, 28; "democratic" façade, 65–66; discipline (*ʾinḍibāṭ*), 88; Diyala Branch, 105, 163; duties (*al-tasarrub*), 5; egalitarianism, 125–127, 134; Euphrates Bureau, 12–13, *13*, 57–58, 103, 119, 121, 136, 186–187; evaluation of members, 88–89; as extension of Hussein, 73; Faith Campaign (*al-ḥamla al-ʾīmāniyya*), 17, 60–61, 130–131, 140; form of government, 7; founding of, 211n22; General Secretary, 26; ideological army (*jaysh ʿaqāʾidī*), 21; ideology, 19, 26–28, 133; indoctrination (*tawʿīyya*), 30, 53–55, 57–62; as institution, 73; intellectual cannon, 36–37; intelligence services, 163–164; internal activities and responsibilities, 87–91; internal control officials (*masʾūl al-raqāba al-dākhiliyya*), 111; internal threats, 157–158; international relations, 131–132; Internet access, 257n3; July 17–30, 1968 revolution (*thawrat 17–30 tamūz*), 20–21, 29, 42, 58–59, 124, 217n7, 217n10, 226n40; Karbala Branch, 113–114; al-Karkh bureau, 81–82; Kirkuk Branch, 83, 233n6; leadership, 73–96, 87*t*, 217n8; as "leading party" (*al-ḥizb al-qāʾid*), 10, 260; legitimacy, 10; literature, 36–37; local organizations, 121; local watchmen (*mukhtārīn*), 4, 105, 184, 236n35; loyalty, 3–17, 169–170; loyalty tests, 90, 101; marriage regulations, 89; mass aspect of party work (*al-jānib al-jamāhīrī*), 91, 118–119; Maysan Branch, 90–91; means of terror, 153–157, 184; means of violence, 7, 15, 148, 184; meetings, 59–60, 87–88, 91; membership, 4, 82–87, 84*t*, 108*t*, 127, 210n8, 230n27, 262; as meta-control, xvi, 208n3; Middle Euphrates Bureau, 85; military, 21; Military Bureau (*al-maktab al-ʿaskarī*), 81, 107–108, 108*t*, 108–110, 159, 255n35; morals, 125–126; National Assembly (*al-majlis al-waṭanī*), 65–66, 104–106, 145, 156, 227n7; National Command (*al-qiyāda al-qawmiyya*), xvi, 37, 208n4; nationalization of Islam, 132–133; National Security Branch Command (*qiyādat furʿ al-ʾamn al-qawmī*), 110; National Security Council (*majlis al-ʾamn al-qawmī*), 155; negative internal party phenomena, 114; Ninth Regional Congress, 29, 40–42; nomination process, 90; Northern Bureau, 73, 85, 98, 119–120, 127; obligation to, 85; Office of Culture and Media (*maktab al-thaqāfa wa-l-ʾiʿlām*), 36–37, 176, 224n9; Office of the Party Secretariat (*maktab ʾimānat sirr al-quṭr*), xix, 3–4, 26; Office of the President (*dīwān al-riʾāsa and riʾāsat al-jumhūriyya*), xvi, 227n7; Office of Public Relations, 22, 219n37; Office of Students and Youth, 42–43, 92, 94; Office of Tribal Affairs (*maktab shuʾūn al-ʿashāʾir*), 145; Office of Unions, 96; opposition parties, 158–164; opposition slogans, *167*, 168; Order of the Party (*shārat al-ḥizb*),

Baʿth Party (*continued*)
175–176, 178, 254n27; organization, 69–71, 80–82, 99, 108*t*, 146; Organization Committee (*al-lajna al-tanẓīmiyya*), 77, 85; Party State (*dawlat al-ḥizb*), 14, 71, 97–115; personnel appointments, 262; "A Plan for the Baʿthification of Society," 12–13, *13*; political commissars, 109; "poster committee" (*lajnat al-jadāriyāt*), 45; power struggles, 22–23; "Practicing responsibility from the lowest position" initiative, 213n37; preparatory schools (*madāris al-ʾiʿdād al-ḥizbī*), 54–55; preservation of the revolution, 39; priorities, 39; Professional and Mass Organizations, xvi, 14, 26, 47, 71, 73, 91–97, 117; propaganda, 165; al-Rasafa Bureau, 81–82; recruitment (*al-kasb*), 5, 26, 119–122, 143, 239n17, 260; public aspect of party work (*al-jānib al-jamāhīrī*), 91, 118–119; regional bureaus, 81; Regional Command, xv–xvi, 22–23, 26, 37, 156, 173, 208n4; Regional Congress, 21, 29, 40–42, 217n10; religious schools, 139; Republic of Fear, 6–7, 15–16, 148–149; retention, 5; Revolutionary Command Council, xvi, 22–23, 74, 102, 155, 173, 217n8, 227n7; revolutionary plan (*al-ʿaql al-mukhaṭṭiṭ*), 42; rituals, 31–32; ruling strategy, 18; Saʿad bin Abi Waqas Branch, 222n39; salaries, 230n31; salutations, 31, 259, 263; security detachments (*mafāriz*), 152; service requirements, 109; slogans, 9–10, 26–27, 48, 55; social welfare system, 23–24; Southern Bureau, 98, 134, 155, 165; strategy and tactics, 16–17, 120, 183–187; structure, 19, 26, 81–82, 110; supporters, 84*t*, 85; support networks, 146; survival in, 187; Ta'amim (Kirkuk) Branch, 83, 233n6; terminology, 31; terror and enticement (*tarhīb wa-targhīb*), 15–16, 147–149, 184, 214n53; *al-Thawra*, 133; totalitarianism, 20; total strategy, 183–187; as tribe of all tribes, 145; as vanguard (*ṭalīʿa*), 10; "A Work Plan for Coordination between the Party and Mass Organizations in the Field of the Baʿthification of Society," 92, 120, 123, 193–201 (text); al-Zubayr Branch, 50. *See also* Popular Army; *and specific directorates*
beggary, 60
Bengio, Ofra, xviii, 6
Berlin, Isaiah, 24
Berlin Wall, 189, 241n52
"Big Deal," 147
Bitar, Salah al-Din, 211n22
blood feuds, 121
blood oaths (*wathīqat ʿahd bi-l-damm*), 4, 32, 48–50, 176, 264
BRCC. *See* Baʿth Arab Socialist Party Regional Command Collection
Brown, Timothy S., 51, 70
Browning, Christopher, 183
Brzezinski, Zbigniew, 57
bureaucracy, xvi–xviii, 44, 94, 114–115, 184; governorate, 104

capitalism, 29
capital offenses, 45–46
carrot and stick policy, 6, 21, 147, 172, 214n53. *See also* terror: and enticement
celebrations, 140, 144, 265
Central Office of the Professional and Popular Bureau (*al-maktab al-markazī li-l-tanẓīm al-mihnī wa-l-shaʿbī*) (Baʿth Party), 91–92, 96, 224n9, 231–232n52
Central Office of Workers, 93, 261
ceremonies, 62–67; Martyr's Day (De-

cember 1), 63–64, 67; mass ceremonies, 63, 67; national (*sāḥat al-ʾiḥtifālāt*), 65
Chamberlin, William Henry, 51–52
children: benefits for, 177–178; Day of the Iraqi Child (*yawm al-ṭifl al-ʿirāqī*), 66; martyrs, 64–65
China, 53, 189–190
civil society, 91–97, 183–184
clan connections, 6, 142–144
cleansing: of enemies, 148, 182, 264; ethnic, 154–155, 162–163
code words, 58, 60–61, 67, 106, 114
cohabitation (*muʿāyisha*), 109, 262
collective leadership (*al-qiyāda al-jamā-ʿiyya*), 11, 35–36
commendations (*kitāb shukr*), 176, 254n35
commissioned spies (*al-ʿuyūn al-mukallafa*), 155
communications, 76–77; Baʿthist correspondence, 31, 259, 263; code words, 58, 60–61, 67, 106, 114; favorite positive adjectives, 58–59; salutations, 31, 259, 263
Communist Party, 21, 89, 99, 159, 164, 249n40
computers, 103
Conflict Records Research Center (CRRC), xvii, 208n7
conservatives, 124–125
conspiracies, 157–158, 179; foreign, *167*, 168
corruption, 112–116, 152, 191, 251n70
Court of the Revolution (*maḥkamat al-thawra*), 75, 170
cowardice, 158
creativity (*ʿibdāʾ*), 75, 228n2, 260
crimes: against honor (*jarāʾim mukhilla bi-l-sharf*), 168–170, 179, 186; against women, 94, 125–127, 169–170
criminals (*mujrimīn*), 144, 148, 152, 170; amnesty for, 256n40; deportations of, 166; families of, 180–182, 203–205; political criminals, 103, 120–121, 178–179, 181, 203–205
cult of personality, 36, 40–50, 62
cultural committees, 53–54; competitions, 54; seminars (*nadwa*), 54
culturalization (*tathqīf*), 30, 32–33, 51–67; mass, 57–58; means of, 54–55; process, 54; rituals, 64–65; self-culturalization (*al-tathqīf al-dhātī*), 54–55; "Ways to Culturalize the Masses (Mass Mobilization)," 57–58
Cultural Revolution (China), 53
Cultural Revolution (Soviet), 147
culture: Baʿthification of, 185–186; Iraqi, 32–33; political, 52–53, 185–186; *thaqāfa*, 53–57

Davis, Eric, 11–12
Daʿwa Party. *See* Islamic Daʿwa Party
Day of the Glorious Victory (*yawm al-fatḥ al-mubīn*), 66
Day of the Iraqi Child (*yawm al-ṭifl al-ʿirāqī*), 66
de-Baʿthification, 191
defections, 229n12
"Degree of Relation," 102–103, 121, 180, 203–205, 231n42, 235n23
democratic facade, 65–66
Democratic National Union of Kurdistan (*al-ʾittiḥād al-qawmī al-dīmuqrāṭī al-kūrdistānī*), 251n58
demonstrations, 162
deportations: Baʿthist (*tasfīr*), 165–166, 179, 184; Nazi, 183
deserters, 5, 59–60, 89–90, 143–144, 154, 168–169, 182, 186–187; deportations of, 166; High Committee for Deserters and Draft Dodgers, 3; pardons to, 256n40
detotalitarization, 9
Dhi Qar, Iraq, 114, 145
dictatorship, xvi, 4, 18, 39–40, 79, 188–189

Directorate of Military Intelligence (DMI, *mudīriyyat al-ʾistikhbārāt al-ʿaskariyya*) (Baʿth Party), 22, 76–77
Directorate of Political Guidance (*mudīriyyat al-tawjih al-siyāsī*) (Baʿth Party), 21
discipline (*ʾinḍibāṭ*), 88, 158
divorce regulations, 89–90
Diyala, Iraq, 162–163
Diyala Branch (Baʿth Party), 105, 163
Diyala Governorate, 162–163
DMI. *See also* Directorate of Military Intelligence
Dujayl, Iraq, 250n43
Duri, Izzat Ibrahim al-, 80

education: Baʿthification of (*tabʿīth al-taʿlīm*), 110–111, 136, 183–184; Baʿth Party benefits, 177–178; elementary school examinations, 48, *49*; essay contests, 47–48; preparatory schools (*madāris al-ʾiʿdād al-ḥizbī*), 54–55; religious schools, 136–137, *137*, 138–139, 141, 243n78
egalitarianism, 125–127, 134
Egypt, 190–191
employment, state, 97, 180
enemies, xx, 11, 15, 25, 38, 42, 56, 74, 79, 204, 259; Baʿth definition of, 148; foreign, 165–168; invention of, 7, 151–152; outside, 246n7; Persian, 165, 259; use of terror against, 154, 163, 170, 181–182
enticement: Baʿthist, 171–182; rewards and benefits, 148–149, 172–178; terror and (*al-tarhīb wa-l-targhīb*), 15–16, 147–149, 184, 214n53
Eskander, Saad, 207n1
espionage, 121, 184; commissioned spies (*al-ʿuyūn al-mukallafa*), 155; informants, 156, 184. *See also* surveillance
ethnic cleansing, 154–155; al-Anfal campaign, 162–163
Euphrates Bureau (Baʿth Party), 12–13, *13*, 57–58, 103, 119, 121, 136, 186–187
Evans, Richard, 70
execution(s), 156, 158, 218n13; of Saddam Hussein, 250n43. *See also* mass executions
expulsions, 162–163, 179
extortion, 152, 169
extremism, religious, 132–133

faith: in Husseini Baʿthism, 14, 32, 54–56, 188; religious (*ʾīmān*), 60–61, 133, 140, 184
Faith Campaign (*al-ḥamla al-ʾīmāniyya*), 17, 60–61, 130–131, 140
families: betrayal within, 3–4, 156, 169–170, 185–186, 209n6; clan connections, 6, 121, 142–144; of criminals, 180–182, 203–205; "Degree of Relation," 102–103, 121, 180, 203–205, 231n42, 235n23; deportations, 165–166; of martyrs, 120–121, 173; monitoring, 121, 260; personnel appointments, 102–103; relatives, 102–103; terror against, 154
Farouk-Sluglett, Marion, xvii, 5–6, 10
fascism, 213n35
Faw Peninsula, 109, 176
Faylī Kurds, 216n4
Faysal bin Hussein al-Hashemi, xi, 19, 217n11
Fedayeen militia, 100, 109–110, 177
Fitzpatrick, Sheila, 187, 226n44
food: distribution of, 140; oil-for-food program (UN), xii, 86–87, 189
foreign agents. *See* agent(s): foreign
freedom, 27–29
Free Officers, xvii
Friedrich, Carl, 57
Friends of Mr. President Leader, Saddam Hussein (God keep him) (*ʾaṣdiqāʾ al-sayyid al-raʾīs al-qāʾid ṣaddām ḥusayn, ḥafẓuhu allāh*), 175, 179, 254n35, 259

future directions, 191–192

GDI. *See* General Directorate of Intelligence
Geertz, Clifford, 185
gender roles, 35–36
General Directorate of Intelligence (GDI, *mudīriyyat al-mukhābarāt al-ʿāma*) (Baʿth Party), 22, 110, 154, 156–158
General Federation of Iraqi Women (GFIW, *al-ʾittiḥād al-ʿām li-l-nisāʾ al-ʿirāq*), 91–95, 123–125, 127–128
General Security Directorate (GSD, *mudīriyyat al-ʾamn al-ʿāma*) (Baʿth Party), 22, 75, 98–100, 110
genocide, 154–155, 162–163
Gentile, Giovanni, 11
GFIW. *See* General Federation of Iraqi Women
Ghannoushi, Rashid al-, 241n52
Giddens, Anthony, 71
Gleichschaltung (coordination), 69–70, 99
Golden Square, xi
governors, 104–105
graffiti, 155, 164, *167*, 168
Great Arab Revolt, 217n11
Great Britain, xi, 19, 216n4
Great Terror, 147
GSD. *See* General Security Directorate
Gulf War. *See* Persian Gulf War

Haddad, Fanar, 134
Hama, Syria, 241n52
Hamas, 241n52
Hamdani, Raad, 128, 152
Hammud, Abd, 79
harassment, sexual, 126
Hashemi, Ghazi bin Faysal bin Hussein al-, xi
Hashemite Monarchy, xvii, 19
Hashim, Jawad, 23
Havel, Vaclav, 36
Hawza, 136–137, *137*, 138, 141, 243n78
heavy metal slogans, *167*, 168
Helms, Christine Moss, 83
Hilla, Iraq, 101
historical trends, 18–24, 41
Hitler, Adolf, 7–8, 51, 69–70, 97
Ḥizb al-Baʿth al-ʿArabī al-ʾIshtirākī in Iraq. *See* Baʿth Party
holidays, 66–67; Day of the Glorious Victory (*yawm al-fatḥ al-mubīn*), 66; Day of the Iraqi Child (*yawm al-ṭifl al-ʿirāqī*), 66; Islamic, 140; Muharram, 44, 130, 134, 139–141
homosexual activity, 169
honor(s): Badge of Honor (*nawṭ al-shujāʿa*), 174–175, 179, 254n35, 255n37; codes, 127, 142, 144; multiple, 174–175; official honors, 175; personal, 112; state, 174; withdrawal of privileges, 178–182. *See also* crimes: against honor
Hoover Institution Archives, xv
housing, 176, 178
ḥusayniyyāt, 139–140
Hussein, Imam, 44–45, 135, 139, 243n76
Hussein, Qusay, 79, 191
Hussein, Saddam: advisory offices (*al-makātib al-ʾistishāriyya*), 22; affection for, 50; allegiance to, 4; assassination attempts, 151–152, 157–158, 246n6, 250n43; attitude toward women, 127; authority, 31, 36, 40, 74; Baʿthification, 16–17, 120–121; and Baʿthist state, 74–80; and Baʿth Party, 47, 73; chronology, xii; as Commander-in-Chief, 74–75; commitment to pan-Arabism, 35–36; on creed, 35; cult of personality, 36, 40–50, 62; as Deputy Chairman, 22–23; as Deputy Secretary-General, 22–23; dictatorship, xvi, 4, 18, 39–40, 79, 188–189; execution of, 250n43; exile, 25; Faith Campaign (*al-ḥamla al-ʾīmāniyya*), 17, 60–61, 130–131,

Hussein, Saddam (*continued*)
140; family, 229n12; as General, 22–23; as General-Secretary, 107; inner circle, 79–80, 228n11; institutional power, 74; invocations, 45, *46*; as "the leader" (*al-qā'īd*), 4, 11, 37–50, 74; leadership, 40–50, 73, 97, 217n8; loyalty to, 22–23; means of terror, 153–157; means of violence, 15, 40; measures and methods, 12–16; micromanagement, 77–78, 115–116, 228n7, 235n33; as military leader, 42–43; monikers for, 259, 262–263; moral legitimacy, 39–40; new theory, 30; Order of the Command (*shārat al-qiyāda*), 173; paranoia, 218n32; on party loyalty, 3, 10; personal authority, 112–113; personality, 18–19, 24–26; personalized politics, 5–6; personnel appointments, 219n43, 228n7, 235n33; power, 18–19, 22–23, 35–36, 73–74; presidency, xv, 10–11, 73–75, 152; psychological profile, 24–25; Republic of Fear, 6–7, 15–16, 148–149; resistance movements against, 159; "The Responsibility of State Departments to Solve the Issues of Citizens," 78; ruling strategy, 16–17, 86, 183–187, 212n34; ruthlessness, 218n32; "Sayings of the Leader Comrade (God save him)," 45, *46*; as Secretary-General, 74; as symbol, 44; symbols or depictions of, 45–47; titles, 44, 74; totalitarianism, 5–30, 146; total strategy of rule, 183–187; tribal policy, 141–146; vendettas against, 23; writings, 37
Hussein, Uday, 79, 151, 175
Hussein al-Tikriti, Saddam. *See* Hussein, Saddam
Husseini Baʿthism, 9–12, 30, 35–50; application of, 36; culture, 32–33, 53; elements of, 36; faith in, 55–56; ideology, 73, 148; measures and methods, 12–16; morality, 156–157; origins of, 18–30; political culture, 53; propaganda, 57–62, 99–100; strategy and tactics, 16–17, 183–187; totalitarianism, 18–30; total strategy, 183–187
Husseini Baʿthist Trinity, 9–10, 16, 31–33, 53, 56, 67, 70, 120, 128–129, 136, 144, 148–149, 169–170, 185–186

ICP. *See* Iraqi Communist Party
identity: national, 129; tribal, 141
ideology, 11–12, 31–33; Baʿthist, 10, 213n41; Baʿth Party, 19, 26–28, 133; Husseini Baʿthist, 73, 148
Ilah, Abd al-, xi
imams, 17, 138–141, 184; Shiʿi, 44
IMF. *See* Iraq Memory Foundation
incentives. *See* enticement
independents (*mustaqill*): and awards and benefits, 177; Baʿthification of, 93, 95, 197; candidates for academies and state positions, 98, 100, 102, 104–107; loyalists, 11, 99, 166, 262; mapping, 119–120, 199; officers, 233n6; preachers, 244n96
indoctrination (*tawʿīyya*), 30, 53–55, 57–62
influence or effect (*ta'thīr*), 103, 180–181, 264. *See also* social influence
informants, 156, 184
information sharing, 76, 114
institutions: social, 128–146; state, 107–112
intellectuals, 225n31
intelligence reports, 31–32, 184, 229n20, 248n29
intelligence services, 163–164. *See also specific services*
internal control officials (*mas'ūl al-raqāba al-dākhiliyya*), 111
international relations, 131–132
Internet access, 190, 257n3
interrogations, 171
Iran: domestic support against, 134;

as enemy, 165; Iraqi invasion of, xii; Islamic Republic of Iran, 130, 132, 160
Iran-Contra affair, 166
Iranians, 101–102; agents, 161, 265; deportation of, 77, 165–166, 201
Iran-Iraq War (Saddam's or second *Qādisiyya*), 24, 107, 109, 112, 160–161, 209n1, 249n40; chronology, xii; domestic support for, 134; honors during, 254n35; martyrs in, 63; rewards and benefits during, 255n35; terminology for, 58–59, 114
Iraq: Air Force, 233n10; Airlines, 233n10; autonomous region (*mantaqat al-ḥukm al-dhātī*), 42, 161–162, 225n36; as Baʿthist State, xi–xii, *xiii*, 74–80; constitution, 161; coup d'etat, xi; Court of the Revolution (*maḥkamat al-thawra*), 75, 170; culture of, 32–33; disintegration of, 11–12; district maps, 119; Diyala Governorate, 162–163; as Eastern Flank of the Arab World, 165; economic conditions, 177–178; governorates, *xiii*, 104; Hashemite Monarchy, xvii, 19; High Committee for Deserters and Draft Dodgers, 3; independence of, xi; invasion of Iran, xii; invasion of Kuwait, xii, 131; as Iraqi region, 258n1; July 17–30, 1968 revolution (*thawrat 17–30 tamūz*), 20–21, 29, 42, 58–59, 124, 217n7, 217n10, 226n40; Kirkuk Governorate (*al-Taʾmīm*), 115; Kurdish region or territories, 42, 161–162, 225n36; local government, 104–105, 114–115, 118; Medal and Badge Law (*qānūn al-ʾawsima wa-l-ʿanwāṭ*), 174, 179; Ministry of Culture and Media, 45, 47, 63–64, 66–67, 140, 213n39; Ministry of Education, 104, 235n22; Ministry of Endowments and Religious Affairs, 135; Ministry of Health, 65; Ministry of Higher Education and Scientific Research, 111, 235n22; Ministry of the Interior, 104, 175; Muthanna Governorate, 233n6; nationalization of, 23; Navy, 233n10; new stage (*marḥala jadīda*), 36–40; nuclear strategy, 42; oil-for-food program (UN), xii, 86–87, 189; oil industry, xi, 23, 29, 42, 190; oil revenues, 23–24, 189; as Party State (*dawlat al-ḥizb*), 14, 71, 97–115; patriotism, 9–10, 66–67; people, 101; population, 216n4; Portsmouth Treaty with Great Britain, xi; Republic of Fear, 6–7, 15–16, 148–149; Republic of Rewards and Dependence, 148–149; Salah al-Din Governorate, 244n96; as shadow state, 6; state honors, 174; state institutions, 107–112; state personnel, 77, 98–107; Sunni triangle, 23; totalitarianism, 5–12; US invasion of, xii
Iraqi Armed Forces, 42, 74; personnel appointments, 98–99. *See also* deserters
Iraqi Central Bank, 227n7
Iraqi Communist Party (ICP), 21, 155, 159, 164, 260
Iraq in Wartime (Khoury), xvii
Iraqi Red Crescent, 64–65
Iraq Memory Foundation (IMF), xv, 208n6
Islam, 129; Baʿthist, 259; holidays, 140; Husseini Baʿthist, 131; nationalization of, 132–133; as revolutionary movement, 60
Islamic Daʿwa Party (*ḥizb al-daʿwa al-ʾislāmiyya*), 89, 103, 121, 130, 132, 140, 159–160; early activities, 250n43
Islamic Jihad, 241n52
Islamic Republic of Iran, 130, 132, 160
Islamic Salvation Front, 241n52
Islamic State in Iraq and the Levant (ISIL), 191

Islamism, 131–132, 159; Shiʿi, 130; Sunni, 131, 138–139, 241n52
Israel, 166

Jabar, Faleh A., 143, 245n114
Jasim, Latif Nisayyif al-, 213n39
Jerusalem (al-Quds) Force, 109–110
Jordan, 241n52
Judicial Institute (*al-maʿahad al-quḍāī*), 233n10
July 17–30, 1968 revolution (*thawrat 17–30 tamūz*), 20–21, 29, 42, 124, 217n7, 217n10, 226n40; Court of the Revolution (*maḥkamat al-thawra*), 75, 170; terminology for, 58–59
Jumaila, 217n8
jurists, 160, 264
just punishment (*qiṣāṣan ʿādilan*), 158, 170, 264

Kailani, Rashid Ali al-, xi
Kamil, Hussein, 113, 215n58
Kamil brothers, 229n12
Kandel, I. L., 52
Karbala, Iraq, 6, 114, 130, 134, 136, 140–141
Karbala Branch (Baʿth Party), 113–114
Kassof, Allen, 188, 192
Kautsky, John, 128, 246n7
Kazzar, Nazim, 22
KDP. *See* Kurdistan Democratic Party
Khadduri, Majid, 10
Khafaji, Isam al-, 101
Khalil, Samir al-, 208n10
Khaniqin, Iraq, 163
Khlevnyuk, Oleg, 147, 246n2
Khoei, Abu al-Qasim al-, 134–135
Khomeini, 133–134, 160
kidnappings, 152, 162
killings. *See* violence
kinship ties, 6, 142
Kirkuk (Ta'mim), Iraq, 162
Kirkuk (Ta'mim) Branch (Baʿth Party), 83, 233n6
Kirkuk (Ta'mim) Governorate, 115
Kolakowski, Leszek, 12, 164
Kurdish region or territories, 42, 161–162, 225n36
Kurdistan, xii, 161, 251n58
Kurdistan Democratic Party (KDP), 159–164, 265
Kurds, 19–20, 42, 101, 154–155, 160–164; expulsion of, 162–163; Faylī Kurds, 216n4; Iraqi population, 216n4; suppression of, 6; surveillance of, 163–164
Kurzman, Charles, 164
Kuwait, Iraqi invasion of, xii, 131

language, 59–60; Baʿthist correspondence, 31, 259, 263; code words, 58, 60–61, 67, 106, 114; invocations for Saddam Hussein, 45, *46*; monikers for Saddam Hussein, 259, 262–263; multivocalities, 60; positive adjectives, 58–59; salutations, 31, 259, 263
leadership: of Baʿth Party, 73–96; collective (*al-qiyāda al-jamāʿiyya*), 11, 35–36; of Saddam Hussein, 40–50, 73, 97, 217n8; Shiʿi sources of emulation (*marājiʿ al-taqlīd*), 130, 134–136, 261; totalitarian, 25–26; tribal, 106
Libya, 190–191
life insurance, 178
limited political pluralism, 8–9
Linz, Juan, 17, 216n1
local government, 104–105, 114–115, 118
local organizations, 121
local watchmen (*mukhtārīn*), 4, 105, 184, 236n35
loyalists, 11, 99, 166, 262
loyalty, 112; absence of (*ʿadam al-wilāʾ*), 179; absolute loyalty (*al-wilāʾ al-muṭlaq*), 12–13; to Baʿthist principles, 97–98; to Baʿth Party, 3, 5, 10, 101–102, 169–170; blood oaths (*wathīqat ʿahd bi-l-damm*), 4, 32, 48–50, 176, 264; extreme, 3–4; familial, 6, 121;

importance of, 101–102; inculcation of, 3–17; kin and clan connections, 6; political, 179; primordial allegiances, 6, 20; tests of, 90, 101; total, 258n2
Lübbe, Herman, 188
Luks, Leonid, 241n54

Mahdi, 249n36
Majid, Ali Hassan al-, 80, 126–127, 158, 162–163, 169, 252n79
Majmai, Diya al-Din al-, 38–39
Makiya, Kanan, xv, xvii, 6–7, 16, 151
Mandate for Iraq, xi
Mao Tse Tung, 8, 53
marāji' al-taqlīd (Shi'i leaders or sources of emulation), 130, 134–136, 261
marja'iyya (the Institution of the *marāji'*), 136–137, *137*, 138
marriage: definition of, 28; forced, 124; as national duty, 28; regulations for, 89–90, 231n42
Marsh Arabs, 155
martyrs, and martyrdom(s), 158, 162; Ba'thist, 73, 120–121, 152, 161, 259; benefits for families of, 120–121, 173; cult of, 63; Shi'i, 225n39; suicide bombings, 210n10
Martyr's Day (December 1), 63–64, 67
masses, the (*al-jamāhīr*), 10; Ba'thification of, 117–128
mass executions, 156, 248n28; al-Anfal campaign, 162–163; genocide, 154–155, 162–163
mass organizations. *See* Professional and Mass Organizations
Maysan Branch (Ba'th Party), 90–91
Medal and Badge Law (*qānūn al-'awsima wa-l-'anwāṭ*), 174, 179
medals, 148–149, 173–174; Badge of Honor (*nawṭ al-shujā'a*), 174–175, 179, 254n35, 255n37; *Rāfidayn* Medal (*wisām al-rāfidayn*), 174, 179, 264; Revolution Medal (*wisām al-thawra*), 174, 179, 254n14, 255n37; Saddam's *Qādisiyya* Medal (*wisām qādisiyyat ṣaddām*), 174, 254n14, 255n37; withdrawal of privileges, 179–180
Media and Cultural Foundation, 180
meta-control, xvi, 208n3
Milgram, Stanley, 185
militant secularism, 131–132
military academies (*al-kulliyāt al-'askariyya*), 99–102, 184, 233n10, 234n12
Military Bureau (*al-maktab al-'askarī*) (Ba'th Party), 81, 107–108, 108*t*, 108–110, 159, 255n35
military training drills, 230n37, 254n23
missing in action (MIA), 120–121
mobilization: mass (*ta'bi'a*), 56–58; popular, 56–58, 105
modernization, 23–24
monitoring. *See* surveillance
Montgomery, Bruce, 207n1
morality, 125–126, 156–157
Mosca, Gaetano, 39, 257n6
mosques, 139–140
Mosse, George, 53
Mosul, Iraq, 229n22, 250n43
Mottahedeh, Roy, 251n70
Muhammad, 60, 133
Muharram, 44, 130, 134, 139–141
mujāhidīn, 241n52
Mukhlis, Muhammad, 217n11
mukhtārīn (local watchmen), 4, 105, 184, 236n35
murder: al-Anfal campaign, 162–163; executions, 156, 158, 218n13, 250n34; genocide, 154–155, 162–163; killing or betrayal, 3–4, 156, 169–170; mass executions, 156, 248n28; violent killings, 151–152
Muslim Brotherhood, 138–139, 159, 241n52
Mustansiriyya University, 122, 152

Muthanna Governorate, 233n6
mythology, 60

Najaf, Iraq, 6, 130, 134, 136, 140–141
narcotics, 168, 252n77
Nasserist movement, 159
National Activism units (*al-nishāṭ al-waṭanī*), 120
National Assembly (*al-majlis al-waṭanī*), 65–66, 104–106, 144, 156, 227n7
national ceremonies (*sāḥat al-ʾiḥtifālāt*), 65
National Computer Center (*al-markaz al-qawmī li-l-ḥāsibāt al-ʾiliktrūniyya*), 103
National Defense Regiments (*ʾafwāj al-difāʿ al-waṭanī*), 6
National Defense University, xvii
nationalism: Arab, 27–28, 60, 208n4; Iraqi-Islamic, 160
nationality, 101
nationalization, xi; of Islam, 132–133; of oil industry, 23, 42
national occasions. *See* occasions
National Security Council (*majlis al-ʾamn al-qawmī*), 155
National Socialism (Nazism), 14, 27, 51–53, 69–70, 183, 213n35, 256n5
National Union of Students and Youth of Iraq (*al-ʾittiḥād al-waṭanī li-ṭalaba wa-shabāb al-ʿirāq*), 93, 110–111, 231n52
Nazification, 70
Nazism (National Socialism), 14, 27, 51–53, 69–70, 183, 213n35, 256n5
neo-tribalism, 142, 146
neutrality, 213n39
new man (*al-ʾinsān al-jadīd*), 9–10
new society (*al-mujtamaʿ al-jadīd*), 9–10
new stage (*marḥala jadīda*), 36–40
Nidal al-Baʿth (The Baʿthist Struggle), 37
Ninewa, Iraq, 162
North Korea, 189
nuclear strategy, 42
nuclear weapons, 166

oaths of loyalty, 4, 32, 48–50, 176, 264
occasions (*munāsabāt*), 31–32, 62–67, 110–111, 135, 140, 145, 164, 176
oil-for-food program (UN), xii, 86–87, 189
oil industry, xi, 23, 29, 42, 190
oil revenues, 23–24, 189
Old Social Classes and the Revolutionary Movements of Iraq, The (Batatu), 208n9
opposition: groups, 185; parties, 158–164; slogans, *167*, 168
Order of the Command (*shārat al-qiyāda*), 173
Order of the Mother of All Battles (*shārat ʾumm al-maʿārik*), 175
Order of the Party (*shārat al-ḥizb*), 175–176, 178, 254n27
organization (*al-tanẓīm*), 69–71, 80–81, 99, 108*t*, 146
Organization of the Awaited Imam Mahdi (*munaẓẓamat al-ʾimām mahdī al-muntaẓar*), 249n36
Organization of Senior Citizens and the Ill (*munaẓẓamat kibār al-sinn wa-l-marḍā*), 177
Organization of the Strugglers (*munaẓẓamat al-munāḍilīn*), 176–177
Osiraq nuclear reactor, 166
Ottomans, 19, 101–102
Overy, Richard, 7, 39, 256n5

Palace of Martyrs school (*madrasat balāṭ al-shuhadāʾ*), 66
pan-Arabism, 7, 27, 35–36, 159; organizations, 95–96
paramilitary organizations, 109–110
paranoia, 166–168, *167*, 168, 218n32
pardons, 256n40

partisans, 262
Party committees (*al-lijān al-ḥizbiyya*), 53–55, 76–77, 111
party preparatory schools (*madāris al-ʾiʿdād al-ḥizbī*), 54–55
paternalism, 125–127
Patriotic Union of Kurdistan (PUK), 159–164, 265
patriotism, 39–40, 66–67, 112; Iraqi, 9–10, 160, 166
patronage, 6, 23–24, 120–121, 217n11; rewards and benefits, 148–149, 172–178, 184
People's Councils (*majālis al-shaʿb*), 65–66, 91–92, 106–107
Persian Gulf War, 16–17, 85, 186–187; chronology, xii; martyrs in, 63; terminology for, 58–59, 264
Persians, 134, 165, 259
Personal Status Law, 124
personnel appointments, 77, 98–107, 184, 219n43, 228n7, 235n30, 235n33, 262; criteria for, 135–136, 263; religious, 135–136, 141
Peterson, Edward N., 215n63
petitions (citizen), xx, xvii, 31, 59, 63, 75, 77–79, 98, 114–115, 126, 156–157, 173, 176, 178, 184, 220n4, 242n64, 247n8, 249n31, 253n87; petitioners, 32, 43–44, 47, 178
phenomena: of banner burning (*ẓāhirat ʾiḥrāq al-ʾiṭārāt*), 225n39; of banquets (*ẓāhirat ʾiqāmat*), 225n39; of beggary, 60; graffiti, 155, 164, *167*, 168; negative, 111, 114, 188–189; of processions (*ẓāhirat al-mashī*), 225n39, 243n87; religious, 60, 123–124; of Shiʿi rituals, 225n39; unnatural, 59–60, 225n32
Piro, George L., 219n43
"Plan for the Baʿthification of Society, A" (*khiṭat tabʿīth al-mujtamaʿ*), 12–13, *13*, 119
plebiscite (*ʾistiftāʾ*), 65–66
pluralism, political, 8–9
poetry, 4, 62
Police Preparatory School (*ʾiʿdādiyyat al-shurṭa*), 101, 233n10
political commissars, 109
political criminals, 103, 120–121, 178–179, 181; pardons to, 256n40; relatives of, 203–205
politics: culture of, 52–53, 185–186; limited pluralism, 8–9; movements, 159; personalized, 5–6; and religions, 52
Popular Army (*al-jaysh al-shaʿbī*), 109–110, 124, 161, 210n8, 236n47, 236n55
Portsmouth Treaty, xi
posters, 45, 222n39
post-totalitarian systems, 189
power, 71; centralization of, 77–78; infrastructural, 14; institutional, 74; resistance to, 215n63; of Saddam Hussein, 18–19, 22–23, 35–36, 73–74; struggles, 22–23
prayer: circles, 139–140; leaders, 235n30
preparatory schools. *See* party preparatory schools
prisoners of war (POWs), xvi, 90, 119–121, 142
privileges: withdrawal of, 178–182. *See also* rewards and benefits
processions: funeral, 64–65; phenomena of (*ẓāhirat al-mashī*), 225n39, 243n87
Professional and Mass Organizations (PMOs, *al-munaẓẓamāt al-mihniyya wa-l-jamāhīriyya*), xvi, 14, 26, 47, 71, 73, 85, 91–97, 117; Baʿthification, 120; Baʿthification Committee (*lajnat tabʿīth*), 93; Central Office, 261; membership, 210n8
Professional and Popular Bureau (Baʿth Party), Central Office (*al-maktab al-markazī li-l-tanẓīm al-mihnī wa-l-shaʿbī*), 91–92, 96, 224n9, 231–232n52
professional unions and associations, 95–96

propaganda, 9–10, 16–17, 45, 50, 57–62, 70, 113–114, 139–140, 183–184; anti-Iran, 165–166; culturalization (*tathqīf*), 30, 32–33, 51–67; effective, 250n50; religious, 135
prostitution, 169
protests: demonstrations, 162; Shiʿi, xi, 130, 133–134; uprisings, 16–17, 23, 85, 186–187
PUK. *See* Patriotic Union of Kurdistan
purification, 163

Qaddafi, Muammar al-, 252n77
Qadhani, Hassan al-, 171
Qādisiyya, original battle, 209n1
Qādisiyya, Saddam's. *See* Iran-Iraq War
Qasim, Abd al-Karim, xi, 19, 25–26, 80, 217n7
Qurʾān, 66

rabble-rousers (*ghūghāʾiyīn*), 133–134
Rāfidayn Medal (*wisām al-rāfidayn*), 174, 179, 264
Ramadan, Taha Yasin, 80, 178
rape, 169
Rashid, Muhyi Abd al-Husain, 40
Rautsi, Inari, 218n32
RC. *See* Baʿth Party, Regional Command
RCC. *See* Revolutionary Command Council
"Reality of the Unions, Federations, and Mass Organizations during the Most Recent Period, The," 85
recruitment, 5, 26, 119–122, 143, 239n17, 260
redactions, 113
Regional Command (RC, *al-qiyāda al-quṭriyya*), xv–xvi, 22–23, 26, 37, 156, 208n4; Order of the Command (*shārat al-qiyāda*), 173
relatives, 102–103; "Degree of Relation," 102–103, 121, 180, 203–205, 231n42, 235n23; "Special Regulations for How to Deal with the Relatives of Criminals Convicted for Political Crimes," 203–205. *See also* families
religion(s), 129–141; Baʿthification of, 183–184; clerics, 135–136, 141; establishments, 129–141; extremism, 132–133; faith (*ʾīmān*), 60–61, 133, 140, 184; phenomena, 60, 123–124; political religions, 52; propaganda, 135; rhetoric, 16–17; schools, 136, 139, 141, 243n78; school teachers, 235n30
"Religious Study about the *marjaʿiyya* (the Institution of the *marājiʿ*), the Hawza, Students and Schools of the Religious Sciences, Recommendations, A" 136–137, *137*, 138
"Report about Why I Do Not Want to Receive the Honor of [Full] Membership, A," 83
Republican Decree (*marsūm jumhūrī*), 174
Republican Guard, 110, 133, 140, 157–158, 236n55
Republic of Fear, 6–7, 15–16, 148–149
Republic of Fear (Makiya), xvii, 151
Republic of Rewards and Dependence, 148–149
resistance movements, 159, 215n63; acts of, 162, 164; graffiti, 155, 164
responsibility, taking (*ḥaml al-masʾūliya*), 75, 228n2, 260
"Responsibility of State Departments to Solve the Issues of Citizens, The" (President's Office), 78
retirement benefits, 176–177
Revolutionary Command Council (RCC, *majlis qiyādat al-thawra*), xvi, 74, 102, 227n7; expansion of, 22–23; membership, 217n8; National Security Council (*majlis al-ʾamn al-qawmī*), 155; Order of the Command (*shārat al-qiyāda*), 173
Revolution Medal (*wisām al-thawra*), 174, 179, 254n14, 255n37

Revolution of 17 July 1968 (*thawrat 17–30 tamūz*), 20–21, 29, 42, 124, 217n7, 217n10, 226n40; Court of the Revolution (*maḥkamat al-thawra*), 75, 170; terminology for, 58–59

rewards and benefits, 148–149, 172–178, 184; for families of martyrs, 120–121, 173; during Iran-Iraq War, 255n35; medals, 148–149, 173–174, 179–180; terror and enticement (*al-tarhīb wa-l-targhīb*), 15–16, 147–149, 184, 214n53; withdrawal of privileges, 178–182

rights: of adultery (*haqq al-ʿihr*), 126–127; women's rights, 124–127, 169–170

Rikabi, Fuad al-, 217n8

rituals: Baʿth Party, 31–32; ceremonies, 62–67; public, 164; Shiʿi, 60, 225n39

Roberts, Stephen H., 57

Rohde, Achim, 124

rumors, 248n29

Saʿad bin Abi Waqas Branch (Baʿth Party), 222n39

saboteurs (*mukharribīn*), 143, 148, 152, 162, 249n36

Sadat, Anwar, 241n52

Saddam Hussein's Baʿth Party (Sassoon), xvii

Saddam River, 59, 225n27

Saddam's Cubs (*ʾashbāl ṣaddām*), 176, 254n23, 259

Saddam's Fedayeen militia, 100, 109–110, 177

Saddam's *Qādisiyya*. *see* Iran-Iraq War

Saddam's *Qādisiyya* Medal (*wisām qādisiyyat ṣaddām*), 174, 254n14, 255n37

Saddam Tapes, The (Woods, Palkki, Stout, eds.), 208n7

Saʿdi, Salah al-, 20

Sadr, Muhammad Baqir al-, xii, 135

Safar Intifada, xi

Said, Nuri al-, xi, 216n7

Salafis, 138–139

Salah al-Din Governorate, 244n96

salaries, 230n31

salutations, 31, 259, 263

Samarrai, Wafiq al-, 156, 248n28

San Remo Conference, xi

Sassoon, Joseph, xvii, 6

"Sayings of the Leader Comrade (God save him)," 45, *46*

schools: elementary school examinations, 48, *49*; preparatory schools (*madāris al-ʾiʿdād al-ḥizbī*), 54–55; religious schools, 136–137, *137*, 138–139, 141, 235n30, 243n78

sectarianism, 132–134

secularism, militant, 131–132

security services, 22, 25; committees, 76–77; detachments (*mafāriz*), 152; General Security Directorate (GSD, *mudīriyyat al-ʾamn al-ʿāma*), 22, 75, 98–100, 110; National Security Branch Command (*qiyādat furʿ al-ʾamn al-qawmī*), 110; National Security Council (*majlis al-ʾamn al-qawmī*), 155; personnel, 101, 233n6; personnel appointments, 98–99; Special Security Organization (SSO, *jihāz al-ʾamn al-khāṣṣ*), 6, 22, 76–77, 219n43

seminars, cultural (*nadwa*), 54

separatism, national, 20

Sessions for Judicial Clerics (*dawrāt li-kuttāb al-ʿudūl fī wizārat al-ʿadal*), 233n10

sexual harassment, 126

Shapiro, Leonard, 215n1

Shatt al-Arab University, 114

sheikhs, 141–146, 184; registration of, 245n114. *See also* tribes

Shiʿi(s), 19, 101, 121, 129–130, 134; Arabs, 216n4; deportations of, 165; Islamist opposition groups, 130; leaders or sources of emulation (*marājiʿ*

Shiʿi(s) (*continued*)
al-taqlīd), 130, 134–136, 261; martyrs, 225n39; processions (*ẓāhirat al-mashī*), 225n39, 243n87; protests, xi, 130, 133–134; as rabble-rousers (*ghūghāʾiyīn*), 133–134; religious schools, 136; rituals, 60, 225n39
shuʿūbiyya, 251n70
Sidqi, Bakr, xi, 216n7
slogans, 9–10, 27, 60, 112, 140, *167*, 168
Sluglett, Peter, xvii, 5–6, 10
social influence, 106, 117, 122, 129, 145, 259
social institutions, 128–146
socialism, 29
social media, 190
society: administered, 189; Baʿthification of, 91–97, 117–146, 183–184; civil, 91–96, 183–184
Society of American Archivists, 207n1
Sousa, Richard, 207n1
Soviet Union. *See* Union of Soviet Socialist Republics (USSR)
Special Protection Apparatus (*jihāz al-himāya al-khāṣa*), 22
Special Republican Guard, 4, 110, 236n55
Special Security Organization (SSO, *jihāz al-ʾamn al-khāṣṣ*), 6, 22, 76–77, 219n43
spying, 121, 184; commissioned spies (*al-ʿuyūn al-mukallafa*), 155. *See also* surveillance
SSO. *See* Special Security Organization
Stalin, Joseph, 7–9, 15, 35, 147, 151
Stalinism, 189
State Company for Internet Services, 190
state personnel, 77, 98–107
Steavenson, Wendell, 128, 171, 187
students and youth (*al-ṭalaba wa-l-shabāb*), 93–94, 191–192; Baʿthification of, 121–123; National Union of Students and Youth of Iraq (*al-ʾittiḥād al-waṭanī li-ṭalaba wa-shabāb al-ʿirāq*), 93, 110–111, 231n52; Office of Students and Youth, 42–43, 92, 94; "A Religious Study about the *marjaʿiyya* (the Institution of the *marājiʿ*), the Hawza, Students and Schools of the Religious Sciences, Recommendations," 136–137, *137*, 138; tests of, 47–48
suicide bombings, 210n10
Sulaiman, Hikmat, 216n7
Sunni(s), 23, 104, 130, 133–134, 191, 241n52; Iraqi population, 216n4; Islamists, 19, 131, 138–139, 241n52; Salafists, 132; Tikriti, 217n8; Wahhabis, 60
Suny, Ronald Grigor, 35
Sura 48 (verse in *Qurʾān*), 66
surveillance, 155–156, 163–164, 184, 260; maps and, 119, 261; public, 121, 123–124; self-monitoring, 155–156
Syria, 166, 190–191, 208n4, 217n9, 241n52, 249n40; Baʿthist, 103–104

Taʾmim (Kirkuk) Branch (Baʿth Party), 83, 233n6
Taʾmim (Kirkuk) Governorate, 115
targhīb, 214n53
taxi drivers, 6, 139, 154, 169
teachers: admission criteria, 99, 102; Baʿthification of (*tabʿīth al-taʿlīm*), 110–111; teaching academies, 99, 102, 184; teaching corps (*al-hayʾa al-tadrīsiyya*, or, *silk al-taʿlīm wa-l-tadrīs*), 99
terminology, 59–60, 259–265; code words, 58, 60–61, 67, 106, 114; invocations for Saddam Hussein, 45, *46*; monikers for Saddam Hussein, 259, 262–263; multivocalities, 60; positive adjectives, 58–59; salutations, 31, 259, 263
terror: Baʿthist, 151–170, 184; and en-

ticement (*al-tarhīb wa-l-targhīb*), 15–16, 147–149, 184, 214n53; Great Terror, 147; indiscriminate, 153; justifications of, 157–170; kidnappings, 152, 162; means and purposes of, 153–157; Republic of Fear, 6–7, 15–16, 148–149; suicide bombings, 210n10; targets of, 157–170; torture, 152–153; totalitarian, 151
terrorist attacks, 250n43
Thursday Word (*kalimat yawm al-khamīs*), 110–111, 261
Tikrit, Iraq, 20, 133, 229n22
Tikriti, Barzan al-, 22
Tikriti, Sabawi al-, 22
Tikriti, Saddam Hussein al-. *See* Hussein, Saddam
torture, 152–153
totalitarianism, 5–30, 51–53, 146, 188–189, 215n1; Baʿthist, 20; defective or arrested, 17; definition of, 7–8, 212n27, 256n5; Husseini Baʿthist, 18–30; Iraqi, 5–12; leadership, 25–26; strategy of rule, 7–8; terror, 151
tourism, 228n2
traditional values, 125, 127, 186
traitors, 148
treason, national, 9–10
tribalism, 16–17, 27, 62, 101, 124–125, 134, 186
tribes, 23, 236n39; Baʿthification of, 141–146; Hussein and, 218n24; leadership of, 106; registration of, 245n114; sheikhs, 141–146, 184
Tripp, Charles, 6
Tunisia, 190–191, 241n52
Turabi, Hassan al-, 241n52

Union of Saddamists (*ʾittiḥād al-ṣaddāmiyīn*), 175
Union of Soviet Socialist Republics (USSR), 9, 51, 128, 213n35, 241n52; Cultural Revolution, 147
unions, 175; professional, 95–96; "The Reality of the Unions, Federations, and Mass Organizations during the Most Recent Period," 85. *See also specific unions*
United Arab Emirates, 77
United Nations, 75; oil-for-food program, xii, 86–87, 189
United States: de-Baʿthification, 191; invasion of Iraq, xii; Iran-Contra affair, 166
uprisings, 16–17, 23, 85, 186–187; popular, 16–17, 23, 186–187

values, traditional, 125, 127, 186
Victory Arch, 222n40
violence: al-Anfal campaign, 162–163; assassinations and attempts, 25, 151–152, 157–158, 162, 246n6, 250n43; Baʿthist terror, 151–170, 184; executions, 156, 158, 218n13, 250n43; genocide, 154–155, 162–163; and Hussein, 40; indiscriminate, 153; kidnappings, 152, 162; killing or betrayal, 3–4, 156, 169–170, 185–186, 209n6; mass executions, 156, 248n28; means of, 6–7, 15, 40, 148; rape, 169; self-mutiliation, 145; suicide bombings, 210n10; terror and enticement (*al-tarhīb wa-l-targhīb*), 15–16, 147–149, 184, 214n53; terrorist attacks, 250n43; torture, 152–153; totalitarian terror, 151

Wahhabis, 132, 138–139, 244n96
"Ways to Culturalize the Masses (Mass Mobilization)" (*ʾasālīb al-tathqīf al-jamāhīrī [al-taʿbiʾa al-jamāhīriyya]*) (Baʿth Party), 57–58
weakness (*al-takhādhul*), 158, 179
weapons, 145–146
Wedeen, Lisa, 217n9
weigh-ins, 90, 231n48
Windawi, Hisham, 97
withdrawal of privileges, 178–182

women, 123–128; in Baʿth Party, 127; emancipation of, 35–36; General Federation of Iraqi Women, 91–95, 123–125, 127–128; as incapable (*qāṣira*), 125; "morally discredited" (*sāqiṭa khalqiyan*), 90; prayer circles, 139–140; rights, 124–127, 169–170, 180; as second-class citizens, 126; "unsuitable" (*lā yaṣluḥ*), 90; in work force, 239n33
Woods, Kevin M., 208n7
"Work Plan for Coordination between the Party and Mass Organizations in the Field of the Baʿthification of Society, A," 92, 120, 123, 193–201 (text)

yawm al-nakhwa, 89, 100–101, 230n37, 254n23
youth. *See* students and youth

Zionism, 132, 166, 168
Zuo, Jiping, 53

Printed and bound by CPI Group (UK) Ltd, Croydon, CR0 4YY

09/06/2025

14685839-0003